CompTIA® A+® Certification

A Comprehensive Approach for all 2006 Exam Objectives

Student Manual
Volume 1

CompTIA® A+® Certification: A Comprehensive Approach for all 2006 Exam Objectives

Part Number: 085820
Course Edition: 1.1

NOTICES

HELP US IMPROVE OUR COURSEWARE

Your comments are important to us. Please contact us at Element K Press LLC, 1-800-478-7788, 500 Canal View Boulevard, Rochester, NY 14623, Attention: Product Planning, or through our Web site at **http://support.elementkcourseware.com**.

4.   Take and pass the CompTIA certification exam(s).

For more information about CompTIA's certifications, such as its industry acceptance, benefits, or program news, please visit **www.comptia.org/certification**.

CompTIA is a not-for-profit Information Technology (IT) trade association. CompTIA's certifications are designed by subject matter experts across the IT industry. Each CompTIA certification is vendor-neutral, covers multiple technologies, and requires demonstrations of skills and knowledge widely sought after by the IT industry. To contact CompTIA with any questions or comments, please call 1-630–678–8300 or email **questions@comptia.org**.

CompTIA® A+® Certification: A Comprehensive Approach for all 2006 Exam Objectives

VOLUME 1

Lesson 1: Personal Computer Components

A. Personal Computer Components 2

    Categories of Personal Computer Components 3

    The System Unit.. 3

    Display Devices 4

    Input Devices 5

    External Devices 6

B. System Unit Components.................................. 8

    The System Board 8

    The Central Processing Unit (CPU) 10

    Memory 10

    The System Bus... 11

    Storage Devices... 12

    Power Supplies 13

    Cooling Systems 15

    Adapter Cards 16

    Riser Cards 17

    System Board Form Factors 18

C. Storage Devices. **27**

    Floppy Disk Drives (FDD). 27

    Hard Disk Drives (HDD) 28

    Optical Disks 28

    Types of Optical Disks and Drives 29

    Tape Drives 30

    Solid State Storage 31

D. Personal Computer Connection Methods. **33**

    Ports. 33

    Personal Computer Connections. 34

    Serial Connections. 35

    Parallel Connections 36

    Universal Serial Bus (USB) Connections 37

    IEEE 1394 and FireWire Connections 38

    Small Computer Systems Interface (SCSI) Connections. 39

    Parallel ATA (PATA) Connections 39

    Serial ATA (SATA) Connections 41

Lesson 2: Operating System Fundamentals

A. Personal Computer Operating Systems **46**

    Microsoft Windows. 47

    Microsoft Windows Versions 47

    UNIX 50

    Linux. 52

    Apple Macintosh Operating Systems. 53

B. Windows User Interface Components **56**

    The Windows Desktop 56

    The Taskbar 57

    The Start Menu 57

    Windows Explorer 63

    My Computer 64

    The My Documents Folder 65

    The Control Panel 68

    The Command Prompt 72

    My Network Places 75

C. Windows File System Management **79**

    Directories and Folders 79

    File Extensions 80

    File Attributes 84

    Windows File System Types 87

    Permissions 87

    NTFS File Permissions 88

    NTFS Folder Permissions 89

    Shares 90

    Windows Shared Folder Permissions 92

D. Windows System Management Tools **97**

    The Computer Management Console 97

    The Registry 102

Lesson 3: PC Technician Professional Best Practices

A. Tools of the Trade **108**

Multimeters 109

Loopback Plugs 110

Types of Hardware Toolkits 111

Software Diagnostic Tools 112

Firmware 113

The System BIOS. 114

CMOS RAM 116

The Power-On Self Test (POST) 118

Hard Drive Self Tests 119

Software Diagnostics Tests 119

B. Electrical Safety **122**

Static Electricity 122

Electrostatic Discharge (ESD) 123

ESD Prevention Techniques 124

An ESD Toolkit 125

Electrical Hazards 125

C. Environmental Safety and Materials Handling **130**

Atmospheric Considerations 130

Situational Hazards 131

Physical Hazards 131

Safety Precautions for Physical Hazards 133

Equipment Moving Safety Recommendations 134

Chemical Hazards 135

Liquid Hazards 135

The Material Safety Data Sheet (MSDS) 136

Incident Reports 137

Hazardous Material Disposal Procedures 138

D. Perform Preventative Maintenance **141**

Preventative Maintenance Theory 141

Computer Component Maintenance Techniques 142

Cleaning Compounds and Materials 144

E. Diagnostics and Troubleshooting **156**

Troubleshooting Theory 156

The Troubleshooting Process 157

F. Professionalism and Communication **164**

Communication Skills 164

Professional Conduct 168

Lesson 4: Installing and Configuring Peripheral Components

A. Install and Configure Display Devices **174**

Display Device Types 175

Display Settings 176

LCD Characteristics 178

Connector Types 180

Device Drivers 182

Display Device Selection Tips 183

Display Device Installation Considerations 183

B. Install and Configure Input Devices **191**

Standard Input Device Types 191

Biometric Input Device Types 194

Specialized Input Device Types 194

Input Device Selection Tips 195

Input Device Installation Considerations 196

C. Install and Configure Adapter Cards **201**

    Internal Bus Architectures 201

    Adapter Card Types 203

    Adapter Card Selection Tips 204

    Adapter Card Installation Considerations 204

    Adapter Card Configuration and Optimization Requirements 204

    Hardware Resources 205

D. Install and Configure Multimedia Devices **215**

    Multimedia Devices 215

    Common Multimedia Devices 216

    Multimedia Connectors 217

    Multimedia Device Selection Tips 218

    Multimedia Device Installation Considerations 220

    Multimedia Device Configuration and Optimization Requirements 221

Lesson 5: Installing and Configuring System Components

A. Install and Configure Storage Devices **228**

    Hard Disk Drive Types 229

    Floppy Disk Drives 233

    Tape Drive Types 234

    Optical Drive Types 236

    Solid State Storage Types 237

    Storage Device Power Connectors 238

    Hot Swapping 239

    Drive Images 240

    Disk Partition Types 240

    The Windows Disk Management Utility 241

    Internal Storage Device Installation Considerations 242

    Storage Device Configuration and Optimization Requirements 242

B. Install and Configure Power Supplies **259**

Power Supply Form Factors 259

Power Requirements 260

Power Supply Safety Recommendations 261

Power Supply Selection Tips 262

C. Install and Configure Memory **269**

Memory Modules 269

Memory Form Factors and Slot Types 270

Memory Types 270

Memory Selection Tips 272

D. Install and Configure CPUs **281**

CPU Chip Types 281

Instruction Sets 281

Cache Memory 282

CPU Operational Characteristics 284

Processor Connections 290

CPU Selection Tips 292

CPU Installation Considerations 293

CPU Configuration and Optimization Requirements 293

E. Install and Configure System Boards **298**

Integrated I/O Port Types 298

Chipsets 298

BIOS Types 299

Complementary Metal Oxide Semiconductor (CMOS) Memory
Settings 300

System Board Selection Tips 301

System Board Installation Considerations 301

System Board Configuration and Optimization Requirements 302

System Board Power Connectors 303

Lesson 6: Maintaining and Troubleshooting Peripheral Components

A. Troubleshoot Display Devices **312**

Common Display Device Issues. 313

B. Maintain and Troubleshoot Input Devices. **321**

Common Input Device Issues 321

Input Device Maintenance Techniques 325

C. Troubleshoot Adapter Cards **330**

Common Adapter Card Issues 330

D. Troubleshoot Multimedia Devices **335**

Common Multimedia Device Issues. 335

Lesson 7: Troubleshooting System Components

A. Troubleshoot Storage Devices **344**

Common Storage Device Issues 345

ATA Drive Troubleshooting Tips 348

SCSI Drive Troubleshooting Tips 349

B. Troubleshoot Power Supplies **368**

Common Power Problems 368

Common Power Supply Issues 369

C. Troubleshoot Memory **377**

Error Checking 377

Common Memory Issues 377

D. Troubleshoot CPUs **381**

Common CPU Issues. 381

E. Troubleshoot System Boards **384**

Common System Board Issues 384

Lesson 8: Installing and Configuring Operating Systems

A. Install Microsoft Windows **390**

Windows System Requirements 391

Hardware Compatibility 393

Installation Methods 393

Installation Options.................................... 395

Windows Update 396

Microsoft Product Activation............................. 397

B. Upgrade Windows **409**

Supported Upgrade Paths 409

Hardware Upgrade Compatibility.......................... 410

Software Upgrade Compatibility 410

C. Add Devices to Windows **422**

Driver Signing....................................... 422

Unsigned Driver Installation Options 423

Installation Permissions................................. 423

D. Optimize Windows...................................... **433**

Virtual Memory...................................... 433

The Virtual Memory Process 434

Windows Services 436

The Windows XP Boot Process 437

Temporary Files 442

Windows Optimization Software Tools...................... 446

Lesson 9: Maintaining and Troubleshooting Microsoft Windows

A. Operating System Utilities **458**

File Management Tools 459

Disk Management Tools................................. 460

System Management Tools 464

B. Maintain Microsoft Windows **475**

    Backup and Restore. 475

    The Windows Backup Utility. 476

    System State Data 478

C. Troubleshoot Microsoft Windows **486**

    System Stop Errors 486

    System Lockup Errors 487

    Input/Output Device Issues 488

    Application Errors. 489

    Boot Errors 489

    Error and Warning Messages in Event Viewer 492

    Registry Error Messages 494

    Remote Diagnostic and Troubleshooting Tools 496

D. Recover Microsoft Windows. **504**

    System Restore 504

    Safe Mode 505

    Last Known Good. 506

    Recovery Console 507

    Windows Boot Disk 508

    Automated System Recovery (ASR) 508

    Repair Installations. 510

    Windows System Issues 510

VOLUME 2

Lesson 10: Network Technologies

A. Network Concepts **534**

Networks 535

Network Models 536

Network Interface Card Characteristics 539

Twisted Pair Cables 540

RJ-45 Twisted Pair Connectors 541

Coaxial Cables 542

Coaxial Cable and Connector Types 543

Fiber Optic Cables 544

Fiber Optic Connectors 545

Other Network Connection Types 547

B. Network Communications **555**

Network Protocols 555

Network Addresses 556

The TCP/IP Protocol 556

IP Addresses 557

Subnet Masks 558

IP Address Classes 559

The IPX/SPX and NWLink Protocols 561

NetBIOS 563

NetBEUI 564

Network Bandwidth 565

Full and Half Duplex Communications 566

C. Network Connectivity **572**

    Local Area Networks (LANs) 572

    Wide Area Networks (WANs) 573

    Ethernet 574

    Dial-up Connections... 574

    Wireless Connections 575

    802.11 Wireless Standards 576

    Wireless Access Points (WAPs)................................ 577

    Bluetooth Communications 578

    Infrared Connections 578

    Cellular WAN Communications 579

    Broadband Communications 580

    Types of Broadband Communications 580

D. Internet Technologies **585**

    Internet Service Providers (ISPs) 585

    SMTP 585

    POP3 586

    IMAP4 587

    HTML 587

    HTTP 588

    SSL 589

    HTTPS 589

    Telnet 590

    FTP 590

    Voice Over IP (VoIP)... 591

Lesson 11: Installing and Managing Network Connections

A. Create Network Connections **598**

    IP Address Configuration Methods............................. 599

    Name Resolution with the Domain Name System (DNS)........... 601

    WINS 602

    Workgroups 603

    Directory Services 604

    Active Directory Domains.................................. 605

    Novell eDirectory 606

    Network Client Options 606

B. Install and Configure Web Browsers **622**

    Web Browsers 622

    Web Browser Settings 623

C. Maintain and Troubleshoot Network Connections............... **632**

    Preventative Maintenance Techniques 632

    Networking Tools and Utilities 633

    Cable Testers 634

    Common Network Issues.................................. 635

Lesson 12: Supporting Laptops and Portable Computing Devices

A. Laptop and Portable Computing Device Components **646**

    Laptop Computers 647

    Portable Computing Devices 649

    Mobile System Boards 650

    Mobile Processors 651

    Mobile Hard Drive Form Factors 654

    Mobile Memory Form Factors 654

    Mobile Adapter Card Form Factors and Expansion Slots. 655

    Mobile Device Ports 658

    Mobile Device Peripheral Components 659

    Power Supplies and Batteries 660

    Mobile Input Devices 663

    Video Sharing. 663

B. Install and Configure Laptops and Portable Computing Devices. . . **665**

    Power Management Technologies. 665

    Power Management Modes 665

    Communication Connection Selection Tips 667

C. Maintain and Troubleshoot Laptops and Portable Computing
Devices **695**

    Maintenance and Handling Techniques 695

    Operating Environment Best Practices 696

    General Mobile Computing Device Issues 697

    Common Stylus Issues 699

    Common Laptop Keypad Issues 699

    Common Wireless Connectivity Issues 700

Lesson 13: Supporting Printers and Scanners

A. Printer and Scanner Technologies **714**

    Printers 715

    Scanners 716

    Multi-function Devices 718

    Laser Printers 719

    Inkjet Printers 720

    Thermal Printers 721

    Types of Thermal Printers 722

    Solid Ink Printers 723

    Impact Printers 723

B. Printer and Scanner Components **728**

    Printer and Scanner Memory 728

    Printer and Scanner Drivers 728

    Printer and Scanner Firmware 729

    Printer and Scanner Interfaces 729

    Consumable Printer Components 730

    Flatbed Scanner Components 731

C. Printer and Scanner Processes **734**

    The Laser Printing Process 734

    The Inkjet Print Process 735

    Thermal Print Processes 736

    The Solid Ink Print Process 736

    The Dot-Matrix Impact Print Process 737

    The Scanning Process 738

D. Install and Configure Printers and Scanners **740**

    Local and Network-based Printers 740

    Network-Connected Printers 741

    The Print Spooler 741

    The Windows Print Process 744

    Windows Print Permissions 745

    Printer Configuration Options................................. 746

    Scanner Performance Factors 747

E. Maintain and Troubleshoot Printers and Scanners **759**

    Preventative Maintenance Techniques 759

    Common Printer Issues 760

    Common Scanner Issues..................................... 763

    Printer and Scanner Troubleshooting Resources 764

Lesson 14: Personal Computer Security Concepts

A. Security Fundamentals **778**

    Corporate Security Policies 779

    Security Incident Reports.................................... 780

    Authentication 781

    Authentication Methods 782

    Biometric Authentication Methods 784

    Password Management 784

    Access Control 785

    User Account Types 785

    Groups 786

    Access Control Measures 787

    Rights... 788

    Auditing 789

B. Security Protection Measures **793**

    Encryption 793

    Data Encryption Methods.................................. 794

    Malicious Software...................................... 797

    Types of Malicious Software................................ 798

    Malicious Software Protection Techniques 799

    Firewalls.. 800

    File System Security Measures 801

C. Data and Physical Security **804**

    Physical Access Controls.................................. 804

    Data Access Policies 805

    Workstation Protection................................... 806

    Backup Security 806

    Data Migration 806

    Data Removal 807

    Media and Hardware Disposal 808

D. Wireless Security.. **811**

    Wireless Encryption Methods 811

    Security Methods for Wireless Access Points 812

    Wireless Client Configuration Options 812

E. Social Engineering **814**

    Social Engineering Attacks................................ 814

    Social Engineering Prevention.............................. 815

Lesson 15: Supporting Personal Computer Security

A. Install and Configure Security Measures **824**

    Windows Security Policies................................. 825

    Windows Firewall....................................... 826

    Software Firewall Configuration Settings...................... 827

    Computer Security Measures 827

B. Maintain and Troubleshoot Security Measures **852**

Common Computer Security Issues 852

Common Software Firewall Issues............................ 853

Common Wireless Client Configuration Issues 854

Common Encryption Issues 856

Appendix A: Mapping Course Content to the CompTIA A+ Essentials 220-601 Exam Objectives

Appendix B: Mapping Course Content to the CompTIA A+ IT Technician 220-602 Exam Objectives

Appendix C: Mapping Course Content to the CompTIA A+ Remote Technician 220-603 Exam Objectives

Appendix D: Mapping Course Content to the CompTIA A+ Depot Technician 220-604 Exam Objectives

Appendix E: A Brief History of Personal Computers

Appendix F: CompTIA A+ Acronyms

Lesson Labs... **945**

Solutions **969**

Glossary **1023**

Index... **1045**

About This Course

If you are getting ready for a career as an entry-level information technology (IT) professional or personal computer (PC) service technician, the *CompTIA® A+®
Certification* course is the first step in your preparation. The course will build on your existing user-level knowledge and experience with personal computer software and hardware to present fundamental skills and concepts that you will use on the job. In this course, you will acquire the essential skills and information you will need to install, upgrade, repair, configure, troubleshoot, optimize, and perform preventative maintenance of basic personal computer hardware and operating systems.

The *CompTIA® A+® Certification* course can benefit you in two ways. Whether you work or plan to work in a mobile or corporate environment where you have a high level of face-to-face customer interaction, a remote-based environment where client interaction, client training, operating systems and connectivity issues are emphasized, or in an environment with limited customer interaction and an emphasis on hardware activities, this course provides the background knowledge and skills you will require to be successful. It can also assist you if you are preparing to take the CompTIA A+ certification examinations, 2006 objectives (exam numbers 220-601, 220-602, 220-603, and 220-604), in order to become a CompTIA A+ Certified Professional.

Course Description

Target Student

The target student is anyone with basic computer user skills who is interested in obtaining a job as an IT professional or PC technician. Possible job environments include mobile or corporate settings with a high level of face-to-face client interaction, remote-based work environments where client interaction, client training, operating systems, and connectivity issues are emphasized, or settings with limited customer interaction where hardware activities are emphasized. In addition, this course will help prepare students to achieve a CompTIA A+ Certification.

Course Prerequisites

Students taking this course should have the following skills:

- End-user skills with Windows-based personal computers, including the ability to:
    - Browse and search for information on the Internet.
    - Start up, shut down, and log on to a computer and network.
    - Run programs.

■ Move, copy, delete, and rename files in Windows Explorer.

● Basic knowledge of computing concepts, including the difference between hardware and software; the functions of software components, such as the operating system, applications, and file systems; and the function of a computer network.

How to Use This Book

As a Learning Guide

Each lesson covers one broad topic or set of related topics. Lessons are arranged in order of increasing proficiency with *CompTIA® A+® Certification*; skills you acquire in one lesson are used and developed in subsequent lessons. For this reason, you should work through the lessons in sequence.

We organized each lesson into results-oriented topics. Topics include all the relevant and supporting information you need to master *CompTIA® A+® Certification*, and activities allow you to apply this information to practical hands-on examples.

Through the use of sample files, hands-on activities, illustrations, and supporting background information, this book provides you with the foundation and structure to learn *CompTIA® A+® Certification* quickly and easily.

As a Review Tool

Any method of instruction is only as effective as the time and effort you are willing to invest in it. In addition, some of the information that you learn in class may not be important to you immediately, but it may become important later on. For this reason, we encourage you to spend some time reviewing the topics and activities after the course. For additional challenge when reviewing activities, try the "What You Do" column before looking at the "How You Do It" column.

As a Reference

The organization and layout of the book make it easy to use as a learning tool and as an after-class reference. You can use this book as a first source for definitions of terms, background information on given topics, and summaries of procedures.

Course Icons

Icon	Description
	A **Caution Note** makes students aware of potential negative consequences of an action, setting, or decision that are not easily known.
	Display Slide provides a prompt to the instructor to display a specific slide. Display Slides are included in the Instructor Guide only.
	An **Instructor Note** is a comment to the instructor regarding delivery, classroom strategy, classroom tools, exceptions, and other special considerations. Instructor Notes are included in the Instructor Guide only.
	Notes Page indicates a page that has been left intentionally blank for students to write on.
	A **Student Note** provide additional information, guidance, or hints about a topic or task.
	A **Version Note** indicates information necessary for a specific version of software.

Certification

This course is designed to help you prepare for the following certification.

Certification Path: A+ Certification

- Exam: Essentials 220-601
- Exam: IT Technician 220-602
- Exam: Remote Technician 220-603
- Exam: Depot Technician 220-604

Course Objectives

In this course, you will install, upgrade, repair, configure, optimize, troubleshoot, and perform preventative maintenance on basic personal computer hardware and operating systems.

You will:

- identify the components of standard desktop personal computers.

- identify fundamental components and functions of personal computer operating systems.
- identify best practices followed by professional personal computer technicians.
- install and configure computer components.
- install and configure system components.
- maintain and troubleshoot peripheral components.
- troubleshoot system components.
- install and configure operating systems.
- maintain and troubleshoot installations of Microsoft Windows.
- identify network technologies.
- install and manage network connections.
- support laptops and portable computing devices.
- support printers and scanners.
- identify personal computer security concepts.
- support personal computer security.

Course Requirements

Hardware

Each student and the instructor will require one computer. The class is designed for each pair of students to work at a student lab station that should consist of one desktop computer, one laptop/portable computer, and one printer. If you do not have enough laptop computers to have one per lab station, provide as many as you can and provide the remaining students with desktop computers. If you do not have enough physical printers to have one per lab station, provide sufficient printers so that students can have adequate hands-on access to the printer mechanisms and components. You will also need to provide other hardware items for students to install; wherever possible provide enough components so that each lab station can install each device. The specifications for the desktop and laptop computers, as well as a list of other hardware items you will need to provide, follow.

- Desktop computers should be ATX-based systems with PCI slots. Additional bus types, such as ISA slots, are a plus. The system should also include the following ports: parallel, VGA, PS/2 keyboard port, PS/2 mouse port, serial, USB, and, if possible, sound ports including Line In, Line Out, Mic, and Game. Any additional ports are a plus. Desktop systems should have bootable CD-ROM drives and floppy drives.

- Portable computers should have a floppy drive and a CD/DVD drive (these can be swappable in a single drive bay, or separate components); at least one PC card slot; a mini-PCI card bay; and an empty memory slot.

- All computers should be 300 Mhz Pentium systems or higher.

- All computers should have 8 GB hard disks or larger.

- All computers should have 128 MB of RAM or more.

- All computers should have a keyboard and mouse.

- All computers should have a 800x600-capable display adapter and monitor.

- Laptop computers should have a docking station or port replicator to support the standard peripherals (keyboard, mouse, monitor).

- All computers should have network adapters and appropriate network cabling.

- Provide printing devices of your choice. You might wish to have different printer types, such as laser printers and inkjet printers, if available.

- The instructor's computer should have a projection system so the students can follow activities and demonstrations and so the instructor can display the course slide presentation.

- Provide two floppy disks for each student and the instructor.

- Each student should have a basic computer toolkit including an anti-static wrist strap, screwdrivers, tweezers and other small tools, and a multimeter. You may wish to provide other sample tools to the students, such as a power supply tester, as well as masking tape and pens. (Some of these items are included in the basic toolkit that is provided with the full courseware kit.)

- Each lab station should have a cleaning kit that includes monitor cleaning wipes, keyboard cleaning wipes, lint-free cloths, rubbing alcohol, cotton swabs, lens cloth, window cleaner, toothpicks, paint brush, compressed air canister, and computer vacuum.

- A classroom Internet connection.

- Each PC should contain the following internal devices that students can remove and reinstall, examine for troubleshooting purposes, or use to perform maintenance techniques: a hard disk; memory modules; power supply; one or more adapter cards; cooling systems.

- If the computers do not have integrated sound support, install sound cards.

- Provide a second, compatible hard drive and a cable that will enable a second hard drive to be added to student computers.

- Provide a multimedia device of some type for students to install.

- Provide the appropriate cabling for all devices.

- Provide as many other samples of different types of computer components as possible to display for the students. This can include adapter cards for various bus types, SCSI, PATA, and SATA storage devices, a variety of ports and cables, USB devices or hubs, multimedia devices such as digital cameras or microphones, gaming devices such as joysticks, various network cables and connectors, different display device types, different printer types, internal or external modems, examples of different motherboards, CPUs, and chipsets, and so on. Although you cannot work hands-on with every conceivable type of PC component within the confines of the classroom, the more different component types students can see and handle, the more beneficial their learning experience will be.

- Some activities and labs might require or suggest additional materials, so be sure to review the activity-specific setup requirements throughout the course prior to teaching this class.

Software

The following software is required for this course:

- Windows XP Professional with appropriate licenses. This will be installed during initial classroom setup, and students will install it again during class. Provide as many copies of the installation CD-ROM as possible. You might also wish to provide a separate classroom server computer, and copy the installation source files to a shared folder on the server.

- Windows XP Home with appropriate licenses. (If you prefer, you may substitute Windows 2000 Professional.) Students will install this operating system in class, so you should provide as many copies of the installation CD-ROM as possible. You might also wish to provide a separate classroom server computer, and copy the installation source files to a shared folder on the server.

- Classroom Internet access. Please configure Internet access and TCP/IP settings as appropriate for your classroom environment.

- Windows XP Professional Service Pack 2 or later and all current security patches. The setup instructions and classroom activities assume that you will obtain these through an Internet connection. Otherwise, you must download all current Windows XP Professional critical updates to installation CD-ROMs and have those available to the students to complete operating system setup.

- Device drivers and software manuals for each device the students will install. You should be able to obtain this live from the Internet during class; if not, you can download the drivers and burn them to a CD-ROM or place them on a network share, or provide the manufacturers' original disks.

Class Setup

For Instructor and Student Desktop and Laptop Operating System Installation:

1. Make sure that all computer components are properly installed and working.

2. Perform a fresh installation of Windows XP Professional. You can boot the computer from the installation CD-ROM, or create a network boot disk and install from a network share. After you configure the first computer of each type, you might wish to create a ghost image and install that to the remaining classroom computers. Regardless of your installation method, use the following installation parameters:

   - Accept the license agreement.

   - Delete existing partitions.

   - Create a 6 GB NTFS C partition. When you do this, make sure that you leave at least 2 GB of free space.

   - Select the appropriate regional settings for your location.

   - Enter the appropriate user name and organization for your environment.

   - Enter the product key.

   - For the instructor's computer, use a computer name of INST. For each of the student computers, use a computer name of CLIENT##, where ## is a unique two-digit number assigned to each student.

   - Set the default administrator account password to !Pass1234.

   - Configure the appropriate date and time for your location.

- Accept the Typical network settings; or, if necessary, configure Custom settings as appropriate to support Internet access or to conform to the network configuration of your classroom environment.

- Install the computer into the default workgroup.

- After the computer restarts, if prompted to turn on Automatic Updates, select Not Right Now. Then, complete the Internet connection portion as appropriate for your environment. If the computer will connect via a LAN connection, you should be able to skip this portion.

- Complete the system activation portion as appropriate for your environment. Training centers are responsible for complying with all relevant Microsoft licensing and activation requirements.

- On the Who Will Use This Computer screen, in the Your Name text box, enter a user account named Admin##, where ## matches the number in the computer name. At the instructor computer, name the account simply Admin. This account will become a member of the local Administrators group by default.

When setup is complete, the system will automatically log you on as Admin## with a blank password.

3. Set the Admin## account password.

   a. From the Start menu, click Control Panel, click User Accounts, and then click the Admin## account.

   b. Click Create a Password.

   c. Enter and confirm !Pass1234 as the password, and then click Create Password.

   d. Click Yes, Make Private and close all open windows.

4. If Service Pack 2 is not slipstreamed into your Windows XP Professional installation media, and you have a Service Pack 2 installation CD-ROM, install Service Pack 2 manually.

5. Choose Start→All Programs→Windows Update. From the Windows Update website, download and install all High Priority updates, including any current service packs and recommended security patches.

6. Configure workgroup networking so that all classroom computers can connect to each other.

   a. From the Start menu, open My Computer→My Network Places.

   b. Click Set Up A Home Or Small Office Network.

   c. In the Network Setup Wizard, click Next twice.

   d. On the Select a Connection Method screen, select Other and click Next.

   e. On the Other Internet Connection Methods screen, select This Computer Belongs To A Network That Does Not Have An Internet Connection and click Next.

   f. Accept the computer name by clicking Next.

   g. On the Name Your Network screen, enter WORKGROUP as the workgroup name and click Next twice.

   h. If prompted, turn on File And Printer Sharing and click Next. Review the parameters and click Next.

   i. On the You're Almost Done screen, select Just Finish The Wizard, click Next, and then click Finish.

7. Use the Start→Run command or My Network Places to verify that all classroom computers can connect without entering a user name or password.

8. To install the course data files, insert the course CD-ROM and click the Data Files button. This will install a folder named 085820Data on your C drive. This folder contains all the data files that you will use to complete this course. It also includes several simulated activities that can be used in lieu of the hands-on activities in the course.

9. Close all open windows and log out.

For Individual Labs and Activities

Prior to teaching the class, review the Setup instructions for the individual labs and activities throughout the course for additional activity-specific equipment requirements and setup procedures.

List of Additional Files

Printed with each activity is a list of files students open to complete that activity. Many activities also require additional files that students do not open, but are needed to support the file(s) students are working with. These supporting files are included with the student data files on the course CD-ROM or data disk. Do not delete these files.

1 | Personal Computer Components

Lesson Time: 2 hour(s)

Lesson Objectives:

In this lesson, you will identify the components of standard desktop personal computers.

You will:

- Identify the major components of personal computers.
- Identify the major components of the system unit.
- Identify the various types of storage devices used in personal computers.
- Identify personal computer connection methods.

Introduction

Before you begin to learn how to install and configure computer hardware and software, you need to know the basic components that constitute most personal computers. In this lesson, we will introduce you to computers by showing you some of the hardware components that make them work.

As you prepare for a career in computer support and maintenance, a good place to start is with some basics, such as a description of some common components, and an explanation of the types of connections that are used to join the components together. With the proper foundation, you'll be ready to tackle the more complex aspects of a computer support professional's job.

This lesson covers all or part of the following CompTIA A+ (2006) certification objectives:

- Topic A:
    - Exam 220–601 (Essentials): Objective 1.1
- Topic B:
    - Exam 220–601 (Essentials): Objective 1.1, Objective 2.1
    - Exam 220–602 (IT Technician): Objective 1.1
- Topic C:
    - Exam 220–601 (Essentials): Objective 1.1
- Topic D:
    - Exam 220–601 (Essentials): Objective 1.1, Objective 4.1, Objective 5.1

TOPIC A
Personal Computer Components

In this lesson, you will investigate many types of hardware components. The first step is to identify the main elements that are used in virtually all computer systems. In this topic, you will identify the major components of personal computers.

If you don't understand the main components of a computer, it can seem like the most elaborate jigsaw puzzle you have ever seen. Like most puzzles, the parts of a computer each have a specific place they need to be, but generally, you will find that the pieces fit together almost exactly the same way. To help you put the puzzle together, you need to understand what the pieces look like and what they do.

Categories of Personal Computer Components

There are four primary categories of components in a typical personal computer: the system unit, a display device, input devices, and external devices.

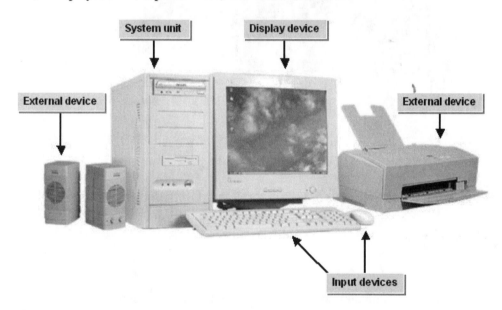

Figure 1-1: A typical personal computer.

The System Unit

Definition:

A *system unit* is the main component of a personal computer, which houses the other devices necessary for the computer to function. It is comprised of a chassis and the internal components of a personal computer such as the system board, the microprocessor, memory modules, disk drives, adapter cards, the power supply, a fan or other cooling device, and ports for connecting external components such as monitors, keyboards, mice, and other devices.

System units are often referred to as boxes, main units, or base units.

Example:

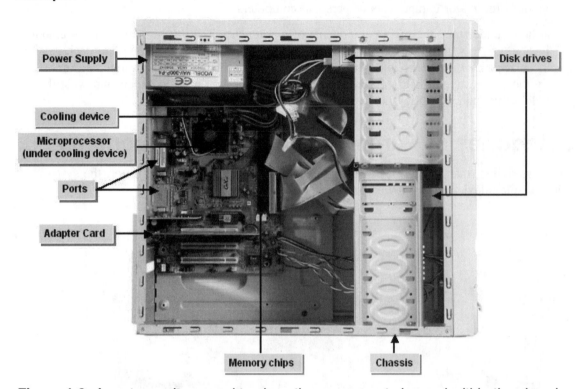

Figure 1-2: A system unit, opened to show the components housed within the chassis.

Display Devices

Definition:

A *display device* is a personal computer component that enables users to view the text and graphical data associated with a computer program. Display devices commonly connect to the system unit via a cable, and they have controls to adjust the settings for the device. They vary in size and shape, as well as the technologies used.

 Common terms for various types of display devices include display, monitor, screen, CRT, LCD, and flat-panel, to name a few.

Example:

Figure 1-3: *A display device.*

Input Devices

Definition:

An *input device* is a personal computer component that enables users to enter data or instructions into a computer. The most common input devices are keyboards and computer mice. Input devices can connect to the system unit via a cable or a wireless connection.

Example:

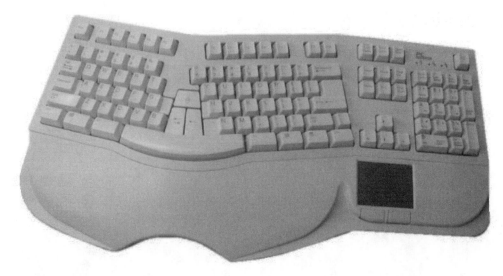

Figure 1-4: *An input device.*

External Devices

A personal computer's functionality can be enhanced by connecting different types of external devices to the system unit. Often called peripheral devices, external devices typically provide alternative input or output methods or additional data storage. External devices are connected to the system unit via a cable or a wireless connection. Some have their own power source and some draw power from the system.

There are several categories of external devices.

External Device	Functionality
Microphone	Provides audio input.
Digital camera	Provides graphical input.
Scanner	Provides graphical input.
Speakers	Provide audio output.
Printer	Provides printed output.
Network device	Enables communication with other computers, such as access to the Internet.
External drive	Provides additional data storage.

ACTIVITY 1-1

Identifying Personal Computer Components

Scenario:
In this activity, you will identify personal computer components.

---

1. **Identify the computer components in the graphic.**

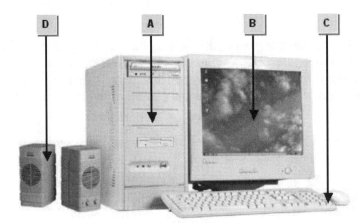

___ A	a.	Display device
___ B	b.	External device
___ C	c.	Input device
___ D	d.	System unit

---

2. **Which computer components are part of the system unit?**

   a) Chassis

   b) Monitor

   c) Internal hard drive

   d) Portable USB drive

   e) Memory

---

3. **Match each external device with its function.**

___ Microphone	a.	Provides audio output.
___ Speaker	b.	Provides graphical input.
___ Scanner	c.	Provides text and graphical output.
___ Printer	d.	Provides audio input.
___ External drive	e.	Provides additional data storage.

TOPIC B
System Unit Components

In the last topic, you identified the main components of personal computers, one of which is the system unit. The system unit itself has several important sub-components. In this topic, you will identify the major components of the system unit.

Being able to recognize a system unit is a good start, but it is not enough for a computer technician. If you need to replace a part within a system unit, you want to be sure that you replace the right one. The ability to identify system unit components is an integral part of the background knowledge that every computer technician should have.

The System Board

Definition:

The *system board* is the personal computer component that acts as the backbone for the entire computer system. Sometimes called the *motherboard,* it consists of a large, flat circuit board with chips and other electrical components on it. Some components are *soldered* directly to the board, and some are slots and sockets where other components can be added and removed easily.

 Another short term for the motherboard is "mobo."

Example:

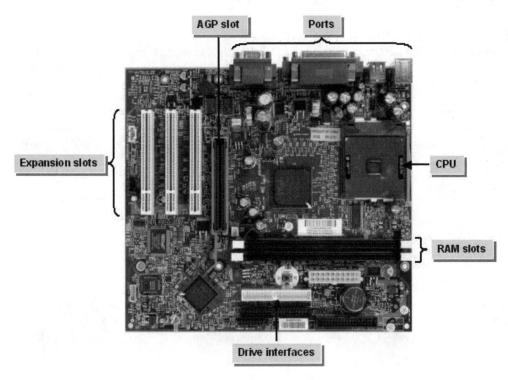

Figure 1-5: A system board.

System Board Features

Because features that are built into the design of the system board cannot be changed without replacing the whole system board, most system boards include only the standard features that most users want—those that will not change much in the near future. By omitting features that some users do not use, such as SCSI connections, system board manufacturers can keep the cost of their boards low. By allowing users to buy components such as a high-end video card with the speed and features they want, and letting the users attach the card to the system board, the designers build in flexibility that most users appreciate.

Sometimes computer makers who sell complete systems find it is cheaper to build a system board with components such as the modem, sound card, video, and all other features built-in, rather than add interface cards to a standard system board. If the integrated components are sufficient for your needs, this is an economical way to purchase this functionality; however, you should not invest money in a board with integrated components if you plan to upgrade these components anyway.

The Central Processing Unit (CPU)

Definition:

The *central processing unit (CPU)*, sometimes called microprocessor or just processor, is the real brains of the computer and is where most of the calculations take place. On most personal computers, the CPU is housed in a single microprocessor chip that is installed on the system board in a slot or socket.

 On larger or more powerful computers, there may be two or more individual CPU chips that work together as a unit.

Example:

Figure 1-6: CPUs.

Memory

Definition:

Memory is the component that provides the electronic storage for the computer. Memory most commonly refers to actual chips that typically store and retrieve information faster than tape or hard drives can. Memory chips contain millions of transistors etched on one sliver of a semiconductor. When a transistor conducts electricity, it represents the binary number 1. When it does not, it represents the binary number 0.

Example:

Figure 1-7: *A sample memory module.*

Volatile and Non-volatile Memory

Memory can be considered either volatile or non-volatile:

- Volatile memory requires a constant source of electricity to keep track of the data stored in it. When the power is no longer available, the data stored in volatile memory is lost. RAM (Random Access Memory) is an example of volatile memory.

- Non-volatile memory retains the information stored on it whether or not electrical current is available. ROM (Read-Only Memory) is an example of non-volatile memory.

The System Bus

Definition:

In computer communications, a *bus* is a collection of wires that connect components and the rules for data transfer through the connection. The *system bus* is the wires, or *traces*, on the motherboard that provide the main communication path between the CPU and memory. The system bus enables data transfer between the CPU, memory, and the other buses in the computer, which connect other system components such as hard drives and adapter cards. It is sometimes referred to as the frontside bus or local bus.

Example:

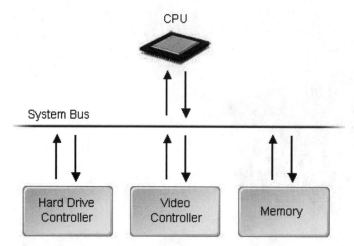

Figure 1-8: *The system bus.*

System Bus Terminology

The terminology used to describe the various buses connecting individual system components to the CPU will vary depending on the motherboard manufacturer. Terminology has also changed and developed as system boards have evolved. You might encounter terms such as the frontside bus, the backside bus, the memory bus, the processor bus, the address bus, and so on. Regardless of its placement and terminology, the basic function of a bus is to enable data transfer between individual micro components at the speed that is appropriate for each component. For definitions of some of the bus types from processor manufacturer AMD, see **http://www.amd.com/us-en/Glossary/0,,238_242,00.html.**

Storage Devices

Definition:

A personal computer *storage device* is a component, such as a hard drive, that enables users to save data for reuse at a later time, even after the personal computer is shut down and restarted. Storage devices can save data magnetically, optically, or electrically, depending on the medium on which the data is stored.

Example:

Figure 1-9: Examples of storage devices.

Power Supplies

Definition:

A *power supply* is an internal computer component that converts AC power from an electrical outlet to the DC power needed by system components. The power supply is a metal box in the rear of the system that is attached to the computer chassis and to the system board. While the power supply is not itself a component of the system board, it is required in order for system components to receive power. The power supply contains the power cord plug and a fan for cooling, because it generates a lot of heat. Some power supplies have a voltage switch that enables you to set the voltage to that used in different countries.

Another commonly used term for the power supply is the Power Supply Unit, or PSU.

Example:

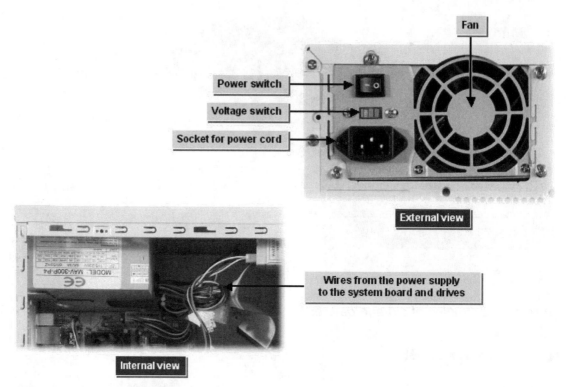

Figure 1-10: A power supply.

Fixed-Input Power Supply Voltage Switch Safety

Power supplies with voltage switches are called fixed-input power supplies. The voltage switches generally have two settings—for example, 220 and 110—depending on the manufacturer. If you set the switch to a higher voltage than supplied by the power source, the system will not receive enough power and will not function properly. However, if you set the switch to a lower setting than supplied by the power source—for example, if you set the switch to 110V while connected to a 220V outlet—you run the risk of burning out the power supply, damaging system components, or more seriously, creating a fire or electrocution hazard.

Auto-switching power supplies do not have a manual voltage switch, but detect the voltage level supplied by the outlet and set themselves to the correct voltage automatically. This can be convenient and safe for people who travel to various countries with portable computers.

Cooling Systems

Definition:

A *cooling system* is a system unit component that prevents damage to computer parts by dissipating the heat generated inside a computer chassis. The cooling system can contain fans and other devices such as a heat sink that service the entire computer as well as individual components such as the power supply and CPU.

Example:

Figure 1-11: A typical cooling system for a CPU.

Components that Require Cooling

Computer systems contain several components that require cooling:

- The computer case
- The CPU
- The power supply
- Some adapter cards
- Some hard disk drives

Cooling System Types

Several types of cooling systems have been developed to protect personal computer components.

Cooling System	Description
Fans	Computer fans provide cooling by simply blowing regular air across heated components. Fans are commonly used to cool the case, power supply, adapter cards, and CPUs.
Vents	Computer cases are designed with vents to facilitate airflow through the case and across all components. A common implementation is to include air vents near the bottom of the front of the case and to place a fan near the top of the rear of the case to pull cooler air through the system.
Heat sinks	A device attached to a processor that addresses the problem of overheating processors. It normally has fins to increase its surface area to aid in heat dissipation. Cool air is blown by a fan onto the device's main elements, keeping the air around the processor cool.
Thermal compound	Thermal compounds are used to connect a heat sink to a CPU. They are designed to provide maximum heat transfer from the CPU to the heat sink.
Liquid cooling systems	CPUs can also be kept cool using a device to circulate a liquid, such as water, around the CPU. The heat from the CPU is absorbed by the cooler liquid, and then the heated liquid is circulated away from the CPU so it can disperse the heat into the air outside the computer. Liquid cooling systems are not as prevalent as heat sinks in most desktop systems or low-end servers.

Although it might seem to be a good idea to remove the chassis cover to provide additional cooling, it is not recommended. Most PC cases have been designed to provide an airflow path, with fans positioned to keep the air moving and blow hot air away from heat-sensitive components. The PC case must be closed for this airflow path to work properly. If the case cover is removed, the fans will blow air around at random. Opening the PC case also allows more dust to accumulate on internal components, causing additional cooling problems.

Adapter Cards

Definition:

An *adapter card* is a printed circuit board that you install into a slot on the computer's system board to expand the functionality of the computer. Each card has a connector that fits into a slot on a system board and circuitry to connect a specific device to the computer. Some adapter cards connect to the system bus instead of a peripheral bus, use different slot types, or are built into the system circuitry instead of being separate physical boards.

An adapter card is also known as an expansion card, add-in, add-on, or simply a board.

Example:

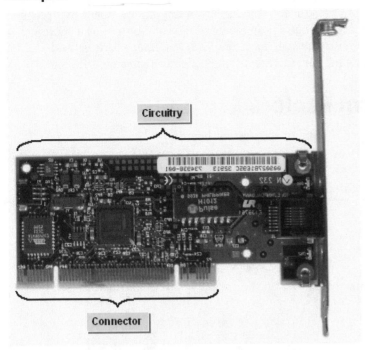

Figure 1-12: An adapter card.

Riser Cards

Definition:

A *riser card* is a board that plugs into the system board and provides additional slots for adapter cards. Because it rises above the system board, it enables you to connect additional adapters to the system in an orientation that is parallel to the system board and save space within the system case.

Example:

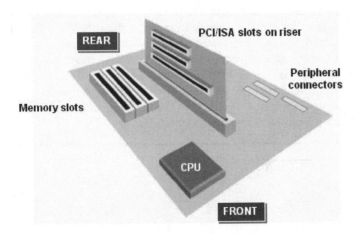

Figure 1-13: A system board with a riser card.

Daughter Boards

Daughter board is a general computing and electronics term for any circuit board that plugs into another. For example, in personal computing, daughter board can be used as a more general term for adapter cards. Sometimes in casual usage the term daughter board is used interchangeably with the term riser card, but technically they are not the same.

System Board Form Factors

The *form factor* describes the size and shape of the system board.

System Board	*Form Factor*
Full-size AT	

This form factor is usually used in older tower systems. Originally, it was designed from an even older system, the original XT motherboard, which itself was designed for use in the second version of the IBM PC, released in 1983. These original full-size systems took up a large amount of desktop space. Vertically-oriented tower systems using the AT board can stand on the floor and not take up desktop space, and they can still use the full-size system board. The board is 12 inches by 13.8 inches. A transfer bus of 16-bit or better is required. It uses CMOS to retain configuration settings. It has a 5-pin DIN keyboard connection.

System Board   *Form Factor*

Baby AT

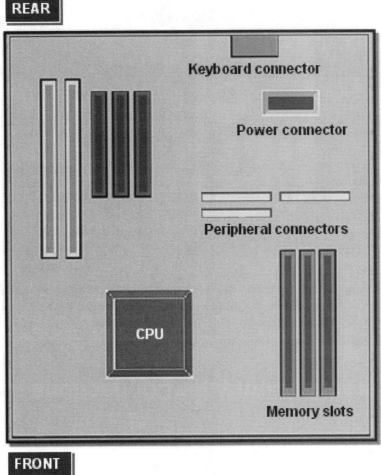

This form factor is usually used in older desktop systems. In an effort to free up desk space, manufacturers wanted to build a computer that was smaller than systems with full-size AT motherboards. The popular AT motherboard was scaled down to create the Baby AT motherboard. It fits into a smaller case than the full-size AT board, but it is otherwise the same. It works in any case except for those considered low profile or slimline. This was an extremely popular design. This board is usually 13 inches by 8.5 to 9 inches. It was never developed as a standard, so there are variations on the size of this particular board.

System Board	Form Factor
ATX	

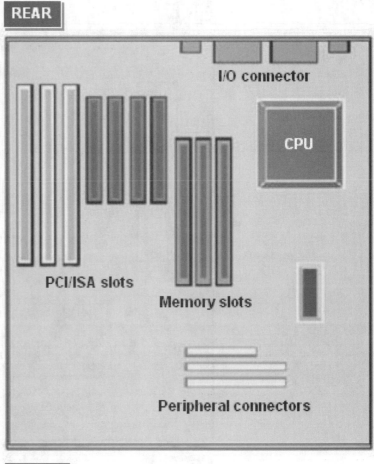

Compared to AT system boards, the ATX form factor boards provide better I/O support, lower cost, easier use, and better processor support. Some of the features of the ATX board are:

● Power supply with a single, keyed 20-pin connector. Rather than requiring Voltage Regulator Modules (VRMs) to reduce voltage down from 5 volts to 3, 3v DC is available directly from the power supply.

● The CPU is closer to the cooling fan on the power supply. Also, the cooling circulation blows air into the case instead of blowing air out of the case.

● I/O ports are integrated into the board along with PS/2 connectors (instead of 5-pin DIN connectors).

● You can access the entire motherboard without reaching around drives. This was accomplished by rotating the board 90 degrees.

● This board cannot be used in Baby AT or LPX cases.

● The board is 12 inches by 9.6 inches.

System Board	**Form Factor**

microATX

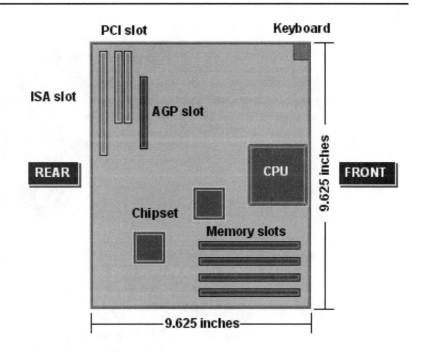

With a maximum size of 9.6 inches x 9.6 inches (244 mm x 244 mm), microATX boards with integrated graphics are often used by system board manufacturers as a basis for small form factor and home entertainment PCs. MicroATX boards can often use the same components as ATX system boards. There are fewer I/O ports available than in ATX systems, so it might be necessary to use external USB hard drives, expansion cards, CD burners, and so forth.

System Board	**Form Factor**

LPX

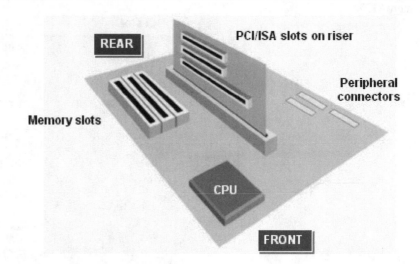

Slimline and low-profile cases, which are today's typical desktop cases, were being developed about the same time as the Baby AT motherboard was introduced. However, these smaller cases could not use even the Baby AT board. The LPX and Mini-LPX motherboards were developed for these cases. A riser card is used to plug expansion cards into the motherboard. This riser card enables the expansion cards to lie sideways, in the same orientation as the system board. Thus, the case does not have to be as high as the card. Another difference in this board is that it uses a PS/2-style keyboard connector rather than the 5-pin DIN connector used on the AT boards. Video, parallel, and two serial ports were placed at the rear of the board in standard locations. This board is 9 inches by 11 to 13 inches. A mini-LPX board was also designed, which was 8 to 9 inches by 10 to 11 inches.

System Board	Form Factor
NLX	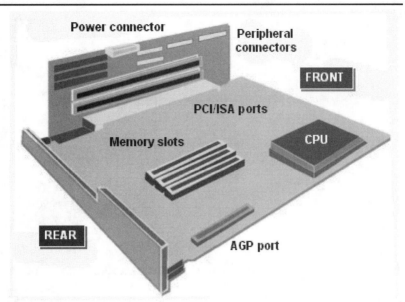

The NLX system board replaces the LPX system board. It is a small form factor designed around the Pentium II processor. It supports advances in memory and graphics technology such as DIMMs and AGP. It is used in newer slimline design systems. The board is 8 to 9 inches by 10 to 13.6 inches.

System Board   Form Factor

BTX

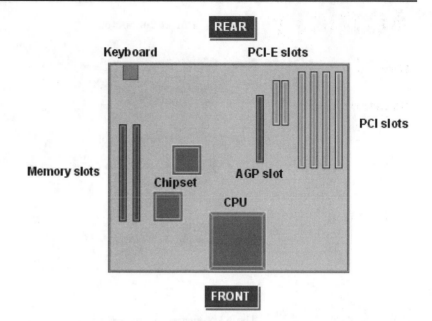

Intended to be the replacement for the ATX system board form factor, the BTX form factor was designed to alleviate some of the issues that arose from using newer technologies (which often demand more power and create more heat) on system boards compliant with the circa-1996 ATX specification. BTX features include:

● Low profile: The backplane is inches lower than the ATX.

● Thermal design: The BTX layout establishes a straighter path of airflow with fewer obstacles, resulting in better overall cooling capabilities.

● Structural design: The emerging need for heat sinks, capacitors, and other components dealing with electrical and thermal regulation has resulted in devices that can physically strain some motherboards. The BTX standard addresses this issue by specifying better locations for hardware mounting points. For example, the chips that make up the system's chipset are located closely to each other and to the hardware they control to reduce delays in data transfer.

ACTIVITY 1-2

Identifying System Unit Components

Scenario:

In this activity, you will identify system unit components.

1. Identify the system unit components in this graphic.

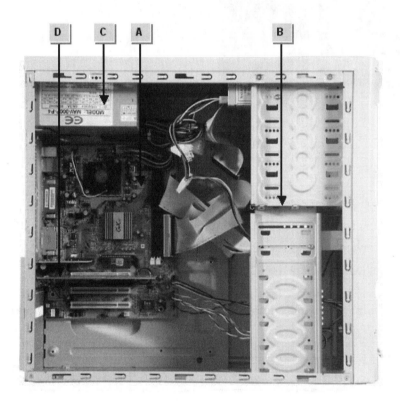

___	A	a. Storage device
___	B	b. Power supply
___	C	c. System board
___	D	d. Adapter card

2. **Identify the system unit components shown in this graphic.**

___	A	a.	Memory
___	B	b.	CPU

3. **What is a system bus?**

   a) The communication path from memory to the adapter card slots.

   b) The communication path between the CPU and memory.

   c) The connection between the power supply and the system board.

   d) The electronic pathway between the CPU and the storage devices.

4. **True or False? There is at least one cooling system inside almost every personal computer.**

   ___ True

   ___ False

TOPIC C
Storage Devices

In the last topic, you identified the main components of the system unit. The next group of major internal computer components are the computer storage devices. In this topic, you will identify the various types of storage devices used in personal computers.

As a computer technician, your responsibilities are likely to include installing and maintaining different types of internal and external computer components, including storage devices. Identifying the types of storage devices found in most personal computers will help when you are asked to work on a personal computer.

Floppy Disk Drives (FDD)

Definition:

A *floppy disk drive (FDD)* is a personal computer storage device that reads data from, and writes data to, removable disks made of flexible Mylar plastic covered with magnetic coating and enclosed in stiff, protective, plastic cases. The vast majority of floppy drives are internal devices that connect to the system board and get their power from the personal computer's power supply.

Example:

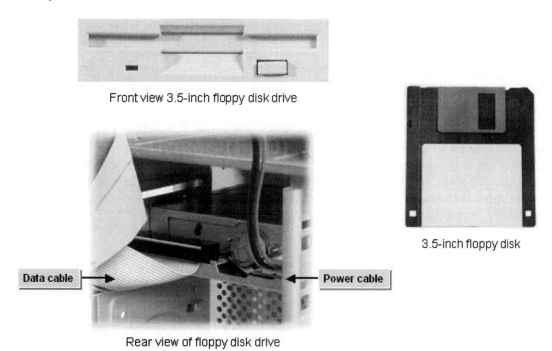

Front view 3.5-inch floppy disk drive

3.5-inch floppy disk

Data cable → ← Power cable

Rear view of floppy disk drive

Figure 1-14: A floppy disk drive (FDD).

Hard Disk Drives (HDD)

Definition:

A *hard disk drive (HDD)* is a personal computer storage device that uses fixed media, which means that the disk is built into the drive and the drive remains in the computer unless you are performing an upgrade or a repair. Hard drives connect directly to the system board via at least one cable for data and one for power. The hard disk itself consists of several metal or hard plastic platters with a magnetic surface coating. Data is stored magnetically and can be accessed directly. Most hard drives are internal, but some are external.

Example:

Figure 1-15: A hard disk drive (HDD).

Optical Disks

Definition:

An *optical disk* is a personal computer storage device that stores data optically, rather than magnetically. The removable plastic disks have a reflective coating and require an optical drive to be read. In optical storage, data is written by either pressing or burning with a laser to create pits (recessed areas) or lands (raised areas) in the reflective surface of the disc. A laser in the optical drive then reads the data off the disc. Optical drives can be internal or external, and they generally have a 5.25-inch form factor.

Example:

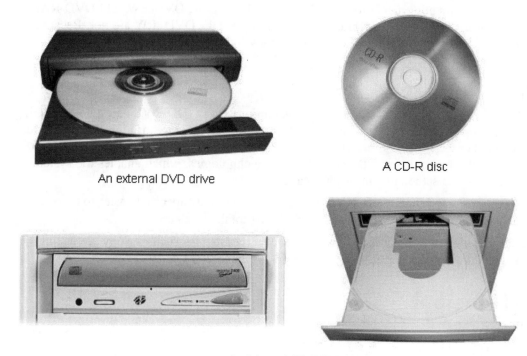

An external DVD drive

A CD-R disc

An internal CD-ROM drive

Figure 1-16: Optical disks and drives.

Types of Optical Disks and Drives

Optical disks and drives come in several types.

Optical Disk Type	Description
CD-ROM	Compact Disc-Read Only Memory. Data is permanently burned onto the disk during its manufacture.
CD-R	CD-Recordable. Data can be written to the disk only once.
CD-RW	CD-Rewritable. Data can be written to the disk multiple times.
DVD-ROM	Digital Video Disc-Read Only Memory, or Digital Versatile Disc-Read Only Memory. Data is permanently burned onto the disk during its manufacture.
DVD-R	DVD-Recordable. Data can be written to the disk only once.
DVD+R	DVD Plus Recordable. Data can be written to the disk only once.
DVD+R DL	DVD Plus Recordable Double Layer. Data can be written to the disk only once.
DVD-RW	DVD-Rewritable. Data can be written to the disk multiple times.
DVD+RW	DVD Plus Rewritable. Data can be written to the disk multiple times.
DVD-RAM	DVD-Random Access Memory. Data can be written to the disk multiple times.

DVD Plus or Dash?

There are several competing DVD formats. DVD-ROM, DVD-R, DVD-RW, and DVD-RAM are approved by the DVD Forum, while DVD+R, DVD+R DL, DVD+RW are not. Because some of the competing formats are incompatible, many hybrid DVD drives have been developed. These hybrid drives are often labeled DVD ±RW.

New Optical Disk Formats

Blu-ray Disk (BD) and High Density (or High Definition) DVD (HD DVD) are two competing next-generation optical disk standards intended for high-density storage of high-definition video as well as data storage. Both use blue laser light to read and store data. The blue laser has a shorter wavelength than existing CD and DVD laser technologies, which enables the system to store more data in the same amount of physical space.

- HD-DVD has less capacity per layer than Blu-ray, but is cheaper and easier to manufacture. Current HD-DVD disks hold 30 GB total.

- Current Blu-ray disks hold 50 GB total. However, companies such as Sony are testing experimental disks that have storage capacities of up to 200 GB.

Tape Drives

Definition:

A *tape drive* is a personal computer storage device that stores data magnetically on a tape that is enclosed in a removable tape cartridge. Data on the tape must be read sequentially. The size of external tape drives varies, but internal drives have a 5.25-inch form factor. Tape drives are most commonly used to store backup copies of data.

Example:

Figure 1-17: A tape drive.

Solid State Storage

Definition:

Solid state storage is a personal computer storage device that stores data in special types of memory instead of on disks or tape. Common types of solid state storage include the USB devices commonly known as jump drives or thumb drives, flash memory cards, and secure digital (SD) memory cards. Solid state storage uses a combination of volatile and non-volatile memory to emulate mechanical storage devices, but solid state storage is usually faster than mechanical storage because there are no moving parts.

Example:

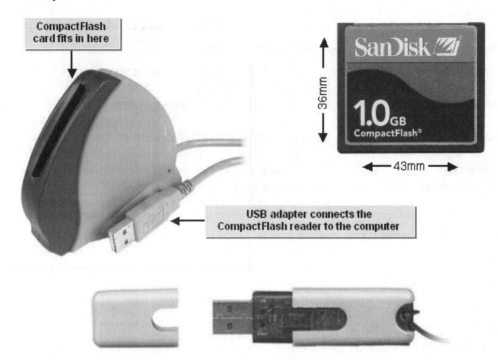

Figure 1-18: Solid state storage.

ACTIVITY 1-3

Identifying Storage Devices

Scenario:

In this activity, you will identify storage devices.

1. **Match the storage type with the appropriate description.**

    ___ Floppy disk drive   a. Records data magnetically; most often used for backups.

    ___ Hard disk drive   b. Records and reads data by using a laser.

    ___ Optical disk drive   c. Records data magnetically on removable disks.

    ___ Tape drive   d. Records data on non-removable disks.

    ___ Solid state storage   e. Records data in memory that emulates a mechanical storage device.

2. **Which optical drive media types enable you to write to an optical disk only once?**

    a) CD-ROM

    b) CD-R

    c) CD-RW

    d) DVD-R

    e) DVD-RW

TOPIC D
Personal Computer Connection Methods

You have now identified the primary components inside the system case. The next thing to do is investigate the means by which those components, and other components, are connected together to form a complete personal computer system. In this topic, you will identify personal computer connection methods.

A personal computer is made up of many different components. To be able to work together effectively to provide users with the computing power they need, these components need to be able to communicate with each other. As personal computers have evolved over the years, different connection technologies have been implemented to provide communication among computer components. As a computer technician, identifying the different connection technologies will enable you to install personal computer components quickly and effectively.

Ports

Definition:

A *port* is a hardware interface where you can connect devices to the computer. The port transfers electronic signals between the device and the system unit. The port is either an electrically wired socket or plug or a wireless transmission device. Ports can vary by shape, the number and layout of the pins or connectors contained within the port, the signals the port carries, and the port's location. There are ports for both internal and external devices.

Example:

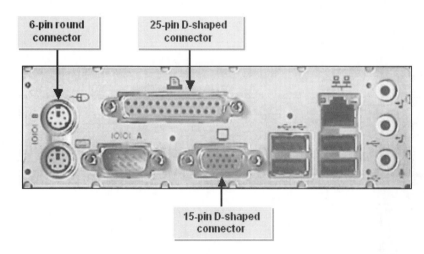

Enable devices to be connected to a personal computer

Figure 1-19: Ports enable devices to connect to a personal computer.

Genders

Ports and the cables that connect to them have genders. For example, if a computer port consists of a plug, the matching cable connection will have a socket. The port in this case would be the male connector and the cable would be the female connector.

Port Shapes

Ports can have different physical shapes such as male, female, round, rectangular, square, and oblong. There is some standardization of physical properties and functions, though. For example, most computers have a keyboard port (currently round, or telephone type), into which the keyboard is connected.

PS/2 Ports

The round 6-pin ports that many keyboards and mice connect to are called PS/2 ports, after the early IBM Personal System/2 personal computer. To avoid confusion between the identical-looking keyboard and mouse ports, PS/2 ports are often color-coded to match the end of the cable on the device: purple for the keyboard and green for the mouse. Or, there will be a sticker with a picture of a mouse and keyboard near the connectors.

PS/2 ports are also called mini-DIN ports. DIN is the abbreviation for a German standards organization. There is an older, larger DIN port with only 5 pins.

Personal Computer Connections

Definition:

A *personal computer connection* is the collection of hardware components that enables the computer to communicate with internal or external devices. It comprises the ports on both the computer and the device plus a transmission medium, which is either a cable with connectors at each end or a wireless technology. Personal computer connections can be categorized by the technology or standard that was used to develop the device.

Example:

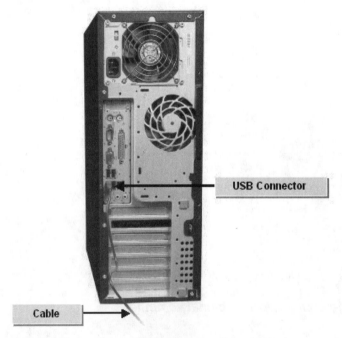

Figure 1-20: Personal computer connections.

Serial Connections

Definition:

A *serial connection* is a personal computer connection that transfers data one bit at a time over a single wire. Serial connections support two-way communications and are typically used for devices such as fax machines or external modems. Serial ports have either 9-pin (DB-9) or 25-pin (DB-25) male connectors. A serial cable ends with a female connector to plug in to the male connector on the system unit. On system units that have color-coded ports, the serial port is teal-colored.

Example:

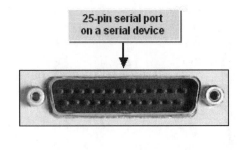

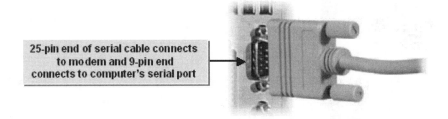

Figure 1-21: Serial connections.

Serial Transmissions

In a serial transmission, data is sent and received one bit at a time over a single wire. To accomplish this, the serial communication process:

1. Disassembles bytes into bits on the sending end of the communication.

2. Sends the bits across the communication wires.

3. Reassembles the bits into bytes at the receiving end.

Serial Ports

Serial ports are typically called COM1, COM2, COM3, and COM4, where COM is short for communications port. In modern systems, only one or two serial ports will be present. This port is being phased out in favor of other standards, so you might find some systems with no serial ports at all.

Other Uses for Serial Connections

Serial connections can be used for direct PC-to-PC connections and to connect some mice, printers, and Personal Digital Assistant (PDA) devices.

Parallel Connections

Definition:

A *parallel connection* is a personal computer connection that transfers data eight bits at a time over eight wires and is typically used to connect a printer to a system unit. Parallel connections in older personal computers support only one-way or unidirectional communications. Most computers now have parallel ports that support bidirectional communications. Standard parallel ports have 25-pin female connectors. A parallel cable has a 25-pin male connector to plug into the system unit and a 36-pin male Centronics connector at the other end to attach to the external device. On system units that have color-coded ports, the parallel port is burgundy or dark pink.

Example:

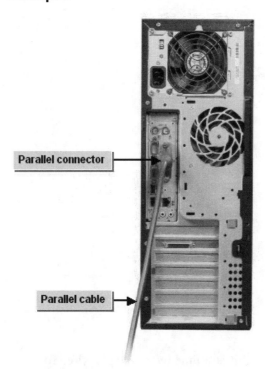

Figure 1-22: Parallel connections.

Parallel Ports

A PC can have up to three parallel ports, referred to as LPT1, LPT2, and LPT3. LPT is short for line printer.

Other Uses for Parallel Connections

In addition to printers, other devices, such as older scanners, some network adapters, CD-ROM drives, and other types of external drives used to be connected to a system unit by using parallel ports. Some devices had piggy-back connections, enabling you to install a second parallel device on a port with the first device.

Universal Serial Bus (USB) Connections

Definition:

A *USB connection* is a personal computer connection that enables you to connect multiple peripherals to a single port with high performance and minimal device configuration. USB connections support two-way communications. Most computers today have one or more USB ports and can, with the use of USB hubs, support up to 127 devices per port. USB cables usually have different connectors at each end. The computer end of the cable ends in a Type A connector. The device end of the cable ends in a Type B connector. The size of the connector varies depending on the device.

Example:

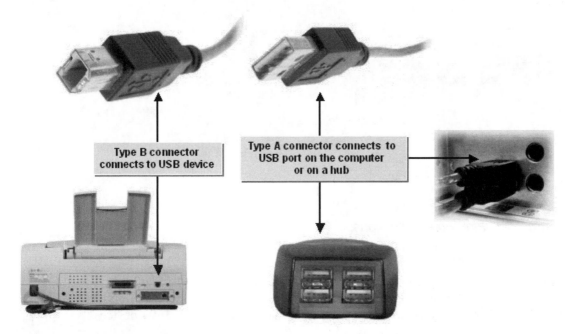

Figure 1-23: *USB connections.*

USB Standards

USB 2.0 is the current standard. It can communicate at up to 480 Mbps. The original USB 1.1 standard is still commonly found in devices and systems. It can communicate at up to 12 Mbps. A USB 2.0 device connected to a USB 1.1 hub or port will only communicate at USB 1.1 speeds, even though it might be capable of faster speeds. Windows XP will inform you of this when you connect the device.

IEEE 1394 and FireWire Connections

Definition:

A *FireWire connection* is a personal computer connection that provides a high-speed interface for peripheral devices that are designed to use the *IEEE* 1394 standard. FireWire can support up to 63 devices on one FireWire port. FireWire 400 transmits at 400 Mbps and uses either a 6-pin bullet-shaped powered connector or a 4-pin square-shaped unpowered connector. FireWire 800 transmits at 800 Mbps and uses a 9-pin connector.

Example:

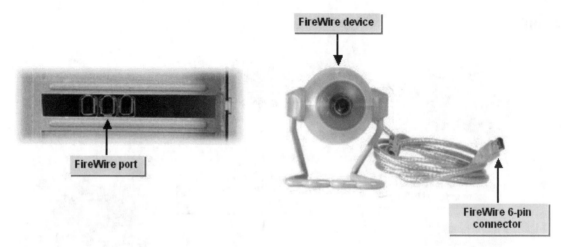

Figure 1-24: FireWire connections.

FireWire Terminology

Apple Computer was the primary vendor to promote the IEEE 1394 standard, and used the FireWire name as a trademark for the IEEE 1394 implementation included in its Macintosh systems. FireWire has since become the common name for all IEEE 1394 devices.

FireWire vs. USB

FireWire predated USB and was faster than the original USB 1.1 standard. USB 2.0, with its increased speed, has largely superseded FireWire. However, although USB 2.0 is faster by the numbers than FireWire, FireWire is actually faster on throughput, making it ideal for video/audio file transfers and external storage devices. A file transfer of 100 separate documents might be slightly faster on USB than FireWire, but a file transfer of a single 2 GB video file will be much faster in FireWire. Also, while USB provides a device up to 5V power, FireWire provides up to 12V power on the wire.

Small Computer Systems Interface (SCSI) Connections

Definition:

SCSI is an older connection standard, typically used for storage devices such as tape and hard drives, that remains in use due to its reliability and high speed. A SCSI adapter has a port for external devices and a connection for internal devices. SCSI devices themselves can have multiple ports, enabling you to connect several devices in a chain to one SCSI adapter. Each device in the chain requires a unique ID, which you configure by using switches or jumpers. SCSI cables have 50-pin, 68-pin, or 80-pin connectors depending upon the type of SCSI in use.

Example:

SCSI connector

SCSI cable

Figure 1-25: SCSI connections.

Parallel ATA (PATA) Connections

Definition:

A *PATA connection* is a drive connection standard that provides a parallel data channel from the drive controller to the disk drives. Originally called IDE, EIDE, or *ATA*, PATA connections are used to connect internal hard drives, optical drives, and tape drives to the system board. On the system board, two sockets provide connections for up to two drives per socket. PATA cables are ribbon cables with 40 or 80 wires and 40-pin connectors.

 You might hear PATA pronounced "Parallel ay-tee-ay," "PEE-ay-tee-ay," "PAY-tuh," or "PAT-uh."

Example:

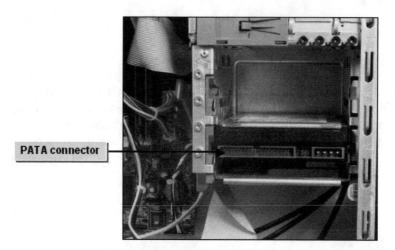

Figure 1-26: PATA connections.

ATA, IDE, and EIDE

IDE (Integrated Drive Electronics) and EIDE (Enhanced IDE) are alternative names for the ATA (Advanced Technology Attachment) standards that are now referred to as PATA. (After Serial ATA drives became popular, the PATA term was coined to refer to the parallel drives.) There have been several versions of the ATA standard, with successive versions providing support for different types of devices, or providing performance enhancements such as higher data rates. For example, ATAPI (Advanced Technology Attachment Packet Interface) provides support for tape drives and CD-ROM drives, while ATA-7 supports data rates up to 133 MB/sec.

Master and Slave Designations

PATA drives are configured in a master/slave hierarchy, usually by setting *jumpers*. Each PATA channel can support one or two devices. Because each PATA device contains its own integrated controller, you need to have some way of differentiating between the two devices. This is done by giving each device a designation as either master or slave, or by using the Cable Select feature to assign master and slave designations, and then having the controller address commands and data to either one or the other.

● In the master/slave configuration scheme, the drive that is the target of the command responds to it, and the other one ignores the command, remaining silent. Each manufacturer uses a different combination of jumpers for specifying whether its drive is master or slave on the channel, though they're all similar. Some manufacturers put this information right on the top label of the drive itself, while others do not. Jumpering information is available in the hard disk's documentation, or by checking the manufacturer's website and searching for the model number.

● With Cable Select, you don't have to set jumpers to designate which device is master and which is slave. The connectors that are connected to the devices take care of the configuration. To set up Cable Select, you need to use a jumper to set both devices on the channel to the Cable Select (CS) setting, along with a special cable. This cable is similar in most respects to the regular PATA cable, except for the CSEL (Cable SELect) signal, which the devices use to determine which is the master and which is the slave.

Serial ATA (SATA) Connections

Definition:

A *SATA connection* is a drive connection standard that enhances PATA by providing a serial data channel between the drive controller and the disk drives. SATA transfer speeds are much higher than PATA for the same drive technologies. SATA's physical configuration is also easier because the SATA serial cables are much smaller, thinner, and more flexible than traditional PATA ribbon cables. SATA connectors have four pins.

 You might hear SATA pronounced "Serial ay-tee-ay," "ESS-ay-tee-ay," "SAY-tuh," or "SAT-uh."

 Although current practice is to use the terms IDE and PATA interchangeably, you should be aware that SATA is also a type of IDE drive.

Example:

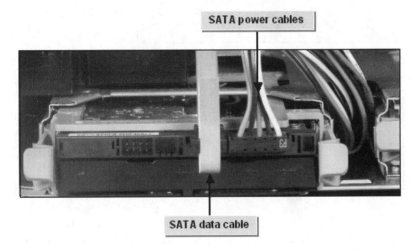

Figure 1-27: SATA connections.

ACTIVITY 1-4

Identifying Personal Computer Connection Methods

Scenario:
In this activity, you will identify personal computer connection methods.

---

1. **Identify the connection types listed.**

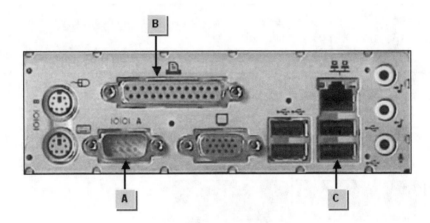

___	A	a.	Parallel
___	B	b.	Serial
___	C	c.	USB

---

2. **Which PC connection type is sometimes called IDE?**

   a) FireWire

   b) PATA

   c) SATA

   d) SCSI

   e) USB

---

3. **Which connection type supports up to 127 peripherals in a single connection?**

   a) IEEE 1394

   b) SATA

   c) Parallel

   d) USB

---

4. **Which cable has the smallest connectors?**

    a) SCSI

    b) PATA

    c) SATA

    d) Parallel

Lesson 1 Follow-up

In this lesson, you have identified the components that make up most standard desktop personal computers. The ability to identify the various parts of personal computers is essential foundational knowledge for every computer technician.

1. **How many of the personal computer components described are familiar to you?**

2. **What is the most important component of a computer?**

2 | Operating System Fundamentals

Lesson Time: 2 hour(s), 15 minutes

Lesson Objectives:

In this lesson, you will identify fundamental components and functions of personal computer operating systems.

You will:

- Identify the major personal computer operating systems.
- Identify the primary components of the Windows user interface.
- Identify the primary tools and functions used in Windows file system management.
- Identify Windows system management tools.

Introduction

In the previous lesson, you identified the hardware components of standard desktop personal computers. The other major element of a personal computer is its operating system software. In this lesson, you will identify the fundamental components and functions of personal computer operating systems.

As a professional IT support representative or PC service technician, your job will entail installing, upgrading, configuring, troubleshooting, and optimizing personal computer operating systems. Before you can perform any of those important functions, you need to understand the basics of what operating systems are, including their various versions, features, components, and technical capabilities. With this knowledge, you can build a career in which you can provide effective support in all types of system environments.

This lesson covers all or part of the following CompTIA A+ (2006) certification objectives:

- Topic A:
    - Exam 220–601 (Essentials): Objective 3.1
    - Exam 220–603 (Remote Technician): Objective 2.1
- Topic B:
    - Exam 220–601 (Essentials): Objective 3.1, Objective 3.3
    - Exam 220–602 (IT Technician): Objective 3.1
    - Exam 220–603 (Remote Technician): Objective 2.1
- Topic C:
    - Exam 220–601 (Essentials): Objective 1.2, Objective 3.1, Objective 3.3
    - Exam 220–602 (IT Technician): Objective 3.1, Objective 5.2., Objective 6.1
    - Exam 220–603 (Remote Technician): Objective 2.1, Objective 4.2, Objective 5.2
- Topic D:
    - Exam 220–601 (Essentials): Objective 3.1, Objective 3.3
    - Exam 220–602 (IT Technician): Objective 1.3, Objective 3.1
    - Exam 220–603 (Remote Technician): Objective 1.3, Objective 2.1

TOPIC A
Personal Computer Operating Systems

In this lesson, you will identify the fundamental components and functions of personal computer operating systems. The first step is to learn about the various operating systems available today, and to identify those that are commonly used on personal computers. In this topic, you will identify the major personal computer operating systems.

Although Microsoft® Windows® is the dominant operating system in the personal computer market today, there are other operating systems that can run on various desktop and laptop computers. These operating systems vary in their popularity, system requirements, and features. As a support professional, you should be familiar with the operating systems that can be installed on personal computers so that you can support a variety of computer environments.

Microsoft Windows

Microsoft Windows is the single most popular and widely deployed operating system on both desktop computers and server systems in the world today. The various versions of Windows all feature a graphical user interface, support for a wide range of applications and devices, a minimum of 32-bit processing, native networking support, and a large suite of built-in applications and accessories such as the Internet Explorer web browser. Windows currently comes pre-installed on many personal computers sold commercially.

Microsoft Windows Versions

Microsoft Windows comes in several different versions and revision levels for use on both personal computers and network servers. They are described in the following table.

Version	Description
Windows XP 	Windows XP is Microsoft's primary operating system for desktop and laptop computers for both home and office use. It comes in several distinct editions. <ul><li>Windows XP Professional, the flagship Windows XP edition, intended for office use in networked corporate environments. It supports individual file-level security and encryption, policy-based configuration management, and domain as well as workgroup membership.</li><li>Windows XP Home Edition, intended for private home users. Windows XP Home is very similar in look and feel to Windows XP Professional, but does not support some of the Windows XP Professional security and management features.</li><li>Windows XP Media Center Edition, optimized for media-based activities such as recording live TV, organizing and playing music, and managing digital photographs.</li><li>Windows XP Tablet PC edition, for tablet-type PCs.</li><li>Windows XP Professional x64 Edition, for computers with 64-bit processors.</li></ul>
Windows Server 2003 	Microsoft's current server-oriented operating system. Windows Server 2003 is currently available as Release 2 (R2). Windows Server 2003 R2 comes in several editions. <ul><li>Windows Server 2003 R2 Standard Edition, for general purpose use as a file server or service host, or to support small and medium business needs.</li><li>Windows Server 2003 R2 Enterprise Edition, optimized to support enterprise network management for large numbers of users, computers, and services.</li><li>Windows Server 2003 R2 Datacenter Edition, for high-availability applications and databases.</li></ul>
Windows 2000 	Windows 2000 was a prior version of Microsoft's enterprise operating system software. It was available in several Server editions as well as in a desktop version, Windows 2000 Professional. The Server version was the first to include Microsoft's standards-based directory service software, Active Directory. Microsoft no longer provides active product support for Windows 2000 Server or Professional.

Version	Description
Windows 9x and Windows Me 	Prior to Windows XP, the Windows 9x group of operating systems were Microsoft's primary products for end-user and home PCs. They were complete operating systems with built-in networking, but used a different code base and a different graphical interface design from the Windows Server computers available at that time, as well as from the later Windows XP operating system family. This group of operating systems is no longer supported. ● Windows 95 was Microsoft's first release of a complete desktop operating system, as opposed to a system shell for lower-level system software. It was the first to provide a graphical interface based around the Start menu and taskbar. ● Windows 98 was a popular and widely adopted version within the Windows 9x product line. It was also released as Windows 98 SE (Service Edition). ● Windows Me (Millennium Edition) was the final release in the Windows 9x code base family. It was released in 2000.
Windows NT versions 	There were several prior versions of Windows Server software, all released under the Windows NT (*aka* New Technology) brand. As a group, they employed the Windows 3.1 graphical interface and implemented network domain configurations on a proprietary Microsoft model. ● Windows NT 3.1 Advanced Server and its client version, Windows NT 3.1, were the first 32-bit versions of Windows. They were released in 1993. ● Windows NT 3.5x and its client version, Windows NT Workstation 3.5x, were the first Windows versions considered to be robust enough for enterprise network support. They were released in 1995. ● Windows NT 4.0 and its client version, Windows NT Workstation 4.0, were the first versions to use TCP/IP as the preferred protocol. They were released in 1996.

Version	Description
Older Windows desktop operating systems 	The first Windows desktop operating systems were "shell" programs that ran on top of the underlying DOS command-line-based operating system. They extended DOS by providing a graphical interface, extended memory support, mouse support, and the ability to have multiple programs open at once. ● Windows 1.0 (released in 1985), Windows 2.0 (released in 1987), Windows/286, and Windows/386 were earlier releases but were not that popular. ● Windows 3.0 was the first commercially successful version of Windows. It was released in 1990. ● Windows 3.1 was the primary end-user desktop version of Windows until the advent of Windows 95. It was released in 1992. ● Windows for Workgroups was an extension of Windows 3.1 that incorporated workgroup networking support using the NetBEUI protocol. It was released in 1992.

 Microsoft is always developing new versions of both its desktop and server editions of Windows. The company released Windows Vista for the desktop in early 2007. It also plans a new version of Windows Server, code-named "Longhorn," for server systems. For more information, see **http://www.microsoft.com/windowsvista/default.aspx** and **http://www.microsoft.com/windowsserver/longhorn/default.mspx**.

 DOS, short for Disk Operating System, was the major operating system for the majority of IBM-style personal computers until the release of Windows 95. DOS supported only 1 MB of memory without additional software enhancements, and did not support running multiple programs simultaneously. Windows has maintained support for running legacy DOS programs and provides a command-line interface at which you can issue standard DOS commands.

UNIX

UNIX® is a trademark for a family of operating systems originally developed at Bell Laboratories beginning in the late 1960s. All UNIX systems share a kernel/shell architecture, with the kernel providing the core functionality and the interchangeable shells providing the user interface. Unlike many operating systems, UNIX is portable to different hardware platforms; versions of UNIX can run on everything from personal computers to mainframes and on many types of computer processors. UNIX also incorporates built-in multitasking, multiuser support, networking functions, and a robust platform for software development.

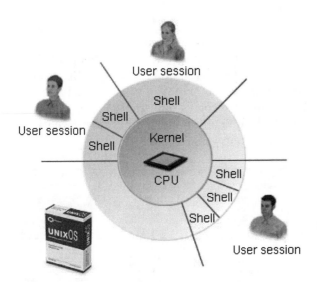

Figure 2-1: *UNIX and its architecture.*

UNIX Versions

Many different companies and organizations have licensed the UNIX name and technology, and marketed their own UNIX versions, leading to a proliferation of different UNIX families, system names, and interfaces. Different hardware manufacturers tend to favor particular versions, or "flavors," of UNIX. The following table lists some of the most important UNIX categories you will encounter.

UNIX Version	Description
Berkeley Software Distribution (BSD) UNIX	Any of a group of UNIX versions that followed the innovations incorporated into UNIX at the University of California at Berkeley.
System V Release 4 (SVR4) UNIX	The standard for UNIX systems that follow the AT&T development architecture. It was issued to unify standards and features in competing versions of UNIX, including BSD UNIX, and it is the foundation for current UNIX-based systems.
Portable Operating System for Computer Environments (POSIX)	A set of IEEE standards for portability of applications from one UNIX environment to another. An application should run identically on any POSIX-compliant platform.
Single UNIX Specification (SUS)	A set of specifications issued by The Open Group (**www.opengroup.org**), setting software standards for operating systems that qualify for the name UNIX.

Linux

Linux® is an open-standards UNIX derivative originally developed and released by a Finnish computer science student named Linus Torvalds. The Linux source code was posted publicly on a computing newsgroup, and the code was developed and tested cooperatively all over the world. Because the source code is open, it can be downloaded, modified, and installed freely. However, many organizations prefer to purchase and implement a *Linux distribution,* which is a complete Linux implementation, including kernel, shell, applications, utilities, and installation media, that is packaged, distributed, and supported by a software vendor.

 Linux is usually pronounced "LINN-ux." It is a combination of Linus Torvalds's first name (pronounced LEEN-us TOUR-valds in Swedish) and UNIX.

 The official symbol of the Linux operating system is "Tux" the penguin, which serves as a mascot for the Linux community and as a Linux logo. For information about the Linux penguin, see **www.linux.org/info/logos.html**.

Open vs. Proprietary

Open standards are any type of software-development standards that are arrived at cooperatively and are not owned, copyrighted, or maintained by any particular organization or commercial enterprise. Open standards are the opposite of *proprietary development.*

Linux Release Versions

The first version of the Linux kernel that was publicly released was version .02, released in 1991. Linux kernel version 2.6.20-rc4 was available as of January, 2007. For more information about Linux and its versions, see the Linux home page at **www.linux.org**.

Popular Linux Distributions

The following table lists some popular Linux distributions.

Vendor	Description
Red Hat® Linux®	A popular USA distribution designed to be easy for new users to install and use.
SuSE®	A popular European distribution, now owned by Novell.
Mandriva® Linux®	A Red Hat variant optimized for Pentium processors. Formerly known as Mandrake Linux.
Debian®	A free distribution assembled by volunteers that contains many utilities and supports many hardware platforms.
Gentoo®	A source-code distribution designed for professional developers and computer hobbyists.

SuSE is properly pronounced ZOO-zuh, but is often pronounced to rhyme with Suzie.

Apple Macintosh Operating Systems

Apple® Computing, Inc. markets the proprietary Macintosh® operating system with its own graphical user interface design. Mac OS® X features:

● Multiple user support.

● Integrated Mac, Windows, and UNIX server, file, and printer browsing in the Finder.

● The Safari™ Web browser.

● Native TCP/IP networking.

● Many file- and network-level security features.

● And, wide hardware device support with a unique Macintosh computer system design.

 OS X is pronounced "Oh Ess Ten."

Mac OS Versions

There have been several versions of the Macintosh operating system.

Version	Description
Mac OS® X Tiger™	A version of the Mac OS operating system that can run on both Intel and PowerPC processors. It features various enhancements to OS X, including Spotlight™ search technology.
Mac OS X	The first Mac operating system to be developed as a UNIX derivative. It is based on an open-source UNIX implementation called Darwin and features a user interface called Expose.
Prior Mac OS versions	Older versions of the Macintosh operating system were based on a proprietary system architecture and utilized the proprietary AppleTalk® file and print services and LocalTalk® network topology. Security was based on user roles, including administrative user accounts, normal user accounts, limited user accounts, and panel user accounts.

 The next release of the Mac OS X operating system will be named Mac OS X Leopard. For more information on Leopard, see **http://www.apple.com/macosx/ leopard/**.

ACTIVITY 2-1

Discussing Operating Systems

Scenario:
In this activity, you will discuss various personal computer operating systems.

1. **Match the version of Windows with its description.**

   ___ Windows XP Professional

   ___ Windows XP Home

   ___ Windows XP Media Center

   ___ Windows 98

   ___ Windows 3.1

   ___ Windows 2000 Professional

   a. A desktop version of Windows that provided a graphical shell for DOS.

   b. The flagship Windows version intended for desktop use in corporate business environments as well as for general use.

   c. A version of Windows that is optimized for activities such as recording live TV, playing music, and managing digital images.

   d. A popular complete Windows operating system including network support, built on a unique code base that is no longer supported.

   e. A version of Windows intended for private users, with a limited set of security and management features.

   f. A desktop version, no longer supported, of Microsoft's enterprise server operating system software.

2. **Which statements about UNIX are true?**

   a) There are many versions of UNIX from different developers and distributors.

   b) All versions of UNIX use the same shell, or user interface.

   c) UNIX versions are proprietary.

   d) UNIX is a multiuser, multitasking system.

   e) It was developed using open-source methodology.

3. **Which statements about Linux are true?**

   a) It was developed as open-source software.

   b) Developers must obtain permission to access and modify the source code.

   c) Development was initiated and managed by Linus Torvalds.

   d) Releases of Linux are unstable.

   e) Linux distributions can provide tools, utilities, and system support.

4. **Mac OS X can:**

   a) Be downloaded and modified freely.

   b) Integrate browsing for files created in other operating systems.

   c) Support many hardware devices.

   d) Run the Windows XP user interface.

TOPIC B
Windows User Interface Components

In the previous topic, you identified the major personal computer operating systems and learned that Microsoft Windows is the most common of those operating systems in use today. Your next step in preparing to support the Microsoft Windows operating system is to identify the elements of Windows that users interact with most often. In this topic, you will identify the primary components of the Windows user interface.

The Windows user interface is the starting point for interacting with the Windows operating system for systems professionals and end users alike. As a professional support technician, you'll need to understand the user interface both so that you can utilize it to interact with Windows efficiently in your own work, and so that you can help users who want to understand the system and use it effectively.

The Windows Desktop

The *Windows desktop* is a general term for the overall contents of the computer screen that displays whenever Windows is running. The desktop always contains the taskbar and Start button as well as desktop icons and shortcuts that users can click to launch programs and documents. The remainder of the screen can display graphic images, patterns, or simply a background color. The desktop is highly configurable, so the specific appearance of it will depend upon the Windows version in use and the user's preferences.

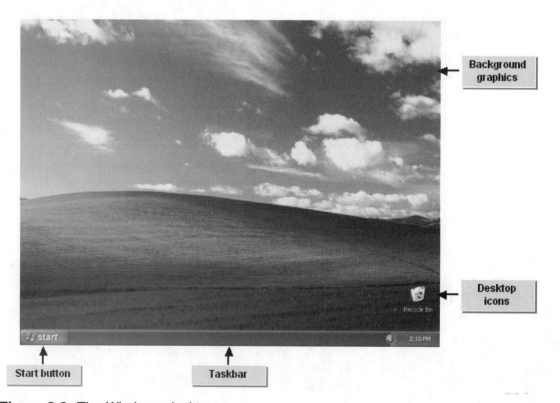

Figure 2-2: The Windows desktop.

The Taskbar

The taskbar is located at the bottom of the Windows XP screen. It contains:

● The Start button.

● The optional Quick Launch toolbar, which provides one-click access to frequently used programs.

● Buttons for any open programs.

● And, the notification area, which includes the clock icon plus icons for various system tools. You can access the properties of these programs by clicking or right-clicking the icons.

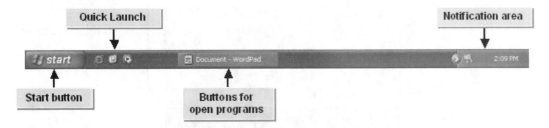

Figure 2-3: The taskbar.

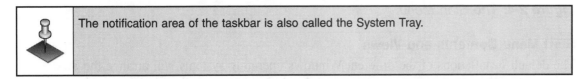

The notification area of the taskbar is also called the System Tray.

The Start Menu

The Start menu is the main entry point into the Windows user interface. You can access programs, tools, and documents by choosing them directly from the Start menu or from one of its sub-menus. The Start menu can display the name of the current user or the Windows version in use. To open the Start menu, click the Start button on the taskbar.

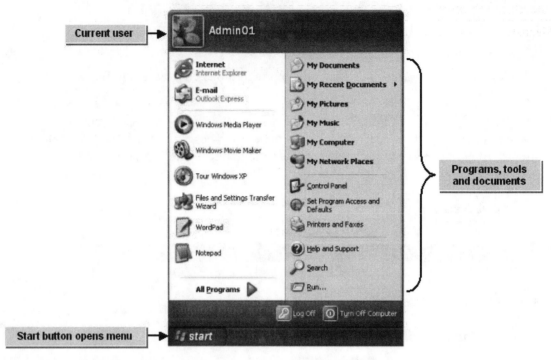

Figure 2-4: *The Start menu.*

Start Menu Contents and Views

The default installations of the different Windows operating systems will arrange the Start menu in slightly different ways. Some programs also add icons to the Start menu when they are installed. The following table shows the default Start menu contents for Windows 2000 Professional and Windows XP Professional.

Operating System	*Default Start Menu Contents*
Windows 2000 Professional	<ul><li>A link to the Windows Update website.</li><li>The Programs menu.</li><li>The Documents menu.</li><li>The Settings menu.</li><li>The Search menu.</li><li>A shortcut to Windows Help.</li><li>The Run command.</li><li>The Shut Down command.</li></ul>

Operating System	*Default Start Menu Contents*
Windows XP Professional	• Program shortcuts that are pinned to the top of the Start menu; by default, these are Internet Explorer and Outlook Express.
	• Shortcuts to frequently used programs; by default, these include MSN® Internet Explorer®, Windows Media® Player, Windows Movie Maker, Tour Windows XP, and the Files and Settings Transfer Wizard.
	• The All Programs menu.
	• The My Documents folder.
	• The My Recent Documents folder.
	• The My Pictures folder.
	• My Computer.
	• My Network Places.
	• Control Panel.
	• Printers and Faxes.
	• A shortcut to Windows Help and Support.
	• The Search function.
	• The Run command.
	Icons for other commonly used programs are added automatically as you use the system. You can also pin items to the Start menu manually.

In Windows XP, users can modify the contents of white areas of the Start menu. The system controls the contents of the blue areas of the Start menu.

If you prefer the Windows 2000-style arrangement of the Start menu, Windows XP offers a similar configuration, called the Classic Start Menu. To use the Classic Start Menu in Windows XP, right-click the taskbar and choose Properties. Click the Start Menu tab, select Classic Start Menu, and then click OK.

ACTIVITY 2-2

Examining the Taskbar and Start Menu

Scenario:

In this activity, you will examine the Windows XP taskbar and Start menu.

 There is a simulated version of this activity available on the CD-ROM that shipped with this course. You can run this simulation on any Windows computer to review the activity after class, or as an alternative to performing the activity as a group in class. The activity simulation can be launched either directly from the CD-ROM by clicking the Interactives link and navigating to the appropriate one, or from the installed data file location by opening the C:\085820Data\Simulations\Lesson#\Activity# folder and double-clicking the executable (.exe) file.

What You Do	How You Do It
1. **Log on to Windows XP Professional.**	a. On the Welcome Screen, **click the Admin## user account.**
	b. In the Type Your Password text box, **type *!Pass1234* and press Enter.**
2. **Examine the Start menu.**	a. **Click the Start menu.**
	b. The name of the current user appears at the top of the Start menu. There are areas for pinned programs, frequently-used programs, and links to applications, folders, and menus. **Point to the All Programs menu.**
	c. The All Programs menu contains several submenus. To run a program and close the Start menu, **choose Accessories→ Notepad.**

3. Identify the areas of the taskbar.

a. Buttons on the taskbar enable you to access running programs and open documents. To minimize Notepad, **click the Notepad button on the taskbar.**

b. To close Notepad from the taskbar, **right-click the Notepad button and choose Close.**

c. The system tray at the right end of the taskbar contains links to system accessories. You can point to the current time in the system tray to display the date and time. **Double-click the current time in the system tray** to open the Clock program.

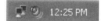

d. Administrators can use the Date And Time Properties box to change the date, time, and time zone. **Click OK.**

e. **Right-click an open area of the taskbar and choose Toolbars→Quick Launch.**

f. The Quick Launch toolbar provides one-click access to frequently-used programs. In the Quick Launch toolbar, **click the Internet Explorer icon.**

g. **Close the Internet Explorer window.**

4. Examine the Start menu and taskbar configuration settings.

a. **Right-click an open area of the taskbar and choose Properties.**

b. You can make various selections to affect the appearance and behavior of the taskbar and notification area. **Click the Start Menu tab.**

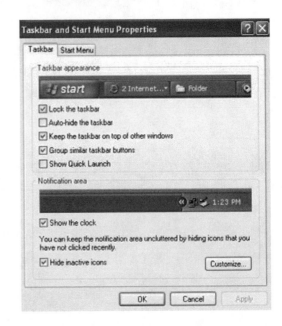

c. You can choose the Start Menu or Classic Start Menu display, and you can customize either one. **Click OK.**

Windows Explorer

Windows Explorer is a graphical tool that enables users to manage files and folders on a computer, including the contents of hard disks, floppy drives, CD and DVD drives, and any other storage devices attached to the computer. The left side of Windows Explorer holds the Explorer bar, which by default displays the folder hierarchy; the right pane displays the contents of the selected item.

 You can run Windows Explorer in Windows 2000 and Windows XP from the Accessories group on the Start menu.

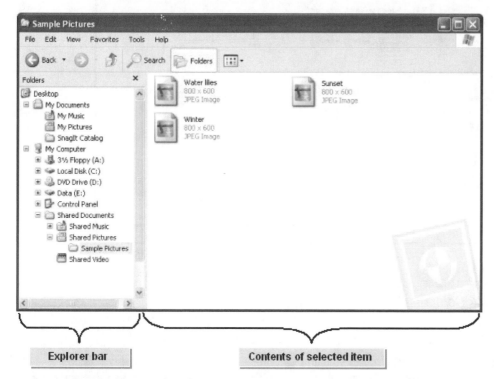

Figure 2-5: Windows Explorer.

 You can also open Windows Explorer by right-clicking an object and choosing Explore. Windows Explorer will open with the object you right-clicked selected in the folder hierarchy. For example, if you right-click the Start menu and choose Explore, Windows Explorer opens and displays the contents of the Start Menu folder on the disk.

 You can choose to display other contents in the Explorer Bar. In Windows Explorer, choose View→Explorer Bar and then choose Search, Favorites, History, Research, or Folders.

My Computer

Like Windows Explorer, My Computer is used to manage files and folders on a computer and on any storage devices attached to the computer. My Computer is simply a single-pane view of Windows Explorer, with a context-sensitive Task Pane on the left instead of the Explorer Bar. The Task Pane contains links to common tasks and resources that relate to the selected item. My Computer can be available as an icon on the Windows desktop and also from the Start menu in Windows XP.

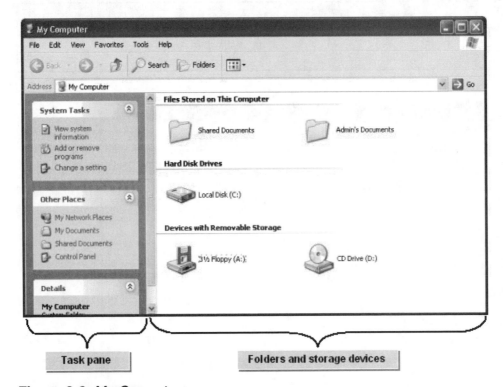

Figure 2-6: My Computer.

 You can switch at any time between the My Computer single-pane view and the Windows Explorer two-pane view by turning the Explorer Bar on or off. To turn the Explorer Bar off, choose View→Explorer Bar and then click whichever Explorer Bar view has a check mark by it.

 You can configure options for how you view and interact with My Computer or Windows Explorer windows by choosing Tools→Folder Options.

The My Documents Folder

Each user on a Windows system has a personal folder named My Documents for storing the user's individual files. The My Documents folder for the current user can be available as an icon on the desktop, and it appears on the Start menu. The My Documents folder is part of a collection of user-specific settings and folders known as the *user profile.* User profile folders are named for each user and are stored on the drive where Windows is installed.

Figure 2-7: My Documents.

 Each user's profile can be found on the disk in the path C:\Documents and Settings*user name.* The My Documents folder is a subfolder within each user's profile folder.

ACTIVITY 2-3

Examining Folder Management Tools

Scenario:

In this activity, you will examine the My Documents folder and other contents of My Computer and Windows Explorer.

 There is a simulated version of this activity available on the CD-ROM that shipped with this course. You can run this simulation on any Windows computer to review the activity after class, or as an alternative to performing the activity as a group in class. The activity simulation can be launched either directly from the CD-ROM by clicking the Interactives link and navigating to the appropriate one, or from the installed data file location by opening the C:\ 085820Data\Simulations\Lesson#\Activity# folder and double-clicking the executable (.exe) file.

What You Do	How You Do It
1. **Examine My Computer.**	a. **Choose Start→My Computer.**
	b. The My Computer window has a blue Task Pane on the left. The window shows the various drives, folders, and other storage areas available on the computer. To open drive C, **double-click the Local Disk (C:) icon.**
	c. You can see the folders on the C drive. The contents of the Task Pane change according to the contents of the folder window. In the Task Pane, under Other Places, **click My Computer.**
	d. The Address bar provides another way to navigate the contents of My Computer. In the Address bar, **click the drop-down arrow.**
	e. In the Address list, **click Local Disk (C:).**
	f. To return to the My Computer view, **click the Address drop-down arrow and choose My Computer.**

2. **Examine My Documents.**

    a. In the Task Pane, under Other Places, **click My Documents.**

    b. By default, the My Documents folder contains two subfolders, My Music and My Pictures. **Click the My Computer link.**

    c. The My Documents folder for the current user appears in My Computer. **Double-click the Admin##'s Documents folder icon.**

    d. **Close the My Documents window.**

    e. My Documents is also available from the Start menu. **Choose Start→My Documents.**

    f. **Close the My Documents window.**

3. **Examine Windows Explorer.**

a. **Choose Start→All Programs→ Accessories→Windows Explorer.**

b. Windows Explorer has a two-pane view that shows the Explorer bar on the left and the folder contents on the right. In the Explorer bar, in the Folders list, **click the plus signs to expand My Computer, Local Disk (C:).**

c. You can see the folder hierarchy for drive C. To see the contents of drive C, **select Local Disk (C:).**

d. To close the Folders list and switch to My Computer view, **click the Close box in the Explorer Bar.**

e. To switch back to Windows Explorer view, **choose View→Explorer Bar→Folders.**

f. **Close Windows Explorer.**

g. You can use the Explore choice to open an Explorer view of any selected item. **Choose Start, right-click My Documents, and choose Explore.**

h. **Close Windows Explorer.**

The Control Panel

The Control Panel is a graphical interface that provides access to a number of utilities that you can use to configure the Windows operating system or the computer's hardware. The following table shows some of the most commonly-used Control Panel utilities.

 Control Panel is available from the Start menu, and as a link in various My Computer views.

Utility	*Use To*
Add Hardware	Install or remove hardware devices from the computer.
Add or Remove Programs	Install or remove application software from the computer.
Display	Configure the wallpaper, screen saver, color scheme, and screen resolution for the computer's monitor.
Mouse	Configure mouse properties, such as whether you're using the mouse left-handed or right-handed, the double-click speed, pointer style, and acceleration.
Network Connections	Manage network and Internet connections.
Printers and Faxes	Manage printers, scanners, and fax settings.
Sounds and Audio Devices	Manage audio settings.
System	Configure hardware profiles, devices, and performance settings such as virtual memory.

Utility	*Use To*
User Accounts	Manage local user accounts on Windows XP.

 In Windows XP, by default, the Control Panel utilities are grouped together in related categories, such as Performance and Maintenance. You can display the utilities as a list by clicking Switch To Classic View in the Task Pane of Control Panel. To switch back to the default, click Switch To Category View.

 The names of the Control Panel utilities vary slightly between Windows 2000 and Windows XP. For example, Windows XP has a utility called Add Hardware; the corresponding utility in Windows 2000 is called Add/Remove Hardware. Some third-party or computer manufacturer's utilities might also add their own icons to Control Panel.

ACTIVITY 2-4

Exploring the Control Panel

Scenario:
In this activity, you will explore the components of the Control Panel.

 There is a simulated version of this activity available on the CD-ROM that shipped with this course. You can run this simulation on any Windows computer to review the activity after class, or as an alternative to performing the activity as a group in class. The activity simulation can be launched either directly from the CD-ROM by clicking the Interactives link and navigating to the appropriate one, or from the installed data file location by opening the C:\ 085820Data\Simulations\Lesson#\Activity# folder and double-clicking the executable (.exe) file.

What You Do	How You Do It
1. **Examine Control Panel utilities.**	a. **Choose Start→Control Panel.**
	b. Control Panel tools are grouped by function. **Click Appearance And Themes.**
	c. Appearance And Themes contains a number of related tools and links, as well as context-sensitive links in the Task Pane. **Click Taskbar And Start Menu.**
	d. The Taskbar And Start Menu Properties dialog box opens. **Click Cancel.**
	e. **Click the Back button.**
	f. **Examine other categories in Control Panel.**

2. **Change the Control Panel view.**

    a. In the Task Pane, **click Switch To Classic View.**

    b. **Click Switch To Category View.**

    c. You might see either one of these views on Windows XP computers. **Close Control Panel.**

The Command Prompt

Windows provides a Command Prompt interface that enables you to enter text-based commands or run command-line tools. Command-line tools accept only text input, and they output information either in text format or by opening a graphic display window. You can use command-line equivalents of graphical tools to create batch programs or scripts that automate administrative tasks. Some administrators and power users might also find command-line management to be more streamlined and efficient than working through a graphical interface.

Figure 2-8: The Command Prompt interface.

 Because you can run DOS-type commands at the Command Prompt, it is sometimes casually called the "DOS prompt."

Command Interpreters

Windows provides two different command interpreters. The typical Command Prompt interface is the Windows XP command interpreter. To access the Command Prompt interface, you can either run cmd.exe or choose the Command Prompt item from the Accessories menu. Windows XP also includes the DOS command interpreter, command.com, to support running DOS-based applications with an MS-DOS subsystem.

Sample Command-line Tools

The following table gives some examples of common command-line tools you can use to manage Windows computers. Because the syntax for a tool might vary slightly between operating systems, you should check online help for the exact syntax. To view online help at the Command Prompt, enter the command followed by a forward slash and a question mark (for example, `format /?`). For a list of all the available commands, type `help` at the command prompt.

Tool	Function and Syntax
Dir	List the contents of a directory (folder). `dir [path] [switches]`
Cd	Change to another directory. `cd drive:path`
Copy	Copy files. `copy source destination`
Del	Delete files. `del filename`
Md	Create a directory. `md foldername`
Rd	Delete a directory. `rd foldername`
Rename	Rename a file. `rename drive:path oldfilename newfilename`
Type	Display the contents of a text file. `type drive:path filename`
Ver	Display the operating system version. `ver`

ACTIVITY 2-5

Running the Command Prompt

Scenario:
In this activity, you will run the Command Prompt interface and enter basic commands.

 There is a simulated version of this activity available on the CD-ROM that shipped with this course. You can run this simulation on any Windows computer to review the activity after class, or as an alternative to performing the activity as a group in class. The activity simulation can be launched either directly from the CD-ROM by clicking the Interactives link and navigating to the appropriate one, or from the installed data file location by opening the C:\ 085820Data\Simulations\Lesson#\Activity# folder and double-clicking the executable (.exe) file.

What You Do	How You Do It
1. Open a Command Prompt.	a. Choose Start→All Programs→ Accessories→Command Prompt.
	b. The default path for the prompt is the user profile folder for the current user (C:\ Documents and Settings*username)*. **Maximize the Command Prompt window.**
2. Enter commands at the prompt.	a. To display the current operating system version, **enter *ver***
	b. To change to the root of the current drive, **enter *cd ***
	c. To see the contents of the current folder, **enter *dir***
3. Create a folder.	a. At the C:\> prompt, **enter *md LocalData* and press Enter.**

b. To verify that the folder was created, **enter**
   dir

```
C:\>md LocalData

C:\>dir
 Volume in drive C has no label.
 Volume Serial Number is E4AD-D8A1

 Directory of C:\

03/23/2006  11:48 AM    <DIR>          Apps
01/21/2005  01:45 PM    <DIR>          Compaq
01/21/2005  01:43 PM    <DIR>          cpqs
09/26/2006  03:24 PM    <DIR>          Documents and Settings
09/27/2006  10:18 AM    <DIR>          General
01/21/2005  01:42 PM    <DIR>          i386
09/27/2006  12:38 PM    <DIR>          LocalData
01/21/2005  11:27 AM    <DIR>          Program Files
09/26/2006  03:53 PM    <DIR>          WINDOWS
               0 File(s)              0 bytes
               9 Dir(s)  34,431,594,496 bytes free

C:\>_
```

c. To close the Command Prompt window,
   enter the command *exit*

My Network Places

My Network Places is a view of My Computer that enables you to connect to other computers and to manage files and folders elsewhere on the network. You can use My Network Places to:

● Display or add shortcuts to network locations or network service providers.

● View and connect to other computers on the network.

● Manage files and folders on a remote computer.

● View the network connections on your local system.

● And, transfer files and folders between your computer and a remote computer.

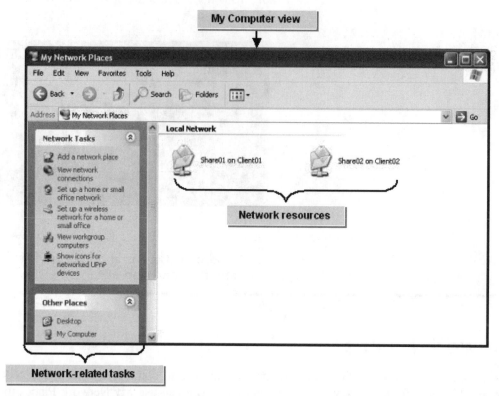

Figure 2-9: *My Network Places.*

 You must have the necessary permissions and access rights to connect to another computer and manage files and folders on that computer.

 Windows will automatically create Network Places for you as you access various resources on your local network. You can use the Add A Network Place wizard to create Network Places manually for network resources you expect to access often.

ACTIVITY 2-6

Exploring My Network Places

Scenario:
In this activity, you will explore the My Network Places interface.

 There is a simulated version of this activity available on the CD-ROM that shipped with this course. You can run this simulation on any Windows computer to review the activity after class, or as an alternative to performing the activity as a group in class. The activity simulation can be launched either directly from the CD-ROM by clicking the Interactives link and navigating to the appropriate one, or from the installed data file location by opening the C:\085820Data\Simulations\Lesson#\Activity# folder and double-clicking the executable (.exe) file.

What You Do	How You Do It
1. Examine Network Places.	a. **Choose Start→My Network Places.**
	b. The Task Pane shows network-related tasks; the window shows any Network Places shortcuts the system has created. **Click View Workgroup Computers.**
	c. You can see the computers in your workgroup, including your computer. **Double-click one of the workgroup computers.**
	d. You can see shared resources on the selected computer. **Click the Address drop-down arrow and choose Microsoft Windows Network.**
	e. The Microsoft Windows Network view enables you to see all workgroups on your local network, including your own. To return to My Network Places, **click the Address drop-down arrow and choose My Network Places.**

2. **Examine the Add A Network Place function.**

   a. In the Task Pane, **click Add A Network Place.**

   b. **Click Next.**

   c. **Verify that Choose Another Network Location is selectedmm, and click Next.**

   d. To see some examples of network place shortcut addresses, click **View Some Examples.**

   Examples:
   \\server\share   (shared folder)
   http://webserver/share   (Web Share)
   ftp://ftp.microsoft.com   (FTP site)

   e. **Click the Examples speech bubble** to close it.

   f. **Click Cancel.**

   g. **Close My Network Places.**

TOPIC C
Windows File System Management

In the previous topic, you identified the primary components of the Windows user interface. Another important Windows system component that users frequently access is the file system. In this topic, you will identify the primary tools and functions used in Windows file system management.

File and folder management is important in users' daily work, because all user data documents are stored on the disk as files. It is also important in system support tasks, as all the components of the operating system and its utilities are also stored as files on the disk. For both of these reasons, you as a support professional will need an understanding of the Windows file system and its structure, as well as the skills to manage Windows files and folders properly and efficiently.

Directories and Folders

Definition:

Directory and *folder* are interchangeable terms for a component in a file system hierarchy that provides a container to organize files and other folders. System software and applications usually create standardized directory structures at the time of installation. Users can create their own directory structures.

 In Windows, the maximum depth of a folder structure is restricted by the 255-character limit in the overall file path, including the character representing the drive and any file name and extension. Otherwise, there is no set limit on the length of a particular file or folder name.

Example:

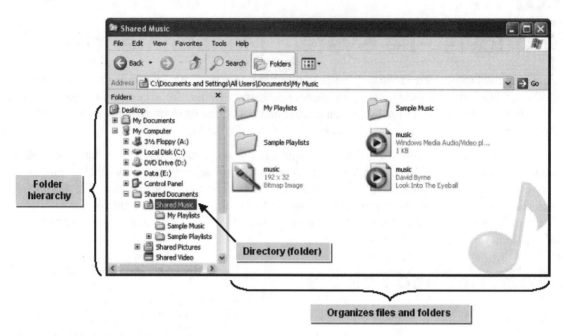

Figure 2-10: Directories and folders.

File Extensions

Standard file extensions following the names of files can indicate whether a particular file is a system, program, or data file. If it is a data file, the extension can indicate the category of application that might be used to edit the file. Many common file extensions are three characters long, although there is no longer a strict character limit for the file name or extension in most modern operating systems. A period separates the extension from the file name itself.

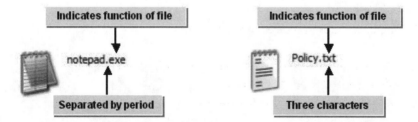

Figure 2-11: File extensions.

 By default, the folder view options in My Computer and Windows Explorer are set so that common file extensions do not display. You can display the extensions by unchecking Hide Extensions For Known File Types on the View page in the Folder Options dialog box.

Common File Extensions

The following table lists a number of common file extensions. Because Windows uses the file extension to determine how the system will use a file, if you alter a file name extension, you might find that a program file will not execute properly or that a data file will not automatically open in the associated application.

File Extension	Typically Indicates
.txt	A plain text file containing no formatting. Can be opened in any text editing program, such as Notepad, or word processing programs such as Microsoft Word.
.rtf	For Rich Text Format, a text file that can include a limited amount of formatting such as bold and italic. Can be opened in various applications such as common word processors or Microsoft's WordPad accessory.
.doc	A data file created in a word-processing program such as Microsoft Word.
.bat	A batch file; a small text file containing a string of system commands that execute in a "batch" rather than requiring the user to type each one in succession.
.bin	A binary file, containing only binary data (1s and 0s), which cannot typically be opened and read by a user application.
.com	A command file or compiled application file.
.exe	Executable files that launch programs and applications.
.dll	A Dynamic Link Library file, containing additional application settings or functions that are loaded by executable files as needed.
.hlp, .chm	Help files used by various applications.
.htm, .html	HyperText Markup Language (HTML) files, used to create web pages.
.inf	Setup configuration settings for operating systems and applications.
.ini	Configuration settings for software and hardware components.
.msi	A Windows Installer package; a file that can specify installation parameters for an application.
.sys	System files.
.tif, .jpg, .jpeg, .gif, .bmp, .png	Graphic image files in various formats.
.xls, .ppt, .mdb	Data files created in Microsoft® Excel®, Microsoft® PowerPoint® and Microsoft® Access™, respectively.

ACTIVITY 2-7

Viewing File Extensions

Scenario:

In this activity, you will view the file extensions of default files on your Windows system.

 There is a simulated version of this activity available on the CD-ROM that shipped with this course. You can run this simulation on any Windows computer to review the activity after class, or as an alternative to performing the activity as a group in class. The activity simulation can be launched either directly from the CD-ROM by clicking the Interactives link and navigating to the appropriate one, or from the installed data file location by opening the C:\ 085820Data\Simulations\Lesson#\Activity# folder and double-clicking the executable (.exe) file.

What You Do	How You Do It
1. Open the folder containing the Windows system files.	a. Choose Start→My Computer.
	b. Double-click the C drive.
	c. Double-click the Windows folder.
	d. Because this is a system folder, the contents do not automatically display. **Click Show The Contents Of This Folder.**

2. **Display the file extensions.**

   a. **Choose Tools→Folder Options.**

   b. **Click the View tab.**

   c. **Uncheck Hide Extensions For Known File Types and click OK.**

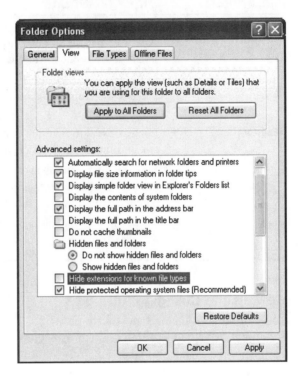

3. **Examine the file extensions.**

   a. The first few files in the window have a number of different extensions. To see all the files in a list, **choose View→List.**

   b. To see similar extensions grouped together, **choose View→Arrange Icons By→Type.**

   c. To return to the default view, **choose View→Arrange Icons By→Name.**

4. **Match the Windows file name with its file type, based on its extension.**

   ___ Notepad.exe   a. Configuration settings.

   ___ Setuplog.txt   b. A graphics file.

   ___ Coffee Bean.bmp   c. An application file.

   ___ System.ini   d. A document containing text but no formatting.

   ___ Twain.dll   e. A file that contains supporting functionality for applications.

File Attributes

There are several standard attributes you can set or clear on files and folders on Windows systems.

File Attribute	Effect When Set
Archive	Indicates that a file has not been backed up. Windows automatically sets the Archive attribute on any file you create or modify. When you back up a computer, you can choose to back up only the files on which the Archive attribute is set.
Hidden	Hides a file from view in file-management tools such as Windows Explorer or My Computer.
Read-Only	Enables users to read the contents of a file or execute it if it's a program file, but prevents users from changing the contents of a file.
System	Indicates that a file is used by the operating system. Some applications use this attribute to restrict user access to these files. The System attribute in Windows automatically hides the file or folder.
Index	This Windows-specific attribute enables the Windows Indexing Service to create an index of the file to speed up the Search function.

Viewing and Changing Attributes

You can view or change most attributes of a file or folder object by opening the properties of the object in Windows Explorer. You can view and manage attributes at the command line by using the `attrib` command. For information on the functions and syntax of the `attrib` command, see the Windows Help system.

File Compression and Encryption

File compression and file encryption are two special features of the NTFS file system that are implemented as advanced attributes.

- File compression is a way to save disk space by removing blank or repeated characters within files. Windows file compression is rarely used, partly because disk space on most systems today is relatively plentiful, and partly because there are other ways to reduce file size, such as with a file-compression utility like WinZip®, that creates a new, compressed file which you can copy to other media or email to other users.

- File encryption is an NTFS security measure that scrambles the contents of a file so that only the person who encrypted the file can open it, even if the disk containing the file is physically removed from the computer and loaded into a different computer system. File encryption is a good way to protect data on portable devices such as laptop computers.

ACTIVITY 2-8

Exploring File Attributes

Setup:

The C:\Windows folder is open in My Computer. There is a C:\LocalData folder on the system.

Scenario:

In this activity, you will explore the attribute settings on a data file.

 There is a simulated version of this activity available on the CD-ROM that shipped with this course. You can run this simulation on any Windows computer to review the activity after class, or as an alternative to performing the activity as a group in class. The activity simulation can be launched either directly from the CD-ROM by clicking the Interactives link and navigating to the appropriate one, or from the installed data file location by opening the C:\085820Data\Simulations\Lesson#\Activity# folder and double-clicking the executable (.exe) file.

What You Do	How You Do It
1. Create a new data file.	a. In My Computer, **click the Address drop-down arrow and choose C:\.**
	b. **Double-click the LocalData folder.**
	c. **Choose File→New→Text Document.**
	d. To accept the default file name, **press Enter.**

2.	**View the basic attributes of a text file.**	a.	In the Windows Explorer window, with the New Text Document.txt file selected, **choose File→Properties.**
		b.	You can set the Read-only and Hidden attributes on the General page. **Click Advanced.**
		c.	You can set the Archive and Index attributes in the Advanced Attributes dialog box. **Click Cancel twice.**
3.	**View attributes from the command line.**	a.	**Open a Command Prompt window.**
		b.	To change to the LocalData folder, **enter cd \localdata**
		c.	To view the current attributes of the file, **enter attrib**
		d.	To add the System attribute, **enter attrib +s**
		e.	To view the current attributes of the file, **enter attrib**

```
Microsoft Windows XP [Version 5.1.2600]
(C) Copyright 1985-2001 Microsoft Corp.

C:\Documents and Settings\Admin04>cd \localdata

C:\LocalData>attrib
A          C:\LocalData\New Text Document.txt

C:\LocalData>attrib +s

C:\LocalData>attrib
A    S     C:\LocalData\New Text Document.txt

C:\LocalData>_
```

		f.	To remove the System attribute, **enter attrib -s**
		g.	To close the Command Prompt window, **click the Close button.**

Windows File System Types

Windows supports several different file systems.

File System	Description
FAT (File Allocation Table)	The FAT file system is an older file system that is best suited for use with drives less than 4 GB in size. The primary advantages of the FAT file system are its extremely low disk overhead (less than 1 MB), and its compatibility with many different operating systems, including all versions of Windows and also MS-DOS and UNIX. You might use the FAT file system if you want to dual-boot a computer between a version of Windows and another operating system. It is primarily used for formatting floppy disks.
FAT32	FAT32 is an enhanced version of the FAT file system. It scales better to large hard drives (up to 2 terabytes in size) and uses a smaller cluster size than FAT for more efficient space usage.
NTFS (NT File System)	NTFS is the recommend file system for today's Windows-based computers. NTFS was introduced with the Windows NT operating system and is sometimes read as New Technology File System. NTFS provides many enhanced features over FAT or FAT32, including file- and folder-level security, file encryption, disk compression, and scalability to very large drives and files.
Media file systems	Windows also supports various types of special media file system formats, such as CD File System (CDFS) for CD-ROM devices.

Disk Clusters and File System Types

When you format drives, you organize the drive into individual data storage areas called *sectors*. Sectors are grouped together into larger units called *clusters* or *allocation units*. The cluster is the smallest unit that the system will use to store data. If a file does not fill a cluster, the extra space in the cluster remains empty.

The size of sectors and clusters is determined by the file system you use to format the drive. Smaller allocation units reduce unused space on the disk, but can also reduce disk read/write performance because there are more locations to access on the disk. The smaller cluster sizes that FAT32 offered were of more benefit when disk space was costly and most drives used FAT; very large hard drives are now relatively inexpensive. In any case, you should use NTFS on most Windows partitions to gain the security benefits.

Permissions

Definition:

Permissions are security settings that control access to individual objects, such as files or folders. Permissions determine which specific actions users can perform on a given object. You assign permissions by modifying an object's properties.

Example:

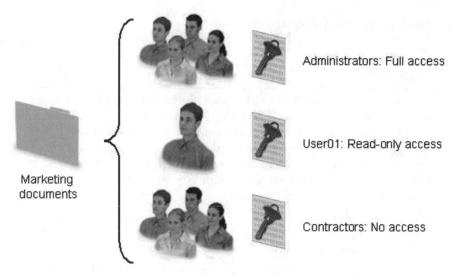

Administrators: Full access

User01: Read-only access

Contractors: No access

Marketing documents

Figure 2-12: *Permissions.*

NTFS File Permissions

There are five standard NTFS permissions you can assign to files.

Permission	Enables the User To
Read	Read the file and view file attributes, ownership, and permissions.
Write	Overwrite the file, change file attributes, and view file ownership and permissions.
Read & Execute	Run applications and perform Read tasks.
Modify	Modify and delete the file and perform Write and Read and Execute tasks.
Full Control	Change permissions, take ownership, and perform all other tasks.

Special Permissions

Each of the standard NTFS permissions is made up of several more granular permissions called special permissions. Standard permissions are the most frequently assigned groups of permissions; special permissions provide you with a finer degree of control.

For example, the standard Read permission is made up of the following special permissions:

● List Folder/Read Data

● Read Attributes

● Read Extended Attributes

● Read Permissions

Workgroup Security Models and File Permissions

By default, when you install Windows XP Professional in a workgroup, the system will use a simple security model called either Simple File Sharing or Guest Only authentication. In this model, the system does not evaluate individual user accounts but grants all users access on the same basis.

To assign NTFS permissions to files or folders on a Windows XP computer in a workgroup, you need to turn off Simple File Sharing and enable local users to authenticate as themselves. You can do this in one of two ways:

- In any My Computer or Windows Explorer window, choose Tools→Folder Options, click the View tab, and in the Advanced Settings list, uncheck Use Simple File Sharing (Recommended).

- Open the Local Security Policy object from Control Panel, select Security Options, and set the value of the Network Access: Sharing And Security Model For Local Accounts policy to Classic.

Once you do this, the Security tab will be available in the file or folder's property sheet.

File Permissions on Windows XP Home

The Classic security model is not available on Windows XP Home, so you will not be able to set individual NTFS permissions on Windows XP Home computers. However, when Simple File Sharing is active, both Windows XP Professional and Windows XP Home provide a rudimentary mechanism for protecting or sharing local files when multiple users use the same computer.

- To protect files, individual users can mark user profile folders such as My Documents as "Private." Other local users will not be able to access these folders.

- To share files, users can place files and folders in the Shared Documents folder in My Computer. All local users will be able to access the contents of Shared Documents. The "Shared Documents" folder is also shared on the network and can be accessed by users at other computers.

NTFS Folder Permissions

There are six standard NTFS permissions you can assign to folders or to drives.

Permission	Enables the User To
List Folder Contents	View the names of files and subfolders in the folder.
Read	View files and subfolders in the folder, folder attributes, ownership, and permissions.
Write	Create new files and subfolders in the folders, change folder attributes, and view folder ownership and permissions.
Read & Execute	Traverse folders and perform Read and List Folder Contents tasks.
Modify	Delete the folder and perform Write and Read & Execute tasks.
Full Control	Change permissions, take ownership, delete subfolders and files, and perform all other tasks.

Permissions you assign to a folder are inherited by files and folders within that folder. It is generally most efficient to group similar files together in a folder and assign permissions to the folder rather than to the individual files. Inherited permissions are indicated by gray check marks in the file or folder's Security properties.

Shares

Definition:

A *share* is any network resource that is available to other computer users on the network. Typical shares include folders, printers, and drives. Because shares enable users to access a computer system from a remote location, you should secure all shared resources against unauthorized access.

Example:

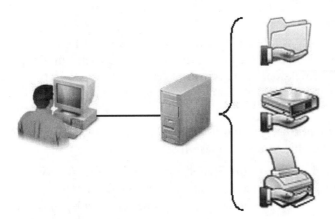

Figure 2-13: *Shared resources.*

File Sharing with Windows

On Windows systems, you can share folders by modifying the folders' properties. When you share a folder, you assign it a share name that can be different from the underlying folder name. You can share the folder more than once using different names.

Users can connect to the shared folder by browsing to the computer in Network Neighborhood, or by choosing Start—>Run and entering the Universal Naming Convention (UNC) path to the folder, in the form *computername\sharename*.

File Sharing with Mac OS X

When you use Mac OS X, you can share files in the Public folder for your user account with up to 10 other network users. (Sharing with more users requires Mac OS X Server.) You will need to make the AppleTalk service active, assign a network name to your computer, and start the File Sharing service. Other Mac OS X users on your local network can then connect to your system by choosing Connect To Server from the Go menu and browsing for your computer's name. They can access files in your Public folder, and place files in your Drop Box folder.

For more information about file sharing in Mac OS X, including information on how to make other folders public, share files with remote users on the Internet, and share with computers running different operating systems, see the technical document "Mac OS X: About File Sharing" on the Apple Computer website at **http://docs.info.apple.com/article.html?artnum= 106461**.

File Sharing with UNIX or Linux

UNIX and Linux are typically used as centralized network file servers, rather than for ad hoc peer-to-peer resource sharing. These systems generally use the Network File Sharing protocol (NFS) to share files with other UNIX and Linux systems. NFS enables clients to see the files on the shared system as if they were part of the client's own local file system.

The specific steps for implementing file sharing with NFS will vary depending on your operating system version, and also depending on whether you use shell commands or your system's Graphical User Interface (GUI) to configure the service. This is also true for the commands or steps the clients will need to use to mount the file systems that NFS exports.

For a sample discussion of exporting and mounting NFS file systems on Red Hat Enterprise Linux, see the Red Hat Enterprise Linux 3 Reference Guide: Chapter 9, Network File System (NFS) at **http://www.redhat.com/docs/manuals/enterprise/RHEL-3-Manual/ref-guide/ch-nfs.html**.

For a sample discussion of sharing folders through a GUI interface using Samba, see "How to Share Folders the Easy Way" in the Unofficial Ubuntu 6.10 (Edgy Eft) Starter Guide at **http://ubuntuguide.org/wiki/Ubuntu_Edgy#How_to_share_folders_the_easy_way**.

Windows Administrative Shares

Certain folders are shared by default on every Windows system. These administrative shares can be deleted, but by default the system will re-create them every time it restarts. The administrative shares are hidden shares, which means that they have the dollar sign ($) appended to the share name. (You can create your own hidden shares by doing the same thing.) You can connect to hidden shares by entering a Universal Naming Convention (UNC) path, but otherwise the shares are not visible on the network.

You can see all shares on a system, including administrative shares, by opening Computer Management, expanding Shared Folders, and selecting the Shares node. You should see the following administrative shares on every Windows XP Professional system:

- The root of each drive on the system is shared with its drive letter. Thus, the C drive is shared administratively as C$, the D drive is shared as D$, and so on.

- The folder where Windows XP is installed, usually the C:\Windows folder, is shared as ADMIN$.

- An InterProcess Communication (IPC) network object is created and shared as IPC$. This doesn't represent a local folder, but enables computers to establish network sessions using the IPC mechanism.

Windows Shared Folder Permissions

You can set three different levels of permissions on shared folders.

Permission	*Enables Users To*
Read	<ul><li>View file and subfolder names.</li><li>View file contents and file attributes.</li><li>Run program files.</li></ul>The Read permission is granted by default to the Everyone group when a folder is shared and to new users when they are added to the permissions list.
Change	<ul><li>Perform all Read permission tasks.</li><li>Add files and subfolders.</li><li>Change file contents.</li><li>Delete subfolders and files.</li></ul>
Full Control	<ul><li>Perform all Read and Change tasks.</li><li>Change NTFS permissions on files and folders inside the shared folder.</li></ul>

Share and File System Permissions Interactions

In Windows, a folder can have NTFS permissions assigned, and then be shared and have share permissions assigned. When a user accesses the folder over the network, both the share and NTFS permissions pertain, and the most restrictive of the two sets of permissions apply. So, if the network user has the Full Control NTFS permission but only the Read share permission, the user will have only the ability to read the contents of the folder.

When a user accesses the file on the local system, however, only the NTFS permissions apply. The fact that the folder is shared is not relevant when accessing the folder locally.

ACTIVITY 2-9

Exploring NTFS Permissions

Setup:
The C:\LocalData folder is open in a My Computer window.

Scenario:
In this activity, you will examine NTFS file and folder permissions.

 There is a simulated version of this activity available on the CD-ROM that shipped with this course. You can run this simulation on any Windows computer to review the activity after class, or as an alternative to performing the activity as a group in class. The activity simulation can be launched either directly from the CD-ROM by clicking the Interactives link and navigating to the appropriate one, or from the installed data file location by opening the C:\ 085820Data\Simulations\Lesson#\Activity# folder and double-clicking the executable (.exe) file.

What You Do	How You Do It
1. Turn off Simple File Sharing.	a. In the C:\LocalData folder window, **choose Tools→Folder Options.**
	b. **Click the View tab.**
	c. **Scroll to the bottom of the Advanced Settings list.**
	d. **Uncheck Use Simple File Sharing (Recommended) and click OK.**
2. Examine NTFS permissions on a drive.	a. To move to My Computer, on the toolbar, **click the Up icon twice.**
	b. **Select the C drive and choose File→ Properties.**
	c. **Click the Security tab.**

d. In the Group Or User Names list, the Administrators group should be selected. **Determine the permissions assigned to the Administrators group.**

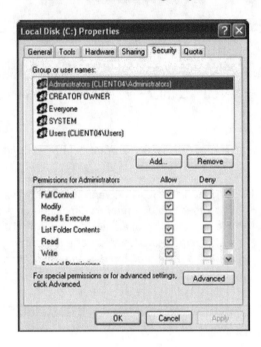

e. **Select the Users group.**

f. **Determine the permissions assigned to the Users group and click Cancel.**

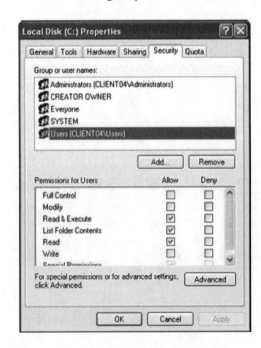

3. **What level of permissions did the Administrators group have?**

   a) Full Control

   b) Modify

   c) Write

   d) Read & Execute

4. **What level of permissions did the Users group have?**

   a) Full Control

   b) Modify

   c) Write

   d) Read & Execute

5. **Examine NTFS folder permissions.**

   a. **Double-click the C drive.**

   b. **Select the LocalData folder and choose File→Properties.**

   c. **Click the Security tab.**

   d. **Select the Administrators group.**

   e. **Determine the permissions assigned to the Administrators group.**

   f. **Select the Users group.**

   g. **Determine the permissions assigned to the Users group and click Cancel.**

6. **How were the permissions on the LocalData folder different from the permissions on the C drive?**

   a) Administrators did not have Full Control to the LocalData folder.

   b) Users could not read files in the LocalData folder.

   c) The permissions on the C drive were set explicitly; the permissions on the LocalData folder were inherited from the C drive.

   d) The available permissions were different.

7. **Examine NTFS file permissions.**

    a. **Double-click the LocalData folder.**

    b. **Select the New Text Document.txt file and choose File→Properties.**

    c. **Click the Security tab.**

    d. **Select the Administrators group.**

    e. **Determine the permissions assigned to the Administrators group.**

    f. **Select the Users group.**

    g. **Determine the permissions assigned to the Users group and click Cancel.**

    h. **Close the window.**

8. **True or False? The permissions on the New Text Document.txt file were inherited from the LocalData folder permissions.**

    ___ True

    ___ False

TOPIC D
Windows System Management Tools

In the previous topic, you identified the primary tools and functions used in Windows file system management. As a final step in understanding the structure and function of the operating system, you should examine some of the key utilities used for general Windows system management. In this topic, you will identify some of the important Windows system management tools.

You should have a good understanding of the tools involved in managing files and folders on a Windows system. Sometimes, however, supporting a Windows system goes beyond file management to more general, comprehensive system management tasks. In addition to your file-management skills, you should also be familiar the most basic Windows system management tools and understand how they reflect the underlying structure of Windows itself.

The Computer Management Console

Computer Management is the primary administrative tool you will use to manage and configure a Windows XP computer. Computer Management combines several administrative utilities into a single console to provide easy access to system properties and tools. The console tree on the left shows a hierarchical view of the various functional nodes within Computer Management; the details pane on the right shows the details for the selected node.

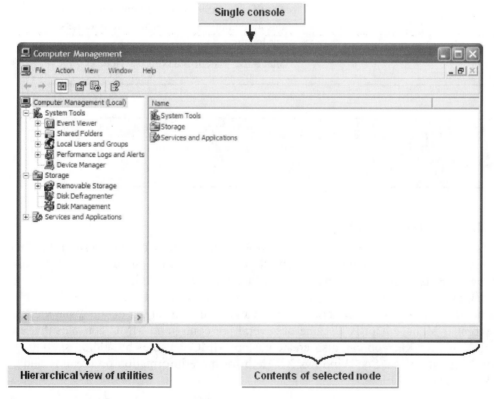

Figure 2-14: *The Computer Management console.*

Computer Management Tasks

You can use the different nodes in Computer Management to perform a variety of tasks. For more information about the specific utilities in Computer Management, see Windows XP Help.

Computer Management Tool	Purpose
Event Viewer	Monitor system events, such as logon times and application errors.
Shared Folders	Create and manage shared resources. View a list of users who are connected to a local or remote computer.
Local Users and Groups	Manage user accounts on the local system.
Performance Logs and Alerts	Document system performance in real time or on a scheduled basis.
Device Manager	View device configurations and add device drivers.
Removable Storage	Manage removable storage devices.
Disk Defragmenter	Defragment system disks.
Disk Management	Set properties for storage devices.
Services	Start and stop system services.
WMI Control	Manage the Windows Management Instrumentation (WMI) interface. WMI is a way to use script files to gather management information about a computer system from a remote network location.
Indexing Service	Manage the system indexing service.

 For more information about WMI Control, visit **http://www.dmtf.org**.

Microsoft Management Console

Computer Management is one example of a Microsoft Management Console (MMC) interface. The MMC interface provides a standard framework for a wide variety of administrative tools within Windows, so that tools with many different functions have a similar look and feel and so that you can access them from within a common application. All MMC consoles have a two-pane structure with a hierarchical console tree view on the left and a details pane view on the right. Computer Management is just one of several pre-configured MMC consoles that are included with Windows XP; you can also create custom MMC consoles by adding snap-in tools into the MMC interface. See Windows XP Help for more information on creating and saving a custom MMC console.

ACTIVITY 2-10

Examining Computer Management

Scenario:

In this activity, you will explore the Computer Management utility.

 There is a simulated version of this activity available on the CD-ROM that shipped with this course. You can run this simulation on any Windows computer to review the activity after class, or as an alternative to performing the activity as a group in class. The activity simulation can be launched either directly from the CD-ROM by clicking the Interactives link and navigating to the appropriate one, or from the installed data file location by opening the C:\085820Data\Simulations\Lesson#\Activity# folder and double-clicking the executable (.exe) file.

What You Do	How You Do It
1. **Open Computer Management.**	a. You can open Computer Management from Control Panel or from the Start menu. **Choose Start, right-click My Computer, and choose Manage.**
	b. **Maximize the Computer Management window.**

2. **Examine the System Tools.**

    a. To view the categories of log files Windows maintains, **select Event Viewer.**

    b. To view the contents of a log file, **double-click System.**

    c. To view tools for managing shared network folders, **select Shared Folders.**

    d. To see the shared folders on the system, **double-click Shares.**

    e. To view tools for managing local computer accounts, **select Local Users And Groups.**

    f. To see the local users on the system, **double-click Users.**

    g. To view tools for logging performance data, **select Performance Logs And Alerts.**

    h. To view the status of devices attached to the system, **select Device Manager.**

3. **Examine the Storage node.**

    a. To examine tools for managing removable storage devices such as CD-ROMs, **select the Removable Storage node.**

    b. To examine the tool for defragmenting hard disks, **select Disk Defragmenter.**

    c. To examine the tool for managing physical disks, **select Disk Management.**

4. **Examine the Services And Applications node.**

    a. **Expand Services And Applications.**

    b. To see a list of available Windows services, **select Services.**

c. To see configuration settings for the WMI Control, **select WMI Control, then right-click and choose Properties.**

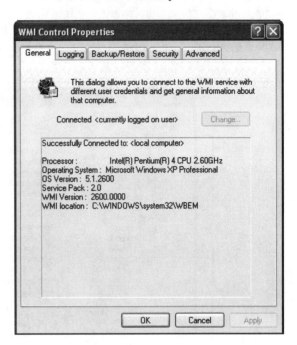

d. **Click Cancel.**

e. To see configuration tools that enable you to create a searchable index of files' contents, **select Indexing Service.**

f. There is a default catalog called System, but indexing is not active. **Close Computer Management.**

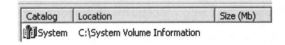

The Registry

The *registry* is the central configuration database where Windows stores and retrieves startup settings, hardware and software configuration information, and information for local user accounts. Logically, the registry is divided into five sections called subtrees; each subtree is further subdivided into keys that contain individual data items called value entries. The registry is stored on the disk as a group of files.

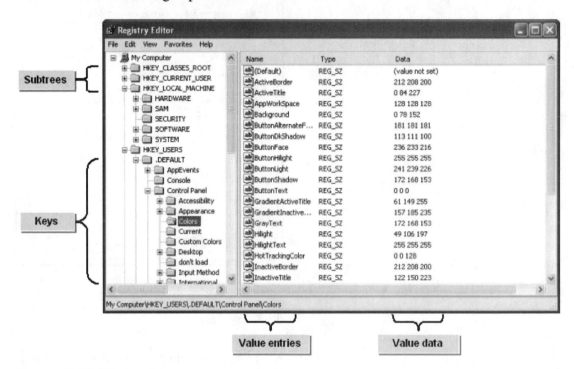

Figure 2-15: The registry.

Editing the Registry

You can view and edit the contents of the registry directly using the Registry Editor tool, regedit.exe. However, most changes to the registry are made automatically by the system, by hardware devices, and by applications. It is rarely necessary to edit the registry directly. If you ever need to do so, use extreme caution and back up the registry files first, because incorrect changes can cause problems with Windows that can be difficult to find and fix.

Versions of Windows prior to Windows XP used an alternate version of the registry editor, regedt32.exe, that had a slightly different user interface. On Windows XP, if you enter the regedt32.exe command, regedit.exe will launch.

Registry Files

The registry consists of five files stored in the \Windows\System32\Config folder: Default, SAM, Security, Software, and System. Plus, there is a registry file named Ntuser.dat, which is unique for each user who logs on to the computer. This file is stored in each user's profile folder.

Registry Subtrees

The registry consists of five subtrees, sometimes also called "hives." Some of the subtrees are temporary pointers to information stored permanently in another registry location. The following table lists and describes the subtrees.

Subtree	Contains
HKEY_CLASSES_ROOT	All the file association information. Windows uses this information to determine which application it should open whenever you double-click a file with a specific extension. For example, Windows automatically opens Notepad whenever you double-click a file with the extension .txt.
HKEY_CURRENT_ USER	The user-specific configuration information for the user currently logged on to the computer. For example, information about the user's selected color scheme and wallpaper is stored in this subtree.
HKEY_LOCAL_ MACHINE	All the configuration information for the computer's hardware. For example, this subtree contains information about any modems installed in the computer, any defined hardware profiles, and the networking configuration.
HKEY_USERS	User-specific configuration information for all users who have ever logged on at the computer.
HKEY_CURRENT_ CONFIG	Information about the current configuration of the computer's hardware. Because Windows supports Plug and Play, the configuration of the hardware can vary even while the computer is running.

Registry Value Entries

An individual registry value entry consists of a name, a data type, and the actual data stored in the value. The data types can be various types of alphanumeric strings, binary data, or hexadecimal data.

Plug and Play

Windows operating systems support Plug and Play (PnP), a set of industry-standard device specifications, originally developed by the Intel Corporation, that enables computers to automatically detect and install various types of devices without user intervention.

ACTIVITY 2-11

Examining the Structure of the Registry

Scenario:

In this activity, you will examine the structure of the Windows registry.

 There is a simulated version of this activity available on the CD-ROM that shipped with this course. You can run this simulation on any Windows computer to review the activity after class, or as an alternative to performing the activity as a group in class. The activity simulation can be launched either directly from the CD-ROM by clicking the Interactives link and navigating to the appropriate one, or from the installed data file location by opening the C:\085820Data\Simulations\Lesson#\Activity# folder and double-clicking the executable (.exe) file.

What You Do	How You Do It
1. **Run the Registry Editor.**	a. **Choose Start→Run.**
	b. To run Registry Editor, in the Open text box, **type *regedit* and click OK.**
	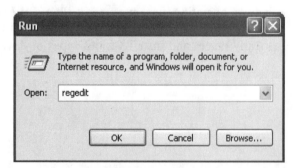
	c. **Maximize the Registry Editor window.**
2. **Examine trees, keys, and value entries.** 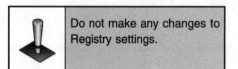 Do not make any changes to Registry settings.	a. **Click the plus sign to expand HKEY_CURRENT_USER.**
	b. This tree contains all the settings that related to the currently-logged-on user. **Expand the Control Panel key.**

   c. **Select the Desktop key.**

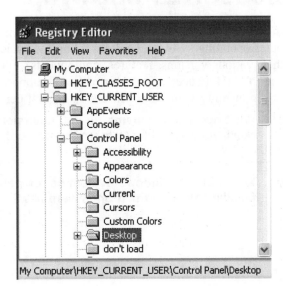

   d. The value entries in this key determine the appearance and settings of the current user's Windows desktop. **Identify the components of several value entries.**

   e. **Explore other areas of the Registry but be careful not to make any changes.**

   f. **Close the Registry window.**

---

3. **Locate the Registry hive files.**

   a. **Choose Start→My Computer.**

   b. **Open the C drive.**

   c. **Open the Windows folder.**

   d. **Open the system32 folder.**

   e. **Click Show The Contents Of This Folder.**

   f. **Open the config folder.**

   g. **Identify the Registry files (Default, SAM, Security, Software, and System), and close the window.**

Lesson 2 Follow-up

In this lesson, you have identified the fundamental components and functions of personal computer operating systems. Understanding the basics of what operating systems are, including their various versions, features, components, and technical capabilities is knowledge you can use to build a successful career as an IT support representative or PC service technician, interact confidently with other professionals, and perform your job duties properly and efficiently.

1. **What operating systems do you have personal experience with? What operating systems would you like to learn more about, and why?**

2. **Which of the Windows system components and tools discussed in this lesson were familiar to you? Which ones were new?**

3 PC Technician Professional Best Practices

Lesson Time: 2 hour(s)

Lesson Objectives:

In this lesson, you will identify best practices followed by professional personal computer technicians.

You will:

- Identify common hardware and software tools used by professional personal computer technicians.

- Identify the best practices for PC technicians to follow to promote electrical safety.

- Identify the best practices for PC technicians to follow to promote environmental safety and proper handling of materials.

- Identify and apply the general preventative maintenance best practices that PC technicians should employ.

- Identify the general diagnostics and troubleshooting best practices that PC technicians should employ.

- Identify best practices for PC technicians to use to communicate appropriately with clients and colleagues and conduct business in a professional manner.

Introduction

In the previous lessons, you gained fundamental knowledge about personal computer components and operating systems. The foundational knowledge that every personal computer technician needs also includes a working knowledge of tools, safety and environmental precautions, general preventative maintenance techniques, and basic diagnostic and troubleshooting techniques. In this lesson, you will identify best practices followed by personal computer technicians.

As an A+ technician, you'll be asked to install, configure, maintain, and correct problems with a variety of PC components. To work with each of these components without damaging it or causing yourself or others physical injury, you'll need the appropriate tools—hardware, software, and a plan to get the job done quickly, safely, and correctly.

This lesson covers all or part of the following CompTIA A+ (2006) certification objectives:

- Topic A:
    - Exam 220–601 (Essentials): Objective 1.1, Objective 1.3, Objective 7.1
    - Exam 220–602 (IT Technician): Objective 1.2
    - Exam 220–604 (Depot Technician): Objective 1.1, Objective 1.2
- Topic B:
    - Exam 220–601 (Essentials): Objective 7.2
    - Exam 220–602 (IT Technician): Objective 1.2, Objective 7.1
    - Exam 220–604 (Depot Technician): Objective 5.1
- Topic C:
    - Exam 220–601 (Essentials): Objective 1.4, Objective 7.1, Objective 7.3
    - Exam 220–602 (IT Technician): Objective 7.1
    - Exam 220–604 (Depot Technician): Objective 1.2, Objective 5.1
- Topic D:
    - Exam 220–601 (Essentials): Objective 1.4, Objective 2.4, and Objective 7.1
    - Exam 220–602 (IT Technician): Objective 1.2, Objective 1.3
    - Exam 220–603 (Remote Technician): Objective 1.3
    - Exam 220–604 (Depot Technician): Objective 1.2, Objective 1.3
- Topic E:
    - Exam 220–601 (Essentials): Objective 1.3, Objective 3.3, Objective 4.3
    - Exam 220–602 (IT Technician): Objective 1.2
    - Exam 220–603 (Remote Technician): Objective 1.2
    - Exam 220–604 (Depot Technician): Objective 1.2
- Topic F:
    - Exam 220–601 (Essentials): Objective 1.3, Objective 8.1, Objective 8.2
    - Exam 220–602 (IT Technician): Objective 1.2, Objective 8.1, Objective 8.2
    - Exam 220–603 (Remote Technician): Objective 6.1, Objective 6.2

TOPIC A
Tools of the Trade

In the last lesson, you learned the basics of operating systems. Knowing what tools are required for certain activities is another important part of an A+ technician's knowledge base. In this topic, you will identify common hardware and software tools used by professional personal computer technicians.

Having the right tool will save you time, trouble, and expense, but you won't usually know what you need until you get to the site. A good collection of software and hardware tools (kept ready to use) will make your life much easier. In this topic, you'll learn what tools you should assemble in toolkits for specific types of jobs.

Multimeters

Definition:

A *multimeter* is an electronic instrument used to measure voltage, current, and resistance. It usually has two wires, one red and one black, that are plugged into two sockets on the meter. The socket you use might depend on what you want to measure. Digital meters have a screen that displays the numeric value of what you are measuring. Analog meters have a thin needle that swings in an arc and indicates the value of what you are measuring.

 Use a digital multimeter whenever possible. It is much more difficult to read and interpret an analog multimeter accurately.

Example:

Digital multimeter

Figure 3-1: *A digital multimeter.*

Analog multimeter

Figure 3-2: *An analog multimeter.*

Loopback Plugs

Definition:

A *loopback plug* is a special connector used for diagnosing transmission problems that redirects electrical signals back to the transmitting system. It plugs into a port and crosses over the transmit line to the receive line. Loopback plugs are commonly used to test Ethernet NICs.

Example:

Figure 3-3: *A loopback plug.*

Types of Hardware Toolkits

Because of the complexity of personal computers, there are several different types of hardware toolkits that are commonly used in PC maintenance and repair.

Toolkit Name	Description and Contents
Basic	This toolkit should contain the tools necessary to remove and install computer components. Each tool should be demagnetized, and the tools hould be stored in a case to protect and organize them. A basic toolkit should include: ● Phillips screwdrivers (small and large, #0 and #1) ● Flat-blade screwdrivers (small and large, eighth inch and three-sixteenth inch) ● Torx driver (size T15) ● Tweezers ● Container for screws ● Nut driver ● Three-prong retriever Basic toolkits can also include: ● Additional sizes of drivers and screwdrivers ● Ratchets ● Allen wrenches ● Cotton swabs ● Batteries ● Flashlight ● Anti-static cleaning wipes ● Anti-static wrist band ● Canister of compressed air ● Mini vacuum ● Pen knife ● Clamp ● Chip extractor ● Chip inserter ● Multimeter ● Soldering iron and related supplies ● Spare parts container ● Pen and/or pencil ● Notepaper or sticky notes

Toolkit Name	Description and Contents
Network	Specialized tools, in addition to those listed previously, are needed to make and install network cables. Kits containing these tools are available, but the prices vary widely depending on the quality of the tools. A network toolkit typically includes: • Cable crimper with dies for a variety of cable styles • Wire stripper for flat and coax cable • Precision wire cutters • Curved forceps • Multi-network LAN cable tester • Digital multimeter
Circuit board	Usually circuit boards are replaced, not repaired. However, sometimes an obviously loose connection can be fixed or a jack with a broken pin can be replaced. A circuit board toolkit typically includes: • 30w ceramic soldering iron • Desoldering braid • Desoldering pump • Solder iron stand with sponge • Solder • Miniature pliers and wire cutters • Heat sink

Software Diagnostic Tools

Definition:

A *software diagnostic tool* or *utility* is a computer repair program that can analyze hardware and software components and test them for problems. Some software diagnostic tools can repair software problems and optimize settings. Most operating systems include several software diagnostic tools, and computer stores generally have an aisle dedicated to utility software developed by other software manufacturers.

Example:

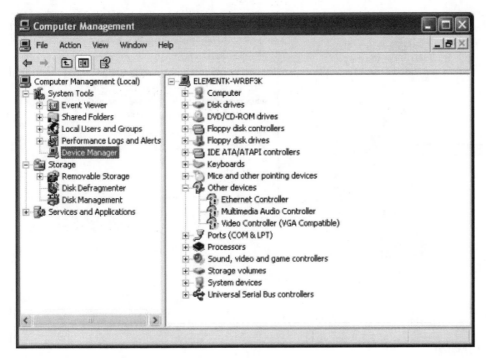

Figure 3-4: *Computer Management includes several software diagnostic tools.*

Firmware

Definition:

Firmware is software stored in memory chips that retains data whether or not power to the computer is on. It is most often written on an electronically reprogrammable chip so it can be updated with a special program to fix any errors that might be discovered after a computer is purchased, or to support updated hardware components.

 Updating firmware is called *flashing.*

Example:

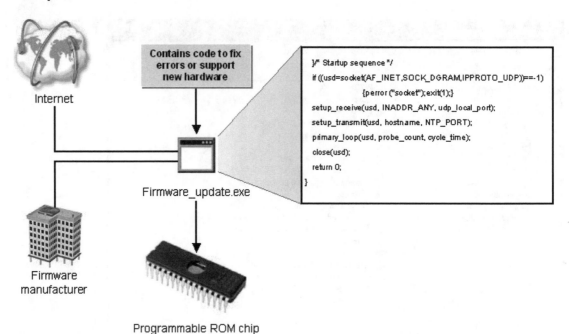

Figure 3-5: Firmware

The System BIOS

Definition:

A *Basic Input/Output System (BIOS)* is a set of instructions that is stored in Read Only Memory and that is used to start the most basic services of a computer system. Every computer has a *system BIOS*, which sets the computer's configuration and environment when the system is powered on. It is located on the system board. Computers can have more than one BIOS to control other system functions.

Example:

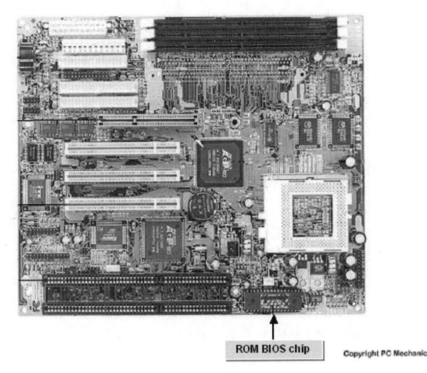

ROM BIOS chip

Copyright PC Mechanic

Figure 3-6: The system BIOS resides on a Read Only Memory chip, and sets the computer's configuration and environment at startup.

The System BIOS and System Startup

On startup, the BIOS tests the system and prepares the computer for operation by querying its configuration settings. It searches for other BIOSs on any adapter cards and configures access to those routines. It then loads the operating system and passes control to it. The BIOS accepts requests from the drivers as well as the application programs.

Accessing the System BIOS

Each BIOS manufacturer has its own method to enable users to access system setup menus and configure BIOS settings. A system setup prompt usually appears while the system is booting; for many manufacturers, it is only displayed during a cold boot. The key or key combination you need to press varies between different BIOS manufacturers. You often need to be very quick to catch it and press the appropriate key or keys. Also, sometimes while the monitor is warming up, the message can pass, so turn the monitor on first if you need to access the BIOS.

Some of the common methods to access system setup are displayed in the following table.

BIOS or Computer Manufacturer	Key Combination for Accessing System Settings
Acer	F1, F2, or Ctrl+Alt+Esc
ALR	F2 or Ctrl+Alt+Esc
AMD	F1
AMI	Delete

BIOS or Computer Manufacturer	Key Combination for Accessing System Settings
ARI	Ctrl+Alt+Esc or Ctrl+Alt+Delete
AST	Ctrl+Alt+Esc or Ctrl+Alt+Delete
Award	Delete or Ctrl+Alt+Esc
Compaq	F10 or F12
CompUSA	Delete
Cybermax	Esc
Dell	Varies according to model. Common keys are F1, F2, F3, F12, Delete
DTK	Esc
Gateway	F1 or F2
HP	F1 or F2
IBM	F1, F2, Delete, or Ctrl+Alt+Insert after Ctrl+Alt+Delete
Micron	F1, F2, or Delete
Packard Bell	F1, F2, or Delete
Phoenix	Ctrl+Alt+Esc, Ctrl+Alt+S, or Ctrl+Alt+Insert
Sony VAIO	F2 or F3
Tiger	Delete
Toshiba	Esc or F1

CMOS RAM

Definition:

Complementary Metal Oxide Semiconductor RAM (CMOS RAM) is special memory that has its own battery to help it keep track of its data even when the power is turned off. CMOS RAM stores information about the computer setup that the system BIOS refers to each time the computer starts. Because you can write new information to CMOS RAM, you can store information about system changes, such as new disk drives that you add to your system. The computer will look for the drive each time it is turned on.

Example:

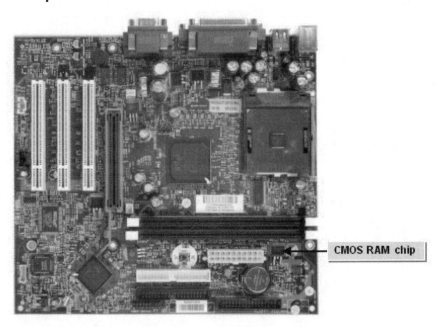

Figure 3-7: CMOS RAM holds system information used by the system BIOS during startup.

CMOS Settings

Prior to the use of CMOS, system settings were configured with jumpers and switches. CMOS was introduced with the AT system boards. Newer computers have CMOSs that allow for more configuration options than the switches and jumpers—or even earlier CMOSs—did, primarily because they use an extended CMOS memory area called the Extended System Configuration Data (ESCD) to hold information about specific hardware devices. Any time you change a hardware component, you should check the CMOS settings to see if they also need to be changed for the system BIOS to recognize the new hardware. Also, you can configure CMOS without needing to open the chassis. The extent to which you can use CMOS to configure a computer depends heavily on the manufacturer of the particular CMOS; however, in most cases, you should be able to configure at least the following—and possibly much more—from the keyboard by using the CMOS Setup program.

Setting	Description
System date and time	You can use the CMOS Setup program to set the PC's real-time clock. (Using DOS date and time commands won't reset the real-time clock, but setting the clock in Windows will.)
Password	You can specify whether a password is required during system startup.
Boot sequence	You can specify the order that drives are checked for the operating system.
Memory	Some systems require you to specify in CMOS how much RAM is installed on the system. You might also be able to specify the type of memory used.
Hard disk drive	You can specify the type and size of the hard disk drives attached to the system.
Floppy disk drive	You can adjust the speed and density settings for the floppy disk drive. You can also disable or enable a floppy disk drive.

Setting	Description
Display	You can specify the monitor type.
Parallel ports	You can specify settings such as unidirectional or bidirectional printing, Extended Capabilities Port (ECP) options, and Enhanced Parallel Port (EPP) options. You can also disable or enable a parallel port. If you know that a parallel or serial port will not be used, you can disable the port, thereby freeing up the resources that would otherwise be unusable by other devices. Conversely, if you connect a device to a port and the device won't work at all, you might want to check the CMOS to ensure that the port hasn't been disabled.
Serial/COM ports	You can specify settings such as what memory addresses and interrupts are used by a port. You can also disable or enable a serial port.
Power management	In most modern computers, you can specify settings such as powering down components (like the monitor, video card, and hard drives) when the components haven't been used for a specified time period, as well as options and time limits for standby and suspend modes. You can also disable or enable global power management.

The Power-On Self Test (POST)

The *Power-On Self Test (POST)* is a built-in diagnostic program that is run every time a personal computer starts up. The POST checks your hardware to ensure that everything is present and functioning properly, before the system BIOS begins the operating system boot process.

The POST process contains several steps to ensure that the system meets the necessary requirements to operate properly.

 The POST process can vary a great deal from manufacturer to manufacturer.

Hardware Component	POST Test Criteria
Power supply	Must be turned on, and must release its reset signal.
CPU	Must exit Reset status mode, and must be able to execute instructions.
BIOS	Must be readable.
CMOS RAM	Must be readable.
Memory	Must be able to be read by the CPU, and the first 64 KB of memory must be able to hold the POST code.
I/O bus or I/O controller	Must be accessible, and must be able to communicate with the video subsystem.

Hard Drive Self Tests

Most hard disk drive manufacturers provide a diagnostic tool that enables the drive to test itself when a personal computer is started up. Some of these hard drive self-tests are built into the firmware for the hard disk drive, while others are separate utilities that are available for download from the drive manufacturer's website. Make sure that you download the specific test utility for your hard disk drive.

Software Diagnostics Tests

Software diagnostics tests are available from many different manufacturers, and they vary widely in their capabilities, but they can all assist you in detecting, repairing, and preventing hardware and software problems. The Windows operating systems also come with their own sets of diagnostic tools that may help you to detect problems.

Examples of Software Diagnostic Tests

Here are just a few examples of applicable software diagnostic tests.

Hardware Component	Examples of Software Diagnostics Test
Entire system	PC-Doctor Service Center, PC-Diag, Norton SystemWorks, QuickTech Pro, McAfee System Mechanic, CheckIt Diagnostics
System board	Motherboard Diagnostic Toolkit
CPU	x86test
Memory	Memtest86+, DocMemory Diagnostics
Fan	SpeedFan
Video adapter card	Video Card Stability Test
Network adapter card	3Com Managed PC Boot Agent, Intel PROset II Utility
Modem	Modem Doctor Diagnostics
Optical drive	CDRoller

ACTIVITY 3-1

Identifying Hardware and Software Tools

Scenario:

In this activity, you will identify hardware and software tools commonly used by PC technicians.

---

1. **You've been asked to repair a system board in a customer's PC. Which set of tools would be best suited for the task?**

   a) Phillips screwdriver (#0), torx driver (size T15), tweezers, and a three-prong retriever.

   b) 30w ceramic solder iron, miniature pliers, wire cutters, and a solder iron stand with sponge.

   c) Wire strippers, precision wire cutters, digital multimeter, and cable crimper with dies.

   d) Chip extractor, chip inserter, rachet, and allen wrench.

   e) Anti-static cleaning wipes, anti-static wrist band, flashlight, and cotton swabs.

---

2. **You've been asked to correct a network cabling problem at a customer site. Which set of tools would be best suited for the task?**

   a) Phillips screwdriver (#0), torx driver (size T15), tweezers, and a three-prong retriever.

   b) 30w ceramic solder iron, miniature pliers, wire cutters, and a solder iron stand with sponge.

   c) Wire strippers, precision wire cutters, digital multimeter, and cable crimper with dies.

   d) Chip extractor, chip inserter, rachet, and allen wrench.

   e) Anti-static cleaning wipes, anti-static wrist band, flashlight, and cotton swabs.

---

3. **You suspect that contaminants from the environment have prevented the fan on a PC from working optimally. Which set of tools would be best suited to fix the problem?**

   a) Phillips screwdriver (#0), torx driver (size T15), tweezers, and a three-prong retriever.

   b) 30w ceramic solder iron, miniature pliers, wire cutters, and a solder iron stand with sponge.

   c) Wire strippers, precision wire cutters, digital multimeter, and cable crimper with dies.

   d) Chip extractor, chip inserter, rachet, and allen wrench.

   e) Anti-static cleaning wipes, anti-static wrist band, flashlight, and cotton swabs.

---

4. **What device has a thin needle that swings in an arc and points to a number that indicates the value of what you are measuring?**

   a) Analog multimeter

   b) Digital multimeter

   c) Loopback plug

5. **Where is the system BIOS stored?**

   a) On the primary hard drive.

   b) In CMOS RAM.

   c) On a ROM chip.

   d) In standard RAM.

6. **Which hardware components are checked during the POST?**

   a) Power supply

   b) CPU

   c) Monitor

   d) RAM

7. **True or False? Windows includes software diagnostic tests that help you find and correct hardware problems.**

   ___ True

   ___ False

TOPIC B
Electrical Safety

In the last topic, you identified hardware tools used by personal computer technicians. Some of these tools are used to promote electrical safety. In this topic, you will identify the best practices for personal computer technicians to follow to promote electrical safety.

The most prevalent physical hazards that computer technicians face are electrical hazards. Although it is necessary to run a computer, electricity can damage computer equipment, and in some cases, pose a danger to humans. Observing best practices with regard to electrical safety will protect both computer equipment and human lives.

Static Electricity

Definition:

Static electricity is a build-up of a stationary electrical charge on an object. It is called static because the charge cannot escape the charged body, but it remains still.

 Static charges can be as small as the sparks that come off a dry blanket in the wintertime or as massive as a lightning strike, with its millions of volts.

Example:

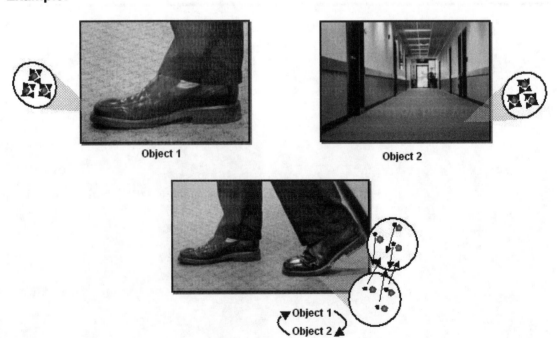

Figure 3-8: The buildup of static electricity.

Sources of Static Electricity

Static electricity is often caused by friction; rubbing one object against another causes a transfer of electrons between the two. Using friction to create a static charge is called *triboelectric generation*. The amount of static that can be built up in this manner depends on various factors, including the types of materials, their surface area and texture, and the ambient humidity. If you have ever rubbed a balloon on your head and stuck it to the wall, you have used triboelectric generation.

Static Electricity and Voltage

Because air has very high resistance, static electric discharge usually requires contact with the statically charged object. For a static discharge to arc through the air, it requires a very high voltage, and no other path to the ground with lower resistance. You can feel a static discharge starting at around 3,000 V. The drier the air, the greater the resistance, which is why static shocks on dry winter days can fall within the range of 10,000 to 20,000 volts. Keeping a room humidified is one way to reduce the risk of static electricity.

If 120 V from a household electrical outlet can kill you, why does a static spark of 20,000 V just startle you? Because, while the voltage might be high, the current is very low; very few total electrons are transferred in a static spark. All the energy of all the electrons in a spark added together cannot hurt you, even though it may surprise you. Each electron in a static discharge has extremely high energy, but the human body is just too big for the very small number of electrons involved in the spark to cause widespread damage. A few cells in your fingertip may be damaged, but they easily grow back.

Electrostatic Discharge (ESD)

Definition:

Electrostatic discharge (ESD) occurs when a circuit is created that allows electrons to rush from a statically charged body to another with an unequal charge. The electricity is released with a spark. The charge follows the path of least resistance, so it can occur between an electrical circuit ground, such as a doorknob or a computer chassis, and a charged body, such as a human hand. ESD can damage sensitive computer equipment.

Example:

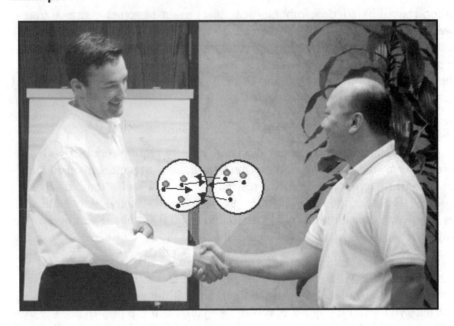

Figure 3-9: *Electrostatic discharge.*

EMI

While ESD is the primary electrical danger to computer equipment, electromagnetic interference (EMI) can also cause problems with microcomputer circuitry. EMI occurs when a magnetic field builds up around one electrical circuit and interferes with the signal being carried on an adjacent circuit.

ESD Prevention Techniques

Charges as low as 10 volts can damage or destroy sensitive electronic circuits. This is why ESD is such an enemy of integrated circuits. Static charges can build up on both conductors and insulators, as well as in the human body. When you work with computer equipment, you must take steps to protect against ESD.

 Anti-static bags that are used for shipping components actually conduct electricity, so keep them away from equipment that is powered on.

ESD Prevention Measures

You can protect against ESD in your work environment by:

- Eliminating unnecessary activities that create static charges.
- Removing unnecessary materials that are known charge generators.
- Using anti-static vacuums for cleaning computer components (such as chassis, power supplies, and fans).
- Using anti-static materials.
- Grounding conductive materials.

- Using anti-static bags to store computer components that are particularly sensitive to ESD.

- Using an air ionizer, which releases negative ions into the air. They attract positively charged particles and form neutrally charged particles.

- Humidifying the air to speed up static discharge from insulators. When the air is extremely dry, more static is likely. A humidity rate of 50 to 60 percent is best.

- And, grounding yourself before touching electronic equipment. To avoid a static shock, touch a grounded object made of a dissipative material. A dissipative material is a conductor, but with high resistance. It loses its electrical charge slowly, so when you touch it, the electron flow is spread over time and you do not feel a shock.

An ESD Toolkit

Some people who work on computer equipment never use a single piece of ESD safety equipment. They discharge themselves by touching an unpainted metal part of the computer case before touching any components. In other instances, the company policy might require that you use a properly equipped ESD-free work area. The minimum equipment in this case would be a grounded wrist strap. Other ESD-protection equipment includes leg straps, grounded mats to cover the work surface, and grounded floor mats to stand on. The mats contain a snap that you connect to the wrist or leg strap. Anti-static bags for storing components can also be included in an ESD toolkit. If the technician's clothing has the potential to produce static charges, an ESD smock, which covers from the waist up, can be helpful.

To ensure that the ESD equipment remains effective, you should test it frequently. A minor shock that you cannot feel can compromise the ESD safety equipment.

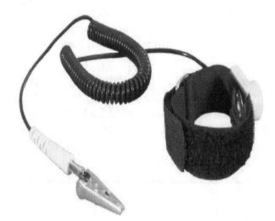

Figure 3-10: A wrist strap is a vital component of any ESD toolkit.

Electrical Hazards

Because personal computers are powered by electricity, there are several potential electrical hazards you should be aware of when servicing them.

Electrical Hazard	Description
Electrocution (fatal)	Electrocution results when the body is exposed to a lethal amount of electrical energy. For death to occur, the body must become part of an active electrical circuit with a current capable of overstimulating the nervous system or damaging internal organs. The extent of injuries received depends on the current's magnitude (measured in Amperes), the pathway through the body, and the duration of flow. The resulting damage to the human body and the emergency medical treatment determine the outcome.
Electric shock	If you come close to a very high-voltage source, the electrons may form an arc or steady spark though the air and flow into your body. When you touch the source of lower electrical voltage directly, or touch it with a conductor like a metal screwdriver, you have decreased the resistance to a point where low-voltage current can start to flow through you. Water is a better conductor than air or dry skin, so touching an electrical contact with wet hands reduces resistance and increases current flow even more. Electricity will flow through you only if your body completes a path to a ground or lower-voltage point.
Burns	Contact with a source of electrical energy can cause external as well as internal burns. Exposure to higher voltages will normally result in burns at the sites where the electrical current entered and exited the body. High voltage contact burns may display only small superficial injury; however, the danger of these deep burns is destruction of internal tissues. Electricity can hurt you even if you are careful and avoid becoming part of an electrical ground circuit. The heat generated by an electric arc or electrical equipment can burn your skin or set your clothes on fire. Anyone who has tried to unscrew a hot light bulb has direct experience with electricity-related thermal burns.
Collateral injuries	Collateral injuries occur when involuntary muscle contractions caused by the shock cause the body to fall or come in contact with sharp edges or electrically live parts. You instinctively pull your hand back from the doorknob when you get a static shock. Electricity flowing through your body can also cause your muscles to twitch uncontrollably. These motions can cause you to hurt yourself on objects around you.

Power Supplies and Electrical Hazards

Most of the internal circuitry in a computer is low voltage (12 V or less) and low current, so there is not much of a threat to your personal safety. However, there are exceptions to this, and these exceptions can be very dangerous. The main exceptions that you need to be aware of are power supplies.

● The computer's power supply has a relatively low voltage, but the current is very high in relation to other components.

● The power supply in a computer monitor increases the voltage, because monitors contain circuits that require 35,000 V with a high current. In any power supply, current is stored on capacitors that do not discharge when the component is turned off or unplugged. Even after months of inactivity, the capacitors may have enough stored electrical energy to kill you. For this reason, leave the internal workings of the monitor to specialists who have the extra training and special equipment that are required to safely remove a monitor cover and make repairs.

ESD and Electrical Hazards

All the precautions used to prevent ESD increase your danger when you work near high voltages. An anti-static wrist band is specifically designed to provide a low-resistance path for electricity to a ground. Do not connect anti-static devices to the electrical system ground or you risk electrocution. You cannot be sure that the electrical system is wired properly or that no devices on the circuit are shorting, sending power through the ground system. If there were ground problems or shorts, your body and your static protection equipment could provide a path from the problem device to ground—the circuit would be completed through your body, causing electrocution.

For the same reason, you must unplug devices that you are servicing. Even when turned off, the power supplies in most devices continue to produce voltage if the device is plugged in to an outlet. You and your anti-static devices could provide a better path to ground than the device's wiring, leading to your electrocution.

Electrical Safety Precautions

Working on a computer can be safe and enjoyable if you protect yourself from electrical hazards by using some common sense and by taking appropriate precautions:

- Perform only the work for which you have sufficient training.

- Don't attempt repair work when you are tired; you may make careless mistakes, and your primary diagnostic tool, deductive reasoning, will not be operating at full capacity.

- Don't assume anything without checking it out for yourself.

- Don't wear jewelry or other articles that could accidentally contact circuitry and conduct current.

- Suspend work during an electrical storm.

- Don't handle electrical equipment when your hands or feet are wet or when you are standing on a wet surface. Perform as many tests as possible with the power off.

- Stand on a totally insulated rubber mat to increase the resistance of the path to ground and provide some protection for yourself. In some cases, workstations are located in areas with grounded floors and workbenches, so static electricity has a low-resistance, non-destructive path to ground.

- When removing circuit boards, place them on a dissipative ground mat or put them in an anti-static bag.

- Use an anti-static wrist strap when handling static-sensitive components like system boards, sound cards, and memory chips, but remove the strap if you are working on any part of a computer monitor.

- After cleaning the keyboard, be very sure it is dry before powering it up.

- Label wires and connectors as you detach them, and make sure you plug them back into the proper sockets in the proper order.

- When you replace the computer's case, make sure all the wires are inside. The case may have sharp edges that can cut through exposed cables.

- Power supplies have a high voltage in them any time the computer is plugged in, even if the computer power is turned off. Before you start working inside the computer case, disconnect the power cord and press the power button to dissipate any remaining power in the system circuitry. Leave the power off until you are done servicing the system unit.

- Never stick anything into the power supply fan to get it to rotate. This approach doesn't work, and it's dangerous.

- Do not take the case off a monitor. The risk to your life is not worth any repairs you might make.

- Don't bang on the monitor screen with your tools; an implosion will propel shards of glass in every direction.

- To clean the monitor, turn it off and unplug it; do not wear an anti-static wrist strap. Use isopropyl alcohol rather than a general-purpose cleaner; it doesn't create a safety hazard if dripped inside the case. Use an anti-static cleaner to clean the glass on the monitor; never wash the glass with the power on.

Following these precautions will help you avoid accidents and prevent personal injury. If you see others working under potentially hazardous conditions, share your knowledge with them to help prevent accidents and injury in your workplace.

ACTIVITY 3-2

Identifying Electrical Safety Issues

Scenario:
In this activity, you will identify electrical safety issues.

---

1. **Which objects can help minimize ESD in a computing environment?**

   a) Air ionizer

   b) Air humidifier

   c) Insulated rubber floor mat

   d) Surge suppressor

---

2. **True or False? If you are using an anti-static floor mat, you do not need any other ESD safety equipment.**

   ___ True

   ___ False

---

3. **Electrical injuries include electrocution, shock, and collateral injury. Can you be injured if you are not part of the electrical ground current?**

---

4. **Which of these computer components present the most danger from electrical shock?**

   a) System boards

   b) Hard drives

   c) Power supplies

   d) Chassis

TOPIC C

Environmental Safety and Materials Handling

In the last topic, you identified best practices for safely dealing with electricity. Environmental factors other than ESD must also be considered to ensure a safe work area. In this topic, you will identify best practices for promoting environmental safety and proper materials handling.

In addition to electrical issues, there are other environmental issues that computer technicians must deal with on a regular basis. For instance, the health and safety of you and those around you should be considered the highest priority—computer equipment can be replaced, but human lives cannot. Recognizing potential environmental hazards and dealing with them safely is an integral part of an A+ technician's job.

Atmospheric Considerations

Atmospheric hazards can be extremely dangerous to you and those around you.

Hazard	Description
Ozone gas	Laser printers produce ozone gas, usually when the corona wire produces an electrical discharge during printing. Depending on the levels, ozone can be a mild-to-severe irritant. Regulatory agencies have established limits regarding the amount of ozone that employees are exposed to. Be sure the printer operates in a well-ventilated area. The laser printer may have a filter to control ozone emissions.
Humidity	Too much moisture can be problematic and cause physical damage to equipment. On the other hand, low humidity can contribute to more electrostatic charge into the air. High humidity levels can also have an effect on tapes and paper media.
Dust	Dust can be a more subtle hazard. Buildup of dust particles over time can cause problems with different types of equipment. Excessive amounts of metallically conducive particles in the air can cause power supplies and other electronic components to shut down. Dusting equipment often can prevent these types of issues. Make sure that printers and paper products are kept in a separate area from computer equipment to prevent paper dust from getting into the equipment.

Situational Hazards

Various workplace situations can be a hazard to you and your coworkers.

Hazard	Description
Falling and tripping	Within your work area alone a number of things can cause you to fall or trip. While working with computer equipment, you need to keep in mind the location of hardware, cables, and devices. Loose cables and cords on the floor can be problematic when moving within your work area.
Equipment storage	CPUs and other hardware should not be stacked on top of one another. Make sure the equipment is secure, whether it is on the floor or on a desk or shelf.
Food and drink	Eating and drinking around computer equipment can be problematic. Food particles and liquids can get inside and harm the inner mechanics of the hardware. Your employer may have no eating or drinking policies in place for these reasons.

Physical Hazards

Potential physical hazards are present in any workplace, including the environment you work in as a computer technician.

Physical Hazard	Description
Cords and cables	In office environments where there are many computers, there will also be many cables and power cords. Sometimes, these cords and cables are lying on the floor and could possibly cause a person to trip on them.
Lasers	Lasers are used in printers, CD drives, and DVD drives. Laser is an acronym for Light Amplification by Stimulated Emission of Radiation. A laser produces an intense, directional beam of light by stimulating electronic or molecular transitions to lower energy levels. This powerful beam can cause damage to the human eye or skin. Lasers have many uses and, like other tools, are capable of causing injury if improperly used. The most likely injury is a thermal burn which will destroy retinal tissue in the eye. Since retinal tissue does not regenerate, the injury is permanent.

Physical Hazard	*Description*
Repetitive Strain Injury (RSI)	Repetitive strain injuries involve damage to muscles, tendons, and nerves caused by overuse or misuse. Computer users suffer mostly from repetitive strain injuries to the hand, wrist, and arm. Unlike strains and sprains, which usually result from a single incident—called acute trauma—repetitive strain injuries develop slowly over time. The type of injury depends on whether the muscle, tendon, tendon sheath, or nerve tissue has been irritated or damaged. Any or all of the following symptoms may appear in any order and at any stage in the development of an injury of RSI: • Aching, tenderness, swelling • Pain, crackling, tingling • Numbness, loss of strength • Loss of joint movement, decreased coordination
Eye strain	Many computer tasks are done at a close working distance, requiring the eyes to maintain active focusing. This can cause stress and strain on the eyes and the muscles that control them. A very common health problem reported by users of computer monitors is eye strain—including the following symptoms: • Blurred vision • Difficulty focusing • Double vision • Tiredness • Headaches • Burning, sore, or itchy eyes Dry eyes can also be a concern for computer operators. The eye surface becomes dry because computer users tend to blink less and tears evaporate faster during monitor use. Symptoms associated with dry eyes are redness, burning, and excess tearing.
Radiation	Radiation is a broad term used to describe energy in the form of waves or particles. Electromagnetic radiation comes from both natural and manufactured sources, including computer monitors. Circuits within the monitor are responsible for the horizontal and vertical movements of the electron beam. This movement occurs tens of thousands of times each second (Very Low Frequency, or VLF) for the horizontal scan, and 50 to 60 times each second (Extremely Low Frequency, or ELF) for the vertical scan. The VLF and ELF field intensities have been extensively evaluated in many different models of monitors for possible biological effects. Computer monitor users have expressed concerns about the possible health effects—including adverse pregnancy outcomes—from the electromagnetic radiation that monitors produce. While the research continues, current scientific information does not identify a health risk from exposure to these electromagnetic fields.
Noise	Noise levels produced by computers and printers are well below those that cause adverse health effects. The equipment has minor noise sources such as the hum of cooling fans and the clicking of keys. Excessive noise from the computer may indicate an internal malfunction.

OSHA

Your employer is obligated to comply with the Occupational Safety and Health Administration (OSHA) and/or state standards regarding employee safety. Employers must provide:

● A workplace that is free from recognized hazards that could cause serious physical harm.

● Personal protective equipment designed to protect employees from certain hazards.

● Communication—in the form of labeling, Material Safety Data Sheets (MSDS), and training about hazardous materials.

Your responsibility—to yourself, your employer, your coworkers, and your customers—is to be informed of potential hazards and to always use safe practices.

Laser Safety Standards

To provide a basis for laser safety, standards are established for Maximum Permissible Exposure (MPE). Lasers and laser systems and devices are grouped into classes:

● Class 1 lasers do not emit harmful levels of radiation and are exempt from control measures.

● Class 2 lasers are capable of creating eye damage through chronic, continuous exposure; this class includes barcode readers.

● Class 3 lasers pose severe eye hazards when viewed through optical instruments (for example, microscopes) or with the naked eye.

● Class 4 lasers pose danger to eyes and skin, as well as being fire hazards.

Frequently, lasers are embedded in laser products or systems with a lower hazard rating. For example, laser printers, CD drives, and DVD drives are Class 1 laser products; however, they contain Class 3 or Class 4 lasers. When the printer or drive is used as intended, the controls for the device's class (Class 1) apply. When the system is opened—for example, for service—and the embedded laser beam is accessible, precautions must be based on the classification of the embedded laser (Class 3 or 4).

Safety Precautions for Physical Hazards

To minimize the physical hazards associated with computing environments, follow the recommended safety precautions and use the appropriate repair tools at all times.

Physical Hazard	Safety Precautions
Cords and cables	If cords and cables must traverse a floor area where people need to walk, it is recommended that cord protectors be used to shield the cords and cables from being damaged by pedestrian traffic, as well as to minimize the chance of someone tripping on the cords and cables.
Lasers	● Never point a laser beam in someone's eyes. ● Never look directly at a laser beam. ● Never disable safety mechanisms when servicing a device with an embedded laser.

Physical Hazard	Safety Precautions
Repetitive Strain Injury (RSI)	If an individual has even mild RSI symptoms, action should be taken. If symptoms are allowed to progress, a person with RSI can develop chronic symptoms. The key to RSI management is to remove an individual from the exposure that causes injury. A period of time away from the keyboard and mouse is followed by a gradual return to keying in an ergonomically correct work setting. Occasionally, a physician will prescribe a medication to help reduce symptomatic inflammation and pain. People with more severe forms of RSI may be referred by their medical provider to an occupational therapist who can do further evaluation and recommend a program of localized treatments, stretches, and exercises. Referral to an orthopedic hand specialist may be needed to determine treatment options. If the individual displays symptoms even at rest, splints may be recommended; while these are useful in the first stages of recovery, they are not the long-term solution. The best treatment for RSI, of course, is prevention by proper arrangement of computer workstations and reasonable project design.
Eye strain	A vision examination is recommended. A specific eyeglass prescription for computer use may help compensate for the strain involved in looking at a close and fixed point for periods of time. Artificial tears—used to supplement the eye's natural tear film and lubricate the dry surface—alleviate dry-eye symptoms for some computer users.
Noise	Printers can be noisy and should be located in rooms away from operators, where possible. Noise reduction hoods are recommended.

Equipment Moving Safety Recommendations

As an A+ IT technician, lifting and moving computer equipment can be one of the more strenuous parts of your job. For example, when you need to work on a CPU, you may have to lift and relocate the machine to your work area. Always assess the situation first to determine if you can lift or move items safely.

Lifting and Moving Equipment Safely

Before lifting anything:

● Know your own strengths and weaknesses. You need to be aware of how much weight you can handle.

● When you lift, bend at your knees and not at your waist. This will prevent strain on your back muscles and pressure on your spine.

● Assess the equipment you are moving. If you feel that physically the equipment is too heavy or awkward for you to move alone, then get help from a coworker, or use a cart to relocate the equipment. If you use a cart, make sure the equipment is tightly secured during transport.

● The equipment may be unstable for lifting. You may need to take special precautions and may require help moving it to a cart.

● Equipment should never be stacked too high while moving to avoid hardware falling and breaking on the floor. This can cause damage to other devices or to yourself.

- Plan ahead. While moving equipment from one area to another, be aware of narrow door-ways or columns that you will encounter on the way. Also, make sure to prep the space before delivering the equipment so that you are not trying to reconfigure the space with all the equipment in the way.

Chemical Hazards

Working with personal computers can cause you to come in contact with some chemical hazards.

Chemical Hazard	Description
Laser printer toner	Made of fine particles of iron and plastic, toner presents its own set of problems due to its reactions with heat. If you spill toner, don't clean it up with a regular vacuum; the particles will get into the motor and melt. Don't use warm water to wash toner off your hands or arms; the toner could fuse to your skin. Instead, brush off as much as you can with a dry paper towel, rinse with cold water, and then wash with cold water and soap. In addition, do not use ammonia-based cleaners on or around laser printers, as the ammonia may react chemically with the toner.
Capacitors	Capacitors store electricity using two or more conducting plates separated by an insulator. There are capacitors in various personal computer components, including microprocessors. The electrolytes in capacitors are very caustic; treat them as you would any hazardous chemical. Thoroughly wash your hands after handling capacitors. **Caution:** The capacitors in power supplies and monitors do not discharge when they are turned off or unplugged, and contain enough charge to kill you. Do not open or attempt to service internal components of power supplies or monitors.
Batteries	Batteries are used to maintain the data in CMOS chips and to supply power to remote controls and portable computers. These batteries may contain mercury, cadmium, and lithium, as well as other dangerous chemicals.

Liquid Hazards

There are many different professional situations when you may come in contact with a hazardous liquid. Some such compounds are used to clean or condition equipment, including the computer's case, contacts and connections of adapter cards, and glass surfaces. They may present safety or environmental problems. Make sure you read the labels and follow instructions carefully when disposing of hazardous materials.

The Material Safety Data Sheet (MSDS)

Definition:

A *Material Safety Data Sheet (MSDS)* is a technical bulletin designed to give users and emergency personnel information about the proper procedures of storage and handling of a hazardous substance. This applies to any situation in which an employee may be exposed to a chemical under normal use conditions or in the event of an emergency. Manufacturers supply MSDSs with the first shipment to a new customer and with any shipment after the MSDS is updated with significant and new information about safety hazards. You can get MSDSs online; the Internet has a wide range of free resources. OSHA regulations govern the use of MSDSs and the information an MSDS must contain.

Required Information in an MSDS

Every MSDS is required to include information about the following items:

- Physical data
- Toxicity
- Health effects
- First aid
- Reactivity
- Storage
- Safe-handling and use precautions
- Disposal
- Protective equipment
- Spill/leak procedures

Example:

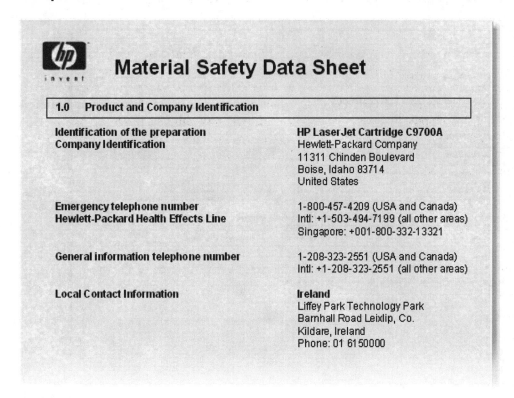

Material Safety Data Sheet

1.0	Product and Company Identification

Identification of the preparation Company Identification	**HP LaserJet Cartridge C9700A** Hewlett-Packard Company 11311 Chinden Boulevard Boise, Idaho 83714 United States
Emergency telephone number Hewlett-Packard Health Effects Line	1-800-457-4209 (USA and Canada) Intl: +1-503-494-7199 (all other areas) Singapore: +001-800-332-13321
General information telephone number	1-208-323-2551 (USA and Canada) Intl: +1-208-323-2551 (all other areas)
Local Contact Information	**Ireland** Liffey Park Technology Park Barnhall Road Leixlip, Co. Kildare, Ireland Phone: 01 6150000

Figure 3-11: An MSDS.

Incident Reports

An *incident report* is a record of any instance where a person is injured or computer equipment is damaged due to environmental issues. The report is also used for accidents involving hazardous materials, such as chemical spills, that could have an impact on the environment. Any time an accident occurs at a work site, you should submit an incident report. Reporting these occurrences is often part of company policy and can help provide protection against liability.

Office Use Only Incident # ______

Actions taken: Copies to:

CITIZENSINFO.ORG

Computer Safety Incident Report

Fill out as completely as possible

1. Nature of incident: ______
2. Location of incident: ______
3. Time of incident: ______
4. Date of incident: ______
5. Your name, position, and phone number: ______
6. Date and time this report was filed: ______
7. Was there any injury? Place an "X" after one – **Yes** __ or **No** __ – and elaborate in description below.
8. Is there an ongoing hazard? Place an "X" after one – **Yes** __ or **No** __ – and elaborate in description below.

Names, addresses, phone numbers, and ID numbers of individuals involved.
Please identify as complainant(s), perpetrator(s), witness(es).

Name	Address	Phone Number	Employee Number	Status (Employee, Guest, Client)

Sequence or Description of Events. Be concise and thorough.

Figure 3-12: *An incident report.*

Hazardous Material Disposal Procedures

Proper disposal of hazardous materials is an essential part of maintaining a safe work environment.

Hazardous Material	***Disposal Recommendations***
Liquid cleaning materials and empty containers	Follow your company's guidelines for disposing of liquid cleaning materials and their containers. Each municipality has its own disposal regulations that you must learn and practice. You can find out about these ordinances by contacting your local government's environmental office or department for trash disposal and recycling.
Toner	Empty toner cartridges should not be tossed into the trash because of the damage the residual chemicals can do to the environment. Used toner cartridges should be refilled or returned to the manufacturer for recycling and/or disposal. Follow your company's guidelines for disposal procedures.
Display devices	The Cathode Ray Tubes (CRTs) in computer monitors contain lead, which is considered a hazardous material. Follow your company's guidelines for disposing of display devices. Many municipalities have regulations for disposal and recycling of monitors and television sets; contact your local government's environmental office or department for trash disposal and recycling to determine if there are specific rules you need to follow.

Hazardous Material	Disposal Recommendations
Ozone filter	Follow the manufacturer's recommendations for replacement and disposal of a laser printer's ozone filter.
Batteries	Used batteries should not be tossed into the trash, but should be disposed of following your company's guidelines.

ACTIVITY 3-3

Identifying Environmental Safety Issues

Scenario:

In this activity, you will identify the best practices for promoting environmental safety and proper handling of materials.

---

1. **Match each physical hazard with the appropriate safety precaution.**

    ___ Cords and cables

    ___ Lasers

    ___ RSI

    ___ Eyestrain

    ___ Noise

    a. Avoid looking directly at them or disabling related safety equipment.

    b. Special glasses and artificial tears are viable precautionary measures.

    c. Keep printer separate from users, and use hoods.

    d. Prevent tripping by using cord protectors.

    e. Rest, therapy, surgery, and prevention are all viable solutions.

---

2. **You are on a service call, and you accidentally spill some liquid cleaner on the user's work surface. What actions should you take?**

    a) Refer to the MSDS for procedures to follow when the material is spilled.

    b) Wipe it up with a paper towel, and dispose of the paper towel in the user's trash container.

    c) Report the incident.

---

3. **Ozone is classified as an environmental hazard. What device produces ozone gas?**

    a) Laser printer

    b) CPU

    c) Laptop

    d) Power supply

---

4. **What substance reacts with heat and ammonia-based cleaners to present a workplace hazard?**

    a) Capacitors

    b) Lasers

    c) Toner

    d) Batteries

TOPIC D
Perform Preventative Maintenance

In the last topic, you identified best practices for promoting environmental safety and proper handling of materials. Best practices for PC technicians also include using preventative maintenance to avoid potential problems. In this topic, you will identify and apply general preventative maintenance techniques.

It's inevitable that computers and their components will require repair or replacement at some point. However, there are a few relatively simple procedures a computer technician can perform to postpone the inevitable. Providing general preventative maintenance resolves problems before they occur and helps to prolong the life of the computer and its components.

Preventative Maintenance Theory

Although different computer components require different levels of preventative maintenance, there are some general considerations that apply to virtually all components.

Task	Description
Visual/audio inspection	By looking at and listening to a computer in operation, you can sometimes tell if a problem is about to occur. During a visual inspection, look for damaged or cracked components, verify that internal and external connections are properly seated, and check cords and cables for fraying. During an audio inspection, verify that the speakers are working properly and that volume controls respond as expected, and listen for any unusual noises coming from within the computer chassis.
Driver/firmware updates	Driver and firmware manufacturers often develop updates to address known functionality issues. By updating device drivers and firmware, you can avoid many potential operational problems.
Scheduling preventative maintenance	The most basic preventative maintenance technique for all components is keeping them clean. Cleaning a personal computer on a regular basis prevents overheating (and therefore damage to internal components) as well as ESD problems. Obviously, this needs to be done on a regular basis to be effective, so if your company does not have a policy that specifies a maintenance interval, you should consider creating a schedule to inspect and clean any computers that are your responsibility.
Using appropriate repair tools and cleaning materials	During preventative maintenance and other service calls, it is imperative that you use the proper tools and materials. Using the wrong tool or material can cause additional problems to occur and can be dangerous.

Task	Description
Ensuring proper environment	Computers operate best in environments with adequate ventilation, little dust, and relatively humid air. • Airflow around a computer and its external devices helps to dissipate the heat generated, so make sure that the components have enough room around them to prevent overheating problems. • The fan that runs to cool the system pulls dust and debris into the interior of the computer. This can lead to shorts and other electrical damage if it is allowed to accumulate. • Computers function best in relative humidity of 50 to 60 percent. Drier conditions are prone to ESD problems, and moister conditions can affect performance. Use humidifiers, air conditioners, and dehumidifiers when possible to control the air quality.

Computer Component Maintenance Techniques

There are a number of preventative maintenance techniques you can use to maintain personal computer components.

Maintenance Technique	Use To
Use a power strip, surge protector, or *Uninterruptible Power Supply (UPS)*.	Protect the computer from power surges, spikes, and brownouts.
Clean peripheral components.	Prevent problems with the computer's peripherals due to dirty conditions.
Clean internal system components.	Prevent problems with internal computer components due to dirty conditions.

Uninterruptible Power Supply

You use an Uninterruptible Power Supply (UPS), a battery-operated device, to save computer components from damage due to power problems such as power failures, spikes, and sags. Computer systems require a steady supply of electricity. Interrupts in that power can cause your systems to fail. All UPSes:

• Use battery power to supply power to the devices connected to the UPS.

• Can be configured through the operating system as to what happens when there is a power failure.

• Keep the computer powered up long enough for you to perform an orderly shutdown of the operating system.

• Have a method for testing that the UPS works properly.

An *online UPS* supplies power to your systems from its batteries at all times. Power from the normal electrical system is used to constantly charge the batteries. Online UPSes usually supply more clean battery power than standby UPSes. However, the batteries usually don't last as long as standby UPS batteries. Online UPSes generally filter power to reduce or remove power spikes. Because online UPSes supply power from the battery at all times, they can prevent power sags or brownouts.

A *standby UPS* (SUPS) uses a battery to supply power when a power problem occurs. At times of normal power operation, power is supplied from the normal electrical system. This method places minimal burden on the batteries and power inverters in the UPS, leading to longer UPS life. These UPSes are rated on their switching time because their batteries are in use only when the regular power is unavailable.

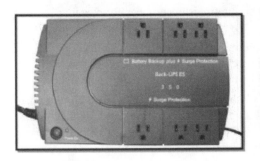 

Figure 3-13: *A standby UPS.*

Determining UPS Size Needs

To determine the size of UPS you need, you can use one of the following techniques:

- Use the tool found on most UPS manufacturers' websites to determine the size you need. By filling out a form about the equipment you will be plugging into the UPS, the tool will recommend the manufacturer's UPSes that meet your needs.

- Perform a manual calculation.

   1. Multiply the volts by amps for each device you will connect to the UPS.

   2. Add together the results of each device in step 1.

   3. Purchase this size UPS.

Surge Suppressor

A surge suppressor helps protect components from power spikes. It does not protect components from power failures or sags, nor does it provide a steady supply of electricity. It also doesn't provide power to components in the case of a power failure.

Cleaning Compounds and Materials

Cleaning materials for computers range from standard household cleaning supplies to supplies specifically designed for computers and electronics.

Cleaning Supply	Description
Wipes and cloths	There are several types of wipes and cloths to use to clean monitors, keyboards, and other equipment.
	• Monitor cleaning wipes are alcohol-based, lint-free, pre-moistened wipes for cleaning monitor screens. These should be used only on CRT or TV monitors and not on plastic-coated LCD screens.
	• Keyboard cleaning wipes are pre-moistened wipes for cleaning keyboards.
	• If you choose not to use pre-moistened wipes, you can use rubbing alcohol applied to a lint-free cloth to wipe down screens and keyboards. They can also be used to clean other components.
	• A toner cloth is a special cloth that you stretch that picks up toner particles that are either in the printer or around the printer. Be careful if using it inside the printer so that the cloth doesn't get caught on any components, leaving fibers behind.
Cleaning solutions	You can use rubbing alcohol on cotton swabs or lint-free cloths to clean many components.
	You can use mild household cleaner to keep the exterior of computer components clean This helps prevent dirt and debris from getting inside the equipment. Never spray the cleaner directly on the equipment. Avoid using ammonia-based cleaners around laser printers; the ammonia may react chemically with the toner.
	For monitors, especially plastic monitors, read the device's manual to determine the cleaning method the manufacturer recommends. While some recommend water or IPA (Isopropyl Alcohol), others claim it's acceptable to use volatile chemicals such as Hexane or Petroleum Benzene, a soft detergent such as Palmolive and water, no suds, or nothing but a dry soft cloth. While some recommend top down motion, others subscribe to the circular method.
	In some cases, you can use standard household window cleaner on various components if you spray it on a lint-free cloth first. You can use this to clean smudges from optical disks. Never use window cleaner on plastic monitor screens, and even on glass screens this cleaner might strip off the anti-glare protection. The best option is a damp, clean, soft cloth with water or a cleaner specifically made for monitors (or that states it is safe for use with monitors) and will not damage anti-glare finishes.
Cleaning tools	Tightly wound cotton swabs are useful in getting cleaning solution into tight places. They are also useful when used dry to get dust and debris out from between keys and around buttons or other tight areas.
	Toothpicks come in handy in getting dirt out from around keys, buttons, and other tight spaces. They are also useful for removing the debris that builds up on the rollers in a mouse. Another use for toothpicks is for when you are trying to retrieve jumpers that have fallen onto the system board.
	A small paint brush can be used to remove dust from between keys on a keyboard. If the brush has long bristles, they can reach under the keys where other cleaning objects would not be able to reach.

Cleaning Supply	Description
Compressed air canister	A canister with a nozzle that can be aimed at components to blow dust out. This is often used when removing dust from the interior of a computer. Be sure to blow the dust away from the power supply and drives. It can also be used to blow dust out of the power supply fan area, from keyboards, and from the ventilation holes on other peripherals. Use caution when working with compressed air. Read the instructions on the can and follow them carefully. Tipping the can too much, something easy to do when trying to maneuver the can into place, can cause the propellant to leave the can in liquid form and at sub-freezing temperatures. The freezing could easily damage components, particularly those which may still be hot from use. There is also the issue of the corrosiveness of the chemical damaging components later on in time. Also, some delicate components on the motherboard can be damaged (literally blown off the board) if used too close to a component. If you use compressed air, take the equipment to a different location, preferably outside, so that the dust does not simply disperse into the air in the work area and settle back on the computer equipment or other devices.
Computer or electronics vacuum	A non-static vacuum that can be used on the chassis, the power supply, fans, and in printers. (Regular vacuum cleaners can create static, which will damage computer equipment.) The vacuum should have a filter and bag fine enough to contain toner particles so that you can use it to clean up toner spills from laser printers or photocopiers. These vacuums can often be used to blow as well as suck, so they can replace the need for compressed air canisters for blowing dust out of machines. Sucking the dust up is usually better, though, since blowing the dust can cause it to get onto or into other components. Sucking it up into a vacuum cleaner bag gets it out of the system without the chance of it getting into something else.
Mask	A mask that fits over your mouth and nose should be worn when using a compressed air canister or working around toner spills. This will keep the particles out of your body.
Latex gloves	You should wear latex gloves when cleaning up a toner spill.

How to Perform Preventative Maintenance

Procedure Reference: Clean Peripherals

To clean peripherals:

1. Shut down the computer, and unplug the peripherals to be cleaned.

2. Clean the keyboard using compressed air, an artist's paint brush or business card, tooth-picks, and rubbing alcohol.

3. Clean the mouse.

    a. Before cleaning the mouse, shut down the system and unplug the mouse.

    b. Remove the ball and clean the rollers with rubbing alcohol and toothpicks.

    c. Clean the mouse interior with compressed air.

    d. Turn on the power and test the mouse.

4. Clean the monitor.

    a. Before cleaning the monitor, shut down the system, turn off the monitor, and unplug the monitor cable and power cord.

    b. For a CRT monitor, spray glass cleaner on a lint-free cloth, and then wipe the glass. (Do not use glass cleaner on an LCD monitor. Use a lint-free cloth.)

    c. Clean the vents using a small vacuum.

    d. Turn on the power and test the monitor.

 LCD monitors are extremely delicate. Unlike glass monitors, LCDs are very susceptible to pressure and pressing hard while cleaning will likely either scratch the plastic or, worse yet, crack the display, a very expensive mistake on someone else's laptop or flat panel display.

5. Clean contacts and connections with a lint-free cloth or an artist's paint brush.

Procedure Reference: Clean the Internal System Components

To clean internal system components:

1. Shut down the computer, and unplug the power cord.

2. Clean the chassis with a damp lint-free cloth.

3. Remove the chassis cover.

4. Clean the system board using a compressed air canister and computer vacuum.

    *   Try to hold the chassis at an angle with the back corner.

    *   Blow the air so the dust is blown away from the drives and power supply.

    *   If it is extremely dusty, you might want to wear a mask over your mouth and nose since the dust particles will fly up when you spray the compressed air.

5. Clean the CD-ROM drive using a CD-ROM cleaning kit and following the enclosed directions.

6. Clean the floppy drive using a floppy drive cleaning kit and following the enclosed directions.

7. Clean removable media drives using the cleaning kit that is compatible with the drive and following the enclosed directions.

 Older Iomega Zip and Jaz drives should not be cleaned. This will damage the drives. Imation SuperDrives can be cleaned. If a removable drive is cleanable, the manufacturer will sell an approved cleaning kit.

Procedure Reference: Configure and Test a UPS in Windows

To configure and test a UPS by using the Power Options tool in Windows:

1. Set up the UPS.

    a. If necessary, connect the battery in the UPS.

    b. Plug the UPS directly into a wall outlet. Do not plug the UPS into a surge suppressor or power strip.

    c. Connect the UPS to the computer (For example, via the USB cable).

    d. Plug the computer components you want to be powered through the UPS into the UPS.

2. If the UPS comes with its own management software, install the software.

3. Configure the steps that you want the UPS to take when a power failure occurs.

    a. Open Control Panel.

    b. Click the Performance And Maintenance link.

    c. Click the Power Options link.

    d. Display the appropriate page of the dialog box to configure the settings.

    • If the UPS tab appears, click it to display the UPS page.

    • If other power-specific tabs appear instead of the UPS tab, such as Alarms or Power Meter, click the appropriate tab to configure each of the UPS settings.

    e. If there is a UPS page, in the Details section of the UPS page, click Select and select the manufacturer and model of the UPS.

    f. If there is a UPS page, click Configure.

    g. Configure the UPS settings.

    • Configure alarm settings to indicate how you want to be notified of a power failure and how often.

    • If desired, configure the UPS to run a program before shutting down the computer.

    • Configure whether the UPS should put the computer in standby mode or shut the computer down completely.

    h. Click OK as needed to apply your changes and close the Power Options Properties dialog box.

4. Test the UPS. You can:

    • Unplug the UPS from the wall outlet and verify that the components remain powered. If you configured it to run a specific program, shut down the computer, or put it into hibernation, you can leave it unplugged until this occurs if you want to test that feature as well. When you are done testing, plug the UPS back into the wall outlet.

- Most models have a Test button. Press the Test button to verify that the UPS can power the components plugged into the UPS.

ACTIVITY 3-4

Performing Preventative Maintenance

Setup:

To complete this activity, you will need a cleaning kit consisting of:

- Monitor cleaning wipes
- Keyboard cleaning wipes
- Lint-free cloths
- Rubbing alcohol
- A mild household cleaner
- Cotton swabs (tightly wound)
- Lens cloth
- Window cleaner
- Toothpicks
- Artist's paint brush
- Compressed air canisters
- Computer vacuum
- CD-ROM cleaning kit
- Floppy drive cleaning kit

Scenario:

In an effort to cut down on the number of peripheral problems that have been occurring, your company has decided to perform preventative maintenance on peripherals each month. To help prevent other system problems, a yearly preventative maintenance plan has also been put in place to clean the internal system components, including the system board, drives, and any adapter cards. As one of the junior members of the support team, you have been assigned the task of cleaning the department's peripherals and internal system components.

 There is a simulated version of this activity available on the CD-ROM that shipped with this course. You can run this simulation on any Windows computer to review the activity after class, or as an alternative to performing the activity as a group in class. The activity simulation can be launched either directly from the CD-ROM by clicking the Interactives link and navigating to the appropriate one, or from the installed data file location by opening the C:\085820Data\Simulations\Lesson#\Activity# folder and double-clicking the executable (.exe) file.

What You Do	How You Do It
1. If you have a keyboard, **clean the keyboard.**	a. **Shut down the system and unplug the keyboard.**
	b. **Turn the keyboard upside down and gently shake it** to remove debris from under the keys.
	c. **Spray compressed air under the keys** to dislodge particles of dust and dirt.
	d. **Drag a small paint brush or a business card between the keys to remove any particles left behind.**
	e. **Wipe each key with keyboard wipes or a soft cloth with rubbing alcohol applied to it.**
	f. **Reconnect the keyboard and restart the system.**
	g. **Verify that all of the keys work.**

2. If you have a mouse, **clean the mouse.**

    a. **Shut down the system and unplug the mouse.**

    b. **Turn the mouse upside down and rotate the cover** to unlatch it. Rotate the cover in the direction indicated on your mouse.

    c. **Place your hand over the cover and ball, and then turn the mouse right side up and the cover and ball should drop out into your hand.** If they don't drop out, gently shake the mouse. If they still don't drop out, make sure that the cover has been turned far enough to unlatch it.

    d. Using a toothpick or your fingernail, **scrape off the line of dirt on each roller.** There should be three rollers and the dirt is usually in the center of each roller.

    e. **Spray compressed air into the mouse** to remove any remaining debris, including the debris you scraped off the rollers.

    f. **Wipe the ball, inside, outside, and the cord of the mouse with mouse cleaning wipes or a soft cloth dampened with rubbing alcohol.**

    g. **Place the ball back inside the mouse.**

    h. **Place the cover over the mouse and rotate it until it locks in place.**

    i. **Reattach the mouse and restart the system.**

    j. **Verify that all of the mouse functions work.**

3. If you have a monitor, **clean the monitor.**

> If you have an LCD monitor, do not use window cleaner on it. Instead, you should use a lint-free cloth to wipe the screen. If more cleaning power is needed, dampen the cloth with rubbing alcohol and wipe the screen.

a. **Shut down the system, turn off the monitor, and unplug the monitor cable and power cord.**

b. **Spray glass cleaner on a lint-free cloth.** Alternatively, you can use specially pre-pared wet monitor wipes and drying wipes.

c. **Wipe the monitor screen using the cloth.**

d. **Vacuum the exterior or wipe with a cloth dampened with a mild household cleaner** to remove dust and debris from the case.

e. **Reconnect the monitor to the system and plug it back in.**

f. **Restart the system and verify that the monitor works.**

4. If you have a complete PC to clean, **clean the case.**

a. **Shut down the system, and then unplug the peripherals and the power cord.**

b. **Remove the cover from the system.**

c. **Wipe the case with a water-dampened, lint-free cloth.** If the case requires addi-tional cleaning power, use a mild household cleaner on the cloth instead of water.

5. If you have a system board, **clean the system board.**

    a. **Position the system so that you can hold the compressed air canister upright.**

    b. **Spray the compressed air so that you blow the dust and debris off the system board and out of the case.**

    c. If you have a computer-safe vacuum, **vacuum any remaining particles from inside the system, being careful not to suck up any jumpers or other components.**

    d. **Reattach the case cover.**

    e. **Reconnect the external devices and power cord.**

---

6. If you have a CD-ROM drive, **clean the CD-ROM drive.**

 Refer to the instructions that come with your cleaning kit and use those steps if they are different from those listed here.

    a. **Power on the system.**

    b. **Insert the CD-ROM cleaner disk in the drive.**

    c. **Access the CD-ROM drive.**

    d. **Remove the CD-ROM cleaner disk from the drive.**

    e. **Test the drive by reading a CD-ROM.**

---

7. Clean the floppy disk drive.

    a. **Insert the floppy disk cleaner disk in the drive.**

    b. **Access the floppy disk drive.**

    c. **Remove the floppy cleaner disk from the drive.**

    d. **Test the floppy disk drive by writing to and reading from a floppy disk.**

ACTIVITY 3-5

Using a UPS

Setup:

To complete this activity, you will need a UPS.

Scenario:

There are periodic power outages at your customer's site due to old power lines and high winds. They have had several corrupted files due to power loss. They have purchased a UPS and have contracted with you to install and test it for them.

 There is a simulated version of this activity available on the CD-ROM that shipped with this course. You can run this simulation on any Windows computer to review the activity after class, or as an alternative to performing the activity as a group in class. The activity simulation can be launched either directly from the CD-ROM by clicking the Interactives link and navigating to the appropriate one, or from the installed data file location by opening the C:\ 085820Data\Simulations\Lesson#\Activity# folder and double-clicking the executable (.exe) file.

What You Do	How You Do It
1. Set up the UPS to power a computer system.	a. If necessary, **connect the battery in the UPS.**
	b. **Plug the UPS into the power outlet.**
	c. **Shut down each of the components that will be powered through the UPS.**
	d. **Unplug the components from the wall or surge protector, and then plug them into the UPS.**
	e. If your UPS is equipped with a cable to connect to a peripheral port on your computer, **connect the UPS to the USB or COM port.**

2. If the UPS comes with its own management software, **install the
software.**

   a. **Insert the UPS software installation
CD-ROM.**

   b. To install the software, **follow the
prompts in the installation wizard.**

3. **Configure what happens when the
UPS encounters a power failure.**

Depending on your UPS, you
might find that you must configure it using its software
rather than the Power
Options within Control Panel.
If this is the case, complete
the tasks in steps f and g
within your UPS's manage-
ment software.

   a. From the Start menu, **choose Control
Panel.**

   b. **Click Performance And Maintenance.**

   c. **Click Power Options.**

   d. If available, **click the UPS tab.**

    If no UPS tab is displayed, **click the tab
related to UPS configuration.**

   e. If necessary, **configure the UPS port,
manufacturer, and model.**

   f. Following the directions that came with
your UPS, or using the UPS tab in the
Power Options Properties dialog box, **configure the computer to sound an alarm
as soon as there is a power failure and
to repeat it every minute.**

   g. **Configure the settings to perform a
shutdown when the critical alarm
threshold is reached.**

   h. **Close all open windows.**

4. **Test the UPS.**

   a. **Turn on the other components** to make
sure they can be powered through the
UPS.

   b. When all of the components plugged into
the UPS have come up to the functional
state, to simulate a power outage, **unplug
the UPS from the power outlet.**

   c. **Plug the UPS back into the wall outlet.**

   d. If your UPS is equipped with a Test button, **press the Test button.**

TOPIC E
Diagnostics and Troubleshooting

In the last topic, you identified general preventative maintenance techniques. Best practices for PC technicians also include using a methodical approach to solving problems. In this topic, you will identify general diagnostic and troubleshooting techniques.

The most elaborate toolkit and expensive diagnostic software can be useless if you don't have a consistent plan of attack for solving problems. Even experienced technicians can sometimes overlook obvious problems or solutions. Troubleshooting is seldom easy, but if you develop or adopt a basic troubleshooting procedure, you will often be able to determine the specific cause of a problem, as well as possible solutions to the problem.

Troubleshooting Theory

A logical, methodical approach to troubleshooting usually leads to quicker solutions, so there are certain general factors that will apply in any troubleshooting situation.

Factor	Description
Backups	Perform backups before making any changes. If the solution you try does not work or leads to additional problems, you can restore the backup and try again.
Assessment	Assess a problem systematically, and divide large problems into smaller components to be analyzed individually. This makes the problem less complex, and helps you to try one solution at a time.
Simple solutions	Verify the obvious, determine whether the problem is something simple, and **make no assumptions.** Trying simple solutions first can save significant time. If a user reports that his monitor does not work and assures you that it is plugged in, connected, and powered on, check for yourself before beginning an exhaustive diagnostic routine.
Research	Research ideas and establish priorities. If the problem is not solved by a simple solution, you might need to do some research, which could result in several possible approaches that need to be tried.
Documentation	Sufficient and proper documentation of setups, configurations, and histories can prove to be invaluable during the troubleshooting process. Document your findings, actions, and the outcomes to help maintain a comprehensive history for future reference.
Environment	Assess the physical environment the equipment is in. Be aware of the location, air flow, and temperature the equipment is operating in.

The Troubleshooting Process

The troubleshooting process moves through logical stages from identifying the problem to solving the problem and verifying user satisfaction.

Stage	Description
Stage 1: Identification	In Stage 1, you will identify the problem, including questioning the user and identifying any recent changes to the computer. Ask the user a series of open-ended questions to help identify the issue behind the symptoms. For instance, instead of asking if the user can start the computer, try asking what happens when the user tries to start the computer. You can also ask the user (and yourself) questions similar to the following, to help identify the problem:

- *Could you do this task before?* If not, maybe the system is simply unable to perform the task without additional hardware or software.

- *If you could do the task before, when did you first notice that you couldn't do it anymore?* If the computer suddenly stops doing what it has always done seamlessly, that might not be the only change. Try to discover what happened immediately before the problem arose, since the source of the problem might be related to other changes.

- *What has changed since the last time you were able to do this task?* Users might tell you that nothing has changed, so you should follow up with leading questions such as "Did someone add something to the computer?" or "Is the procedure you followed this time different in any way from the way you normally do this?"

- *Were error messages displayed?* If you can get the exact text of any error messages displayed, you can try searching the manufacturer's website to get an explanation of the message and to see if any problem reports have been logged related to this message.

- *Is the problem always the same, no matter what conditions apply?* Determining if the problem is consistent or intermittent can help you narrow down possible causes. For instance, if a user can't open a specific spreadsheet file stored on the hard drive, ask if he or she can open a different spreadsheet stored on the hard drive, or even stored on a network drive, if the computer is connected to a network. If the other files open without any trouble, it's fairly safe to assume that the problem lies with the file and not the application or the hard drive.

Stage	Description
Stage 2: Analysis	In Stage 2, you will analyze the problem, including potential causes, and make an initial determination as to whether the problem is being caused by software or hardware, or a combination of both.
	1. Whenever possible, attempt to re-create the problem so that you can determine exactly what actions were taken and what results were received. If you can, watch the user to ensure that he or she is following the correct procedures. If the problem occurs in the same place, the problem will be easier to solve than if it's an intermittent problem. You can also try to re-create the problem by trying to perform the task yourself, at the user's computer and at a similarly configured computer or by having another user try the task, at the user's computer and at a similarly configured computer.
	2. After you reproduce the problem, try to determine what's causing it. Use a systematic approach to eliminate possible causes, starting with the most obvious cause and working back through other potential causes.
	3. Depending on the cause you've isolated, determine at least one way to correct the problem. For instance, if you've isolated the cause as a corrupt spreadsheet file, one possible correction would be to restore the file from a backup. Draw on your own experiences, review support websites, and confer with your colleagues to come up with possible corrections, and prioritize them according to their likelihood of success and ease of implementation.
Stage 3: Testing	In Stage 3, you will test related components, including inspection, connections, hardware and software configurations, Device Manager, and consulting vendor documentation, to solve the problem or identify a likely solution.
	1. Examine and, if possible, listen to the component that appears to be causing the problem to determine if the part needs to be reconfigured or replaced altogether.
	2. Check all connections to ensure that they are properly seated.
	3. If possible, open Device Manager and review the configuration details provided. Make sure that you check both hardware and software configurations—what appears to be a hardware problem can be caused by a software glitch, and vice versa. And, in some cases, a combination of hardware and software can be causing the problem you are trying to solve.
	4. Review vendor documentation to determine if the issue is a known problem with an identified solution. Manuals often contain troubleshooting sections, and vendor websites usually provide searchable databases that can provide answers to many questions.
Stage 4: Implementation	In Stage 4, you will implement your solution. When you do, you need to ensure that productivity doesn't suffer and that downtime is minimized. For example, you might need to provide a loaner machine to a user whose PC needs to be rebuilt.

Stage	Description
Stage 5: Evaluation	In Stage 5, you will evaluate results, and take additional steps if needed, such as consultation with colleagues or vendor support and use of alternative resources and manuals. Make sure that the solution you've implemented actually solved the problem and didn't cause any new ones. Use several options and situations to conduct your tests; for instance, try the task yourself, and then have the user try the task while you observe the process, or test the computer both before and after it's connected to a network, if applicable. Sometimes, you'll need to conduct the testing over a period of time to ensure that the solution you implemented is the right one. Remember to verify that the user agrees that the problem is solved before you proceed.
Stage 6: Documentation	Documenting your activities and their outcomes in Stage 6 is crucial, because detailed descriptions of computer problems and their solutions can be a helpful part of the overall documentation plan for your company's computers. Not only will this provide you with an ever-growing database of information specific to the computers you're responsible for, it also will be valuable reference material for use in future troubleshooting instances.
Stage 7: Verification	In Stage 7, you will verify that the user agrees that the problem is solved. Don't underestimate the importance of this stage. You should never consider a problem to be resolved until the customer considers it to be solved. You'll probably also need to inform others of the outcome of the situation, especially in cases where the person reporting the problem is not actually the person experiencing the problem. When you can, provide a brief explanation of the problem and how you fixed it, but make sure that you don't overwhelm the user with information, and never blame the user directly for the problem. Your explanation should always be geared to the knowledge and interest level of the person you're addressing. What you tell the user might differ substantially from what you tell another technician.

Troubleshooting Models

Several troubleshooting models have been developed for servicing computers and computer networks. Following one of these models can be helpful because it gives you a basis for a systematic approach to troubleshooting. There is no surefire method that will work 100 percent of the time, since troubleshooting often requires you to make intuitive guesses based on experience, but using a model can help you identify causes and solutions in areas where you don't have the required type of experience. Ultimately, the troubleshooting process that you follow will be a mix of these models, plus methods that you find useful. If you get stuck on something you've never encountered before, ask your colleagues if they have seen similar problems.

Troubleshooting Model	Description
CompTIA Network+ Troubleshooting Model	Although this troubleshooting model is designed primarily for network troubleshooting, its basic tenets can be used for troubleshooting PCs. 1. Identify the exact issue. 2. Re-create the problem. 3. Isolate the cause. 4. Formulate a correction. 5. Implement the correction. 6. Test the solution. 7. Document the problem and the solution. 8. Provide feedback.
Novell Troubleshooting Model	Similar to the CompTIA Network+ troubleshooting model, this model was also designed primarily for network troubleshooting, although its basic tenets can also be used for troubleshooting PCs. 1. Try some quick fixes. 2. Gather basic information. 3. Develop a plan of attack to isolate the problem. 4. Execute the plan. 5. Verify user satisfaction. 6. Document the problem and the solution.

Troubleshooting Model	*Description*
Collect, Isolate, and Correct Troubleshooting Model	Another popular troubleshooting model is the Collect, Isolate, and Correct method. This model divides troubleshooting into three large stages, with several steps incorporated into each stage. Ultimately, it achieves the same goal as the other methods, which is to solve computer-related problems.
	1. Collect. In this stage, you gather information, gather user reports, document the process, and keep track of known problems. The key to this stage is to gather a sufficient amount of high-quality information, rather than simply a large amount of information. The experience you gain from troubleshooting your systems will help you determine what data you need to maintain. Note that some of the steps in the Collect stage are done long before trouble is reported. Being prepared is the best way to solve problems quickly and easily when they do arise.
	2. Isolate. This stage relies on the proper completion of the Collect stage. The Isolate stage is a balancing act between a methodical series of steps and a best-guess attempt at solving problems. In some cases, an intuitive reaction will lead you quickly to the source of the trouble. In other cases, you'll need to methodically proceed with the troubleshooting process to discover the root of the problem. The Isolate stage is often completed nearly simultaneously with the Correct stage.
	3. Correct. This stage involves the steps that actually fix the problem, as well as preventative measures. The prioritized list you created in the Isolate stage can help you set a plan for solving the trouble. Follow your plan. Proceed down your list of potential causes, step by step, from top to bottom. Document your progress, and don't skip any steps.

Troubleshooting Template Forms

You might want to create a troubleshooting template form so that you can ensure that the necessary information is included on all trouble reports, and that all reports are consistent, no matter who completes them. Many organizations have help desk software or similar forms or tools that allow you to enter this information. Some of the things you might want to include in a troubleshooting template or help desk form include:

- A general section, listing a description of the trouble call, the date and time the call was received, the person who reported the problem, and the person who has the problem (if the report was made by someone else).

- A description of the conditions surrounding the problem, such as the type of computer, information about any expansion cards or peripherals connected to the computer, the operating system and version, the name and version of any applications mentioned in the problem report, and, if the computer is part of a network, the network operating system and version, as well as whether or not the user was logged on to the network when the problem occurred.

- The exact issue identified during the troubleshooting process.

- Whether or not the problem could be consistently reproduced.

- The possible cause or causes identified during the troubleshooting process.
- The correction or corrections formulated during the troubleshooting process.
- The results of implementing each of the corrections that were tried.
- The results of testing each solution.
- Any external resources that were used, such as vendor documentation, addresses for vendor and other support websites, names and phone numbers for support personnel, and names and phone numbers for third-party service providers.

Troubleshooting Tips

Whenever you are attempting to resolve a problem, you need to keep some general points in mind. The first is to use your common sense. Some solutions are very obvious if you examine the equipment. For example, a cable might be loose or disconnected. Be sure to look for these obvious problems before delving too deeply into troubleshooting mode.

These are the basic troubleshooting steps you will want to take almost every time you face a device problem:

- Check the physical connections. This might involve making sure the device is plugged in and connected to the computer, that it is connected to the right port, that an adapter card is fully seated in the slot, and so forth.
- Check the adapter to which the device is connected. If you are having trouble with a device, it might not be a fault in the device. It might be a problem with the adapter or the adapter card to which it is connected. Be sure to troubleshoot the entire interface including the card, port, cable, and device.
- Check Device Manager. An exclamation point (!) or X in red or yellow over a device indicates there is a problem. The Properties sheet of devices has a Device Status box that indicates whether the device is working properly. This box also contains a Troubleshoot button which accesses topics in the Help And Support Center.
- Use the Help And Support Center utility to have Windows guide you through the things you should check when troubleshooting a particular device problem.

Many times when you are troubleshooting a problem, you will find that there is more than one cause for the problem. In this case, you might need to combine several troubleshooting strategies to resolve the problem. Often you will need to reboot to test whether your attempt to fix the problem has actually worked. If it did, great! If it didn't, just keep trying to work your way through the rest of the list of possible solutions. If none of the solutions work for your problem, ask a colleague for help. Sometimes that second set of eyes sees the solution that you don't.

ACTIVITY 3-6

Identifying Troubleshooting Best Practices

Scenario:
In this activity, you will identify general diagnostics and troubleshooting best practices that PC technicians should employ.

---

1. **When you receive notice that a user is having trouble with his computer, which is the best first step?**

   a) Determine how many users are having similar troubles.

   b) Isolate the cause of the problem.

   c) Ask the user leading questions to gather information.

   d) Check for simple solutions.

---

2. **When is a problem considered to be solved?**

   a) When the device is working correctly.

   b) When the problem has been documented.

   c) When the user is satisfied that the problem is solved.

   d) When standards are developed to prevent future occurrences of the problem.

---

3. **When troubleshooting a device problem on a Windows-based computer, what common troubleshooting tips are helpful to try first?**

TOPIC F

Professionalism and Communication

So far in this lesson, you have identified best practices for working directly with computer equipment. On almost every service call, you will also need to interact with users who are experiencing problems. In this topic, you will identify best practices for PC technicians to use to communicate appropriately with clients and colleagues and conduct business in a professional manner.

You are a representative of your profession, as well as your company. The way you conduct yourself professionally directly influences the satisfaction of your customer, which in turn influences the productivity of your company.

Communication Skills

Using the proper communication skills when dealing with clients and colleagues provides a professional environment that is conducive to solving the problem at hand.

Communication Skill	*Description*
Verbal communication	• Use tact and discretion in all your communications. • Use clear, concise, and direct statements. This will help you get to the crux of the matter more quickly, and it will help the user understand what you are saying. • Avoid using jargon, abbreviations, and acronyms. Many users will not have the same level of technical knowledge as you and your colleagues, and using terminology that is beyond their level of knowledge can confuse or upset them. • Use timing to set the pace of a conversation. A pause may be more valuable than an immediate answer, as it allows you time to formulate your response. If a situation escalates and your customer becomes agitated, you may ask him or her to slow down so that you can get all the information. When a customer is having difficulty ending a call to the help desk, you may gently step up the pace to indicate your need to move on.

Communication Skill	Description
Non-verbal communication	<ul><li>Be aware of the non-verbal clues you use, whether you are talking or listening. Body language communicates more than actual words. Studies show that up to 70 percent of a message is conveyed through actions. Even when you are talking on the phone, non-verbal characteristics—such as tone of voice—will add meaning to your message and help you interpret your customer's concerns.</li><li>Use the proper level of eye contact. You and your customer will make, maintain, and break eye contact as you talk with each other. When attention is directed to the problem at hand, eye contact may be minimal. Avoid staring directly at your customer—a form of invading personal space—or letting your gaze wander, which indicates disinterest, or even worse, inappropriate interest.</li><li>Use gestures and facial expressions to reinforce the spoken message. Broad, friendly gestures indicate being open to the conversation, while sharp or jabbing gestures usually mean anger. The variety, intensity, and meaning of facial expressions are almost endless. You and your customer read each other's faces to gain insight into the spoken words. Your expression must match the content of your words; if there is a mismatch, your customer will believe the message in your face rather than what you say.</li><li>Use non-verbal encouragement to gather information. Encourage your customer to continue with "Mm-hmm" and a slight nod of your head. You convey that you are listening and want to know more.</li><li>Be aware of physical positioning and posture. Respect your customer's personal space. Depending on the circumstances, you may be from 1.5 to 4 feet away from your customer. If the customer backs up, you're too close. You may be working in close quarters; ask permission before you move into your customer's personal space—for example, sitting in the office chair. Messages are conveyed by body position. Slouching indicates "I'm bored with this conversation." Holding one's arms across the chest says "I'm closed to what you are saying." Watch your body's signals, as well as those of your customer.</li><li>Be aware of the effect of tone of voice. The tone of voice indicates many internal moods: excitement, boredom, sarcasm, fear, or uncertainty. A rise in your voice at the end of a sentence makes it sound like a question, implying lack of assurance instead of competence. Listen to your customer's tone. Volume—loudness or softness—colors the spoken message. If your customer's agitation escalates, try lowering your volume to re-establish a sense of calm.</li><li>Use the appropriate level of physical contact. A firm handshake is appreciated and may be expected in some business dealings. Other forms of touching are generally unnecessary, inappropriate, and risky.</li></ul>

Communication Skill	Description
Listening skills	• Listen to the user. If you do not, you run the risk of missing some important information that can help you solve the problem.
	• Allow the user to complete statements—avoid interrupting. This will convey the message that you respect the user and want to hear what he or she is saying.
	• Employ passive listening techniques. Your message is: "I'm listening. Tell me more." You are alert, attentive, and accepting, but do not participate actively in the conversation. Your silence may help your customer to collect his or her thoughts, especially if he or she is upset or angry. Listen for factual data and be alert for feelings and attitudes, which are conveyed non-verbally. It may be difficult to keep from jumping in with a question or a "Yes, but...". Resist the temptation by writing down your thoughts to refer to later.
	• Employ active listening techniques. When your customer is describing the problem, listen actively to elicit as much information as you can. Clarify user statements by asking pertinent questions.

Active Listening

Active listening techniques can enhance your communications skills. These techniques may feel awkward at first, so you might want to try them out in a situation outside your job. With practice, you will use active listening skills more easily and creatively.

Action	Description
Questioning	Ask questions to gain information, clarify what you have heard, and direct the conversation. Open-ended questions can elicit a lot of information. Close-ended questions limit the amount of information by giving a choice of answers. Yes/no questions further limit information exchange and can be used when you need to get to the point. Examples of each of these question styles are:
	• Open-ended: "What happened after you pressed Ctrl+Alt+Delete?"
	• Close-ended: "What kind of a printer do you have, laser or inkjet?"
	• Yes/no: "Are you on a network?"
	What if the answer to your open-ended question is "I don't know" or "I'm not sure"? Go down the list—using close-ended and then yes-no—until you reach the customer's level of expertise. Examples of less helpful question styles:
	• Confusing multiple questions: "What did you do next? Did you try...? What happened?"
	• Accusations: "What did you do that for?"

Action	Description
Empathizing	Let your customer know that you perceive and support what he or she is feeling. Try to be specific in naming the emotion and link it to the customer, using "you," not "I." Examples of helpful empathetic responses include: ● "This delay is frustrating for you." ● "You're afraid you'll lose business while your computer is down." ● "You must be worried about the cost." Examples of less helpful empathetic responses include: ● "I know how you're feeling." ● "I can identify..."
Paraphrasing	Restate what the customer says in your own words to make sure that you interpreted correctly, to bring order to the customer's thoughts, and to relay that their message is important. Use statements, not questions, and don't add or change anything. Examples of starters for paraphrasing include: ● "You're saying that..." ● "It sounds like..." ● "I'm hearing you say..."
Summarizing	Outline the main points of your conversation to summarize what has been said. You can begin by summarizing your understanding of the problem and then checking for clarification. During the conversation, you can re-establish the focus by listing the important facts. Bring closure by summing up the work performed. If a follow-up plan is needed, restate the responsibilities and timeline. Helpful starters for summarizing include: ● "Let's see what we have so far." ● "Why don't we back up a minute and go through that again?" ● "Let's go over our plan."

Here are some examples of statements and their associated active listening skills.

When You Say	Skill Demonstrated
"Is your computer back up and running?"	Yes/no question
"Did the power go off before you saved, during the save, or after you saved your data?"	Close-ended question
"You must really be nervous right now."	Empathy
"You're saying that the computer was in the process of writing to the disk when the power went off. Is that accurate?"	Paraphrase
"What happens when you try to open the presentation?"	Open-ended question
"Before I come over, let's make sure of our game plan. You won't do anything more on the computer, and I'll bring some recovery software that may rescue your presentation."	Summarization

Professional Conduct

Acting in a professional manner when dealing with colleagues and clients provides a work environment where problems can be solved efficiently.

Facet	Description
Appearance	Exhibit a professional appearance. Your work environment may be in a repair shop, at a help desk, or on-site at the customer's business. Whatever the situation, you will want to present a neat, clean, business-like appearance. On-site work may take you into many settings, from muffler repair shops to executive offices. You may be asked to remove your shoes or put on a hard hat. Be aware of the corporate culture and respond accordingly.
Respect	Be respectful of the customer and the environment in which you are working.
	• Maintain a positive attitude when talking with users. Arguing or getting defensive with users will make it harder for you to solve the problem to the users's satisfaction.
	• Never minimize the customer's problem. What seems simple to you could be a mission-critical problem to the user.
	• Never insult a customer or call the customer names. No matter how frustrating a service call might become, rudeness is never the answer.
	• When dealing with customers, avoid distractions and interruptions. Repeatedly answering a cell phone or pager while you are supposed to be working on a problem sends the message that the user's problem is unimportant to you.
	• Be sure to keep your work area at the customer site neat. Don't pile materials on your customer's books and files. Clean up after yourself; a customer who doesn't know a multimeter from a memory module may chase after you with the anti-static bag you left behind. When on-site, ask where to dispose of materials; find out where the recycling bin is for printer test-run paper.
	• Be respectful of the property at the customer site. Always ask permission before entering an office or workspace, using the telephone, sitting down at a computer, or adjusting the workspace.
Accountability	Be accountable. Do not misrepresent your credentials, competence, or training. Take responsibility for your actions, and admit your mistakes. In questions of conflict of interest between your company and the customer, refer to your supervisor or follow your company's procedure. Be aware of your company's policy for accepting gifts or samples, and socializing with customers.

Facet	*Description*
Confidentiality	Be circumspect. Many fields—including medicine, social work, and special education—are regulated by state laws concerning the confidentiality of their consumers. All companies have personal information about their employees. Many corporations have sensitive information about the development of their products or services. Treat any information you learn about your customer's business as confidential. Know your company's policies concerning confidential information and follow them.
Ethics	Practice ethical conduct. You have an obligation to take responsibility for ethical conduct within your delivery of service. The issues involved are complex and ever-changing in the computer industry. An unethical practice may become so routine that it is falsely assumed to be acceptable behavior. Learn your company's policies and adhere to them.
Honesty	Be forthright with your customers about what is occurring and the actions you will take. Clients have a right to understand the process you are following and how it will affect them.
	Discourage software pirating. Software copyright infringement, or pirating, relates to the legal issues surrounding the distribution and use of software. The Federal Copyright Act of 1976 protects the rights of the holder of a copyright. Typically, a backup copy of software is allowed and a site license allows for multiple use at one facility. You are responsible for upholding the law by complying with the license agreements that both your company and your customer hold. Learn your company's policies and adhere to them. Pirating carries penalties and risks, including fines, imprisonment, corrupted files, virus-infected disks, lack of technical support, and lack of upgrades.
Prioritizing	Set priorities. You will often need to set priorities and make judgment calls. You will recommend whether your customer should repair or replace equipment. You will rank the urgency of your customers' needs. Base your decisions on common courtesy, fundamental fairness, and keeping promises. Be familiar with your company's policies and follow them.

ACTIVITY 3-7

Identifying Communication and Professionalism Best Practices

Scenario:
In this activity, you will identify communication and professionalism best practices.

---

1. **Match each communication skill or behavior with the appropriate example.**

    ___ Verbal communication

    ___ Non-verbal communication

    ___ Listening skills

    ___ Respect

    ___ Ethical behavior

    ___ Confidentiality

    ___ Appearance

    a. Allow the user to complete statements without interruption.

    b. Project professionalism by being neat and clean.

    c. Do not use information gained during a service call for your personal benefit.

    d. Keep sensitive client information to yourself.

    e. Ask permission before sitting down in a user's chair or touching a user's computer.

    f. Use clear, concise, and direct statements.

    g. Maintain the proper amount of eye contact.

---

2. **Using clarifying questions to gather more information from a user is an example of what type of technique?**

    a) Passive listening

    b) Non-verbal communication

    c) Active listening

---

3. **Which are examples of displaying respect during a service call?**

    a) Asking permission before changing display settings.

    b) Asking "What happened just before you noticed the problem?"

    c) Sitting in a user's chair without permission.

    d) Turning off your pager or cell phone.

Lesson 3 Follow-up

In this lesson, you identified best practices that are followed by professional PC technicians. With the proper toolset, awareness of safety and environmental issues, general preventative maintenance techniques, and basic diagnostic and troubleshooting processes, you are prepared to do your job in a safe, effective, and professional manner.

1. **Which of the best practices discussed in this lesson apply in your workplace?**

2. **Of the best practices that are not applicable to your work environment, which would you consider adopting?**

4 Installing and Configuring Peripheral Components

Lesson Time: 2 hour(s), 30 minutes

Lesson Objectives:

In this lesson, you will install and configure computer components.

You will:

- Install and configure display devices.
- Install and configure input devices.
- Install and configure adapter cards.
- Install multimedia devices.

Introduction

In the last lesson, you identified general best practices for personal computer technicians. Now that you have a solid base of background information, it's time to start working on some hardware components. In this lesson, you will install and configure peripheral computer components.

Much of the work that you will perform as a personal computer technician will involve installing and configuring various hardware and software components. Installing and configuring peripheral components is one of the more common tasks an A+ Technician has. If you configure the peripherals correctly, users will be able to complete their daily tasks more efficiently.

This lesson covers all or part of the following CompTIA A+ (2006) certification objectives:

- Topic A:
    - Exam 220–601 (Essentials): Objective 1.1, Objective 1.2, Objective 2.1, Objective 2.3
    - Exam 220–602 (IT Technician): Objective 1.1, Objective 2.1, Objective 2.3
    - Exam 220–603 (Remote Technician): Objective 1.1
    - Exam 220–604 (Depot Technician): Objective 1.1, Objective 2.1, Objective 2.3
- Topic B:
    - Exam 220–601 (Essentials): Objective 1.1, Objective 1.2, Objective 2.1
    - Exam 220–602 (IT Technician): Objective 1.1
    - Exam 220–603 (Remote Technician): Objective 1.1
    - Exam 220–604 (Depot Technician): Objective 1.1
- Topic C:
    - Exam 220–601 (Essentials): Objective 1.1, Objective 2.1, Objective 5.2
    - Exam 220–602 (IT Technician): Objective 1.1
    - Exam 220–603 (Remote Technician): Objective 1.1
    - Exam 220–604 (Depot Technician): Objective 1.1
- Topic D:
    - Exam 220–601 (Essentials): Objective 1.1, Objective 1.2
    - Exam 220–603 (Remote Technician): Objective 1.1
    - Exam 220–604 (Depot Technician): Objective 1.1

TOPIC A
Install and Configure Display Devices

In this lesson, you will install and configure peripheral components. Generally, one of the simplest peripherals to install is the display device. In this topic, you will install and configure display devices.

The display device is a user's window into the computer system. Without the display device, you can't see the computer interface to issue commands, and you can't see the results of your work. Correctly installing and configuring the display system enables you to meet these basic user needs. The information in this topic will enable you to install a range of different display devices correctly.

Display Device Types

Common display devices that you might be asked to install include CRT monitors, LCD monitors, and projection systems, which are described in the following table.

Display Device	Description
CRT monitor	Cathode Ray Tube (CRT) monitors are the traditional type of computer display. Starting with IBM's Video Graphics Array (VGA) standard, CRTs used analog color, which uses three consecutive signals—one each for red, green, and blue. Super VGA (SVGA) is the later standard. Cathode ray tube (CRT) monitors can have curved or flat screens. However, they should not be confused with flat-panel monitors.
LCD monitor	Liquid Crystal Display (LCD) flat-panel displays are a compact, light-weight alternative to traditional CRT monitors and are the most common monitors sold today. LCDs now come in large-screen sizes of 17 inches and more, with high screen resolution and high color capacity. Older LCDs have two disadvantages: they are not as bright as CRT monitors, and the user must sit directly in front of the LCD screen to see the display properly. LCDs consume much less energy than CRTs and do not emit electromagnetic radiations as CRTs do.
Projection system	Video projectors are often used to display the contents of a monitor onto a white board or other surface so that an audience can see the output from a computer screen.

Monochrome, Color, and Enhanced Graphics

The original personal computers were designed to use television as video displays, but televisions at that time were limited to about 40 characters per line. The first personal computer monitors could display up to 80 characters per line and 25 lines of text in bright green or white on a black background. The computer's graphic card only displayed black and white. It was the monitor that used either green or amber phosphor to change the color for the end user.

As demand for color graphics increased, the monochrome standard of the Monochrome Display Adapter (MDA) was replaced by the Color Graphics Adapter (CGA), which could show from two to 16 colors at resolutions from 160 x 200 to 640 x 200 pixels (picture elements or unique dots on the screen). The Enhanced Graphics Adapter (EGA) could show up to 640 x 350 pixels. Monitors of this vintage used digital video signals—TTL for transistor-to-transistor logic—and are completely incompatible with today's computers.

Other Display Devices

Virtual reality games and special-purpose imaging needs led to the development of glasses that substitute for a monitor. Touchscreen monitors enable input by touching images on the screen. This technology is used in bank ATM machines, some point-of-sale terminals at fast food restaurants, and other situations where a separate keyboard for input is not appropriate. Video display systems can be used to display one image to several monitors (often used in training situations) or display an image covering a huge screen (often used at trade shows).

Display Settings

You can configure a number of display characteristics for each video output device, either through a dialog box in Windows or through controls on the physical monitor.

Display Setting	Description
Resolution	The maximum number of pixels on a monitor. A pixel is the smallest discrete element on a video display. A single pixel is composed of a red, a blue, and a green dot. The resolution value is given as horizontal pixels by vertical pixels, usually in the ratio 4:3. Common resolutions are 640 x 480, 800 x 600, 1024 x 768, and 1600 x 1200. The higher the resolution, the more objects or information you can fit on the screen at once.
Refresh rate	The number of times per second that the entire monitor is scanned to illuminate the pixels. Each scan is referred to as a frame. The rate is expressed in Hertz (Hz). Typical refresh rates are 60-70 Hz or 60-70 times per second. Any setting lower than 60 Hz usually produces noticeable flickering.
Color depth (quality)	The number of bits used to store the color of a pixel: the more bits per pixel, the more colors can be displayed. The following are the color depths you will likely encounter:

- 4-bit color depth requires 0.5 bytes per pixel and can display 16 colors. This is standard VGA mode. At 640 x 480 resolution, this requires 0.5 MB of memory.

- 8-bit color depth requires 1 byte per pixel and can display 256 colors. This is 256-color mode. At 800 x 600 resolution, this requires 2 MB of memory.

- 16-bit color depth requires 2 bytes per pixel and can display 65,536 colors. This is High Color mode. At 1024 x 768 resolution, this requires 4 MB of memory.

- 24-bit color depth requires 3 bytes per pixel and can display 16,777,216 colors. This is True Color mode. At 1600 x 1200 resolution, this requires 8 MB of memory.

- 32-bit color depth is actually 24-bit color with 8 extra bits that can be left empty or used for an alpha channel to create composite images.

Display Setting	Description
Font	A size and style of typeface. Computers use fonts to display text on the screen. To use a different set of screen fonts, you will have to install the fonts and restart the system. Configurable in Windows XP.
Brightness	The amount of white in a display image. If the brightness is set too high, you might get an "aura" effect displayed on the screen. If it is set too low, you might not see anything on the screen.
Contrast	The difference in intensity between adjacent colors in an image. If the contrast is not set correctly for the monitor and the lighting conditions in the room (for example, a really bright or really dark room), you might not be able to see anything on the screen, or you might get strange results.
Image position	The location or size of the display in relation to the physical monitor. Sometimes the image is not centered on the monitor. Other times the image doesn't fill the screen, leaving a black band around the edge. Or, part of the image can scroll off the screen. There are usually separate buttons or menu options to adjust each of these issues.
Distortions	Curves or waves in the video image. These are typically caused by Moire patterns, electromagnetic interference, or a defect with hardware, such as the video card. If lines don't appear straight on the monitor, you might need to adjust settings. Electromagnetic issues, however, are resolved by eliminating the source of interference. Refer to the monitor documentation for how to resolve such issues. Configure on the display device itself.
V-hold	The maintenance of vertical hold. Adjusting the V-hold will stop a monitor's display from rolling up or down off the screen. This option is not always available. Depending on the device, there may be a knob on the back to adjust the vertical hold on the display.
Degaussing	This option is available on CRT monitors and is used to demagnify the monitor.

Power Management

Power management settings can affect the performance of monitors and other peripherals. You configure power management in CMOS by specifying when power conservation settings take effect. You then specify which components are automatically powered down and under what conditions.

With the power management enabled in CMOS, you can then use Windows XP Power Schemes to reduce power consumption of specific devices or the computer as a whole. Windows XP comes with several preconfigured power options you can choose from, or you can create your own settings. These features must be supported by the hardware in order for Windows XP to implement them. After a specific interval, you can:

- Turn off components such as the monitor or hard drive.

- Go into Standby Mode. This puts devices in a low power state and turns off some devices.

- Go into Hibernate Mode. This saves the contents of RAM to disk, and then turns off the monitor, drives, and, finally, the computer itself.

LCD Characteristics

LCD devices have some unique characteristics.

LCD Characteristic	Description
Components	LCDs consume much less energy than CRTs and do not emit electromagnetic radiation. An LCD display consists of a number of pixels placed in an array in front of a light source. Each pixel is made up of a layer of liquid crystal molecules suspended between two transparent electrodes and two polarizing filters; the polarizing filters are placed such that one's polarity is perpendicular to the other. The electrodes and polarizing filters enable the monitor to "twist" the liquid crystals within each pixel, and thus control how much light passes through the pixels. An *inverter* is used to convert DC power to AC power for the LCD display. When an inverter fails, depending on the laptop model, it may be necessary to simply replace the LCD display rather than replace the inverter. In addition, replacing the inverter requires you to get an exact match, both electrically and mechanically (connectors, size/shape, and mounting).
Screen type	There are several types of LCD devices, but only two types are in widespread use. • Active Matrix is also known as Thin-Film Transistor or TFT. It uses one transistor for each pixel. It requires more power than a passive matrix monitor, but provides a better quality image with a wider viewing angle and faster screen updates. • Passive Matrix uses two groups of transistors combined with a wire matrix to produce images. Screen updates are slow as they are drawn line by line, and there can be issues with contrast and refresh speeds.

LCD Characteristic	Description
Resolution	Unlike CRT devices, LCD devices have a single, fixed resolution. This is called the native resolution. As an LCD display consists of a fixed raster, it cannot change resolution to match the signal being displayed as a CRT monitor can, meaning that optimal display quality can be reached only when the signal input matches the native resolution. Different video standards and specifications offer different resolutions.

- Extended Graphics Array (XGA) is a high-resolution graphics standard introduced by IBM in 1990. XGA was designed to replace the older 8514/A video standard. It provides the same resolutions (640 x 480, 800 x 600, or 1024 x 768 pixels), but supports more simultaneous colors (65,536 as opposed to 256). In addition, XGA allows monitors to be non-interlaced.

- Super Extended Graphics Array (SXGA) provides a standard monitor resolution of 1280 x 1024 pixels. This resolution is an enhancement of the standard XGA resolution. This resolution is not the standard 4:3 aspect ratio but 5:4. A standard 4:3 monitor using this resolution will have rectangular rather than square pixels, distorting the picture and causing circles to appear elliptical. SXGA is the most common resolution on 17-inch, 18-inch, and 19-inch desktop LCD monitors. The majority of these monitors have a physical 5:4 aspect ratio, avoiding any distortion.

- Super Extended Graphics Array (SXGA+) is a variation of the SXGA display specification that is capable of displaying 1400 x 1050 resolution. SXGA+ display is commonly used on 14-inch or 15-inch laptop LCD screens. SXGA+ displays usually cost more due to their higher resolution. SXGA+ is also the maximum resolution native to many high-end video projectors.

- Widescreen SXGA (WSXGA+) provides a resolution of 1680 x 1050 pixels. This is the native resolution of nearly all 20-inch and 21-inch wide-aspect LCD monitors and is available in laptop displays that are 15.4 inches or larger.

- Ultra Extended Graphics Array (UXGA) is a display specification that is capable of displaying 1600 x 1200 resolution, or four times the default resolution of SVGA.

- Widescreen UXGA (WUXGA) provides a resolution of 1920 x 1200 pixels with a 16:10 screen aspect ratio. It is a wide version of UXGA and is appropriate for viewing North American HDTV content (ATSC).

Contrast ratio	The contrast ratio is a metric of a display system, defined as the ratio of the luminosity of the brightest and the darkest color the system is capable of producing. High contrast ratio is a desired aspect of any display.
Backlighting/frontlighting	A backlight is the typical form of illumination used in a full-sized LCD display. Backlights differ from frontlights because they illuminate the LCD from the side or back, where frontlights are in front of the LCD. Frontlights are used in small displays such as on MP3 players to increase readability in low light conditions, and in computer and television displays to produce light in a manner similar to a CRT display.

LCD Characteristic	Description
Pixelation	Pixelation is the display of a digitized image where the individual pixels are apparent to a viewer. This can happen unintentionally when a low-resolution image designed for an ordinary computer display is projected on a large screen and each pixel becomes separately viewable.

Aspect Ratio

The aspect ratio is the ratio of width to height of a display. Most software expects a 4:3 ratio, and the display will appear to be distorted if other ratios are used. The aspect ratio is found by determining the proportion of the number of pixels across the screen to the number of pixels down the screen. For example, a resolution of 640 x 480 has a 4:3 aspect ratio.

Resolution/Number of Pixels	Aspect Ratio
320 x 200/64,000	8:5
640 x 480/307,200	4:3
800 x 600/480,000	4:3
1,024 x 768/786,432	4:3
1,280 x 1,024/1,310,720	5:4
1600 x 1200/1,920,000	4:3

Interlacing

If you have an interlaced display adapter, every other line is scanned during each pass until the entire screen has been covered. This method improves resolution, but produces a noticeable flicker as the phosphors lose luminescence before they are hit again.

Connector Types

Display devices can use several different types of connectors.

Connector Type	Description
VGA	The DB 15 high-density Video Graphics Array connector is the most common connector for LCD monitors. Pins 4, 11, 12, and 15 receive information from the monitor, while pins 1, 2, 3, 13, and 14 send information to the monitor.

Connector Type	Description
 DVI	Digital Video Interface cables keep data in digital form from the computer to the monitor. There is no need to convert data from digital information to analog information. LCD monitors work in a digital mode and support the DVI format. • DVI-digital (DVI-D) is a digital-only format. It requires a video adapter with a DVI-D connection and a monitor with a DVI-D input. The connector contains 24 pins/receptacles in 3 rows of 8 above or below a flat blade, plus a grounding slot for dual-link support. For single-link support, the connector contains 18 pins/receptacles. • DVI-integrated (DVI-I) supports both digital and analog transmissions. This gives you the option to connect a monitor that accepts digital input or analog input. In addition to the pins/receptacles found on the DVI-D connector for digital support, a DVI-I connector has 4 additional pins/receptacles to carry an analog signal.
 HDMi	High-Definition Multimedia Interface is the first industry-supported uncompressed, all-digital audio/video interface. HDMI uses a single cable to provides an interface between any audio/video source, such as a set-top box, DVD player, or A/V receiver and an audio and/or video monitor, such as a digital television (DTV).
 S-Video	Separate Video is an analog video signal that carries the video data as two separate signals (brightness and color). S-Video works in 480i or 576i resolution.

Connector Type	Description
 Component/RGB	Component video is a type of analog video information that is transmitted or stored as two or more separate signals. Analog video signals (also called components) must provide information about the amount of red, green, and blue to create an image. The simplest type, RGB, consists of three discrete red, green, and blue signals sent down three coaxial cables.
 Composite video	Composite video is the format of an analog (picture only) signal before it is combined with a sound signal and modulated onto an RF carrier.

Device Drivers

Definition:

A *device driver* is a type of software that enables the operating system and a peripheral device to communicate with each other. Also referred to as a driver or driver software, a device driver takes generalized commands from the system software or an application and translates them into unique programming commands that the device can understand. It also provides the code that allows the device to function with the operating system, and it is generally installed as part of the installation process for a new piece of hardware. Device drivers can be generic for a class of device or specific to a particular device.

Example:

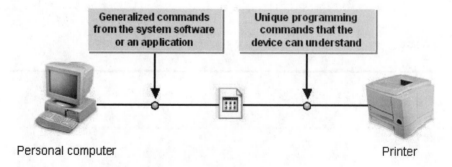

Figure 4-1: Device drivers.

Where to Get Device Drivers

Device drivers can be:

- Included with the Windows XP operating system. New operating systems include thousands of drivers that let them work with all current, popular devices. Peripherals that are designed after the operating system comes out must supply their own drivers.
- Supplied with the device on a CD-ROM or floppy disk when you purchase the hardware.
- Downloaded from the Internet from the hardware manufacturer's website.

Display Device Selection Tips

There are a number of display devices from which you can choose, depending on your (or the user's) needs. CRT monitors offer more features and potentially better resolution, which might make them a better choice for users who work in high-end graphics applications such as Photoshop. In addition, CRT monitors are also less expensive than flat-panel monitors. On the other hand, flat-panel monitors take up less space and many users prefer them.

Display Device Installation Considerations

When you're ready to install a display device, keep the following considerations in mind.

Display Device Component	Description
Drivers	Before you attempt to install any display device, make sure that you have the correct device drivers for the operating system installed on the computer. If necessary, download the most current drivers from the manufacturer's website. If you're also installing a video adapter, you will need its drivers as well.
Digital Video Interface	Be sure to select the proper DVI cable and connector.
	• DVI-analog (DVI-A) can be used to convert the digital signal from the video card to analog signals an analog monitor can display. DVI-A is analog only and uses one row of 5 pins, one row of 3 pins, and one row of 4 pins, along with 2 contacts above and below a flat blade.
	• Typically, monitors that support the DVI-D interface do not include the cable. If you purchase a monitor that uses this interface, be sure to determine whether you need to also purchase the DVI-D cable.
	• Remember that DVI-I can be used to transmit digital signals from the video card to a digital monitor, or analog signals from a video card to an analog monitor, but it cannot convert digital signals to analog or vice versa.
	DVI-D and DVI-I cables can be single or dual-link. Dual-link cables double the transmission power of a single-link cable, thus increasing the transmission speed and signal quality.

Display Device Component	Description
Video Adapter	Video adapters have different features that increase the performance of displaying graphics. Types of video adapters you might encounter now include VESA Local-Bus (VL-Bus), Accelerated Graphics Port (AGP), and PCI Express (PCIe). Keep in mind that if you plan to use a DVI-D connector to connect a monitor to a computer, the video adapter must have a DVI-D port. If you have an analog monitor (VGA connector) and a video card with DVI-D output, you can purchase an inexpensive DVI adapter to make a connection. In some cases, when you have digital monitor and analog output on the video card, you will need to use a conversion box. A simple adapter will not work in this case because the digital display will not be able to interpret the analog signals from the card.

How to Install and Configure Display Devices

Procedure Reference: Install a Monitor

To install a monitor:

1. Turn off the computer, and unplug the monitor from the computer and the power source.

2. Locate the monitor port on the computer. It will likely be a 15-pin VGA adapter or a 29-pin DVI adapter.

3. Align the pins on the monitor cable with the holes in the adapter port, and plug in the monitor.

4. Secure the monitor to the port by tightening the screws on each side of the port.

5. Plug in the monitor power cord.

6. Turn on the computer.

7. Turn on the monitor.

8. Verify that the monitor works.
   - Check that the power light is on, that it is green, and that it is not blinking.
   - Make sure the colors display correctly (they are not washed out or the wrong colors).
   - Make sure there are no lines or distortion in the image displayed on the monitor, and no waviness in the display.

Procedure Reference: Adjust Video Output Settings

To adjust video output settings:

1. Use the control buttons located on the physical monitor to adjust the display size and location. Through these buttons you can change the:
   - Vertical display position.
   - Horizontal display position.
   - Display height.
   - Display width.

2. Use the control buttons located on the physical monitor to adjust brightness and contrast.

3. Use the Windows Display Properties Control Panel to adjust the screen resolution.
   a. Right-click the desktop and choose Properties to display the Display Properties Control Panel.
   b. Click Settings.
   c. Drag the Screen Resolution slider to the desired setting. If your video card and monitor support only one resolution, you won't be able to change it. If the video card supports only two resolutions, instead of dragging the indicator, click above the desired resolution to change it.
   d. Click Apply.
   e. Click OK.
   f. If prompted to retain the settings, click Yes. If you don't click within the allotted time, the setting reverts to the previous setting.

4. Use the Windows Display Properties Control Panel to adjust the font size.
   - To select a standard font size:
     a. Right-click the desktop and choose Properties.
     b. In the Display Properties Control Panel, click the Appearance tab.
     c. Display the Font Size drop-down list.
     d. Select the desired font size. Choices include Normal, Large, and Extra Large.
     e. Click OK.
   - To select a custom font size by adjusting the dpi setting for the monitor:
     a. Right-click the desktop and choose Properties.
     b. In the Display Properties Control Panel, click the Settings tab.
     c. Click Advanced.
     d. From the DPI Setting drop-down list, select a size: Normal (96 DPI), Large (120 DPI), or Custom Setting.
     e. If you selected Custom Setting, either select a percentage of normal font size from the drop-down list or drag the ruler to the desired scale. Click OK, and then click OK again to acknowledge that you will need to install the fonts and restart.
     f. Click OK.
     g. If prompted to use existing files, click Yes.
     h. Click Close, and then click Yes to restart the computer.

ACTIVITY 4-1

Installing Display Devices

Setup:

You have a working computer with either a 15-pin VGA-style monitor port and a computer equipped with a digital video interface, or you have a digital flat-panel LCD monitor that uses the 29-pin DVI connector. The computer is turned off and the monitor is unplugged.

Scenario:

The marketing department of your company is moving to new offices, and you've been assigned the task of setting up the computers in their new offices. The computers and standard VGA CRT monitors or LCD monitors with 29-pin DVI connector have been delivered to each office. Employees want to begin using their computers as soon as possible.

 There is a simulated version of this activity available on the CD-ROM that shipped with this course. You can run this simulation on any Windows computer to review the activity after class, or as an alternative to performing the activity as a group in class. The activity simulation can be launched either directly from the CD-ROM by clicking the Interactives link and navigating to the appropriate one, or from the installed data file location by opening the C:\ 085820Data\Simulations\Lesson#\Activity# folder and double-clicking the executable (.exe) file.

What You Do	How You Do It

1. Install the monitor.

    a. **Verify that the power is off at the computer.**

    b. **Locate the monitor cable and examine the connector.**

    c. If you have a standard VGA CRT monitor, **locate the VGA adapter port on the computer.** If you have an LCD monitor with 29-pin DVI connector, **locate the DVI port on the computer.**

    d. **Insert the monitor connector into the appropriate port, being sure to align the pins carefully.**

 It's easy to bend the pins, so align them carefully. Bent pins can result in poor video display or no video display at all.

    e. **Tighten the screws.**

    f. **Plug in the monitor.**

2. Verify that the monitor is functional.

    a. **Turn on the computer power.**

    b. **Turn on the monitor power.**

    c. After the system has started to boot, **verify that the power light on the monitor is green and is not flashing.**

    d. **Watch the monitor and verify that the display is clear.**

ACTIVITY 4-2

Configuring Display Devices

Setup:

Your instructor has altered the display settings for your monitor. The computer is running, and the Welcome screen is displayed.

Scenario:

A monitor was recently moved from the old location to the new location. The employee reports that the display does not appear in the center of the monitor. The images are too dark, making it difficult to see, and he can't see as much on the screen as he would like. The icons on the screen are too small and the font is too big. The employee needs you to resolve these issues so that he can get back to work.

There is a simulated version of this activity available on the CD-ROM that shipped with this course. You can run this simulation on any Windows computer to review the activity after class, or as an alternative to performing the activity as a group in class. The activity simulation can be launched either directly from the CD-ROM by clicking the Interactives link and navigating to the appropriate one, or from the installed data file location by opening the C:\085820Data\Simulations\Lesson#\Activity# folder and double-clicking the executable (.exe) file.

What You Do	How You Do It
1. Adjust the monitor display.	a. Log on as Admin##.
	b. Referring to documentation as necessary, **locate the control to adjust the brightness of the display image.**
	c. **Adjust the brightness so that the monitor is comfortable to view.**
	d. **Adjust the contrast so that you can view all screen elements easily.**

2. **Adjust the horizontal and vertical position of the image.**

   a. Referring to documentation as necessary, **locate the controls to adjust the size and centering of the display image.**

   b. **Adjust the vertical display position so that the display is centered top-to-bottom on the screen.**

   c. **Adjust the horizontal display position so that the display is centered side-to-side on the screen.**

   d. **Adjust the height and width of the image so that there is either no border or the smallest border allowed.**

3. **Change the resolution.**

   a. To open the Display Properties Control Panel, **right-click the Desktop, and choose Properties.**

   b. **Click the Settings tab.**

   c. In the Screen Resolution box, **drag the slider to the left or click to select a screen area that is less than the one currently set.**

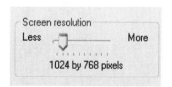

   d. **Click Apply.**

   e. If prompted, **click OK to acknowledge the informational message.**

   f. In the Monitor Settings prompt box, **click Yes.**

4. Reduce the font size.

a. Click the Appearance tab.

b. Display the Font Size drop-down list.

c. Select Normal.

d. Click OK.

TOPIC B

Install and Configure Input Devices

In the last topic, you installed and configured display devices so that users could see computer output. Users also need to be able to issue commands to the computer software by using input devices. In this topic, you will install and configure input devices.

Computers need user input before they can do anything useful. In the early days of computing, user input involved physically rewiring the computers. Later computers could accept input on cards and paper tape. Keyboards and pointing devices are now the standard input devices for personal computers, but there are others available that streamline the process of providing input to the computer. As an A+ technician, part of your responsibilities will include installing and configuring input devices so that users can perform their assignments in the most efficient manner possible.

Standard Input Device Types

Common input devices include mice and keyboards, but these two components come in a variety of implementations.

Input Device	Description
 XT Keyboard  AT (Standard)  AT (Enhanced)	Standard keyboards are rectangular in shape, and have 84 or 101 keys. • The original PC keyboard, the XT, has 84 keys. A numeric pad is integrated to the right of the alphabetical keys. Function keys are along the left side of the keyboard. • The AT keyboard also has 84 keys and is very similar to the original PC keyboard. However, on the AT keyboard, the numeric pad is separate from the alphabetical keys. • The AT Enhanced keyboard has 101 keys. The function keys are integrated across the top. Arrow keys have been added, as well as a set of six keys—Insert, Delete, Home, End, Page Up, and Page Down. There are also additional command keys such as Esc and Ctrl.

Standard keyboards

Input Device	Description
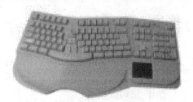 Ergonomic keyboard  Dvorak keyboard	Natural or ergonomic keyboards usually split the keyboard in half so each hand can comfortably use its own set of keys. Built-in wrist rests are common, and some ergonomic keyboards also have an integrating pointing device such as a track ball or touchpad. Dvorak keyboards rearrange the keys into a more natural arrangement that makes faster typing possible.
 Mouse	A mouse is a small object that contains a ball on the underside that is run across a flat surface and at least one, but typically two or three, buttons that send electronic signals to the GUI. Its name is derived from its appearance—a small rounded rectangle shape with a single cord attached at one end. Mice can be: ● Mechanical—Mechanical sensors detect the direction the ball is rolling and move the screen pointer accordingly. ● Opticalmechanical—Optical sensors detect motion of the ball and move the screen pointer accordingly. ● Optical—A laser detects the mouse's movement as you move it along a special mat with a grid. The special mat provides the optical mechanism with a frame of reference. Optical mice have no mechanical moving parts, but they respond more quickly and precisely than other types of mice.

Input Device	Description
 Trackball	A trackball is basically an upside down mouse. The ball is mounted on the top of the case instead of the bottom and signals are sent to the computer by moving the ball with your fingers or palm instead of by rolling the ball across a flat surface. Like a mouse, a trackball has at least one button that is used to send electronic signals to the computer.
 Touch pad	A touchpad is a small, touch-sensitive pad where you run your finger across the surface to send electronic signals to the computer to control the pointer drawn on the screen. Touchpads can have buttons like a mouse or trackball, or the touchpad can be configured to detect finger taps on its surface and process those signals like a button click.

Specialty Keyboards

Specialty keyboards include:

- Keyboards for children or users with special needs may have enlarged or specially constructed keys.

- Foreign language keyboards have a variety of different keys.

- Custom application keyboards can have multimedia access buttons, video/audio editing software buttons, and gaming devices.

Ports, Cables, and Connections

Keyboards and mice can use several types of ports and connections:

- Serial

- Standard DIN (5-pin)

- PS/2 (6-pin mini-DIN)

- USB

- Wireless infrared

- Wireless RF

- Bluetooth

Biometric Input Device Types

Biometrics is an automated method of recognizing a person based on a physiological or behavioral characteristic, such as retina pattern, fingerprints, or voice recognition. Biometric technologies are becoming the foundation of an extensive array of highly secure identification and personal verification solutions. Common implementations in the computing environment include fingerprint scanners on input devices such as keyboards and mice. Using these input devices ensures the security of a user's data.

Figure 4-2: A biometric keyboard.

Figure 4-3: A biometric mouse.

Specialized Input Device Types

Although keyboards and mice are the most popular of the input devices for personal computers, there are some specialized input devices that you might encounter in your workplace.

Input Device	Description
Bar code readers	Bar codes provide a simple and inexpensive method of encoding text information that is easily read by inexpensive electronic readers. A bar code reader decodes a bar code by scanning a light source across the bar code and converting the pattern of reflected light to an electronic signal that is decoded back to the original data by electronic circuits. There are currently four different types of bar code readers available: pen-type readers (or bar code wands), laser scanners, Charge Coupled Device (CCD) readers, and camera-based readers. Bar code readers provide either keyboard wedge output or RS-232 output. The bar code readers with keyboard wedge output plug directly into the keyboard port on the PC, and they also provide a pigtail connector so that you can plug in a keyboard at the same time. An RS-232 or serial interface bar code reader is connected to an available serial port on the PC. A program called a software wedge is required to direct the data from the bar code reader to the application.

Input Device	Description
Touch screens	Touch screens enable users to enter input by touching areas on a monitor screen. Touch screens are composed of:

- Touch sensors. The sensors can be a panel that lays over a standard monitor or can be built into a special touch screen monitor where the user actually touches the glass on the monitor.

- Controller. If using an overlay panel, the controller connects to the panel and then to a PC port. Many use a COM or USB port, although there are special instances where the controller connects to a drive or other device or port. For touch screens with built-in touch sensors, the controller is built into the monitor. In this case, the monitor contains two cables—one to the monitor port and one to the COM or USB port (or other port).

- Device driver or specialized software. This enables the operating system to receive and interpret information from the touch screen device.

Touch screens can gather input using technologies such as infrared, capacitive touch, resistive touch, or surface acoustic wave. They can be finger touch or stylus touch.

Input Device Selection Tips

The Windows operating systems support a variety of input devices, so you should select an input device based on user requirements.

Input Device	Description
Keyboard	When selecting a keyboard for a user, in addition to considering its ergonomics, you should also consider whether the keyboard offers additional features (such as customizable hot keys and scrolling) as well as wireless connectivity. Many users now prefer wireless keyboards as it gives them the freedom to locate the keyboard anywhere on their desks. In some cases, users might be able to use a Bluetooth-enabled keyboard to communicate with both their desktop computers and a personal data assistant (PDA) or mobile phone. Be sure to determine the potential keyboard's connector requirements; if the keyboard uses USB, you'll need to make sure the user's computer has an available USB port.
Pointing device	When choosing a mouse for a user, most users prefer optical mice because they're less susceptible to problems such as dirt interfering with moving the pointer. As with keyboards, you'll also find that users prefer wireless mice over wired mice because of the freedom it gives them to move around while working. Besides these factors, choosing between a mouse, a trackball, and a touchpad comes down to the personal preference of the user.

Input Device Installation Considerations

Before you attempt to install an input device, you should consider certain factors.

Factor	Considerations
Drivers	Be sure that you have the most current drivers for the input device and the operating system of the computer on which you plan to install it.
Ports	Make sure that the computer has an available port to which you can connect the device. Input devices can use PS/2, serial, parallel, USB, SCSI ports, Infrared, and FireWire/IEEE 1394.
Manufacturer's instructions	Review the manual that came with the device. In some cases, the manufacturer might require you to install the device drivers before connecting the device to the computer.

How to Install and Configure Input Devices

Procedure Reference: Install Input Devices

To install input devices:

1. Examine the input device that you need to install, paying particular attention to the connection type.

2. If necessary, shut down the computer, and unplug the power cord and any network or modem cables.

3. If necessary, unplug the current keyboard or mouse from the system unit.

4. If the new input device has a USB connector, plug the device into an available USB port.

5. If the new input device has a PS/2 connector, align the pins on the cable with the openings in the PS/2 port on the computer and plug the device into the port, being sure to plug the keyboard in to the keyboard port and the mouse in to the mouse port. The rectangular plastic piece at the end of the cable helps you align the pins. The color coding of the ports (purple for the keyboard, green for the mouse) can help you connect the ports correctly.

6. Reconnect the power cord and any network or modem cables.

7. Verify that the new input devices work properly.

    a. Restart the computer.

    b. Check for error messages when the system boots. If you see a keyboard error message, the keyboard and mouse cables are probably switched. Power down the system and switch the cables, and then try powering on again.

    c. Enter text from the keyboard.

    d. Move the mouse to different parts of the screen and click an icon or text to verify that the mouse pointer moves where you point it and that the buttons work properly.

8. If necessary, install device drivers for the new input device.

Procedure Reference: Configure the Keyboard

To configure the keyboard:

1. If necessary, log on to Windows.

2. Open the Keyboard Control Panel. The Keyboard Properties Control Panel contains a Speed tab and a Hardware tab.

3. On the Speed tab, adjust the Character Repeat Delay and Character Repeat Rate as needed by using the slider bars.

4. Use the text box below the slider bars to test the Character Repeat settings.

5. Adjust the Cursor Blink Rate by using the slider bar. The sample cursor at the left of the slider bar indicates the speed at which the cursor will blink.

6. On the Hardware tab, click Properties to display the properties of the specific keyboard.

7. On the Driver tab, use the buttons to view, update, roll back, or uninstall the device driver.

8. Click OK twice.

Procedure Reference: Configure the Mouse

To configure the mouse:

1. If necessary, log on to Windows.

2. Open the Mouse Control Panel. The Mouse Properties Control Panel contains four tabs: Buttons, Pointers, Pointer Options, and Hardware.

3. On the Buttons tab, you can use the controls to change the primary mouse button, the double-click speed, and the ClickLock Feature.

4. On the Pointers tab, you can select a pointer scheme and customize it as necessary. You can also enable or disable a shadow for the pointer and change the default pointer that is displayed.

5. On the Pointer Options tab, you can adjust the speed at which the pointer moves across the screen and enhance the pointer positioning, enable the Snap To feature, and modify how the pointer is displayed on the screen.

6. On the Hardware tab, you can use the Properties button to access the mouse's properties. In this dialog box, you can set advanced settings and work with the device driver. Click OK to return to the Mouse Properties Control Panel.

7. Click OK.

ACTIVITY 4-3

Installing Input Devices

Setup:

For this activity, you will need a replacement keyboard and mouse or other pointing device.

Scenario:

You have received a service call to replace a user's mouse and keyboard.

 There is a simulated version of this activity available on the CD-ROM that shipped with this course. You can run this simulation on any Windows computer to review the activity after class, or as an alternative to performing the activity as a group in class. The activity simulation can be launched either directly from the CD-ROM by clicking the Interactives link and navigating to the appropriate one, or from the installed data file location by opening the C:\ 085820Data\Simulations\Lesson#\Activity# folder and double-clicking the executable (.exe) file.

What You Do	How You Do It
1. Replace the keyboard.	a. Shut down the computer, and remove the power cord.
	b. Determine the connection type used by the replacement keyboard.
	c. Unplug the old keyboard from the system unit.
	d. Plug the new keyboard into the appropriate PS/2 or USB port.
2. Replace the mouse or pointing device.	a. Determine the connection type used by the replacement mouse.
	b. Unplug the old mouse from the system unit.
	c. Plug the new mouse into the appropriate PS/2 or USB port.

ACTIVITY 4-4

Configuring Input Devices

Scenario:

You just replaced a user's mouse and keyboard. The user is left-handed and prefers a slow-blinking cursor. She also has a hard time distinguishing the mouse pointer from other screen elements, and asks if you can adjust the pointers to something more easily discernible.

 There is a simulated version of this activity available on the CD-ROM that shipped with this course. You can run this simulation on any Windows computer to review the activity after class, or as an alternative to performing the activity as a group in class. The activity simulation can be launched either directly from the CD-ROM by clicking the Interactives link and navigating to the appropriate one, or from the installed data file location by opening the C:\085820Data\Simulations\Lesson#\Activity# folder and double-clicking the executable (.exe) file.

What You Do	How You Do It
1. Configure the keyboard setting.	a. Choose Start→Control Panel. Click Printers and Other Hardware, and then click Keyboard.
	b. On the Speed tab, **drag the Cursor Blink Rate slider to the third tick mark from the left.**

c. **Click OK.**

2. **Configure the mouse settings.**

   a. In the Printers And Other Hardware Control Panel, **click Mouse.**

   b. On the Buttons tab, **check Switch Primary And Secondary Buttons.**

   c. **Right-click the Pointers tab.**

   d. In the Scheme drop-down list, **select Magnified (System Scheme).**

   e. **Click OK.**

   f. **Readjust the mouse settings to suit your personal preferences.**

   g. **Close the Control Panel window.**

TOPIC C
Install and Configure Adapter Cards

In the previous topic, you installed input devices, such as a mouse and a keyboard, that use standard ports. You can expand the functionality of your computer by adding adapters to provide additional ports for a variety of peripheral devices. In this topic, you will install and configure adapter cards.

When a user needs access to a peripheral for which the computer doesn't have an existing interface, you must install an adapter. As an A+ technician, your responsibilities will likely include upgrading users' computers by installing a variety of components. By mastering the skills to install an adapter, you'll be prepared for whatever device a user asks you to install.

Internal Bus Architectures

System boards include several buses, or data paths, to transfer data to and from different computer components, including all adapter cards.

Internal Bus Architecture	Description
8-bit	The original IBM PC and its successor, the PC/XT, used simple expansion buses. Its architecture provided an 8-bit data bus, with minimal support circuitry. This bus has a clock speed of 4.77 MHz. It supports eight interrupts and four DMA channels; however, except for IRQ 2 and DMA 3, all resources were already assigned, so you didn't have many choices when you installed additional cards. The cards for an 8-bit slot have only one edge connector. Because they are so outdated, you typically won't encounter these cards in the field.
ISA	The *ISA (Industry Standard Architecture) bus* was originally developed for the IBM PC/XT and PC/AT. Many computers still have some ISA slots along with the newer types of buses. Features of ISA adapters include: ● 8-bit or 16-bit edge connectors. ● Support either manual or automatic PnP configuration. ● 8-bit or 16-bit data lines. ● Configured either manually or automatically through PnP.
EISA	The *EISA (Extended Industry Standard Architecture) bus* was a higher-speed bus designed for PCs starting with the Intel 80386 processor. EISA has never been widely adopted. Features of EISA adapters include: ● Compared to ISA cards, they contain an additional row of connectors and additional guide notches. ● Software configurable. ● 32-bit data lines. ● Supports bus-mastering, which enables one adapter to take control of the bus during a data transfer. ● Configured automatically through software configuration utility.

Internal Bus Architecture	Description
MCA	IBM developed the *Micro Channel Architecture bus*, or Micro Channel bus, for its PS/2 line of computers. This bus operates at 10 MHz and can accept 16- and 32-bit adapter cards. However, you cannot use cards for ISA or EISA systems in Micro Channel systems, and IBM required the payment of royalties for implementations of the architecture—both cards and system boards. Because few vendors were willing to pay such royalties, this bus was never widely adopted. You configure MCA adapters using an IBM reference disk.
VL-Bus	In 1992, the Video Electronics Standards Association (VESA) introduced the *VESA Local-Bus (VL-Bus)* standard. A motherboard can contain up to three VL-Bus slots. Bus mastering is supported by the VL-Bus standard. A 32-bit or 64-bit slot is located next to an ISA, EISA, or Micro Channel Architecture slot and enables vendors to design adapters that use the local bus or both buses simultaneously. You typically configure VL-Bus cards through software.
PCI	The *PCI* (Peripheral Component Interconnect) bus is the most common system bus found in today's PCs. • Physical characteristics of cards: 33 or 66 MHz. 133 MBps throughput at 33 MHz. Up to eight functions can be integrated on one board. Card size varies, but must have a PCI edge connector. Slot on the system board is white. • Configuration: Supports up to five cards per bus and a system can have two PCI buses for a total of 10 devices per system. Can share IRQs. Uses PnP. • Used for: All current adapters in client and server systems. • Number of data lines: 64-bit bus often implemented as a 32-bit bus. • Communication method: Local bus standard. 32-bit bus mastering. Each bus uses 10 loads. A load refers to the amount of power consumed by a device. PCI chipset uses three loads. Integrated PCI controllers use one load. Controllers installed in a slot use 1.5 loads. • Pronounced: Pea-Sea-EYE.
AGP	The *AGP* (Accelerated Graphics Port) bus was developed by Intel specifically to support high-performance video requirements, especially fast 3D graphics. • Physical characteristics of cards: Brown slot on the system board. AGP 1.0 is a 1x/2x slot. This is the shortest of the AGP slots with a small separator that divides it into two sections. AGP 2.0 is a 2x/4x slot that has extra pins at one end. There is also an AGP Pro Slot. See **www.tomshardware.com/graphic/20000922/agppro-01.html** for a complete description of the AGP Pro slot. • Used for: Video cards in systems that support the AGP chipset. The system board needs an AGP bus slot or an integrated AGP chip. • Number of data lines: 32 bits wide with a throughput of 266 MBps for AGP 1.0. Faster modes with throughput of 533 MBps are available on AGP 2.0 and 1.07 GBps for AGP Pro. • Communication method: Directly accesses RAM rather than needing to transfer data to video RAM first. • Pronounced: A-G-P.

Internal Bus Architecture	Description
PCI-E	The *PCI Express* bus is an implementation of the PCI bus that uses a faster serial physical-layer communications protocol. ● Physical characteristics of cards: A PCI Express slot is designated by the number of lanes it supports: An x1 slot supports a single lane, an x2 slot supports two lanes, and so on. Theoretically, slots may be x1, x2, x4, x8, x12, or x16. ● Used for: High-speed graphics cards and high-speed network cards. ● Number of data lines: Each device has a serial connection consisting of one or more lanes. Each lane offers up to 250 MBps of throughput. An x16 slot can handle 4 GBps of bandwidth in one direction. ● Communication method: Local serial interconnection.
AMR	An Audio/Modem Riser supports both audio and modem functionality. The slot and its associated cards have two rows of 23 pins each and were primarily used for software-based sound cards and modems (Winmodems). This technology has been superseded by CNR.
CNR	A Communications/Networking Riser supports audio, modem, and local area network (LAN) functionality. ● Physical characteristics of cards: Two rows of 30 pins, with two possible pin configurations. CNR Type A uses an 8-pin network interface, while Type B uses a 16-pin interface. Both types carry USB and audio signals. The slot is often brown and is usually located in the lower-left corner of the system board. ● Used for: Connecting audio, network, and modem cards, but is being phased out in favor of on-board or embedded components.

Adapter Card Types

Adapter cards extend the capabilities of a computer.

Adapter Card Type	Description
Video adapters	A video adapter provides the interface necessary to connect a monitor for visual output. Generally, these adapters connect to the system board through PCI, AGP, or PCI-E slots.
Multimedia adapters	Multimedia adapters provide the interfaces necessary to connect microphones, speakers, electronic musical devices, and some gaming devices for audio input and output.
Input/output adapters	Input/output adapters provide the interfaces necessary to connect SCSI, serial, USB, and parallel devices for data input and output.
Network adapters	Network adapters provide the interface necessary for network communications.
Modem adapters	Modem adapters provide the interface necessary for remote communications over phone or data lines.

Adapter Card Selection Tips

Before selecting an adapter card for a computer, you must verify that its bus type is compatible with the computer. In addition, you must also make sure that the adapter card's drivers are compatible with the computer's operating system. Finally, most adapters on the market today support PnP. If you want to use PnP to automatically configure the card's hardware resources, make sure that the computer's BIOS and operating system support it.

 The PCI slots in a computer are often shared PCI/ISA slots. They share a single opening on the back of the case, so if you install an ISA card in one of the slots, you cannot use the PCI slot unless you first remove the ISA card.

Adapter Card Installation Considerations

Before you attempt to install an adapter card, verify that the computer has an available slot that matches the adapter card's bus type and that you have the device's latest drivers for the computer's operating system. Be sure to unplug the computer and discharge any static electricity before installing the card.

Adapter Card Configuration and Optimization Requirements

When you are installing an adapter card, there is a detailed step-by-step process to follow for configuration and optimization needs.

Step	Description
Plug-and-play installation	For the most part, PnP BIOS and Windows XP automatically configure all PnP adapters for you.
Manufacturer driver	In the event that Windows doesn't automatically detect an adapter, you can point to a driver from the manufacturer on floppy disk or CD-ROM, or get the driver from the manufacturer's website.
Add Hardware Wizard	You can use the Add Hardware Wizard to install and configure PnP devices. You find the Add Hardware Wizard by opening Control Panel, clicking the Printers And Other Hardware link, and then clicking the Add Hardware link.
Hardware Scan	When using the wizard, you should initially let Windows try to scan for new hardware (this is the default selection).
Device list	If Windows can't find the device, you can then choose the device from a list of devices offered by Windows and Windows will install the appropriate driver.

Read the installation instructions for the adapter card to determine if any software is required prior to the installation. Failure to do so could cause the installation to fail or the adapter and system to behave erratically.

Hardware Resources

All hardware added to the system needs to have resources assigned to enable it to store information and communicate with the CPU. Modern computer systems manage assignment of hardware resources automatically, but in older computers, it was necessary to assign them manually using jumper or *DIP switches* or software settings. Conflicting hardware settings often caused device problems, but resource conflicts are rarely an issue now.

There are several categories of hardware resources.

Hardware Resource	Description
IRQ	*Interrupt Request (IRQ) lines* are hardware lines connected to a controller chip and assigned to a device. When the device needs to request the attention of the computer processor, it sends a signal, called an *interrupt*, over the IRQ line.
I/O address	An *I/O address,* also called a base I/O address or I/O port, marks the beginning of a range of memory, usually in the lowest portions of memory (conventional memory), that a device uses to communicate with the processor. Each device must have its own unique, non-overlapping I/O address space.
DMA	*Direct Memory Access (DMA)* is a system that uses specialized circuitry or dedicated microprocessors that transfer data from devices to memory without using the CPU. This relieves the processor from some duties. The DMA controller communicates with the devices to facilitate transferring data from them directly to system memory. Devices must each use a unique DMA channel to communicate with the DMA controller.
Base memory address	A *base memory address* is the memory address of any memory that might be on the device itself. This configurable area is usually associated with adapters that contain their own BIOS chips or memory. Memory addresses for these on-board memories are most often mapped to the upper memory block (UMB) range on the host computer, which falls between 640 kilobytes (KB) and 1 megabyte (MB).

IRQ Settings

This table shows the default IRQ assignments for the early 8-bit ISA bus and for the current 16-bit systems. Note that some IRQs are shared between two components.

IRQ	8-bit Defaults	16-bit Defaults
0	System timer	System timer

IRQ	8-bit Defaults	16-bit Defaults
1	Keyboard	Keyboard
2	Available	Cascade to IRQ9
3	COM2	COM2 & COM4
4	COM1	COM1 & COM3
5	Hard disk controller	LPT2
6	Floppy drive controller	Floppy drive controller
7	LPT1	LPT1
8		Real Time Clock (RTC)
9		Cascade to IRQ2
10		Available
11		Available
12		Bus mouse port
13		Math coprocessor
14		Hard disk controller
15		Available

An IRQ controller chip manages the first eight IRQs. The CPU answers the interrupts in numerical priority order, starting with IRQ 0 (the system clock) and cycling through IRQ 7. On a 16-bit system, the eight additional IRQs reside on a second IRQ controller chip, which itself uses interrupt 2 on the first controller chip. Thus, the IRQ priority order becomes 0, 1, (8, 9, 10, 11, 12, 13, 14, 15), 3, 4, 5, 6, 7.

DMA Assignments

The following table shows the standard DMA assignments for various system components.

DMA Channel	Default DMA Assignments on an 8-bit Bus	Default DMA Assignments on a 16-bit Bus
0	Dynamic RAM refresh	Available
1	Hard disk controller (XT)	Available
2	Floppy drive controller	Floppy drive controller
3	Available	Available
4	n/a	2nd DMA controller
5	n/a	Available
6	n/a	Available
7	n/a	Available

Memory Address Assignments

The following table shows the standard base memory address assignments for various system components.

Port	Base Memory Address
LPT1	378h
LPT2	278h
COM1	3F8h
COM2	2F8h
COM3	3E8h
COM4	2E8h
Primary IDE	1F0
Secondary IDE	170
Floppy disk drive	3F0
Network adapter	300–310

ACTIVITY 4-5

Identifying System Parameters

Scenario:

In preparation for adding a new device to your system, you want to check the current communication parameter assignments.

 There is a simulated version of this activity available on the CD-ROM that shipped with this course. You can run this simulation on any Windows computer to review the activity after class, or as an alternative to performing the activity as a group in class. The activity simulation can be launched either directly from the CD-ROM by clicking the Interactives link and ·navigating to the appropriate one, or from the installed data file location by opening the C:\ 085820Data\Simulations\Lesson#\Activity# folder and double-clicking the executable (.exe) file.

What You Do	How You Do It
1. **Open Device Manager.**	a. **Choose Start→Control Panel.**
	b. **Click Performance And Maintenance.**
	c. **Click System.**
	d. **Click the Hardware tab.**
	e. **Click Device Manager.**
2. **View the current DMA, IRQ, I/O address, and base memory assignments.**	a. **Choose View→Resources By Type.**
	b. To examine the current DMA assignments on your computer, **expand Direct Memory Access (DMA).**

Direct memory access (DMA)
   2   Standard floppy disk controller
   4   Direct memory access controller

c. To examine the current I/O address assignments on your computer, **expand Input/Output (IO).**

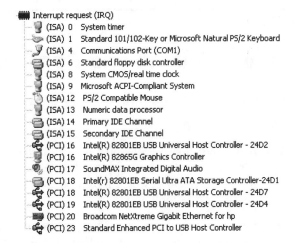

d. **Collapse Input/Output (IO).**

e. To examine the current IRQ assignments on your computer, **collapse Direct Memory Access (DMA), and expand Interrupt Request (IRQ).**

Interrupt request (IRQ)
   (ISA) 0 System timer
   (ISA) 1 Standard 101/102-Key or Microsoft Natural PS/2 Keyboard
   (ISA) 4 Communications Port (COM1)
   (ISA) 6 Standard floppy disk controller
   (ISA) 8 System CMOS/real time clock
   (ISA) 9 Microsoft ACPI-Compliant System
   (ISA) 12 PS/2 Compatible Mouse
   (ISA) 13 Numeric data processor
   (ISA) 14 Primary IDE Channel
   (ISA) 15 Secondary IDE Channel
   (PCI) 16 Intel(R) 82801EB USB Universal Host Controller - 24D2
   (PCI) 16 Intel(R) 82865G Graphics Controller
   (PCI) 17 SoundMAX Integrated Digital Audio
   (PCI) 18 Intel(r) 82801EB Serial Ultra ATA Storage Controller-24D1
   (PCI) 18 Intel(R) 82801EB USB Universal Host Controller - 24D7
   (PCI) 19 Intel(R) 82801EB USB Universal Host Controller - 24D4
   (PCI) 20 Broadcom NetXtreme Gigabit Ethernet for hp
   (PCI) 23 Standard Enhanced PCI to USB Host Controller

f. **Collapse Interrupt Request (IRQ).**

g. To examine the current base memory assignments on your computer, **expand Memory.**

```
Memory
    [00000000 - 0009FFFF] System board
    [000A0000 - 000BFFFF] Intel(R) 82865G Graphics Controller
    [000A0000 - 000BFFFF] PCI bus
    [000CC600 - 000DFFFF] System board
    [000E0000 - 000FFFFF] System board
    [00100000 - 3F7FFFFF] System board
    [3F800000 - 3F8FFFFF] System board
    [40100000 - FEBFFFFF] PCI bus
    [F0000000 - F7FFFFFF] Intel(R) 82865G Graphics Controller
    [FC400000 - FC47FFFF] Intel(R) 82865G Graphics Controller
    [FC480000 - FC4803FF] Standard Enhanced PCI to USB Host Controller
    [FC480400 - FC4805FF] SoundMAX Integrated Digital Audio
    [FC480600 - FC4806FF] SoundMAX Integrated Digital Audio
    [FC500000 - FC50FFFF] Broadcom NetXtreme Gigabit Ethernet for hp
    [FEBFFC00 - FEBFFFFF] Intel(r) 82801EB Parallel Ultra ATA Storage Controller-24DB
    [FEC00000 - FEC00FFF] Advanced programmable interrupt controller
    [FEC01000 - FFFFFFFF] System board
```

3.	**Close Device Manager, System Properties, and Control Panel.**	a.	**Close Device Manager.**
		b.	**Click Cancel.**
		c.	**Close Control Panel.**

How to Install and Configure Adapter Cards

Procedure Reference: Install an Adapter Card

To install an adapter card:

1. If the card doesn't support PnP, determine unused IRQ, DMA, and I/O addresses that you can assign to the card if needed. You can use Device Manager in Control Panel to print a list of the resources by choosing View→Resources By Type and then clicking the Print button on the toolbar.

2. Shut down the computer. Then, referring to your system documentation for the procedure, remove the system cover and access the slots on the system board.

3. Remove the slot cover from an empty slot. Traditionally, slot covers are secured by a screw to the chassis, but some newer ones slide out or are punched out of the metal case. Save the slot cover so that if you decide to remove the adapter card later, you can replace the slot cover. This helps keep dust and dirt out of the computer and helps with cooling the interior of the computer.

4. If card resources are set with DIP switches or jumpers, configure the card prior to installing it into the system.

5. Holding the card where there are no metal contacts (by the upper edge), firmly press the card into the slot.

Often, it will be easier to insert one end of the card first, then tilt the card down into place along the rest of the connector. It is best to start by inserting the end of the connector away from the cover plate.

6. Connect any necessary internal cables.

7. Secure the card to the chassis with the screw from the slot cover (or another screw if the slot cover was not screwed to the case). Secure the cover back on to the system when you are through working.

8. Configure the card for the system by installing any drivers required for operation. If you must configure the card's resources through software, configure DMA, I/O addresses, or interrupts as required using the card's installation software or Device Manager.

9. Verify that the card is functioning properly.

Procedure Reference: Verify an Installed Adapter Card

To verify that an installed adapter card is functioning properly:

1. Open Device Manager.

2. Review the list of hardware installed in the computer. If any device isn't functioning properly (due to problems such as a hardware resource conflict), you'll see an exclamation point surrounded by a yellow dot on the device. If you see a red X on the device, this indicates that Windows (or the user) has disabled the device. If you don't see either icons, the new adapter is functioning properly.

3. Connect any devices to the card that are required for testing the card functionality. Access or use the device connected to the card.

Procedure Reference: Remove a PC Bus Adapter

To remove an adapter:

1. Shut off the computer, unplug it, and open the case.

2. Disconnect all cables, making a note of where they were installed and the orientation (such as white wire on left pin).

3. Unscrew the card from the chassis.

4. Gently rock the card front to back (not side-to-side) to remove it from the slot.

5. Place the card in an anti-static bag to prevent electrostatic damage to the card. Always store the card with its documentation and driver disks.

6. Replace the slot cover. If necessary, screw down the slot cover.

7. Replace the cover, plug in the computer, and turn it on.

ACTIVITY 4-6

Installing Adapter Cards

Setup:

You have open ISA, PCI, and AGP slots on the system board. You have been given one or more of the following card types and device drivers: ISA, PCI, or AGP card.

Scenario:

You have been asked to install several expansion cards in a user's system. The appropriate drivers for the card are also available to you should you need them.

 There is a simulated version of this activity available on the CD-ROM that shipped with this course. You can run this simulation on any Windows computer to review the activity after class, or as an alternative to performing the activity as a group in class. The activity simulation can be launched either directly from the CD-ROM by clicking the Interactives link and navigating to the appropriate one, or from the installed data file location by opening the C:\ 085820Data\Simulations\Lesson#\Activity# folder and double-clicking the executable (.exe) file.

What You Do	How You Do It
1. Open the system cover and access the slots.	a. Turn off the system power.
	b. Unplug the computer from the electrical outlet.
	c. Unplug peripherals from the system.
	d. Remove the cover.
	e. Determine if you need to move or remove any components in order to access the slots.

2. Insert the card in an available slot.

 Do not rock the card side-to-side when installing or removing it.

     a. **Locate an open slot.**

     b. **Remove the slot cover.**

     c. **Firmly press the card into the slot.**

     d. **Secure the card to the chassis with the screw from the slot cover.** Normally, you would now secure the cover back on to the system, but since you will be doing more work inside the system, leave it off.

---

3. Configure the card for the computer.

     a. **Reconnect the peripherals and cables you disconnected in step 1.**

     b. **Power on the system.**

     c. **Install any required drivers.**

     d. **Configure DMA, I/O addresses, and/or interrupts as required for the device.**

---

4. Verify that the card is functioning properly.

     a. **Connect any devices to the card that are required for testing the card functionality.**

     b. **Access or use the device connected to the card.**

     c. In Device Manager, **verify that the device's properties show that the device is working properly and that there are no IRQ, I/O address, or DMA conflicts, and then click Cancel.**

DISCOVERY ACTIVITY 4-7

Examining Adapter Cards

Scenario:

In this activity, you will examine adapter cards.

1. Which of the following adapter cards provide interfaces necessary to connect SCSI, serial, USB, and parallel devices for data input and output?

   a) Input/output adapters

   b) Multimedia adapters

   c) Video adapters

   d) Modem adapters

2. True or False? Before attempting to install an adapter card, verify that the computer has an available slot that matches the adapter card's bus type.

   ___ True

   ___ False

3. What is the first step when installing an adapter card?

   a) Refer to the system documentation for the procedure for the specific adapter card.

   b) Remove the system cover and access the slots on the system board.

   c) Remove the slot cover from an empty slot.

   d) Determine the unused IRQ, DMA, and I/O addresses that can be assigned to the card if needed.

TOPIC D

Install and Configure Multimedia Devices

In the last topic, you installed and configured adapter cards to support additional computer functionality. Once you have the right adapters in place, you can add other peripheral components to enable users to take full advantage of the capabilities of their personal computers. In this topic, you will install multimedia devices.

As an A+ technician, you might support corporate users, such as marketing or sales representatives, who will need to create multimedia business presentations. Or, you might work for a retail computer outlet, supporting home users who like to play music and games on their PCs. In either case, the users will need a lot of different devices, connected to a number of different computer ports that are often poorly marked. In either case, the users will rely on you to connect and configure their multimedia devices, such as speakers and microphones, to the PC.

Multimedia Devices

Definition:

A *multimedia device* is a computer peripheral or internal component that transfers sound or images to or from a personal computer. These kinds of devices are often connected to a personal computer by a sound card. Multimedia devices can be input devices or output devices.

Example:

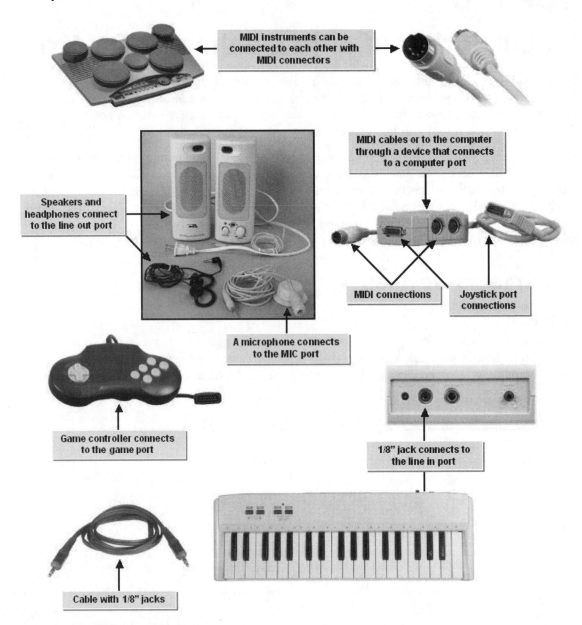

Figure 4-4: Multimedia devices.

Common Multimedia Devices

Common multimedia devices include different types of cameras and sound devices.

Multimedia Device	Description
Digital cameras	A camera that uses electronic signals to capture and store photographic images or video images. The resulting files are often stored on embedded memory cards, removable memory cards, or optical disks. Connecting the digital camera or its removable memory card to a PC enables you to save, manipulate, print, and otherwise work with the images.

Multimedia Device	Description
Web cameras, or webcams	A camera that is used to send periodic images or continuous frames to a website for display. Webcam software usually captures the images as JPEG or MPEG files and uploads them to a web server. Webcam images can also be accessed using some instant messaging software and by some video applications. Some corporations use webcams as a security measure.
Video-conferencing cameras	Video-conferencing cameras are usually a small camera connected directly to a PC. Used in conjunction with microphones and speakers, they enable people at remote locations to see and speak with each other in real time.
MIDI devices	The Musical Instrument Digital Interface (MIDI) connection enables you to connect and control musical devices such as electric keyboards (also known as electric pianos), synthesizers, guitars, and drum kits. Sound cards usually include built-in synthesizers as well, to produce MIDI sounds. If the MIDI connection is made through the game port, then the MIDI cable usually includes an additional port so that a game controller can still be added to the system. Other ports can also be used to establish MIDI connections. MIDI devices can be connected to each other and then to the computer.
Microphones	A computer microphone can be connected to the MIC port of any sound card. If the card is color-coded, it will be pink. Otherwise, it will be marked MIC or have a picture of a microphone.
Speakers and subwoofers	Speakers are connected to the Line Out port on the sound card. Some speaker sets are permanently connected to each other. Other speaker sets are connected by the user to each other or to a subwoofer. A cable runs from one of the speakers to the Line Out port to connect both speakers to the computer. If the card it is color-coded, the speaker port will be green or lime. The port might be marked with Line Out, Spkr, Speaker, or have a marking indicating the direction of the audio (out).

Multimedia Connectors

There are several types of cables and connectors used with common multimedia devices.

Multimedia Device	Connectors and Cables
Digital cameras	If the digital camera has a removable memory card, the connector is the card reader or adapter. If the digital camera uses optical disks, the optical drive is the connector. Other digital cameras use USB and FireWire cables and connections.
Webcams	Webcams commonly use USB or FireWire cables and connectors.
Video-conferencing systems	If the video-conferencing system uses a composite display device that is built to the S/PDIF (Sony/Philips Digital Interface Format), the cable can be coaxial, with a standard phono jack, or optical, with a standard optical jack.

Multimedia Device	Connectors and Cables
MIDI devices	MIDI connectors are also known as AT DIN5 connectors. AT DIN5 connectors were originally used on older AT style computers as the keyboard connector; now, MIDI devices use them. MIDI adapters have a DIN5 connector at one end, and a 15-pin connector (for connecting to the game port) at the other end. MIDI adapters do not always have a joystick connector at one end. A MIDI to USB interface, even MIDI to Serial or MIDI to FireWire, are more commonly used, allowing for faster communication between the musical instrument and the computer or controller device. In fact, not having a game port on a PC has become quite commonplace, since most new joysticks/game controllers use USB.
Microphones	Microphones typically have a 1/8-inch connector built into the attached cable.
Speakers	Speakers typically have a 1/8-inch connector built into the attached cable.

Multimedia Device Selection Tips

The most common multimedia devices you will be expected to install are cameras, sound cards, microphones, and speakers.

Device	Considerations
Digital cameras	What type of output does the user need from the camera? If the user plans to use the images only for viewing online, you can select a lower quality (fewer megapixels) camera. If the user also wants to print the images, particularly if the user wants large prints (such as 11" x 17" and higher), you should select a camera with as many megapixels as the user can afford. Keep in mind that you also need to have a strategy for the user to download the camera's photos to the computer. Common techniques you can use include: ● Connecting the camera directly to the computer via a USB or FireWire port. ● Using a memory card reader that connects to a USB or FireWire port. Be aware that FireWire connections provide you with the fastest transfer speeds.

Device	Considerations
Sound cards	Sound cards are responsible for translating digital music into analog signals. Sound cards differ in five basic areas: <ul><li>Processor: Handles the communications between the music application, Windows, and the processor. Higher-end processors offload the processing of music from the CPU and thus provide better performance. You should also look for mid- to higher-end processors that support surround sound (assuming the user needs this capability).</li><li>Number of speakers supported: Higher-end sound cards add support for five or more speakers, including a subwoofer. If the user needs (or wants) surround sound, make sure you get a sound card with support for at least five speakers.</li><li>Recording quality: Higher-end sound cards eliminate substantial amounts of noise recorded through a microphone. Look for the sound card's signal-to-noise ratio; this number, which is measured in decibels, indicates the quality of the signal. A lower number indicates a lower quality for recording. Mid-range sound cards offer a signal-to-noise ratio of 30 to 50 decibels; high-end cards offer a 96 to 100 signal-to-noise ratio, which is very close to ratios for equipment used by professional musicians.</li><li>Jacks: Sound cards come with a minimum of three connections—one for speakers (typically green), one for a microphone (typically pink), and one for secondary output called Line Out (typically green) that enables you to connect devices such as a CD player. Higher-end sound cards offer connections for components such as rear surround sound speakers, digital speaker systems, and joysticks or MIDI devices. Newer sound cards can also have a Digital Audio output, sometimes an input, jack. These can be either RCA type, or S/PDIF (Sony/Phillips Digital Interface).</li><li>Additional features: Because so many computer manufacturers now build sound capabilities into motherboards, many sound card manufacturers add extended features to their cards in order to justify their purchase. These features might include digital output so that you can integrate the computer into a home entertainment system or FireWire connections so that you can play MP3 recordings directly from an MP3 device. Higher-end sound cards also offer higher-quality recordings from musical instrument digital interface (MIDI) devices.</li></ul>
Microphones	Users use microphones to complete tasks such as making phone calls via the Internet and to dictate to the computer using voice recognition software. For such users, the higher the quality of the microphone, the better they will be able to accomplish these tasks.

Device	Considerations
Speakers	If users plan to listen to music or play games on a computer, it's important to help them select higher-quality speakers. Key speaker standards include: ● Stereo: Specifies a left and right speaker that connect directly to a single jack in a sound card. These types of speakers are usually the least expensive. ● 2.1 Systems: Specifies a pair of stereo speakers plus a subwoofer. These systems do not support surround sound. ● 5.1 Systems: Specifies five channels of sound, including front-left, front-center, front-right, rear-left, and rear-right speakers, plus a subwoofer. ● 7.1 Systems: Specifies seven channels of sound, including front-left, front-center, front-right, middle-left, middle-right, rear-left, and rear-right speakers, plus a subwoofer.

Multimedia Device Installation Considerations

There are some considerations you should be aware of when installing multimedia devices.

Consideration	Description
Adapter card slots	If you're installing a sound card, do you have an available slot on the motherboard? Also, try to locate this adapter in such a way as to avoid reducing the airflow in the computer.
Device drivers	Do you have the appropriate device drivers for the computer's operating system? If not, download them before starting the installation.
Cables	Do you have the necessary cables (and long-enough cables) to connect devices such as speakers and locate them where the user wants them?
Cameras and card readers	Although you can connect a digital camera directly to a computer to download its photos, doing so increases the wear and tear on the camera. You should use a memory card reader instead. The user will also see faster download performance when downloading photos using a memory card reader.

 Read the installation instructions for the device to determine if any software is required prior to the installation. Failure to do so could cause the installation to fail or the device and system to behave erratically.

Multimedia Device Configuration and Optimization Requirements

You can use multimedia device-specific software and Device Manager to configure multimedia devices. Options you can configure for these devices within Device Manager include:

- Enabling and disabling a device's audio features.
- Updating the device's driver.
- And, specifying hardware resources used, as long as the device is non-PnP.

How to Install Multimedia Devices

Procedure Reference: Install Multimedia Devices

To install multimedia devices:

1. If necessary, install a sound card.
    a. Shut down the computer, unplug the power cord, and open the computer case.
    b. Locate an available expansion card slot.
    c. Remove the slot cover.
    d. Insert the sound card into the open slot.
    e. Use the screw from the slot cover to secure the sound card to the system unit.
    f. To test the sound card, restart the computer, install the device driver if you are prompted to do so, and use Device Manager to verify that no resource conflicts have been caused by the addition of the sound card.

2. Connect the speakers to the jack on the sound card marked for speakers. Some speakers use an external AC adapter for power, some are powered by the computer, some use batteries, and some contain a standard electrical plug. If necessary, connect the speakers to their power source.

3. Connect any external devices to the Line In jack.

4. Connect a microphone to the MIC jack.

5. Connect MIDI devices or game controllers through the game port. If necessary, connect the AC adapter to the device and to an electrical outlet.

6. If necessary, use Device Manager to configure MIDI device or game controller settings.

7. Test the components by powering on the system and using each device. Verify that Mute is not checked in the Volume Controls. If Microphone is not listed, choose Options→ Properties. Select Recording, check Microphone, and then click OK. You can then adjust the sound levels for it.

ACTIVITY 4-8

Installing Multimedia Devices

Setup:

If your computer does not have integrated (onboard) sound support, a sound card has been installed in your computer.

Scenario:

A group in the marketing department is responsible for creating and presenting audio visual presentations. These users have sound cards installed in their systems. They all have speakers and microphones connected to their sound cards. Some of them also have MIDI instruments and instruments that connect through an eighth-inch stereo jack. The users have just received these sound devices and want to begin using them.

 There is a simulated version of this activity available on the CD-ROM that shipped with this course. You can run this simulation on any Windows computer to review the activity after class, or as an alternative to performing the activity as a group in class. The activity simulation can be launched either directly from the CD-ROM by clicking the Interactives link and navigating to the appropriate one, or from the installed data file location by opening the C:\085820Data\Simulations\Lesson#\Activity# folder and double-clicking the executable (.exe) file.

What You Do	How You Do It
1. Connect the speakers to the computer.	a. Determine if you need to connect the speakers to each other, and if so, connect them to each other.
	b. Locate the speaker jack on the computer.
	c. Plug the speaker cable into the jack.
2. Connect a microphone to the MIC jack.	a. Locate the MIC jack on the computer.
	b. Connect the microphone to the MIC jack.

3. If you have a MIDI device, **connect the MIDI device through the game port.**

   a. **Locate the game port.**

   b. **Connect the MIDI adapter to the game port.**

   c. If necessary, **connect MIDI cables to the MIDI adapter.**

   d. **Connect the MIDI cable to the MIDI instrument.**

   e. If necessary, **install drivers for the MIDI instrument.**

4. **Connect an external device to the Line In jack.**

   a. **Locate the Line In jack.**

   b. **Connect an eighth-inch stereo jack from the device to the computer.**

5. **Test the sound components.**

   a. To test the microphone, **choose Start→ All Programs→ Accessories→ Entertainment→Sound Recorder.**

   b. In the Sound Recorder window, **click the Record button.**

   c. **Speak a few words into the microphone.**

   d. **Click the Stop button.**

   e. To test the speakers, **click the Play button.** The words you just recorded should be played back.

   f. If you installed a MIDI device, **play a few notes to verify that it works correctly.**

   g. **Close the Sound Recorder without saving changes.**

DISCOVERY ACTIVITY 4-9

Examining Multimedia Devices

Scenario:
In this activity, you will examine multimedia devices.

1. When installing multimedia devices, how do you connect an external device to the system?

   a) Connect it to the line jack.

   b) Connect it to the MIC jack.

   c) Connect it through the game port.

   d) Connect it to the jack on the sound card.

2. True or False? When installing a sound card, you don't have to worry about the available slots on the motherboard.

   ___ True

   ___ False

Lesson 4 Follow-up

In this lesson, you installed and configured peripheral computer components. The ability to successfully install and configure computer components is an integral part of a computer technician's job.

1. **What types of peripheral components will you be required to install most often in your job?**

2. **Will you be responsible for configuring specialty input devices at your workplace?**

5 Installing and Configuring System Components

Lesson Time: 5 hour(s)

Lesson Objectives:

In this lesson, you will install and configure system components.

You will:

- Select, install, and configure storage devices.
- Install and configure power supplies.
- Install and configure memory.
- Install and configure CPUs.
- Install and configure system boards.

Introduction

In the last lesson, you installed and configured peripheral components such as display devices, input devices, adapter cards, and multimedia devices. As an A+ technician, you will also be asked to install internal system components such as storage devices, power supplies, memory, processors, and system boards. In this lesson, you will install and configure system components.

Much of the work that you will perform as a personal computer technician will involve installing and configuring various hardware and software components. These skills are particularly important for internal system devices that users cannot install themselves. It will be your professional responsibility to know the technical specifications for these components and to install and configure them correctly.

This lesson covers all or part of the following CompTIA A+ certification objectives:

- Topic A:
  - Exam 220-601 (Essentials): Objective 1.1, Objective 1.2, Objective 2.2, Objective 3.1
  - Exam 220-602 (IT Technician): Objective 1.1, Objective 3.1
  - Exam 220-603 (Remote Technician): Objective 2.1
  - Exam 220-604 (Depot Technician): Objective 1.1, Objective 2.2
- Topic B:
  - Exam 220-601 (Essentials): Objective 1.1
  - Exam 220-602 (IT Technician): Objective 1.1, Objective 1.2
  - Exam 220-604 (Depot Technician): Objective 1.1, Objective 1.2
- Topic C:
  - Exam 220-601 (Essentials): Objective 1.1
  - Exam 220-602 (IT Technician): Objective 1.1
  - Exam 220-604 (Depot Technician): Objective 1.1
- Topic D:
  - Exam 220-601 (Essentials): Objective 1.1
  - Exam 220-602 (IT Technician): Objective 1.1
  - Exam 220-604 (Depot Technician): Objective 1.1
- Topic E:
  - Exam 220-601 (Essentials): Objective 1.1
  - Exam 220-602 (IT Technician): Objective 1.1
  - Exam 220-604 (Depot Technician): Objective 1.1

TOPIC A

Install and Configure Storage Devices

In this lesson, you will install and configure system components. Storage devices such as hard disks are one of the most common system components you will install. In this topic, you will install and configure storage devices.

Users rely on local storage devices to keep their applications and data current and available. As an A+ technician, your responsibilities are likely to include installing and configuring different types of storage devices to provide your users with the data-storage capabilities that they need to perform their jobs.

Hard Disk Drive Types

There are many types of hard disks as well as the hard disk controllers that enable the disk to connect to the system board.

Hard Drive Type	Features
Parallel ATA (also known as IDE, EIDE, and ATA)	• Controller is built into the drive. • Limited to two channels, each with up to two devices. Supports single-drive only configuration (for one drive on a channel) and master/slave configurations (for two drives). The master device is the boot disk; it is first on the chain and controls the second device, which is the slave. • If the drive type is not automatically detected, it must be set in system BIOS. • Several revisions to the standard, each supporting different data transfer rates.
SCSI (Small Computer Systems Interface)	• No controller, but is actually a separate bus within the computer system. • Supports up to seven devices (15 devices in more recent versions). • Must configure separate SCSI ID settings for each device. • May need to set system BIOS to no drive, and then configure SCSI software to recognize drive to boot from. • Several variations on the interface, each supporting different data transfer rates.
Serial ATA	• Supports one device per channel. • Data transfer rates: 150 MB/sec for SATA I and 300 MB/sec for SATA II. • Supports hot swapping of drives.

When you install PATA drives, you use jumpers to set the master/slave or Cable Select configuration. Most drives today come preset for Cable Select, which allows the BIOS to configure itself as needed.

Extending IDE Drive Capabilities

The original IDE specification limits hard drive size to 504 MB. Three ways were developed to overcome this limitation.

- You can extend the drive size limit to 8.4 GB through the use of Logical Block Addressing (LBA) or Extended CHS (ECHS). With LBA or ECHS, hard drives can be up to 8.4 GB in size. LBA and ECHS are methods of sector translation (translating a hard drive's logical geometry into physical geometry) that essentially give the BIOS incorrect information about the geometry of the drive so that larger hard-drive capacities can be supported, while staying within BIOS limitations. The cylinder value after translation never exceeds 1,024. LBA was developed by Western Digital. ECHS was developed by Seagate. They differ only in the sector translation results they produce. If you want to move a hard drive from one computer to another, then the other computer must support the same sector translation method as the computer from which you are removing the hard drive. Otherwise, you will lose the data on the disk if you move the drive. This is a problem mostly if one computer is significantly older than another. But you do want to check and always back up your data before moving a drive. Today's hard disks and BIOSs all support LBA and ECHS to accommodate the need for large disk capacity.

- To address the need for even larger hard drive capacities, Phoenix Technologies developed Interrupt 13h (INT13h) extensions. Developed in 1994, INT13h extensions are a newer set of BIOS commands that enable support for hard drives larger than 8.4 GB. This support is made possible by using 64 bits for addressing, instead of 24 bits, and by using 1,024 cylinders. This expands hard drive support for drives up to 137 GB. INT 13h extensions are supported by modern hard drives and Windows 95 and newer operating systems, but must also be supported by the system BIOS or the hard-disk controller.

- If you need to support hard disks greater than 137 GB, you can use large LBA translation mode. It uses 48 bits for addressing instead of 24 bits.

PIO Modes

The ATA and ATA-2 standards use the Programmed Input/Output Mode (PIO Mode) to indicate the speed of data transfer between two devices that use the computer's processor as a part of the datapath. The PIO Mode is set in the BIOS. It is originally set when you install an IDE or EIDE drive. The following table lists the transfer rate for several ATA and ATA-2 standards.

Standard/PIO Mode	Data Transfer Rate
ATA/0	3.3 MBps
ATA/1	5.2 MBps
ATA/2	8.3 MBps
ATA-2/3	11.1 MBps
ATA-2/4	16.6 MBps

IDE Drives and ATA Specifications

For IDE drives, ATA was the formal name chosen by the American National Standards Institute (ANSI) group X3T10. It specifies the interface specifications for the power and data signals between the system board, the drive controller, and the drive.

The manufacturer can use any physical interface, but must have an embedded controller that uses the ATA interface controller to connect the drive directly to the ISA bus.

The original IDE specification did not support CD-ROMs or hard drives larger than 528 or 504 MB. However, revisions of the specifications over the years have extended the capabilities to provide support for faster and larger hard drives. The following table describes ATA specifications.

Standard	Description
ATA	The original ATA specification supported one channel, with two drives configured in a master/slave arrangement. PIO modes 0, 1, and 2 were supported, as well as single-word DMA modes 0, 1, and 2 and multi-word DMA mode 0. No support for non-hard disk devices was included, nor were block mode transfers, logical block addressing, and other advanced features.
ATA-2	Also known as the Advanced Technology Interface with Extensions. Western Digital's implementation was called Enhanced IDE (EIDE). Seagate's implementation was called Fast ATA or Fast ATA-2. Supports PIO modes 3 and 4 and two multi-word modes, 1 and 2, all of which are faster than the modes supported by the original ATA specification. Support for 32-bit transactions. Some drives supported DMA. Could implement power-saving mode features if desired. Specification also covered removable drives.
ATA-3	Minor enhancement to ATA-2. Improved reliability for high-speed data transfer modes. Self Monitoring Analysis And Reporting Technology (SMART) was introduced. This is logic in the drives that warns of impending drive problems. Password protection available as a security feature of the drives.
ATAPI	AT Attachment Packet Interface is an EIDE interface component that includes commands used to control tape and CD-ROM drives.
ATA-4	Also known as Ultra-DMA, UDMA, Ultra-ATA, and Ultra DMA/33. Doubled data transfer rates. Supported ATAPI specification.
ATA-5	The ATA-5 specification introduced Ultra DMA modes 3 and 4, as well as mandatory use of the 80-pin, high-performance IDE cable. Additional changes to the command set were also part of this specification. Supports drives up to 137 GB.
ATA-6	Supports Ultra DMA/100 for data transfers at up to 100 MB/second. Supports drives as large as 144 PB (petabytes), 144 million MB, or 144 quadrillion bytes.
PIO	Programmed Input/Output is a data transfer method that includes the CPU in the data path. It has been replaced by DMA and Ultra DMA.
DMA	Direct Memory Access is a data transfer method that moves data directly from the drive to main memory. Ultra DMA Transfers data in burst mode at a rate of 33.3 MB per second. The speed is two times faster than DMA.
Ultra DMA 100	Also known as ATA-100, this standard supports data transfers in burst mode at a rate of 100 MB per second.

Standard	Description
Serial ATA	Uses serial instead of parallel signaling technology for internal ATA and ATAPI devices. Serial ATA employs serial connectors and serial cables, which are smaller, thinner, and more flexible than traditional parallel ATA cables. Data transfer rates are 150 MB per second or greater.
Serial ATA II	Also known as SATA 3.0, SATA 3.0 Gb/s, and SATA/100. Provides data transfer rates of 300 MB/sec.

SCSI Standards

SCSI standards have been revised repeatedly over the years. The following table describes current SCSI standards.

SCSI Standard	Description
SCSI-1	Features an 8-bit parallel bus (with parity), running asynchronously at 3.5 MB/s or 5 MB/s in synchronous mode, and a maximum bus cable length of 6 meters, compared to the 0.45-meter limit of the Parallel ATA interface. A variation on the original standard included a *high-voltage differential (HVD)* implementation with a maximum cable length of 25 meters.
SCSI-2	Introduced the Fast SCSI and Wide SCSI variants. Fast SCSI doubled the maximum transfer rate to 10 MB/s, and Wide SCSI doubled the bus width to 16 bits to reach 20 MB/s. Maximum cable length was reduced to 3 meters.
SCSI-3	The first parallel SCSI devices that exceeded the SCSI-2 capabilities were simply designated SCSI-3. These devices were also known as Ultra SCSI and Fast-20 SCSI. The bus speed doubled again to 20 MB/s for narrow (8 bit) systems and 40 MB/s for wide (16-bit). The maximum cable length stayed at 3 meters.
Ultra-2 SCSI	This standard featured a *low-voltage differential (LVD)* bus. For this reason Ultra-2 SCSI is sometimes referred to as LVD SCSI. LVD's greater immunity to noise allowed a maximum bus cable length of 12 meters. At the same time, the data transfer rate was increased to 80 MB/s.
Ultra-3 SCSI	Also known as Ultra-160 SCSI, this version was basically an improvement on the Ultra-2 SCSI standard, in that the transfer rate was doubled once more to 160 MB/s. Ultra-160 SCSI offered new features like cyclic redundancy check (CRC), an error correcting process, and domain validation.
Ultra-320 SCSI	This standard doubled the data transfer rate to 320 MB/s.
Ultra-640 SCSI	Also known as Fast-320 SCSI, Ultra-640 doubles the interface speed yet again, this time to 640 MB/s. Ultra-640 pushes the limits of LVD signaling; the speed limits cable lengths drastically, making it impractical for more than one or two devices.

SCSI Standard	Description
Serial SCSI	Four versions of SCSI (*SSA*, *FC-AL*, IEEE 1394, and *Serial Attached SCSI*, or *SAS*) perform data transfer via serial communications. Serial SCSI supports faster data rates than traditional SCSI implementations, hot swapping, and improved fault isolation. Serial SCSI devices are generally more expensive than the equivalent parallel SCSI devices.
iSCSI	*iSCSI* provides connectivity between SCSI storage networks over an IP-based network without the need for installing Fibre Channel.

Storage Area Networks

In addition to the technologies you see for increasing the drive space on workstations, many companies now implement technologies such as *storage area networks (SANs)*. A SAN is a *Fibre Channel* network designed to attach storage devices such as drive arrays and tape libraries to servers. Most SANs use the SCSI protocol to communicate with these devices, along with the high-speed Fibre Channel interface. The advantage to a SAN is that you can easily move its storage from one server to another. In addition, you can configure a server to boot from a SAN, which means that if the server fails, you can quickly configure another server to use the SAN and thus replace the failed server.

Network-Attached Storage

In contrast to Storage Area Networks, *network-attached storage (NAS)* refers to storage devices that are dedicated storage servers. These devices enable users to access their data even when other servers are down. The drawback to NAS devices is that their performance depends on the speed of and traffic on your existing network.

Floppy Disk Drives

Internal floppy drives connect to the system board through a floppy disk controller. The drive can access data on the disk directly and spins at about 360 RPM. The form factor of floppy drives is usually 3.5 inches. Depending on the number of sectors per track on the disk, 3.5-inch floppy disks can hold 720 KB or 1.44 MB of data; the floppy drive can accommodate either disk capacity.

 Although 3.5 inches is the current standard for floppy disks and drives, 5.25-inch floppy disks and drives were once standard, but are now seen on only the very oldest computers still in use.

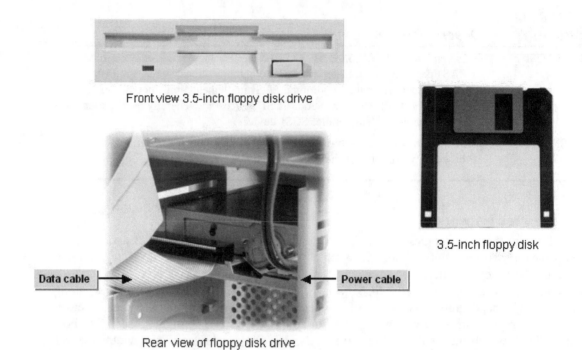

Front view 3.5-inch floppy disk drive

3.5-inch floppy disk

Data cable

Power cable

Rear view of floppy disk drive

Figure 5-1: *Floppy disk drives.*

How Floppy Disk Drives Work

When you insert a floppy disk into a floppy disk drive:

1. The metal door on the disk slides open, revealing the Mylar disk surface.

2. The controller motor spins the floppy disk at about 360 RPMs.

3. A worm gear operated by a stepper motor (a motor that moves in fixed increments) moves the read/write heads (one on each side of the disk) to the desired track.

Write Protection

Floppy disks can be protected so that you cannot write over data on the disk. On the back side of the floppy disk, you will see a slider in the upper-left corner. If the slider is pushed down, it blocks the write-protect hole and enables you to write to the floppy disk. If the slider is pushed up and the write-protect hold is visible, you will not be able to write to the disk.

Tape Drive Types

Tape drives come in several formats.

Tape Drive	Specifications
Quarter-inch cartridge (QIC)	Quarter-inch cartridge (QIC) technology is among the oldest, most standardized, and most reliable of the tape technologies. QIC drives are available for most computer platforms and are usually used for backing up personal computers or small networks. QIC cartridges are available in 60 MB, 150 MB, 250 MB, 525 MB, and larger sizes. Most of the drives designed to read the higher-capacity cartridges can also read the lower-capacity cartridges. The original width was 0.25-inch, but they are also available in 3.5-inch (Travan) and 5.25-inch cartridges. Two of the biggest detractions to QIC technology are cost and speed. QIC drives are inexpensive; however, the cartridges are expensive when dollars per megabyte is considered. Quarter-inch cartridge drives are slow, having about the slowest transfer rates of any of the tape technologies.
4 mm Digital Audio Tape	Originally adapted from the audio market, the 4 mm DAT tape format offers higher storage capacities at a lower cost than does QIC technology. DAT cartridges are about the size of an audio tape, so they are quite small compared with QIC cartridges, and therefore, are much easier to store and use. Capacities for 4 mm tapes range from 1 GB to 12 GB and more, which makes them popular for use in many different sized networks. DAT tapes are considered to be less reliable than QIC tapes. They are especially vulnerable to heat and moisture. Because the tape is pulled out of the cartridge during operation, to be wrapped around the spinning read/write head, the tapes wear more quickly than do QIC tapes. Due to lack of strict standards, 4 mm tape drives are not always compatible: tapes from one drive might not be readable in another drive. This will probably only be a problem for larger installations with a large variety of computing equipment.
8 mm tape (Exabyte)	The 8 mm tape format was originally developed by Exabyte, which continues to be the only manufacturer of 8 mm drives. Many other manufacturers purchase raw drives from Exabyte and integrate them into internal or external 8 mm tape drives. This arrangement ensures compatibility between 8 mm drives. These 8 mm tape drives offer storage capabilities between 2.2 GB and 10 GB per cartridge. The tape cartridges are only slightly larger than DAT tapes. They are often considered more reliable than 4 mm drives; however, the drives and tapes are more expensive than 4 mm units. The 8 mm tape drives are popular in the UNIX and workstation industry. These drives have only recently become popular with network administrators as the amount of data on LANs has grown.
Digital linear tape	Digital linear tape (DLT) was developed by DEC, who sold this technology to Quantum. The tape is a half-inch cartridge with a single hub and is used mainly in mid- to large-size networks for network backups. There are 128 or 208 linear tracks, holding 10 to 35 GB of data. Another DLT format, Super DLT, holds up to 600 GB. Currently, DLT transfer rates are in the 1.25 MB to 72 MB per second range. The forecast is for DLT to soon hold up to 1500 GB with up to 100 MB per second transfer rates.
Linear Tape Open	Linear Tape Open (LTO) was developed by IBM, HP, and Seagate. LTO's primary format is called Ultrium. The newest version, Ultrium-3, has a maximum capacity of 800 GB on a single tape with a transfer rate of 160 MB per second.

How Tape Drives Work

While hard drives, floppy drives, and removable cartridge drives are direct-access devices, tape drives are sequential access devices. Rather than being able to go to a specific file directly, with a tape, you have to read past every file on the tape until you get to the one you want. For this reason, tape drives are typically used to store backup copies of information, as opposed to for live data access. When you insert a tape cartridge in a tape drive and perform a backup of files from your hard drive:

1.   The computer reads the file system table on the hard drive, locates the files that you want to back up, and begins reading file data into RAM.

2.   Data is then dumped from RAM to the tape drive controller buffer as memory fills.

3.   The controller sends commands to the drive to start spooling the tape.

4.   The capstan in the center of the supply reel turns the rollers in the cartridge. The belt around the tape and the rollers provide resistance and keep the tape taught and tight to the drive heads.

5.   Data is sent from the controller to the read/write heads.

6.   The tape is composed of parallel tracks. Data is written from the center out towards the edge on each pass. Holes in the end of the tape signal when the direction of the tape needs to be reversed. When it gets to the end, it reverses and moves out one track.

Optical Drive Types

Optical drives include CD and DVD drives. They can be connected via IDE, SCSI, USB, FireWire, or parallel interfaces. Some optical drives provide only read capabilities, while others enable users to write, or burn, data to optical disks. Optical drives can be internal or external. Internal optical drives have a 5.25-inch form factor. The following table describes optical drive specifications.

CD and DVD drives have varying characteristics and specifications.

Optical Drive	Specifications
CD	Compact discs store data on one side of the disc and most hold up to 700 MB of data, although older discs may only hold up to 650 MB of data. (Some CDs can hold up to 1 GB.) CDs are widely used to store music as well as data. To meet the audio CD standard, the CD drive on a computer must transfer data at a rate of at least 150 kilobytes per second (150 KB/sec). Most CD drives deliver higher speeds: at least twice (2X, or double speed) or four times (4X, or quad speed) the audio transfer rate. There are also drives with much higher transfer rates. CD drives use one of two special file systems: CDFS (Compact Disc File System) or UDF (Universal Disc Format).
DVD	Digital video discs can typically hold 4.7 GB on one side of the disc; it is possible to write to both surfaces of the disc, in which case the disc can hold up to 9.4 GB. DVD drives access data at speeds from 600 KB/sec to 1.3 MB/sec. Because of the huge storage capacity and fast data access, DVD discs are widely used to store full-length movies and other multimedia content. DVD drives use UDF as the file system.

Solid State Storage Types

Solid state storage comes in several formats, many of which are used in external devices such as digital cameras or personal digital assistants (PDAs). The following table describes solid state storage device specifications.

Solid State Storage Device	Specifications
USB flash drives	USB flash drives come in several form factors, including thumb drives and pen drives. Thumb drives are small, varying from 50 to 70 mm long, 17 to 20 mm wide, and 10 to 12 mm tall. Data-storage capacities vary, from 128 MB up to 16 GB. Data-transfer rates also vary, from 700 KB/sec to 28 MB/sec for read operations, and from 350 KB/sec to 15 MB/sec for write operations.
Flash drives	Flash-memory-based disks do not need batteries, allowing makers to replicate standard disk drive form factors (2.5-inch and 3.5-inch). Flash Solid State Disks (SSDs) are extremely fast since these devices have no moving parts, eliminating seek time, latency, and other electromechanical delays inherent in conventional disk drives.
CompactFlash cards	CompactFlash cards are flash memory cards that are 43 mm long x 36 mm wide. Type I is 3.3 mm thick and Type II is 5 mm thick. They hold 8 MB to 8 GB or more and have a 50-pin contact. Transfer speeds up to 66 MB/sec are possible.
SmartMedia cards	SmartMedia cards are flash memory cards that are 45 mm long x 37 mm wide x 0.76 mm thick. They can hold from 2 to 128 MB and can transfer data at speeds up to 8 MB/sec.
xD-Picture Cards	xD-Picture Cards (xD) are flash memory cards that are 20 mm long x 25 mm wide x 1.7 mm thick. They can hold from 16 MB to 2 GB with plans for up to 8 GB. Data transfer rates range from 4 to 15 MB/sec for read operations and from 1.3 to 9 MB/sec for write operations.
Memory Sticks	Memory Sticks (MS) are flash memory cards that are 50 mm long x 21.5 mm wide x 2.8 mm thick. They can hold from 4 MB to 8 GB and are used extensively in Sony products. Data transfer rates are 2.5 MB/sec for read operations and 1.8 MB/sec for write operations. Other versions include Memory Stick Pro (50.0 mm x 21.5 mm x 2.8 mm, holds up to 4GB, 20 MB/sec transfer rate, 1.875 MB/sec for write operations), Memory Stick Duo (31.0 mm x 20.0 mm x 1.6 mm, holds up to 128 MB, 20 MB/sec transfer rate), Memory Stick Pro Duo (31.0 mm x 20.0 mm x 1.6 mm, holds up to 2 GB, 20 MB/sec transfer rate, 1.875 to 10 MB/sec for write operations), and Memory Stick Micro (15.0 mm x 12.5 mm x 1.2 mm, holds up to 1 GB, 20 MB/sec transfer rate).
Secure Digital (SD) cards	The original SD Memory Card is 32 mm long, 24 mm wide, and 2.1 mm tall. The miniSD Card measures 21.5 mm by 20 mm by 1.4 mm, and the microSD/TransFlash Card measures 15 mm by 11 mm by 1 mm. SD Memory Cards are currently available in several capacities, up to 4 and 8 GB. Data transfer rates range from 10 MB/sec to 20 MB/sec.

Solid State Storage Device	Specifications
MultiMediaCards (MMC)	MultiMediaCards are 32 mm long by 24 mm wide by 1.5 mm tall. Reduced Size MMCs (RS-MMCs) and MMCmobile cards are 16 mm by 24 mm by 1.5 mm. MMCmini cards are 21.5 mm by 20 mm by 1.4 mm, and MMCmicro cards are 12 mm by 14 mm by 1.1 mm. These cards can hold up to 8 GB, and data transfer rates can reach 52 MB/sec.

Storage Device Power Connectors

Every internal storage device uses one of several types of power connectors to get electrical power from the computer's power supply.

Power Connector	*Internal Storage Devices that Use It*
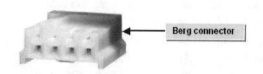 Berg	Berg connectors are used to supply power to floppy disk drives and some tape drives.
 Molex	Molex connectors are used to supply power to Parallel ATA drives, optical drives, and SCSI drives.
 SATA power connector	SATA power connectors are used to supply power to Serial ATA drives.

Hot Swapping

Definition:

Hot swapping is a type of hardware replacement procedure where a component can be replaced while the main power is still on. Also called hot plug or hot insertion, hot swap is a feature of USB and FireWire devices, enabling you to install an external drive, network adapter, or other peripheral without having to power down the computer. Hot swapping can also refer to the system's ability to detect when hardware is added or removed.

 Windows Plug and Play facilitates hot swapping by recognizing new devices and installing the needed drivers.

Example:

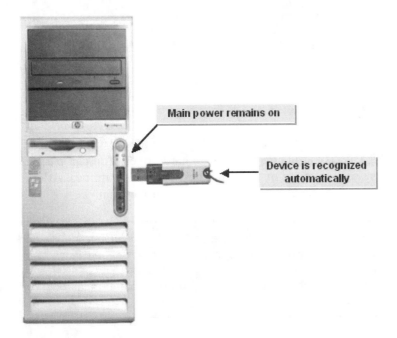

Main power remains on

Device is recognized automatically

Figure 5-2: Hot swapping.

Warm Swap and Cold Swap

Similar to hot swapping, warm swapping enables you to replace components without turning the power off, but the component that you're replacing should not be functioning during the swap. Cold swap refers to powering down the system before replacing a component or installing a component and having to force the operating system to detect the new hardware.

Drive Images

Definition:

A *drive image* is a computer file containing the complete contents and structure of a data-storage medium or device. Often used in *disk cloning*, or the transfer of one hard disk's contents to another disk, drive images can streamline the setup of new computers, the installation of operating systems and applications, and the replacement of an installed hard drive. Disk imaging software is sometimes included when you buy a hard disk drive, and more generic third-party solutions are also available.

Example:

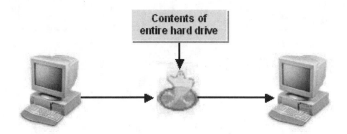

Figure 5-3: *Drive images.*

Disk Partition Types

A *disk partition* is an isolated section of a disk that functions like a separate physical drive. Partitions enable you to create a logical disk structure to organize hard drives. You can partition a drive through the operating system software or by using third-party disk utilities. After you create a partition, you must format it to be able to store data on that partition.

 To create a dual-boot system, you might need to create a partition for each operating system that you want to install. However, you could also implement what is known as hardware virtual machines, where virtualization software can enable you to run several different operating systems on one machine. Examples of virtualization software include VMware® and Microsoft Virtual PC.

There are several types of disk partitions.

Disk Partition Type	Description
Primary	A disk partition that can contain one file system or logical drive. Sometimes referred to as volumes.
Active	A primary partition that is bootable and holds the operating system.
Extended	An extended partition can contain several file systems, which are referred to as logical disks or logical drives.
Logical	A part of a physical disk drive that has been partitioned and allocated as an independent unit and functions as a separate drive.

You are generally limited to four partitions per hard disk. If you need more partitions on a disk, you can make one of them an extended partition, and then create logical drives within it as necessary.

Format Types

There are two types of formatting for hard disks:

- *Low-level formatting* is the process of writing track and sector markings on a hard disk. This level of formatting is performed when the hard disk is manufactured.

- *High-level formatting* is an operating system function that builds file systems on drives and partitions. It tests disk sectors to verify that they can be reliably used to hold data. It marks any unreliable sectors as bad sectors which cannot be used.

The Windows Disk Management Utility

The Windows Disk Management utility, located in the Computer Management console, enables you to create, view, and manage disks. You can perform disk-related tasks such as creating partitions and volumes, formatting them, and assigning drive letters.

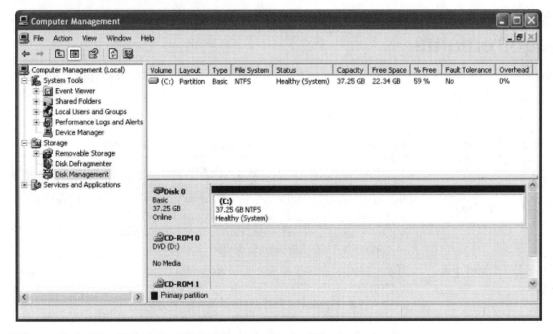

Figure 5-4: The Windows Disk Management utility.

Internal Storage Device Installation Considerations

There are a number of factors you should keep in mind when attempting to install an internal storage device.

Factor	Description
Placement	Make sure you place the storage device where it will get good air flow to avoid overheating the device.
Total air flow	Make sure there's enough total air flow to handle whatever heat the new storage device will add to the computer.
Power	Make sure that the storage device won't cause the computer to exceed the capacity of its power supply.
Device drivers	Make sure that you have the appropriate device drivers for the operating system of the computer on which you plan to install the new storage device. If necessary, download the device drivers from the device manufacturer's website.

Storage Device Configuration and Optimization Requirements

There are several configuration and optimization requirements you must review before installing a storage device.

Storage Device	Configuration and Optimization Requirements
External USB device	If you plan to install a USB external storage device, you will get the best possible performance from the device if you connect it to a port or hub that supports USB 2.0. Keep in mind that many hubs drop all ports down to the slower USB 1.1 speed if you connect any USB 1.1 devices. Try not to connect a slower speed device to the same hub in which you plan to connect a USB 2.0 storage device.
Internal PATA hard disk drive	If you plan to install an internal PATA hard drive, make sure you jumper it properly. If the drive is the only drive in the computer, you must jumper it as a single drive. If the drive is the second drive in the computer, you must jumper the drive as the second (slave) drive in a two-drive configuration and the first drive as the master drive.
Internal or external SCSI device	If you plan to install a SCSI storage device, keep in mind that SCSI devices require unique SCSI IDs. Some storage devices require you to configure this ID using a jumper or the device's installation software. Some SCSI controllers require you to manually install a terminator on the last device in the SCSI chain. Make sure you review the documentation for the SCSI controller and the new device you are installing to determine whether you need to install a terminator.

Storage Device	Configuration and Optimization Requirements
Any storage device	Most computers automatically detect newly installed hard drives when you power them on. If a computer doesn't, run the computer's CMOS setup program to configure the computer to recognize the new hard drive. In some cases, particularly with SCSI hard drives, you might have to run manufacturer-specific installation software before the computer will recognize the new hard drive.

How to Select, Install, and Configure Storage Devices

Procedure Reference: Select Storage Devices for Installation

There are a number of factors you should consider when choosing a storage device for a computer. To select a storage device for installation:

1. Do you want to install an internal or an external device?

2. If you want to install an internal device, ask yourself the following questions:

    a. Does the computer have existing internal storage devices? If it does, what interface do these devices use (PATA, SCSI, or SATA)? Is there room on the controller of these devices for an additional device? For example, if the computer uses devices with the SATA interface, are there already two devices connected to the controller? If there are, you will need to purchase an additional SATA controller before you can add another SATA device. If you do not have room on the controller for an additional storage device, you must purchase both the storage device and a controller. In addition, make sure that the computer has an available slot for the controller.

     Keep in mind that you can't install a SATA hard drive on a PATA controller.

    b. Does the computer have an available power supply cable to supply power to the device? If it doesn't, you can't add another internal storage device to the computer. You must add an external device.

    c. Does the computer have an available drive bay for the storage device? Most hard drives require a 3.5" drive bay; most tape drives, optical drives, and floppy drives require a 5.25" drive bay. If you want to install a hard drive in a 5.25" drive bay, you will need *drive rails*.

    d. Do you have the necessary data cables to connect the storage device to the controller?

3. If you want to install an external storage device, ask yourself the following questions:

    a. What interface does the external storage device require (USB, FireWire, or SCSI)?

    ● If the external storage device uses USB 2.0, does the computer support it?

- If the external storage device uses FireWire, is there an available FireWire port in the computer? If not, you must buy and install a Firewire controller. Make sure the computer has an available slot for the FireWire controller before purchasing one.

- If the external storage device uses SCSI, is there room on the SCSI chain for an additional device?

b.   Do you need a cable to connect the external storage device to the computer?

c.   Do you have an available source of power for the storage device?

4.   If you are installing additional hard drives in order to increase the computer's reliability, do you have a controller that supports a *Redundant Array of Independent Disks (RAID)*? If not, the computer must use an operating system that supports RAID (Windows 2000, Windows XP, Windows Server 2003, or Windows Vista). Note that it would be quite unusual to implement RAID on a desktop system.

Procedure Reference: Install a Parallel ATA Hard Disk Drive

To install a Parallel ATA (IDE) hard disk drive:

1.   If necessary, shut down the computer, unplug all peripherals and the power cord, and open the computer case.

2.   If necessary, remove the original Parallel ATA disk drive.

a.   Disconnect the data and power cables from the drive.

b.   Unscrew the drive from the bay and slide it out of the bay.

c.   If you are removing the master drive, reset the jumpers on other drives if necessary.

3.   Locate an available drive bay, Parallel ATA data connection on the Parallel ATA data cable, and a power connector.

4.   Set the jumpers for cable select, master, or slave, as appropriate to your needs. There is usually a sticker on the top of the drive that specifies the jumper settings for each of these functions. If there is not a sticker, then the documentation for the drive will include this information.

- If the drive is the first drive on the channel, it should be configured as cable select or the master.

- If the drive is the second drive on the channel, it should be configured as cable select or the slave.

- If cable select is not available on your system, you should use the slave setting.

5.   If necessary, attach rails to the drive to fit in the drive bay.

6.   Slide the drive into the bay, and then connect the data and power cables.

7.   Restart the system, and if necessary, access CMOS setup to specify the drive type. You might need to know the number of cylinders, heads (tracks), and sectors on the disk as part of the CMOS setup procedure. You can usually find this information printed on a label on the drive or in the documentation that came with the drive.

8. Prepare the new hard disk drive for use. If you are installing an additional hard drive, you can use Windows Disk Management to prepare the new drive.

   a. Log on to Windows.

   b. Open Computer Management.

   c. In the left pane, click Disk Management.

   d. Right-click the new disk, and choose New Partition.

   e. Follow the New Partition Wizard prompts to partition and format the new drive.

   f. Close the Computer Management console.

9. If necessary, transfer data to the new disk. You can use disk imaging software to accomplish this.

Procedure Reference: Install an Internal SCSI Hard Disk Drive

To install an internal SCSI hard drive:

1. If necessary, shut down the computer, unplug all peripherals and the power cord, and open the computer case.

2. Set the drive ID on the drive. A sticker on the drive or the drive documentation will show how to set the ID and any other settings required to successfully install the drive.

3. Determine which device is at the end of the chain and terminate each end of the chain. Remove termination from any other devices in the SCSI chain. Termination is accomplished by changing jumper settings, switches, or by physically inserting a termination plug into the port. Refer to the documentation for the device to determine how termination is accomplished on the particular device you are working with.

4. Insert the drive in an available drive bay. If you are using a 5.25-inch drive bay and a 3.5-inch drive, you will need to install the drive using rails to adapt the drive to the larger bay.

5. Connect the SCSI cable from the host bus adapter to the drive.

6. Connect the power cable to the drive. Most modern systems have plenty of power connectors for all of the internal devices you might install. Some systems might run out of connectors, though. If this happens, you can purchase splitters to enable two (or more) devices to be connected to one existing power connection to the power supply.

7. Restart the system. If prompted, access CMOS setup and set the disk type, and then exit CMOS and save the settings.

   Prepare the new hard disk drive for use. If you are installing an additional hard drive, you can use Windows Disk Management to prepare the new drive.

   a. Log on to Windows.

   b. Open Computer Management.

   c. In the left pane, click Disk Management.

   d. Right-click the new disk, and choose New Partition.

   e. Follow the New Partition Wizard prompts to partition and format the new drive.

   f. Close the Computer Management console.

8. If necessary, transfer data to the new disk. You can use disk imaging software to accomplish this.

Procedure Reference: Install an External SCSI Drive

To install an external SCSI drive:

1. Connect the SCSI cable to the device and the other end of the cable to the SCSI port on the computer, being sure not to confuse the SCSI port with the parallel port.

2. If the SCSI device is the last device in the SCSI chain, terminate the device; if it is not the last device in the chain, remove termination from the device.

3. If you are adding additional SCSI devices to the chain, repeat steps 1 and 2, being sure to only terminate the last device in the chain.

4. Test that all devices in the chain function properly.

5. Prepare the new hard disk drive for use. If you are installing an additional hard drive, you can use Windows Disk Management to prepare the new drive.

    a. Log on to Windows.

    b. Open Computer Management.

    c. In the left pane, click Disk Management.

    d. Right-click the new disk, and choose New Partition.

    e. Follow the New Partition Wizard prompts to partition and format the new drive.

    f. Close the Computer Management console.

6. If necessary, transfer data to the new disk. You can use disk imaging software to accomplish this.

Procedure Reference: Install a Serial ATA Hard Disk Drive

To install a Serial ATA hard disk drive:

1. If necessary, shut down the computer, unplug all peripherals and the power cord, and open the computer case.

2. Locate an available drive bay, power connector, and the Serial ATA interface connector on the system board or Serial ATA host adapter.

3. Attach the drive interface and power cables to the drive.

4. Attach the drive interface cable to the Serial ATA interface connector.

5. Attach the power cable to the power supply.

6. If necessary, attach rails to the drive to fit in the drive bay.

7. Slide the drive into an available drive bay, and secure it using the supplied mounting screws.

8. Restart the system, and if necessary, access CMOS setup to force the system to recognize the drive. Because Serial ATA is a relatively new interface type, some systems might recognize the drive as a SCSI device if you are using a Serial ATA host adapter. This does not affect the performance or capacity of the drive, so you do not need to take any action.

9. Prepare the new hard disk drive for use. If you are installing an additional hard drive, you can use Windows Disk Management to prepare the new drive.

   a. Log on to Windows.

   b. Open Computer Management.

   c. In the left pane, click Disk Management.

   d. Right-click the new disk, and choose New Partition.

   e. Follow the New Partition Wizard prompts to partition and format the new drive.

   f. Close the Computer Management console.

10. If necessary, transfer data to the new disk. You can use disk imaging software to accomplish this.

Procedure Reference: Install a Floppy Disk Drive

To install a floppy disk drive:

1. If necessary, shut down the computer, unplug all peripherals and the power cord, and open the computer case. You might also need to remove the front cover.

2. If necessary, remove the original floppy disk drive.

   a. Disconnect the power connector from the rear of the floppy disk drive.

   b. Disconnect the controller cable from the rear of the floppy disk drive.

   c. Remove the screws, brackets, or clips that mount the floppy disk drive in the chassis bay.

   d. Slide the floppy disk drive out of its bay.

 If the floppy disk drive is inside a cage, removing the drive can be more complicated than this.

3. Insert the floppy disk drive into its bay.

4. Mount the floppy disk drive to the chassis using the appropriate screws, brackets, or clips.

5. Connect the controller cable to the rear of the floppy disk drive.

6. Connect the power connector to the rear of the floppy disk drive.

7. Start the system and verify that the floppy disk drive works properly.

Procedure Reference: Install an Optical Drive

To install an optical drive:

1. Determine whether the optical disc drive should be installed internally within the PC by Parallel ATA (IDE) or SCSI connection, or externally by USB, FireWire, or Parallel interface.

2. If the optical drive should be installed internally, shut down the computer, unplug all peripherals and the power cord, and open the computer case. You might also need to remove the front cover.

3. If necessary, install the Parallel ATA optical drive.

   a. Locate an available drive bay, Parallel ATA data connection on the Parallel ATA controller cable, audio cable, and a power connector.

   b. Set the jumpers for cable select, master, or slave, as appropriate to your needs. There is usually a sticker on the top of the drive that specifies the jumper settings for each of these settings. If there is not a sticker, then the documentation for the drive will include this information.

   c. If necessary, attach rails to the drive to fit in the drive bay.

   d. Slide the drive into the bay, and then connect the controller, audio, and power cables.

   e. Restart the system, and if necessary, access CMOS setup to specify the drive type. You might need to know the number of cylinders, heads (tracks), and sectors on the disk as part of the CMOS setup procedure. You can usually find this information printed on a label on the drive or in the documentation that came with the drive.

   f. Verify that you can read data from the optical drive.

4. If necessary, install the SCSI optical drive.

   a. Set the drive ID on the drive. A sticker on the drive or the drive documentation will show how to set the ID and any other settings required to successfully install the drive.

   b. Determine which device is at the end of the chain and terminate each end of the chain. Remove termination from any other devices in the SCSI chain.

   c. Insert the drive in an available drive bay. If you are using a 5.25-inch drive bay and a 3.5-inch drive, you will need to install the drive using rails to adapt the drive to the larger bay.

   d. Connect the SCSI cable from the host bus adapter to the drive.

   e. Connect the power cable to the drive.

   f. Restart the system. If prompted, access CMOS setup and set the disk type, and then exit CMOS and save the settings.

   g. Verify that you can read data from the optical drive.

5. If necessary, install the external optical drive.

   a. Some devices require that you install the drivers before connecting the device to the system. Read the documentation that came with your device before proceeding.

   b. With the computer and device turned off, connect the appropriate cable between the device and the system.

   c. If necessary, connect the AC adapter to the device and plug it into an electrical outlet.

   d. Turn on the device and the computer.

   e. If necessary, install appropriate drivers for the device.

   f. Verify that you can read data from the optical drive.

Procedure Reference: Install a Tape Drive

To install a tape drive:

1. Determine whether the tape drive should be installed internally within the PC by Parallel ATA (IDE) or SCSI connection, or externally by USB, FireWire, or Parallel interface.

2. If the tape drive should be installed internally, shut down the computer, unplug all peripherals and the power cord, and open the computer case. You might also need to remove the front cover.

3. If necessary, install the Parallel ATA tape drive.

   a. Locate an available drive bay, Parallel ATA data connection on the Parallel ATA controller cable, and a power connector.

   b. Set the jumpers for cable select, master, or slave, as appropriate to your needs. There is usually a sticker on the top of the drive that specifies the jumper settings for each of these settings. If there is not a sticker, then the documentation for the drive will include this information.

   c. If necessary, attach rails to the drive to fit in the drive bay.

   d. Slide the drive into the bay, and then connect the controller and power cables.

   e. Restart the system, and if necessary, access CMOS setup to specify the drive type.

   f. Verify that you can write data to and read data from the tape drive.

4. If necessary, install the SCSI tape drive.

   a. Set the drive ID on the drive. A sticker on the drive or the drive documentation will show how to set the ID and any other settings required to successfully install the drive.

   b. Determine which device is at the end of the chain and terminate each end of the chain. Remove termination from any other devices in the SCSI chain.

   c. Insert the drive in an available drive bay. If you are using a 5.25-inch drive bay and a 3.5-inch drive, you will need to install the drive using rails to adapt the drive to the larger bay.

   d. Connect the SCSI cable from the host bus adapter to the drive.

   e. Connect the power cable to the drive.

   f. Restart the system. If prompted, access CMOS setup and set the disk type, and then exit CMOS and save the settings.

   g. Verify that you can write data to and read data from the tape drive.

5. If necessary, install the external tape drive.

   a. Some devices require that you install the drivers before connecting the device to the system. Read the documentation that came with your device before proceeding.

   b. With the computer and device turned off, connect the appropriate cable between the device and the system.

   c. If necessary, connect the AC adapter to the device and plug it into an electrical outlet.

   d. Turn on the device and the computer.

   e. If necessary, install appropriate drivers for the device.

   f. Verify that you can write data to and read data from the tape drive.

Procedure Reference: Install an Internal Solid State Storage Device

Solid state storage devices vary widely in implementation. Read the documentation that accompanies the solid state storage device you are installing before you attempt the installation. To install an internal solid state storage device:

1. If necessary, shut down the computer, unplug all peripherals and the power cord, and open the computer case.

2. Determine if the device uses a Parallel ATA or SCSI connection.

3. If necessary, install the Parallel ATA solid state storage device.

    a. Locate an available drive bay, Parallel ATA data connection on the Parallel ATA controller cable, and a power connector.

    b. Set the jumpers for cable select, master, or slave, as appropriate to your needs. There is usually a sticker on the top of the drive that specifies the jumper settings for each of these settings. If there is not a sticker, then the documentation for the drive will include this information.

    c. If necessary, attach rails to the drive to fit in the drive bay.

    d. Slide the drive into the bay, and then connect the controller and power cables.

    e. Restart the system, and if necessary, access CMOS setup to specify the drive type.

    f. Verify that you can write data to and read data from the solid state drive.

4. If necessary, install the SCSI solid state drive.

    a. Set the drive ID on the drive. A sticker on the drive or the drive documentation will show how to set the ID and any other settings required to successfully install the drive.

    b. Determine which device is at the end of the chain and terminate each end of the chain. Remove termination from any other devices in the SCSI chain.

    c. Insert the drive in an available drive bay. If you are using a 5.25-inch drive bay and a 3.5-inch drive, you will need to install the drive using rails to adapt the drive to the larger bay.

    d. Connect the SCSI cable from the host bus adapter to the drive.

    e. Connect the power cable to the drive.

    f. Restart the system. If prompted, access CMOS setup and set the disk type, and then exit CMOS and save the settings.

    g. Verify that you can write data to and read data from the solid state drive.

DISCOVERY ACTIVITY 5-1

Selecting a Storage Device

Scenario:

You're servicing a customer's computers. You have been asked to order storage devices to upgrade a number of the computers.

1. You have been asked to order an internal hard drive for one of the customer's computers. The customer has heard about the increased performance of SATA drives and would like you to purchase one for the computer. What question should you ask first before ordering a new SATA hard drive?

    a) Does the computer have an available drive bay for the drive?

    b) Does the computer have an available power supply cable for the new drive?

    c) Does the computer have existing storage devices?

    d) Do you have the necessary data cable to connect the drive to the controller?

2. True or False? You can attach a Serial ATA hard drive as a second drive on a Parallel ATA data cable.

    ___ True

    ___ False

3. A user wants to transfer several megabytes of data between two computers that are not connected by a network. What storage device would you recommend?

    a) A USB thumb drive.

    b) A floppy disk.

    c) An external tape drive.

    d) An internal optical drive.

ACTIVITY 5-2

Installing Internal Storage Devices

Setup:

To complete this activity, you will need the following hardware components. If you do not have these available, you can remove and reinstall the existing hardware.

- A second hard drive and an empty drive bay. If you have a Parallel ATA drive, you will also need an available connection on the Parallel ATA cable. If you have a SCSI drive, you will also need an installed SCSI host bus adapter (HBA).

- A floppy disk drive that is compatible with your system.

- An optical drive that is compatible with your system.

- Available power connections for the devices you are adding to the system.

- Optionally, rails to allow smaller drives to fit into larger drive bays.

Scenario:

You have been assigned the task of refurbishing a computer for a user. This computer has a single functioning hard drive, a floppy disk drive that needs to be replaced, and an optical drive that needs to be replaced. The user needs a significant amount of local storage space, and the following internal storage devices have been allocated for use in this project:

- A second hard disk drive

- A floppy drive

- A Parallel ATA optical drive

 There is a simulated version of this activity available on the CD-ROM that shipped with this course. You can run this simulation on any Windows computer to review the activity after class, or as an alternative to performing the activity as a group in class. The activity simulation can be launched either directly from the CD-ROM by clicking the Interactives link and navigating to the appropriate one, or from the installed data file location by opening the C:\ 085820Data\Simulations\Lesson#\Activity# folder and double-clicking the executable (.exe) file.

What You Do	How You Do It

Add a hard disk drive to the system

1. **Locate available bay, power, and data connection resources for the new hard disk drive.**	a. **Power off the system, unplug all peripherals and the power cord, and open the computer case.**
	b. **Locate an available drive bay and determine if the bay is the same form factor as the drive.** If you are using a 5.25-inch drive bay and a 3.5-inch drive, you will need to install the drive using rails to adapt the drive to the larger bay.
	c. **Locate an available data connection on the data cable.** If necessary, **connect a Parallel ATA data cable to the Parallel ATA controller connection on the system board.**
	d. **Locate an available power connector.** If necessary, **connect a power splitter to an existing power connection.**
2. **Prepare the drive for installation.**	a. If you are installing a Parallel ATA drive, **set the jumpers or switches to Cable Select or Slave.**
	b. If you are installing a SCSI drive, **set the SCSI ID to an unused ID number.** If the drive is at the end of the SCSI chain, **terminate the device** and, if necessary, **remove termination from the previously terminated device.**
	c. If necessary, **attach rails to the drive to fit in the bay.**
3. **Install the hard disk drive into the system.**	a. **Slide the drive into the bay.**
	b. **Connect the data cable to the drive.**
	c. **Connect the power cable to the drive.**
	d. **Secure the drive to the bay chassis with screws.**

4. **Verify that the drive is accessible.**

a. **Plug all peripherals back into the system.**

 You can leave the case open until the end of the activity.

b. **Restart the system.**

c. If prompted, **access CMOS, set the disk type according to the drive documentation, and then exit CMOS and save your settings.**

5. Partition and format the new drive as an NTFS drive.

a. **Log on to Windows as Admin##.**

b. **On the Desktop, right-click My Computer and choose Manage.**

c. In the left pane, **click Disk Management.**

d. **Right-click the unallocated space for Disk 1.** The new disk is all unallocated.

e. **Choose New Partition.** The New Partition Wizard starts.

f. **Click Next.**

g. **With Primary Partition selected, click Next.**

h. **Accept the defaults for partition size and click Next.**

i. **Accept the default drive letter and click Next.**

j. **Format the partition as NTFS using Default as the Allocation Unit Size and New Volume as the Volume Label. Click Next.**

k. **Click Finish.**

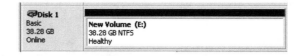

l. **Close Disk Management.**

Replace the floppy disk drive

6. **Remove the floppy disk drive from the computer.**

   a. **Shut down the computer, and unplug the power cord from the power supply.**

   b. **Disconnect the power connector from the rear of the floppy disk drive.**

   c. **Disconnect the controller cable from the rear of the floppy disk drive.**

   d. **Remove the screws, brackets, or clips that mount the floppy disk drive in the chassis bay.**

   e. If necessary, **remove the front cover.**

   f. **Slide the disk drive out of its bay.**

   g. **Examine the controller cable connectors and power cable connector on the rear of the drive.** This data cable and power cable are different than those used on the hard drives.

7. **Connect the new floppy drive to the system.**

   a. **Insert the floppy disk drive into its bay.**

   b. **Mount the floppy disk drive to the chassis using the appropriate screws, brackets, or clips.**

   c. **Connect the controller cable to the rear of the floppy disk drive.**

   d. **Connect the power connector to the rear of the floppy disk drive.**

   e. **Reconnect the power cord to the power supply, start the system, and verify that the floppy disk drive was properly installed.**

 To verify the floppy disk drive is functional, you can try to access data from a floppy disk or open My Computer to verify that the A drive is visible.

Replace the optical drive

8. Remove the old optical drive from the computer.

    a. Shut down the computer, and unplug the power cord from the power supply.

    b. Disconnect the power connector from the rear of the optical drive.

    c. Disconnect the controller cable from the rear of the optical drive.

    d. Disconnect the audio cable from the rear of the optical drive.

    e. Remove the screws, brackets, or clips that mount the optical drive in the chassis bay.

    f. Slide the optical drive out of its bay.

9. **Install the new optical drive in the computer.**

a. If you are installing a Parallel ATA optical drive, **examine the controller cable connectors and the jumper block for master/slave configuration on the rear of the drive. Verify that the optical drive is set as master/single.**

b. If you are installing a SCSI optical drive, **set the SCSI ID to an unused ID number. If the drive is at the end of the SCSI chain, terminate the device** and, if necessary, **remove termination from the previously terminated device.**

c. **Insert the optical drive into its bay.**

d. **Mount the optical drive to the chassis using the appropriate screws, brackets, or clips.**

e. **Connect the controller cable to the rear of the optical drive. Make sure the colored stripe on the controller cable lines up with Pin 1 on the drive.**

f. **Connect the audio cable to the audio out connector at the rear of the optical drive.**

g. **Connect the power connector to the rear of the optical drive.**

Reconnect the power cord to the power supply, and start the system.

h. **Verify that you can read data from the optical drive.**

i. **Close the computer case.**

TOPIC B

Install and Configure Power Supplies

In the previous topic, you installed and configured storage devices. The next system components you'll focus on are power supplies. In this topic, you will install and configure a power supply in a computer.

Underpowered systems, especially older systems with relatively small power supplies, can experience lockups, random reboots, and other quirky behavior. If you are upgrading components, you might exceed the capacity of the current power supply. Replacing it with an adequate power supply can prevent system power problems and keep the number of support calls down.

Power Supply Form Factors

Like system boards and other components, there are several form factors available for power supplies.

Power Supply Form Factor	Description
AT	Used in AT form factor cases and with AT or Baby AT system boards. Dimensions are 213 x 150 x 150 mm. Found in older desktops and towers. AT power supplies have physical on-off switches.
ATX	Used in ATX and NLX cases and with ATX and NLX system boards. Dimensions are 150 x 140 x 86 mm. Found in desktops and towers. ATX power supplies do not have physical on-off switches. The system board actually controls the power state of the ATX power supply.
Proprietary	Some computer manufacturers use system board form factors that do not conform to standards such as ATX, NLX, and BTX. It's likely that these proprietary system boards will require nonstandard power supply form factors as well, although you might be able to use an ATX power supply.

Power Supply Wattage

Power supply specifications are given in watts. A watt is volts times amps (voltage x amperes). Older systems typically had power supplies under 200 watts and often even under 100 watts. Newer power supplies typically have wattages ranging from 200 to 500 watts. Because of their increased power demands, computers designed for games can have power supplies with wattages from 500 watts up to 1 kilowatt.

Power Requirements

Each component in a personal computer has different power requirements.

Component	Voltage and Power Requirements
ISA bus	• Voltage: 5 V • Power: 12.1 watts
PCI bus	• Voltage: 3.3 or 5 V • Power: 56.1 watts
AGP bus	• Voltage: 3.3 or 5 V • Power: 25, 50, or 110 watts
PCI card	• Voltage: 3.3 or 5 V • Power: 5 watts
AGP card	• Voltage: 3.3 or 5 V • Power: 20 to 30 watts
SCSI PCI card	• Voltage: 3.3 or 5 V • Power: 20 to 25 watts
Floppy drive	• Voltage: 5 V • Power: 5 watts
RAM	• Voltage: 3.3 V for DIMMs, 5 V for SIMMs • Power: 10 watts for every 128 MB of RAM
7200 RPM hard drive	• Voltage: 5 V for logic, 12 V for motor • Power: 5 to 15 watts
1 GHz Pentium III CPU	• Voltage: 3.3 V • Power: 34 watts
1.7 GHz Pentium 4 CPU	• Voltage: 3.3 V • Power: 65 watts
300 MHz Celeron CPU	• Voltage: 3.3 V • Power: 18 watts
600 MHz AMD Athlon CPU	• Voltage: 3.3 V • Power: 45 watts
1.4 GHz AMD Athlon CPU	• Voltage: 3.3 V • Power: 70 watts

 Although most devices require specific voltages, some devices have different voltage requirements depending on use. This is particularly true of memory chips, which vary in voltage requirements from 1.8 V to 3.3 V, and some can actually function at different voltages (voltage range).

Calculating Power Needs

In order to calculate whether your power supply meets your power needs, you will need to add up the maximum power you might use at one time. A range of maximum power consumption for various components has been established. Most components use much less than the maximum. You can check the documentation for the component to determine how much power it actually will use.

AC Power for Peripherals

Although internal system components rely on the power supply, other devices such as printers and external modems require their own direct supply of AC power. In such a case, you must plug the device directly into a source of AC power such as a wall socket or power strip.

CPU Voltages

Even some of the most powerful current CPUs, such as the Intel Core2 Extreme and the AMD Opteron Dual Core, only use 1.1-1.3 V. Necessary voltage for CPU and RAM is usually detected by the motherboard (BIOS) and configured appropriately, but sometimes you have to manually configure it, by accessing the BIOS and entering the appropriate values. The Power supply will supply 3.3 V for the CPU, RAM, and other devices, but the motherboard regulates how much they actually get.

Power Supply Safety Recommendations

There are a number of safety precautions you should observe when working with power supplies.

Safety Precaution	Explanation
Check for certification	Be sure to purchase power supplies that are certified by the Underwriters Laboratories, Inc. (UL). UL standard #1950, the "Standard for Safety of Information Technology Equipment, Including Electrical Business Equipment, Third Edition," regulates computer power supplies (along with other components). When it comes to electricity, you don't want to take a chance with a non-certified power supply. The risk of electrocution or fire from a malfunctioning power supply is simply not worth saving a few dollars by purchasing a low quality power supply.
Replace instead of repairing the power supply	You run the risk of electrocution if you open a power supply to attempt to repair it. Even when you unplug a computer, the power supply can retain dangerous voltage that you must discharge before servicing it. Because power supplies are relatively inexpensive, it's easier (and safer) to simply replace a failed power supply rather than attempting to repair it.
Keep the computer case on	Make sure that you run computers with their cases on. The fans inside power supplies are designed to draw air through the computer. When you remove the cover, these fans simply cool the power supplies and not the computer's components. Leaving the case open puts the computer at risk of overheating.

Safety Precaution	Explanation
Protect the power supply	Use a power protection system such as an uninterruptible power supply (UPS) or surge suppressor to protect each computer's power supply (and thus the computer) from power failures, brownouts, surges, and spikes. You should also make sure that the computer's power cord is plugged into a properly grounded electrical outlet. (Three-pronged outlets include grounding; never use an adapter to plug a computer's power cord into a two-pronged electrical outlet.) You can buy a socket tester (available at hardware stores) to test your outlets if you suspect that they aren't properly grounded.

 You should also make sure to cover empty slots in the system board with filler brackets. If you do not install a filler bracket, you reduce the efficiency of the power supply's fan and increase the chances of the computer overheating.

Power Supply Selection Tips

There are several criteria you should use when selecting a power supply for a computer.

Criteria	Explanation
Power supply rating	Make sure that you don't overload the power supply. Add up the total system requirements for power and then select a power supply that can meet the computer's demands.
Form factor	Verify that the power supply will fit in your computer's case and conform to your system board's form factor.
Cooling	Ensure that the power supply you select can adequately cool the components within the computer's case.

Power Supply Fan

Some power supplies enable you to see the revolutions per minute (RPMs) of the power supply fan. You can then adjust the fan speed to run at only the speed needed to cool your system. This can reduce power consumption and save wear and tear on the fan.

How to Install and Configure Power Supplies

Procedure Reference: Calculate Power Needs

To calculate the amount of power needed for a computer system:

1. Determine the number of watts used by each component in the computer. Make sure you include the following components:
   - System board
   - CPU
   - RAM
   - Hard drives
   - CD drives
   - DVD drives
   - Floppy drives
   - Expansion cards

2. Add up all of the power needed by the system components.

3. Look at the label on the power supply to see what the maximum wattage output is.

4. Compare your computation with the power supply output. If you have not exceeded the power available, you do not need to upgrade. If you have, you will need to obtain a suitable power supply and install it.

Procedure Reference: Install and Configure Power Supplies

To install a power supply:

 When installing new equipment, always follow the instructions included with the device from the manufacturer.

1. Remove the existing power supply.
   a. Shut down and turn off the system.
   b. Toggle the power switch on the computer on and off to discharge any remaining electricity stored in the computer's capacitors.
   c. Unplug the electrical power cord from the electric outlet and from the power supply.
   d. Remove any components needed to access the power supply and its connection to the system board. Some systems are very cramped inside and components—for example, drive bay assemblies—might cover the power supply to system board connections, part of the power supply, or both.
   e. Unplug all power connections from devices. Be sure to label each connection to make it easier for you to reconnect them when you are finished installing the new power supply.
   f. Unplug the power supply from the system board.
   g. Unscrew the power supply from the case.
   h. Remove the power supply from the case.

2. Install the replacement power supply.

    a.   Insert the power supply into the case.

    b.   Secure the power supply to the case.

    c.   Plug all power connections to devices.

    d.   Plug the power supply into the system board.

    e.   Reinstall any components you removed to access the power supply.

    f.   Connect the power cord from the power supply to the electrical outlet.

3. Test the new power supply.

To test it, turn on the system, and then try using the components to verify that they are properly powered. Be sure to test all drives, network connections, and any powered devices. You can also test the output with a multimeter.

ACTIVITY 5-3

Replacing a Power Supply

Setup:

You have a power supply to install into the system. If you don't have another power supply, you can just reinstall the one you take out.

Scenario:

After calculating the power needed for all of the components added to a user's system, you have determined that it exceeds the capacity of the installed power supply.

There is a simulated version of this activity available on the CD-ROM that shipped with this course. You can run this simulation on any Windows computer to review the activity after class, or as an alternative to performing the activity as a group in class. The activity simulation can be launched either directly from the CD-ROM by clicking the Interactives link and navigating to the appropriate one, or from the installed data file location by opening the C:\ 085820Data\Simulations\Lesson#\Activity# folder and double-clicking the executable (.exe) file.

What You Do	How You Do It
1. Remove the existing power supply.	a. Shut down and turn off the system.
	b. Unplug the power cord from the electrical outlet.
	c. To discharge any remaining electricity stored in the computer's capacitors, **toggle the power switch on the computer on and off.**
	d. Remove any components necessary in order to access the power supply and its connection to the system board.
	e. Unplug all power connections from devices, marking where each connection went to as you go.
	f. Unplug the power supply from the system board.
	g. Unscrew the power supply from the case.
	h. Remove the power supply from the case.
2. Install the replacement power supply.	a. Insert the power supply into the case.
	b. Secure the power supply to the case.
	c. Plug all power connections into the devices.
	d. Plug the power supply into the system board.
	e. Reinstall any components you removed to access the power supply.
	f. Plug the power cord from the power supply to the electrical outlet.

3. **Test the power supply.**

    a. **Turn on the system.**

    b. **Log on as Administrator.**

    c. **Test all components.**

DISCOVERY ACTIVITY 5-4

Examining Power Supplies

Scenario:
In this activity, you will examine power supplies.

---

1. **When determining the amount of power needed for a computer system, which components should you include?**

   a) CPU

   b) RAM

   c) System board

   d) Expansion cards

   e) Peripheral devices

---

2. **When installing and configuring a power supply, what step should you complete first?**

   a) Unplug the power supply from the system board.

   b) Unplug the electrical power cord from the electric outlet and from the power supply.

   c) Toggle the power switch on the computer on and off to discharge any remaining electricity stored in the computer's capacitors.

   d) Shut down and turn off the system.

TOPIC C
Install and Configure Memory

In the last topic, you installed a power supply. Providing sufficient electrical power is one way to ensure that system components run at an acceptable performance level, but it is not the only solution you should consider. In this topic, you will install and configure memory.

Just as some people say you can never be too rich or too thin, you can never have too much memory. Adding memory is one of the simplest and most cost effective ways to increase a computer's performance, whether it's on a brand-new system loaded with high-performance applications or an older system that performs a few basic tasks. One way or the other, upgrading the memory is a frequent task for any computer service professional.

Memory Modules

Definition:
A *memory module* is a printed circuit board that holds a group of memory chips that act as a single memory chip. Memory modules reside in slots on the system board, and they are removable and replaceable. Memory modules are defined by the number of chips they contain.

Example:

Figure 5-5: A typical memory module.

Memory Form Factors and Slot Types

Memory modules come in several form factors, and each module will connect to the system board through a memory slot of a compatible type.

Memory Form Factor	Description
Single In-line Memory Module (SIMM)	Generally found in older systems, SIMMs have a 32-bit data path. Because most processors now have a 64-bit bus width, they required that SIMMs be installed in matched pairs so that the processor could access the two SIMMs simultaneously. SIMMs generally have 8 memory chips per module. Only SIMMs can be installed into SIMM slots on the system board.
Dual In-line Memory Module (DIMM)	DIMMs are found in many systems, and they have a 64-bit data path. The development of the DIMM solved the issue of having to install SIMMs in matched pairs. DIMMs also have separate electrical contacts on each side of the module, while the contacts on SIMMs on both sides are redundant. DIMMs generally have 16 or 32 chips per module. Only DIMMs can be installed into DIMM slots on the system board.
Rambus Inline Memory Module (RIMM)	RIMMs have a metal cover that acts as a heat sink. Although they have the same number of pins, RIMMs have different pin settings and are not interchangeable with DIMMs and SDRAM. RIMMs can be installed only in RIMM slots on a system board.

Memory Types

Random Access Memory (RAM) is the main memory. The computer can both read the data stored in RAM and write different data into the same RAM. Any byte of data can be accessed without disturbing other data, so the computer has random access to the data in RAM. RAM is volatile and requires a constant source of electricity to keep track of the data it is storing. If the electricity is cut off, RAM forgets everything.

There are several types of RAM.

Type of RAM	Description
SRAM	Static RAM is used for cache memory, which is high-speed memory that is directly accessible by the CPU. It does not need to be refreshed to retain information. It does not use assigned memory addresses. It is faster than Dynamic RAM, but it is also more expensive.
DRAM	Dynamic RAM is used on single and dual in-line memory modules (SIMMs and DIMMs). It is the most common type of RAM. It needs to be refreshed every few milliseconds. Uses assigned memory addresses. Can be implemented using Synchronous DRAM, Direct Rambus DRAM, or Double Data Rate SDRAM.
DRDRAM	Direct Rambus DRAM is implemented on a RIMM memory module.
SDRAM	Synchronous DRAM runs at high clock speeds and is synchronized with the CPU bus. SDRAM was originally packaged on a 168-pin DIMM.

Type of RAM	Description
DDR SDRAM	Double Data Rate SDRAM transfers data twice per clock cycle. It is a replacement for SDRAM. DDR uses additional power and ground lines and is packaged on a 184-pin DIMM module.
DDR2 SDRAM	DDR2 chips increase data rates over those of DDR chips. DDR2 modules require 240-pin DIMM slots. Although DDR2 chips are the same length as DDR, they will not fit into DDR slots.
Sequential Access Memory (SAM)	*SAM* is volatile memory that holds data in a sequential order. When accessing data, each storage cell is checked until the desired information is found. Often used for memory buffers where data is stored in the order it will be used.

RAM Speed

RAM speed is the time needed to read and recharge a memory cell. It's measured in nanoseconds (ns). A nanosecond is one-billionth of a second. The smaller the number, the faster the RAM. For example, 10 ns RAM is faster than 60 ns RAM.

RAM comes in ever-increasing speeds. The RAM on sale at the local computer store might work just fine in your system, or it might be older, slower RAM they are trying to move out of stock.

One of the popular memory manufacturers has an article on the speed of SDRAM at **http://crucial.com/library/sfiles4.asp**. They also have another article on the PC100 Standard, including a discussion on the speed of memory, at **http://crucial.com/library/sfiles5.asp**.

Older EDO RAM was often 60- to 70-ns speed RAM. Modern RAM that you are likely to find runs at clock speeds of 100 MHz and 133 MHz. The 100 MHz RAM has a RAM speed of 10 ns. The 133 MHz RAM has a RAM speed of 6 ns.

The SDRAM used in 168-pin DIMMs has access times in the 6 to 12 nanosecond range.

You need to check what RAM speed is currently installed. All of the RAM in the system runs at the lowest common speed. It is backward-compatible, so it can run at the lower speed if it finds slower RAM. Some systems will not run with mixed RAM speeds, but these are not common. Either way, the RAM will not run any faster than the system board's bus speed.

DRAM Banks

You can combine multiple rows of DRAM into a cluster called a *bank*. Each row of DRAM can then be accessed simultaneously. When creating banks, the goal is to match the width of the DRAM to the width of the CPU's external *data bus*, which will generally be 8-bit, 16-bit, 32-bit, or 64-bit. Expressed another way, the number of SIMMs or DIMMs needed to create a bank is the width of the CPU's data bus divided by the width of the SIMM or DIMM. So, for a CPU with a 32-bit data bus, you need four SIMMs to create a bank.

Types of ROM

ROM is memory that is non-volatile. The original ROM chips could not be altered after the program code was placed on the ROM chip. As time went on, though, users needed the ability to update the information stored on ROM chips. Over the years, various chips have been created that perform the function of ROM, but can be updated one way or another. These are referred to as programmable ROM (PROM). Types of ROM include:

● PROM: A blank ROM chip that is burned with a special ROM burner. This chip can be changed only once. After the instructions are burned in, it cannot be updated or changed.

● EPROM (erasable PROM): Like PROM, except that the data can be erased through a quartz crystal on top of the chip. After removing the chip from the system, a UV light is used to change the binary data back to its original state, all 1s.

● EEPROM (electronically erasable PROM): A chip that can be reprogrammed using software from the BIOS or chip manufacturer using a process called flashing. Also known as Flash ROM. The chip does not need to be removed in order to be reprogrammed.

Memory Selection Tips

There are several factors you should consider when purchasing RAM for a computer.

RAM Characteristics	Questions to Ask
Size	What is the maximum RAM size supported by the computer's system board?
Speed	What is the current speed of the RAM in the computer? What is the bus speed of the computer?
System Board Configuration	Do you need to install RAM in pairs of memory modules? What is the size of the connector for RAM chips?

DISCOVERY ACTIVITY 5-5

Determining the Appropriate Type of RAM

Scenario:

You've been asked to help another A+ technician determine the type and quantity of RAM to be ordered. He has several questions he needs you to answer before he is able to place the order with the vendor.

---

1. **Match the type of RAM with its description.**

   ___ VRAM
   ___ DDR SDRAM

   ___ SRAM

   ___ DRAM

   ___ SAM

   a. A replacement for SDRAM.
   b. A special type of DRAM used on video cards that can be written to and read from at the same time. It also requires less refreshing than normal DRAM.
   c. Volatile memory that holds data in a sequential order.
   d. Used for cache memory. It does not need to be refreshed to retain information. It can use synchronous, asynchronous, burst, or pipeline burst technologies.
   e. Used on SIMMs and DIMMs. It needs to be refreshed every few milliseconds. Uses assigned memory addresses.

---

2. **True or False? RAM will not run any faster than the system board's bus speed.**

   ___ True

   ___ False

---

3. **True or False? A nanosecond is one-trillionth of a second.**

   ___ True

   ___ False

---

4. **In a system that contains RAM modules that run at 6 ns and 10 ns, what speed will the RAM run at?**

    a) 4 ns

    b) 10 ns

    c) 6 ns

    d) 16 ns

5. **On a typical system with RAM that runs at a speed of 10 ns, you could add RAM that runs at which speed?**

    a) 6 ns

    b) 10 ns

    c) 12 ns

6. **The number of SIMMs or DIMMs needed to create a bank is the width of the CPUs data bus divided by the width of the _____ __ _____ .**

7. **On a system with a CPU with a 64-bit data bus, how many SIMMs would you need to create a bank?**

    a) 2

    b) 4

    c) 8

    d) 16

8. **On a system with a CPU with a 32-bit data bus, how many SIMMs would you need to create a bank?**

    a) 2

    b) 4

    c) 8

    d) 16

How to Install and Configure Memory

Procedure Reference: Add RAM to a Computer

To add RAM to a computer:

 Steps may vary depending on your specific system's documentation.

1. Review the computer's current configuration to make sure that the computer's memory slots aren't already full.

2. Determine how much RAM is currently installed so that you can determine afterwards if the new RAM you installed is recognized. You can check the CMOS settings or use the System Properties dialog box in Windows XP to verify the amount of RAM.

   To check the RAM through System Properties:

   a. From the Start menu, choose My Computer.

   b. In the System Tasks box on the left side of the window, click View System Information.

3. Shut down your computer and disconnect the power cord. Press and hold the power button down for 10–30 seconds to release any stored energy in the system.

4. Discharge any static electricity from yourself or your clothes. Although this is always important to do, it is especially important to do when working with memory cards. These components are more delicate and more easily damaged by static charges than other system components.

5. Locate an empty memory expansion socket on the system board, or, if there are no empty slots, remove a smaller memory module to make room for one containing more memory.

   To remove an existing memory module:

   a. Press down on the ejection tabs.

   b. Firmly grasp the memory module and pull it out of the slot.

6. Align the notches in the connector edge of the memory module with the notches in the memory expansion socket, and then firmly press the memory module down into the socket.

7. If the ejection tabs did not lock into the notches on the ends of the memory module, push them up until they lock.

8. Restart the computer.

9. Follow any on-screen prompts or perform any steps described in your computer's documentation for getting the computer to recognize additional memory. This is not required on all computers.

10. Verify that the additional memory was recognized by the system.

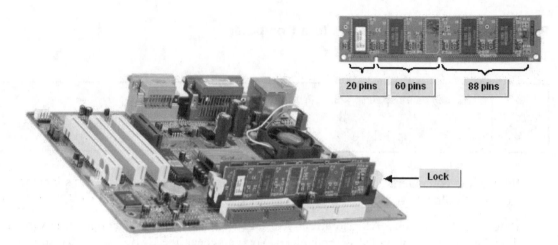

Figure 5-6: Adding RAM to a computer.

ACTIVITY 5-6

Adding RAM to a Computer

Scenario:

The computers your organization purchased have been performing sluggishly. Additional RAM has been purchased for these computers.

 There is a simulated version of this activity available on the CD-ROM that shipped with this course. You can run this simulation on any Windows computer to review the activity after class, or as an alternative to performing the activity as a group in class. The activity simulation can be launched either directly from the CD-ROM by clicking the Interactives link and navigating to the appropriate one, or from the installed data file location by opening the C:\085820Data\Simulations\Lesson#\Activity#folder and double-clicking the executable (.exe) file.

What You Do	How You Do It
1. **Determine how much RAM is currently installed.**	a. If necessary, **log in to the computer as Admin## with a password of !Pass1234** (where the ## is your student number).
	b. From the Start menu, **choose My Computer.**
	c. **Click View System Information.**

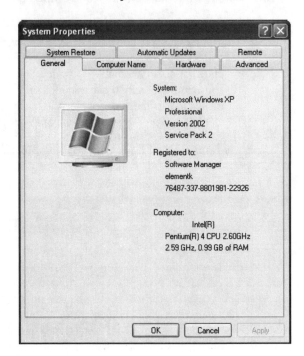

2. **How much memory is currently installed?**

3. **Install more memory in the system.**

    a. **Shut down your computer.**

    b. **Disconnect the power cord.**

    c. **Discharge any static electricity from yourself and your clothes.**

    d. **Locate the memory expansion sockets in your system.**

    e. If there are no empty memory expansion sockets or you don't have a memory module to practice with, **push the ejector tabs on each end of the memory module out** to release the memory module, **and then remove the memory module.**

    f. **Align the notched edge of the memory module with the memory expansion slot, and then firmly press the module down into the socket.**

    g. If the ejector tabs did not automatically lock into each end of the memory module, **push both ejector tabs up until they lock into the notches on each end of the memory module.**

4. **Verify that the additional memory is recognized by the system.**

    a. **Plug in the power cord and restart the system.**

    b. If prompted at startup, **follow any on-screen prompts** to make the system recognize the memory.

    c. **Display the System Properties dialog box and record the amount of memory shown.** If the additional memory isn't recognized, you can check documentation to see if any steps need to be performed. Also, verify that the memory was correctly seated in the slots and was the correct type of memory for the system.

DISCOVERY ACTIVITY 5-7

Examining Memory

Scenario:
In this activity, you will examine how memory is installed and configured.

---

1. **True or False? If there are no empty memory expansion sockets on the system board, you will need to remove an existing module and replace it with a module that contains more memory.**

   ___ True

   ___ False

---

2. **Where can you verify how much RAM is currently installed on your computer?**

   a) System Properties

   b) Component Services

   c) Services

   d) CMOS Settings

TOPIC D
Install and Configure CPUs

In the previous topics, you installed RAM. Another way to increase the performance of a personal computer is to install a second processor or upgrade the existing processor. In this topic, you will install and configure processors.

Have you ever tried to get a new piece of software or a game to run only to find out that your processor is too slow? If this happens to the users you support, they will want you to fix the problem, which might mean upgrading the CPU. This might seem like a drastic measure, and it can be expensive, but in some cases, it is less expensive to upgrade the CPU than it is to purchase a new system if everything else in a user's computer provides acceptable performance.

CPU Chip Types

CPU chips are developed by several different manufacturers.

CPU Manufacturer	Sample CPUs
Intel	Intel CPUs include 8086, 8088, 80286, 80386SX, 80386DX, 80486SX, 80486DX, Pentium, Pentium MMX, Pentium Pro, Pentium II, Pentium III, Pentium 4, Celeron, Xeon, Duo core, and Itanium, to name a few.
AMD	AMD CPUs include the K5, K6, Duron, Athlon, Opteron, and Althon 64 processors.
Cyrix	While no longer in business, Cyrix manufactured the MediaGX and M II processor, among others.

Instruction Sets

An *instruction set* is the collection of commands that is used by a CPU to perform calculations and other computing operations. Every manufacturer has its own instruction set.

There are three main categories of instruction sets used.

Instruction Set	Description
Complex Instruction Set Computer (CISC)	A design strategy for computer architectures that depends on hardware to perform complicated instructions. Does not require instructions to be of a fixed length. Allows for more complicated functions to be executed in one instruction. Most Intel processors fall into this category.

Instruction Set	Description
Reduced Instruction Set Computer (RISC)	A design strategy for computer architecture that depends on a combination of hardware and software to perform complicated instructions. Requires instructions to be of a fixed length. RISC instructions are simpler and fewer than CISC, but more instructions are required to carry out a single function. IBM, Motorola, and Sun manufacture RISC chips. IBM RS/6000, Sun Microsystems, and some Macintosh computers use RISC.
Explicitly Parallel Instruction Computing (EPIC)	A design strategy for computer architecture that is meant to simplify and streamline CPU operation by taking advantage of advancements in compiler technology and by combining the best of the CISC and RISC design strategies. EPIC-based processors are 64-bit chips. Intel IA-64 architecture, including Intel Itanium processors, is based on EPIC.

Cache Memory

Definition:

Cache memory, or CPU cache, is a type of memory that services the CPU. It is faster than main memory and allows the CPU to execute instructions and read and write data at a higher speed. Instructions and data are transferred from main memory to the cache in blocks to enhance performance. Cache memory is typically static RAM (SRAM) and is identified by level. Level 1 (L1) cache is built into the CPU chip. Level 2 cache (L2) feeds the L1 cache. L2 can be built into the CPU chip, reside on a separate chip, or be a separate bank of chips on the system board. If L2 is built into the CPU, then level 3 cache (L3) can be present on the system board.

Example:

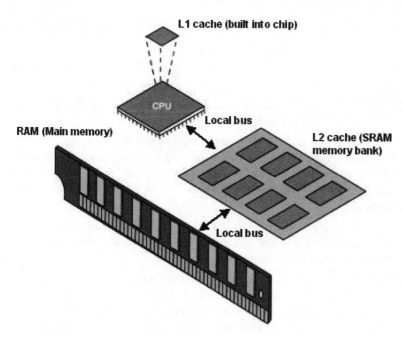

Figure 5-7: Cache memory.

Cache Write Policy

The cache's write policy determines how it handles writes to memory locations that are currently being held in cache. There are two policy types.

Cache Policy Type	Description
Write-back cache	When the system writes to a memory location that is held in cache, it writes only the new information to the appropriate cache line. When the cache line is needed for another memory address, the changed data is written back into system memory. This type of cache provides better performance than a write-through cache, because it saves write cycles to memory.
Write-through cache	When the system writes to a memory location that is held in cache, it writes the new information simultaneously to the appropriate cache line and to the memory location. This type of caching provides lower performance than write-back, but it is easier to implement and has the advantage of internal consistency, because the cache and memory are identical at all times.

CPU Operational Characteristics

There are many different characteristics and technologies that can affect a CPU's performance.

CPU Characteristic or Technology	Description
Bus width	A CPU's internal bus width is either 32 or 64 bits.
Clock speed	The number of processing cycles that a microprocessor can perform in a given second. Some CPUs require several cycles to assemble and perform a single instruction, whereas others require fewer cycles. The clock speed is a technical rating; actual performance speeds can vary from the published clock speed rating.
Overclocking	Configuring your system board to run at a speed greater than your CPU is rated to handle. Doing so can cause the CPU to overheat, produce random results, or be damaged or destroyed.
CPU speed	CPU speed is an umbrella term for the overall rate at which instructions are processed. There are two factors that affect the CPU speed. One is the core clock speed, which is the internal speed at which instructions are processed within the CPU. The other is the bus clock speed, which is the speed at which instructions are transferred to the system board.
Throttling	To adjust CPU speed. A CPU throttle is typically used to slow down the machine during idle times to conserve battery or to keep the system running at a lower performance level when hardware problems have been encountered.
Hyperthreading	A feature of certain Pentium 4 chips that makes one physical CPU appear as two logical CPUs. It uses additional registers to overlap two instruction streams to increase the CPU's performance by about 30%.
Dual core	A single chip that contains two distinct CPUs that process simultaneously. The first dual core chips for x86-based PCs and servers were introduced in 2005.
Cache	Dedicated high-speed memory for storing recently used instructions and data.
Voltage Regulator Module	VRM is a replaceable module used to regulate the voltage fed to the CPU.
Multimedia Extensions	MMX is a set of additional instructions, called microcode, to support sound, video, and graphics multimedia functions.

Processor Specifications

The following table summarizes some of the specifications for popular processors.

Name	Characteristics
80386DX	<ul><li>No L2 cache</li><li>Internal Bus Width: 32 bits</li><li>System Data Bus Width: 32 bits</li><li>System Address Bus Width: 32 bits</li><li>Clock Speed: 16–40 MHz</li><li>Addressable RAM: 4 GB</li></ul>
80386SX	<ul><li>No L2 cache</li><li>Internal Bus Width: 32 bits</li><li>System Data Bus Width: 16 bits</li><li>System Address Bus Width: 24 bits</li><li>Clock Speed: 16–33 MHz</li><li>Addressable RAM: 16 MB</li></ul>
80486DX	<ul><li>Up to 256 KB L2 cache on the system board</li><li>Internal Bus Width: 32 bits</li><li>System Data Bus Width: 32 bits</li><li>System Address Bus Width: 32 bits</li><li>Clock Speed: 25–50 MHz</li><li>Addressable RAM: 4 GB</li></ul>
80486SX	<ul><li>Up to 256 KB L2 cache on the system board</li><li>Internal Bus Width: 32 bits</li><li>System Data Bus Width: 32 bits</li><li>System Address Bus Width: 32 bits</li><li>Clock Speed: 16–33 MHz</li><li>Addressable RAM: 4 GB</li></ul>
80486DX2	<ul><li>Up to 256 KB L2 cache on the system board</li><li>Internal Bus Width: 32 bits</li><li>System Data Bus Width: 32 bits</li><li>System Address Bus Width: 32 bits</li><li>Clock Speed: 50–80 MHz</li><li>Addressable RAM: 4 GB</li></ul>
80486DX4	<ul><li>Up to 256 KB L2 cache on the system board</li><li>Internal Bus Width: 32 bits</li><li>System Data Bus Width: 32 bits</li><li>System Address Bus Width: 32 bits</li><li>Clock Speed: 75–120 MHz</li><li>Addressable RAM: 4 GB</li></ul>

Name	Characteristics
AMD 5x86	<ul><li>Up to 256 KB L2 cache on the system board</li><li>Internal Bus Width: 32 bits</li><li>System Data Bus Width: 32 bits</li><li>System Address Bus Width: 32 bits</li><li>Clock Speed: 133 MHz</li><li>Addressable RAM: 4 GB</li></ul>
Cyrix 5x86	<ul><li>Up to 256 KB L2 cache on the system board</li><li>Internal Bus Width: 32 bits</li><li>System Data Bus Width: 32 bits</li><li>System Address Bus Width: 32 bits</li><li>Clock Speed: 100–200 MHz</li><li>Addressable RAM: 4 GB</li></ul>
Pentium	<ul><li>256 KB to 512 KB L2 cache on the system board</li><li>Support for the installation of up to two processors on the system board</li><li>Internal Bus Width: 32 bits</li><li>System Data Bus Width: 64 bits</li><li>System Address Bus Width: 32 bits</li><li>Clock Speed: 60–200 MHz</li><li>Addressable RAM: 4 GB</li></ul>
Pentium MMX	<ul><li>256 KB to 512 KB L2 cache on the system board</li><li>Support for the installation of up to two processors on the system board</li><li>Internal Bus Width: 32 bits</li><li>System Data Bus Width: 64 bits</li><li>System Address Bus Width: 32 bits</li><li>Clock Speed: 166–233 MHz</li><li>Addressable RAM: 4 GB</li></ul>
Cyrix 6x86	<ul><li>256 KB to 512 KB L2 cache on the system board</li><li>Internal Bus Width: 32 bits</li><li>System Data Bus Width: 64 bits</li><li>System Address Bus Width: 32 bits</li><li>Clock Speed: 100–150 MHz</li><li>Addressable RAM: 4 GB</li></ul>
AMD K5	<ul><li>256 KB to 512 KB L2 cache on the system board</li><li>Internal Bus Width: 32 bits</li><li>System Data Bus Width: 64 bits</li><li>System Address Bus Width: 32 bits</li><li>Clock Speed: 75–116 MHz</li><li>Addressable RAM: 4 GB</li></ul>

Name	Characteristics
Pentium Pro	• 256 KB to 1 MB L2 cache integrated within the CPU • Support for the installation of up to four processors on the system board • Internal Bus Width: 32 bits • System Data Bus Width: 64 bits • System Address Bus Width: 36 bits • Clock Speed: 150–200 MHz • Addressable RAM: 64 GB
Pentium II	• 512 KB L2 integrated cache • Support for the installation of up to two processors on the system board • Internal Bus Width: 32 bits • System Data Bus Width: 64 bits • System Address Bus Width: 36 bits • Clock Speed: 233–333 MHz • Addressable RAM: 64 GB
AMD K6	• 256 KB to 1 MB L2 cache on the system board • Internal Bus Width: 32 bits • System Data Bus Width: 64 bits • System Address Bus Width: 32 bits • Clock Speed: 166–266 MHz • Addressable RAM: 4 GB
Cyrix 6x86 MX	• 256 KB to 512 KB L2 cache on the system board • Internal Bus Width: 32 bits • System Data Bus Width: 64 bits • System Address Bus Width: 32 bits • Clock Speed: 150–187 MHz • Addressable RAM: 4 GB
Celeron	• 128 KB L2 cache on–die • Internal Bus Width: 32 bits • System Data Bus Width: 64 bits • System Address Bus Width: 32, 36 bits • Clock Speed: 266 MHz–1.3 GHz • Addressable RAM: 4 GB, 64 GB
Pentium II Xeon	• 512 KB to 2 MB L2 cache on the system board • Support for the installation of up to eight processors on the system board • Internal Bus Width: 32 bits • System Data Bus Width: 64 bits • System Address Bus Width: 36 bits • Clock Speed: 400–450 MHz • Addressable RAM: 64 GB

Name	Characteristics
Pentium III	• 256 KB on-die, 512 KB L2 cache on the system board • Support for the installation of up to two processors on the system board • Internal Bus Width: 32 bits • System Data Bus Width: 64 bits • System Address Bus Width: 36 bits • Clock Speed: 450 MHz–1.4 GHz • Addressable RAM: 64 GB
Pentium III Xeon	• 256 KB to 2 MB L2 integrated cache • Support for the installation of up to eight processors on the system board • Internal Bus Width: 32 bits • System Data Bus Width: 64 bits • System Address Bus Width: 36 bits • Clock Speed: 600–1 GHz • Addressable RAM: 64 GB
Pentium 4	• 256 KB on-die L2 cache • Internal Bus Width: 32 bits • System Data Bus Width: 64 bits • System Address Bus Width: 32 bits • Clock Speed: 1.3 GHz–2.4 GHz • Addressable RAM: 4 GB
Itanium	• 96 KB on-die, plus 2 to 4 MB L3 cache • Support for the installation of up to 14 processors on the system board • Internal Bus Width: 64 bits • System Data Bus Width: 64 bits • System Address Bus Width: 44 bits • Clock Speed: 733–800 MHz • Addressable RAM: 16 TB
AMD Athlon	• 64 – 512 KB integrated L2 cache • Support for the installation of up to eight processors on the system board • Internal Bus Width: 32 bits • System Data Bus Width: 64 bits • System Address Bus Width: 43 bits • Clock Speed: 500 MHz–2.133 GHz • Addressable RAM: 8 TB

Name	Characteristics
Pentium M	• Developed for laptops to consume less power and generate less heat; part of Intel Centrino platform • 2 *Mebibyte (MiB)* L2 cache • Internal Bus Width: 32 bits • System Data Bus Width: 64 bits • System Address Bus Width: 36 bits • Clock Speed: 1.5 GHz–2.1 GHz • Addressable RAM: 64 GB
Pentium D	• The first *multi-core* processor developed by Intel • 1 MiB L2 cache per core (2 MiB L2 cache total) • Internal Bus Width: 64 bits • System Data Bus Width: 64 bits • System Address Bus Width: 64 bits • Clock Speed: 2.8 GHz–3.2 GHz • Addressable RAM: 1 TB
Intel Core Solo/ Duo	• Fesigned to replace the Pentium M processor • Reduced power consumption • Intel Core Duo is a multi-core processor • 2 MiB L2 cache shared by both processors • Internal Bus Width: 32 bits • System Data Bus Width: 64 bits • System Address Bus Width: 36 bits • Clock Speed: 1.06 GHz–2.33 GHz • Addressable RAM: 64 GB
Intel Core 2 Duo	• Multi-core processor • Significantly reduced power consumption as compared to Pentium chips • Replaces the Pentium product line • 1 to 2 MiB L2 cache per core (2 to 4 MiB L2 cache total) • Internal Bus Width: 64 bits • System Data Bus Width: 64 bits • System Address Bus Width: 64 bits • Clock Speed: Up to 2.66 GHz • Addressable RAM: 1 TB

Name	Characteristics
Intel Core 2 Duo Extreme	• Multi-core processor • Significantly reduced power consumption as compared to Pentium chips • 2 MiB L2 cache per core, but comes with a multiplier that increases this cache to simulate 4 MiB per core • Internal Bus Width: 64 bits • System Data Bus Width: 64 bits • System Address Bus Width: 64 bits • Clock Speed: Up to 2.93 GHz • Addressable RAM: 1 TB

Processor Connections

Different CPUs use different connection methods to connect to the system board, including various sockets, slots, and connection methods.

- Older slot-based processors plugged into a system board in much the same way as an expansion board.

- And, socketed processors plug into a system board using a grid array of pins.

Many varieties of sockets and slots have been developed over the years.

Slot Types

The following table describes some of the slots you might encounter.

Slot Type	Description
Slot 1	Contains a 242-pin edge connector. Used for Celeron SEPP (Single Edge Processor Package), Pentium II SECC (Single Edge Contact Cartridge) and SECC2, and Pentium III processors.
Slot 2	Contains a 330-pin edge connector. Used for Pentium II Xeon and Pentium III Xeon processors. Designed for multi-processor systems.
Slot A	Contains a 242-pin edge connector. Used for AMD Athlon processors. Pinouts are incompatible with Slot 1.
Slot M	Used for Itanium processors.

Socket Types

The following table describes some of the sockets you might encounter.

Socket Type	Description
Socket 7	• Pin layout: 321 pin staggered arranged in 37 x 37 SPGA grid • Processor used for: Later Pentium, AMD K6, and Cyrix 6x86

Socket Type	Description
Super 7	• Pin layout: 321 pin staggered arranged in 37 x 37 SPGA grid • Processor used for: AMD K6-2 and K6-III
Socket 8	• Pin layout: 387 pin staggered ZIF arranged in 24 x 26 SPGA grid • Processor used for: 3.3v Pentium Pro
Socket 370	• Pin layout: Supports PPGA • Processor used for: Original Celeron
Socket 423	• Pin layout: SPGA • Processor used for: Pentium 4
Socket 478	• Pin layout: SPGA • Processor used for: Pentium 4
Socket A	• Pin layout: Supports PPGA • Processor used for: AMD Athlon, Duron, Athlon XP, and Sempron
Socket 603	• Pin layout: 603 pins arrayed around the center of the socket • Processor used for: Xeon
Socket 754	• Pin layout: 754 pin PGA • Processor used for: Athlon 64, Sempron, Turon 64
Socket 771	• Pin layout: 771 pin LGA • Processor used for: Intel Xeon
Socket 775 (or LGA 775, or Socket T)	• Pin layout: 775 pin LGA • Processor used for: Pentium 4, Celeron D, Pentium Extreme Edition, Core 2 Duo, Core 2 Extreme
Socket 939	• Pin layout: 939 pin PGA • Processor used for: Athlon 64, Athlon 64FX, Athlon 64X2, Opteron 100–series
Socket 940	• Pin layout: 940 pin PGA • Processor used for: Opteron, Athlon 64FX
Socket F (or Socket 1207)	• Pin layout: 1207 pin LGA • Processor used for: Opteron
Socket AM2	• Pin layout: 940 pin PGA • Processor used for: Athlon 64, Sempron, Turon 64, Athlon 64FX, Athlon 64X2, Opteron 100–series
PAC418	• Pin layout: 418 pin VLIF • Processor used for: Itanium
PAC611	• Pin layout: 611 pin VLIF • Processor used for: Itanium, Itanium 2

Socket Type	Description
FCPGA6	• Pin layout: 479 pin PGA • Processor used for: Core Solo, Core Duo, Dual-Core Xeon, Core 2 Duo

CPU Selection Tips

There are two key factors you must consider when selecting a CPU for a computer.

Factor	Considerations
Hardware compatibility	The key factor you must consider when selecting a CPU for a computer is its system board. The design of the computer's system board determines the type of CPU you can install. For example, you can't install an AMD processor into a system board designed to support an Intel processor. Most importantly, you should review the documentation for the computer's system board to determine its compatibility with other CPUs. Keep in mind that most original equipment manufacturers (OEMs) such as Dell and Gateway don't typically provide you with the system board's documentation. To obtain this documentation, try contacting the computer's manufacturer or the manufacturer of the system board. (You can typically identify the manufacturer of the system board by examining it.)
Performance	In addition, you should keep in mind that there is a trade-off between price and performance when selecting a CPU. The greater the performance requirements of the user, the more powerful CPU you should select. And more powerful CPUs are simply more expensive. When selecting a CPU for a user, you should ask the user his budget for the purchase. This budget can help you narrow down the choices for selecting a processor.

CPU Installation Considerations

There are several factors you should keep in mind when installing CPUs.

Factor	Description
Power	Make sure to review the CPU's power requirements to verify that you aren't overloading the computer's power supply.
Removal	Review the computer's documentation to determine how to properly remove the existing processor from the system board. Most newer processors use *Zero Insertion Force (ZIF)* sockets, which is a type of processor socket that uses a lever to tighten or loosen the pin connections between the processor chip and the socket. So there is no force required when you insert or remove the chip.
Cooling	Verify that you have the necessary equipment to cool the new processor. Some CPUs come equipped with a heatsink and fan; others don't. If necessary, follow the new CPU manufacturer's instructions to install any fan or heatsink on the new CPU.

Figure 5-8: A ZIF socket.

CPU Configuration and Optimization Requirements

It's critical that you configure the system board properly to support the new CPU. Most importantly, for older systems, you might need to configure the system board to use the correct voltage. This is done by using the jumper settings on the system board or the computer's CMOS setup program. Setting the voltage on the system board too high can destroy the CPU.

How to Install and Configure CPUs

Procedure Reference: Install and Configure CPUs

To install a new CPU or replace an existing CPU:

 When installing new equipment, always follow the instructions included with the device from the manufacturer.

1. Shut down the system and remove the existing CPU.

   a. Shut down the system.

   b. Unplug the power cord.

   c. Ground yourself (wear a wrist strap) to dissipate any static electricity you might be carrying.

   d. Pull up the lever on the side of the ZIF-socket CPU. If you have a different style CPU, refer to the system documentation for how to remove it.

   e. Pick the CPU straight up so that you don't bend any pins.

   f. Place the old CPU in a safe location in an appropriate container to prevent damage to the CPU should you need or want to reinstall it later.

2. Install the new CPU.

   a. Align the pins on the CPU with the holes in the ZIF socket on the system board.

   b. Press the CPU lever back down to lock the CPU in place.

   c. Connect any power connections to the appropriate power connectors.

3. Reboot and verify that the CPU works. If the system boots, then the CPU was installed correctly. To verify that the CPU is reporting the correct information, view the System Properties dialog box and verify that the specifications listed match those of your CPU.

Procedure Reference: Install a Second CPU

To add a second processor to a computer:

1. Shut down the system, disconnect the power, and ground yourself.

2. Remove the terminator from the second processor socket.

3. Insert a CPU that is identical to the processor in the first processor socket.

4. Restart the system and verify that both processors are recognized in System Properties.

ACTIVITY 5-8

Upgrading the CPU

Scenario:

One of your clients has an older computer that needs to be upgraded. The CPU in the computer doesn't meet the requirements for the application the client needs to run. The client has purchased a CPU upgrade and would like you to install it.

 There is a simulated version of this activity available on the CD-ROM that shipped with this course. You can run this simulation on any Windows computer to review the activity after class, or as an alternative to performing the activity as a group in class. The activity simulation can be launched either directly from the CD-ROM by clicking the Interactives link and navigating to the appropriate one, or from the installed data file location by opening the C:\ 085820Data\Simulations\Lesson#\Activity# folder and double-clicking the executable (.exe) file.

What You Do	How You Do It
1. Remove the existing CPU.	a. **Shut down the system and unplug the power cord.**

 If you have a slot based CPU, follow your instructor's recommendations to remove and then install the processor.

b. If necessary, **undo the clip to remove the heat sink and fan from the top of the CPU.**

c. If necessary, **unplug the power cable from the CPU fan.**

d. **Pull up the lever on the side of the ZIF-socket CPU.** If you have a different style CPU, refer to the system documentation for how to remove it.

e. Now that the CPU has been released, **pick the CPU straight up** so as not to bend any pins.

f. **Place the old CPU in a safe location in an appropriate container** to prevent damage to the CPU should you need or want to reinstall it later.

2.	**Install the replacement CPU.**	a. **On the system board, align the pins on the CPU with the holes in the ZIF socket.**
		b. **Press the CPU lever back down** to lock the CPU in place.
		c. **Lock the heat sink and fan clip.**
		d. **Plug the CPU fan power plug in to the system board.**
		e. **Connect any power connections to the appropriate power connectors.**
3.	**Verify that the CPU is recognized.**	a. **Restart the system.**
		b. **Display the System Properties dialog box.**
		c. **Verify that the CPU listed on the General page matches what you just installed.**

DISCOVERY ACTIVITY 5-9

Examining CPUs

Scenario:

In this activity, you will examine CPUs.

---

1. **When you install a new CPU in a system, what is the first thing you should do?**

   a) Shut down the system.

   b) Ground yourself to dissipate any static electricity.

   c) Unplug the power cord.

   d) Pull up the lever on the side of the ZIF-socket CPU.

---

2. **True or False? When installing a CPU, verify that you have the necessary equipment to cool the new processor.**

   ___ True

   ___ False

TOPIC E
Install and Configure System Boards

In the last topic, you installed and configured CPUs. The final system component that you might need to install is the system board. In this topic, you will install and configure a system board.

The most important system component in a computer is the system board. Although you can argue a case for almost any system component as being most important, without the system board, the computer simply cannot run. It's possible that you will be asked to either build a computer from scratch or to replace the system board in a failed computer. In either case, whether you are building a computer from scratch or repairing a failed computer, you must be prepared to install and configure a new system board.

Integrated I/O Port Types

System boards can include any or all of a number of integrated controllers or ports:

- Sound.
- Video.
- Network.
- Modem.
- USB.
- Serial.
- IEEE 1394/FireWire.
- And, parallel.

Most integrated devices provide basic functionality that does not approach the capabilities of the associated add-in cards.

Chipsets

Definition:

A *chipset* is a system board component that includes the CPU and other chips that support basic functions of the computer. PC chipsets are housed on one to four chips and include built-in controllers for almost all common peripherals.

Example:

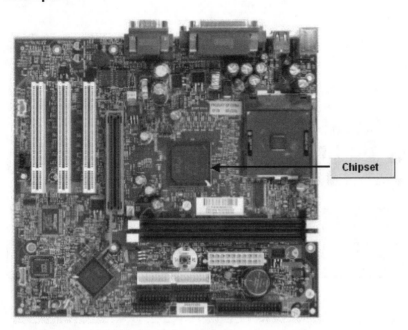

Figure 5-9: A chipset on a system board.

Chips in Chipsets

Chipset architecture, including the number, function, name, and placement of the various chips in a chipset, will vary depending on the type and manufacturer of the system board. For example, on many Intel Pentium computers, the two main chips in the chipset, other than the CPU, are known as the Northbridge and the Southbridge.

- The Northbridge controls the system memory and the AGP video ports, and it may also control cache memory. The Northbridge is closer to the processor and communicates directly with it using the system bus.

- The Southbridge controls input/output functions, the system clock, drives and buses, APM power management, and various other devices. The Southbridge is further from the CPU and uses the PCI bus to communicate with the Northbridge.

Newer Intel systems employ the Intel Hub Architecture (IHA) chipset. This also has two main chips, now named the Graphics and AGP Memory Controller Hub (GMCH) and the I/O Controller Hub (ICH), which perform functions roughly analogous to the Northbridge and Southbridge.

BIOS Types

Types of BIOSes found on system boards include the system BIOS and the BIOS and device drivers for any expansion cards. There are many system BIOS types.

System BIOS Types

There are many different manufacturers of system BIOS:

- American Megatrends.
- Award BIOS.
- Phoenix BIOS.
- IBM SurePath BIOS.

- Microid Research (Mr. BIOS).
- BootControl Pro.
- MicroFirmware.
- SystemSoft.
- And, Unicore.

Complementary Metal Oxide Semiconductor (CMOS) Memory Settings

Most CMOS settings can be configured from the keyboard by using the CMOS Setup program.

 The extent to which you can use CMOS to configure a computer depends heavily on the manufacturer of the particular CMOS.

CMOS Setup Setting	Description
System date and time	You can use the CMOS Setup program to set the PC's real-time clock. Using DOS date and time commands won't reset the real-time clock, but setting the clock in Windows will.
Password	You can specify whether a password is required following the POST.
Boot sequence	You can specify the order that POST checks drives for the operating system.
Memory	Some systems require you to specify in CMOS how much RAM is installed on the system. You might also be able to specify whether the system uses parity memory or non-parity memory.
Hard drive	You can specify the type and size of the hard drives attached to the system.
Floppy drive	You can adjust the speed and density settings for the floppy drive. You can also disable or enable a floppy drive.
Display	You can specify the monitor type.
Parallel ports	You can specify settings such as unidirectional or bidirectional printing, ECP options, and EPP options. You can also disable or enable a parallel port. If you know that a parallel or serial port will not be used, you can disable the port, thereby freeing up the resources for use by other devices. Conversely, if you connect a device to a port and the device won't work at all, you might want to check the CMOS to ensure that the port hasn't been disabled.
Serial/COM ports	You can specify settings such as what memory addresses and interrupts are used by a port. You can also disable or enable a serial port.
Power management	In most modern computers, you can specify settings such as powering down components (such as the monitor, video card, and hard drives) when the components haven't been used for a specified time period, as well as options and time limits for standby and suspend modes. You can also disable or enable global power management.

System Board Selection Tips

You choose a system board based on whether it supports the components you need for the computer.

System Component	Questions To Ask
RAM	Does the system board support enough RAM to meet the user's needs?
CPU	What type of processor can you install? Can you install more than one CPU?
Ports	Does the system board have the necessary ports to meet the user's needs? Specifically, does it have the parallel, serial, USB, and possibly even FireWire ports needed?
Expansion slots	How many expansion slots will the user need? What types of slots does it include?
Drive interfaces	Does the system board include drive interfaces? If not, does it have enough available expansion slots to accommodate the user's hard disk requirements?
Form factor	Will the system board fit inside the case of the computer?
Clock speed	Does the system board operate at a high enough frequency to support the processor you want to use?

System Board Installation Considerations

When you are replacing a system board, specific requirements need to be considered and can also depend on the manufacturer's requirements for the system. You need to make sure you get one that fits your case. This is because the holes in the system board need to line up with the connections in the case. The system board is secured to the case using these connections. Also, when replacing the cover on the case, you must make sure the cover is properly aligned. If the cover isn't properly aligned, it might affect the cooling system and the operation of the internal drives.

Computer Cases

The computer case is the enclosure that holds all of the components of your computer. Computer cases come in several formats. Some are designed to hold many internal components and have a lot of room to work around those components. These cases are usually tower cases and take up a good deal of room. Other cases are designed to use a minimum amount of space. The trade-off is that the interior of the case is often cramped, with little room for adding additional components. Because the tower proved to be popular, there are now several versions of the tower model. These include:

- Full tower, which is usually used for servers or when you will be installing many drives and other components.

- Mid tower, which is a slightly smaller version of the full-size tower.

- Micro tower, which is the size that replaces the original desktop case in most modern systems.

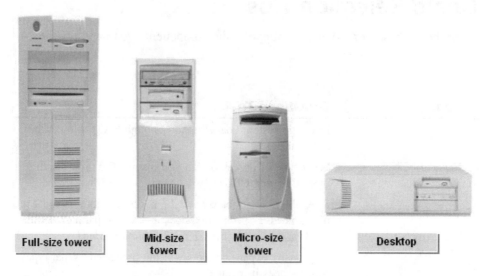

Figure 5-10: *Computer case enclosure styles.*

System Board Configuration and Optimization Requirements

When you replace or install a new system board, you must ensure that it is properly configured to match the processor that it will host. In essence, you must configure the system board so that the internal and external frequencies of the processor are compatible. You accomplish this by specifying a frequency multiple. Most system boards operate at a specific speed, but some enable you to select the speed via DIP switches, jumpers, or the BIOS setup software.

DIP Switches and Jumpers

To configure older system boards, you used either *DIP switches* or *jumpers*. You might have used these switches to specify the multiplier and the CPU bus frequency. Newer system boards enable you to use software to configure these values (through the BIOS Setup program).

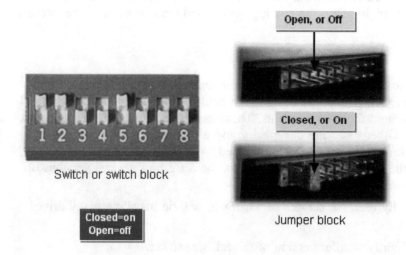

Figure 5-11: *Examples of DIP switches and jumpers.*

System Board Power Connectors

The power supply connection to the system board is a keyed or unkeyed connection that enables the power supply to supply power to the internal components of the system. Keyed connectors are designed so that the plug and socket have notches that must line up in order for the plug to fit into the socket. The connection also might use a single connector or two connectors. If there are two connectors, they are labeled P8 and P9. Be sure not to switch them when you plug them in or you could damage the system board. Most systems have a single, keyed connector that is inserted only one way, which avoids damage to the system board.

Power supplies have connections to other internal components as well. There are Berg and Molex connections and a connection to the power switch for the system.

A single keyed connector

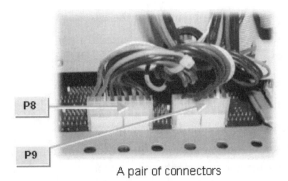

A pair of connectors

Figure 5-12: *System board power supply connectors.*

Specific Connectors

There are specific connectors, depending on the motherboard requirements, usually tied to the CPU type. There's the 20-pin (ATX), a 24-pin ATX connector, and the 20+4 combo (which you can separate, or not, depending on the motherboard). This includes a 20-pin for the main power, plus a 4-pin connector for additional CPU power. This 4-pin is sometimes known as the Intel Pentium 4 connector. There's also an 8-pin CPU connector that requires an ATX 2.02, or EPS12V, PSU.

How to Install and Configure System Boards

Procedure Reference: Install or Upgrade a System Board

To install or upgrade the system board:

 When installing new equipment, always follow the instructions included with the device from the manufacturer.

1. If you are upgrading the computer's system board, remove the original system board.

    a. Shut down the system and unplug the power cord.

    b. Disconnect all external devices.

    c. Remove the system cover.

    d. Remove all expansion cards and store them in anti-static bags. (Before removing components from the system board, you might want to take a picture of the assembled board so that you can use it as a reference when you reconnect the components later.)

    e. Disconnect cables from the system board, marking each cable as to what it connects to and where it goes.

    f. Unscrew the system board from the case.

    g. Lift the system board out of the case. On some systems, after lifting the system board over the pin(s), you will need to slide it out of the case.

2. Install the new or replacement system board.

    a. Place the new system board into the case and align the mounting holes.

    b. Secure the system board to the case.

    c. Install RAM and processor(s) on the new system board. Some sources recommend installing these components prior to installing the system board. If you do this, be careful not to bend the board or mash any connectors on the bottom side of the system board as you insert the components.

    d. Reinstall cards and cables removed from the old system board.

    e. Replace the system cover.

    f. Test the system.

ACTIVITY 5-10

Upgrading the System Board

Scenario:

A lightning storm destroyed the system board in one of your customers' systems. You have been assigned the task of replacing the system board. While doing so, the customer would like you to put in an upgraded system board to improve system performance.

 There is a simulated version of this activity available on the CD-ROM that shipped with this course. You can run this simulation on any Windows computer to review the activity after class, or as an alternative to performing the activity as a group in class. The activity simulation can be launched either directly from the CD-ROM by clicking the Interactives link and navigating to the appropriate one, or from the installed data file location by opening the C:\ 085820Data\Simulations\Lesson#\Activity# folder and double-clicking the executable (.exe) file.

 When installing new equipment, follow the instructions included with the device from the manufacturer.

What You Do	How You Do It
1. Remove cards and cables.	a. Shut down the computer and unplug the power cord.
	b. Disconnect all external devices.
	c. Open the computer case.

 You may find it helpful at this point to take a picture of the inside of the computer to use as reference later.

d. **Remove all cards from the expansion slots and store them in appropriate anti-static containers.**

e. As you disconnect each cable in the computer, **attach a piece of masking tape to each cable and record where each connection goes as you remove it.**

f. If you need the room, **unplug the power and data cable connectors for all drives in the computer. Mark which cable is connected to the primary and which to the secondary IDE connector.**

g. **Unplug connectors attached to any front-panel switches or LEDs.**

h. **Unplug the power supply and data cables from the system board.**

i. If necessary, **remove the drive bay assembly and any other components needed to access all the screws on the system board.**

2. **Remove the existing system board.**

a. **Unscrew the system board from the case.** Be sure to set the screws aside to use in mounting the new system board.

b. **Lift the system board,** and then if necessary, **slide it forward, and then lift it up and out of the case.**

3. **Install the new system board.**

 Be sure not to screw the system board in too tightly to avoid damaging the system board.

a. **Slide the new system board into the case, aligning the mounting holes.**

b. **Secure the system board to the case using the screws you removed from the old system board.**

 Start all the screws before you begin tightening them.

4.	**Install RAM and a processor on the new system board.**	a.	**Install the memory modules beginning with the first memory slot (Bank 0).**
		b.	**Install the CPU according to the manufacturer's directions.**

5.	**Reinstall the cards and cables.**	a.	**Reconnect all internal cables and cards, including any LED or front-panel switch connections.**
		b.	**Reinstall adapter cards.**
		c.	If you needed to remove any drive bay assemblies or other components to access the system board, **replace any of those components.**
		d.	**Reconnect the power supply to the system board.**
		e.	**Reconnect all external devices.**

6.	**Test the computer.**	a.	**Plug in the power cord.**
		b.	**Start the computer.** If all went well, it should boot. Windows might attempt to reboot several times as it discovers new components.

DISCOVERY ACTIVITY 5-11

Examining System Boards

Scenario:

In this activity, you will examine system boards.

---

1. **True or False? Often when you are examining a system board, you will find that there are very few components on the board that are actually repairable.**

   ___ True

   ___ False

2. **When you are installing or upgrading a system board, what should you do as you are disconnecting the cables from the board?**

   a) Remove them completely from the case, so they are out of the way.

   b) Mark each cable as you go, so you can easily reconnect them later.

   c) Unscrew the system board from the case.

   d) Disconnect all external devices.

Lesson 5 Follow-up

In this lesson, you installed and configured system components. The ability to successfully install and configure hardware components is an integral part of a computer technician's job.

1. **What types of internal system hardware will you be required to install most often at your workplace?**

2. **Have you encountered any problems with installing and configuring a computer component?**

6 | Maintaining and Troubleshooting Peripheral Components

Lesson Time: 2 hour(s)

Lesson Objectives:

In this lesson, you will maintain and troubleshoot peripheral components.

You will:

- Test and troubleshoot display devices.

- Maintain and troubleshoot input devices.

- Test and troubleshoot adapter cards.

- Troubleshoot multimedia devices.

Introduction

In the last two lessons, you installed and configured various computer components. After components are installed, maintenance and troubleshooting are required to reap the maximum benefits from the equipment. In this lesson, you will maintain and troubleshoot peripheral components.

It's inevitable—at some point in time, problems with computer hardware will arise. As an A+ technician, maintaining and troubleshooting computer hardware, including peripheral components, will be an integral part of your job duties. Your ability to quickly and effectively solve problems with peripherals will be essential in providing your users with the computing environments that they need to be able to perform their jobs.

This lesson covers all or part of the following CompTIA A+ (2006) Examination objectives:

- Topic A:
    - Exam 220-601 (Essentials): Objective 1.3
    - Exam 220-603 (Remote Technician): Objective 1.2
- Topic B:
    - Exam 220-601 (Essentials): Objective 1.3, Objective 1.4
    - Exam 220-602 (IT Technician): Objective 1.2, Objective 1.3
    - Exam 220-603 (Remote Technician): Objective 1.2
- Topic C:
    - Exam 220-601 (Essentials): Objective 1.3
    - Exam 220-602 (IT Technician): Objective 1.2
    - Exam 220-603 (Remote Technician): Objective 1.2
    - Exam 220-604 (Depot Technician): Objective 1.2
- Topic D:
    - Exam 220-602 (IT Technician): Objective 1.2
    - Exam 220-603 (Remote Technician): Objective 1.2

TOPIC A
Troubleshoot Display Devices

In the last lesson, you installed and configured computer hardware components. The next step is to troubleshoot hardware, and a good place to start is with the monitor. In this topic, you will start by troubleshooting display devices.

Display issues can be very disconcerting for users; after all, if they cannot see output on the monitor, it is as if they are flying blind. Most display device problems have simple causes that you can help users resolve easily. However, if the user cannot determine how to solve a particular issue, or if the symptoms indicate more extensive problems, you will need to step in to correct the situation.

Common Display Device Issues

There are many problems you might encounter when troubleshooting display devices.

Symptom	Possible Problems and Solutions
Monitor is dark or power indicator light is not lit.	This indicates general power problems, such as the power is not turned on, the power cable is disconnected, or the power is on but the monitor is plugged into a power strip, surge protector, or UPS that is not turned on. To correct the problem, turn on the power or power strip and reconnect the cables and cords. If a circuit breaker has tripped, reset it. Press or jiggle the power button on the monitor itself. A fuse in the monitor may have blown. **Do not open the monitor** to change a fuse; send the monitor out for repair, or replace it.
No image.	If there is no power light, check for and correct power problems. The data cable to the VGA port on the PC may be disconnected. Except on very old monitors, you will see an On Screen Display (OSD) message in this case, indicating a signal problem. Connect or re-seat the cables and connectors. If the cable is disconnected, and you do not see an OSD message, the monitor is bad. Brightness or contrast may be adjusted improperly. Adjust the settings using the monitor controls. (The OSD message is not affeted by brightness or contrast.) The monitor may be in power saving mode. The power light will typically change from green to solid or blinking amber. Press a key or move the mouse to wake up the monitor.

Symptom	*Possible Problems and Solutions*
Flickering or distortion.	The monitor cable may not be securely connected to the video port or there are bent or broken pins. Straighten bent pins and re-seat the cable. Use caution; a severely bent pin may break, in which case you will need to replace the monitor. A few cables are removable, in which case you can replace the cable.
	Incorrect display adapter and monitor device drivers may be in use. Through Device Manager, verify that the correct display adapter and monitor device drivers are in use.
	Refresh rate may be too low or too high. For viewer comfort, set the refresh rate as high as supported by the monitor and adapter card, but no higher. If the rate is too high, it can damage the monitor, and the monitor may go into power-saver mode.
	If the monitor is interlaced, replace it with a non-interlaced monitor. (Interlaced monitors refresh the pixel display with multiple passes of the electron beam; non-interlaced monitors refresh the entire display in a single pass. Generally, interlaced monitors have less flicker, but only if they support as high a refresh rate as a non-interlaced monitor.)
	There may be magnetic buildup. Degauss (demagnetize) the monitor by turning it off and on or by pressing the Degauss button.
	The monitor may be too close to other electronic or magnetic equipment. Relocate the monitor.
	The color depth setting may be incorrect. Adjust the color depth.
Monitor turns itself off.	Power management is enabled. You can adjust this either in CMOS settings or in the operating system Display Properties:
	• In CMOS, if the ACPI power settings are enabled, you can use the Display Properties Screen Saver and Monitor Power settings to control when the power is lowered or turned off to the monitor.
	• In Display Properties, on the Screen Saver page, adjust the Wait Time to meet the user's needs. Click the Power button to access the Power Schemes and settings for the Power Options Properties dialog box and set those as appropriate to the user's needs as well.
Application-specific problems.	If the screen goes blank, flickers, or acts erratic when a specific application is active, the application may require different color quality (also known as color depth) or screen resolution. Adjust settings on the Settings page of the Display Properties dialog box.
Display is all white.	This unusual state could be due to multiple bent or broken pins.
Monitor crackles or whines.	Crackling can be caused by dirt: clean the monitor. If there is dust inside the monitor, to avoid electrical hazards, **do not open the monitor!** If necessary, send it to a monitor repair facility for more in-depth cleaning.
	Crackling can be caused by failing electrical components; you will smell burning wire. Shut off and disconnect the monitor to eliminate fire and health hazards, and send the monitor for repair or replacement.
	If it whines, try moving the monitor away from sources of EMI, or replacing it with a quieter monitor. This can also be caused by damaged components, in which case you will need to send the monitor for repair or replacement if it is under warranty.

Symptom	Possible Problems and Solutions
Physical damage.	If the display device has been dropped or tipped, it may have sustained internal or external physical damage that cannot be corrected by any other troubleshooting technique. It is generally more economical and certainly safer to replace the device rather than attempting repair. However, if you must attempt repair on internal monitor components, avoid electrical hazards and **do not open the monitor.** Send the monitor to an authorized repair facility.

How to Troubleshoot Display Devices

Procedure Reference: Troubleshoot Monitor Problems

To troubleshoot monitor problems:

1. If the monitor will not come on and the power light is not lighting up either, verify that the monitor power cord is plugged in. Some steps to take in resolving this problem might include:

   - Plugging in a lamp or other device to the electrical outlet to verify that the outlet is working. If it is not, contact the electrician to fix the outlet and plug the monitor in to another outlet.

   - If the monitor is plugged in to a UPS, power strip, or surge protector, verify that the unit is turned on and has power.

   - Verify that the connections of the power cord and monitor cable are secure on the monitor as well as on the PC and electrical outlet.

   - If there is a fuse on the back of the monitor, remove the fuse and check for a broken wire. Replace the fuse with a good fuse or put the fuse back in if it isn't blown.

   - If the monitor still is not working, replace it with a known good monitor. Unplug the video cable from the monitor port on the computer and unplug the monitor electrical cord from the electrical outlet.

2. If the monitor is flickering and the display is distorted, you might try:

   - Verifying that the monitor cable is firmly plugged in to the monitor and to the computer.

   - If the monitor has one, press the Degauss button. A monitor with a Degauss button lets you demagnetize the monitor in an attempt to resolve color blotching problems or distortions. Most monitors automatically degauss when they are turned on.

   - Check the monitor cable for any bent pins and straighten them if necessary.

   - Move the monitor away from florescent lights, speakers, other monitors, or other electronic devices with powerful motors.

3. If the monitor power light is on, but nothing is displayed on the screen, you might:

- Determine if the power light is glowing green or orange. If the power light is orange, the monitor is in energy-saving mode or is getting no data from the computer. A green power light indicates that the monitor is on and is receiving data.

- Verify that the cable is connected to the monitor and to the PC.

- Adjust the contrast using the buttons on the monitor.

- Adjust the brightness using the buttons on the monitor.

- If it is still not working, swap the monitor with a known good monitor.

4. If the monitor comes on, but then goes blank after a few moments, you should:

- Determine if the monitor power light is glowing green or orange.

- If the light is orange, press a key to arouse the system from energy-saving mode. Some monitors only seem to wake up when the Windows key is pressed on the keyboard.

- Change the Power Management settings in CMOS to disable sleep or doze mode. The exact steps for this vary based on your system BIOS, so the setting might not be called Power Management and could be under a variety of different options.

- Temporarily change the power scheme settings within Windows. After you have determined that the monitor is not shutting down due to electrical malfunctions, the user can adjust these settings to meet his or her needs.

  a. Right-click the Windows Desktop and choose Properties.

  b. Display the Screen Saver page and click Power.

  c. From the Power Schemes drop-down list, select Always On.

  d. Change all settings in the Always On power scheme to Never.

5. If the monitor is making noises, determine whether it is making a crackling or whining noise:

- If it is a crackling noise, clean the monitor and try to vacuum or blow dust out of monitor vents. Remember, **do not open the monitor!** If necessary, send it to a monitor repair facility for more in-depth cleaning.

- If it is a whining noise, try moving the monitor. You might also try changing the refresh rate. If it is still whining, send it out to a monitor repair facility for adjustment and replace it with a quieter monitor.

6. If none of your attempts to correct the problem are successful, it might be because the monitor has failed and needs to be replaced. It is usually less expensive to replace the monitor than to send it out for repairs. To replace the monitor:

  a. Remove the existing monitor.

    1. Shut down the computer.

    2. Turn off the power on the computer and the monitor.

    3. Unplug the monitor from the electrical outlet.

    4. Unplug the monitor data cable from the monitor port.

  b. Install the new monitor.

    1. Connect the data cable from the monitor to the computer's monitor port.

    2. Plug the monitor power cable into an electrical outlet.

    3. Turn on the monitor and computer power.

4. Start the computer and verify that the new hardware was detected.

ACTIVITY 6-1

Troubleshooting Display Devices

Scenario:

Several users have opened trouble tickets with the support center about problems with their monitors. All of the users need their systems fixed before they can continue with their work. You need to resolve the problems. The following is a list of the trouble tickets you are responding to.

Ticket No.	Location	User Name	Issue
296001	Main building, 31H21	Robert Allen	The user's monitor is not coming on. The power light is not lighted. The user has checked that the monitor is plugged in and the monitor is connected to the system.
296002	Main building, 13B19	Althea Gavin	User's monitor is flickering and the display is distorted.
296003	Elmwood Place, cube 32	Chris Parker	The monitor power light is on, but there is no display.
296005	Main building, 62B35	Joan Paris	The monitor is making noises.

There is a simulated version of this activity available on the CD-ROM that shipped with this course. You can run this simulation on any Windows computer to review the activity after class, or as an alternative to performing the activity as a group in class. The activity simulation can be launched either directly from the CD-ROM by clicking the Interactives link and navigating to the appropriate one, or from the installed data file location by opening the C:\085820Data\Simulations\Lesson#\Activity# folder and double-clicking the executable (.exe) file.

What You Do	How You Do It
1. Resolve trouble ticket 296001.	a. **Unplug the monitor from the electrical outlet and plug in a lamp or other device** to verify that the monitor is plugged into a working outlet. If the device works, **plug the monitor back into the outlet.** If the device does not work, **contact the electrician to fix the outlet and plug the monitor in to another outlet.**
	b. If the outlet is on a UPS, surge protector, or power strip, **verify that the unit is turned on.**
	c. **Verify that the connections of the power cord and monitor cable are secure on the monitor as well as on the PC and electrical outlet.**
	d. **Try to turn on the monitor again.**
	e. If the monitor still doesn't come on, **replace the monitor with a known good monitor.**
2. Resolve trouble ticket 296002.	a. **Verify that the monitor cable is firmly plugged in to the monitor and to the computer.**
	b. If available, **press the Degauss button.**
	c. **Check the monitor cable for any bent pins and straighten if necessary.**
	d. **Move the monitor away from florescent light, speakers, other monitors, or other electronic devices with powerful motors.**

3. **Resolve trouble ticket 296003.**

   a. **Verify that the monitor cable is connected to the monitor and to the PC.**

   b. **Adjust the contrast using the buttons on the monitor.**

   c. **Adjust the brightness using the buttons on the monitor.**

   d. If it still is not working, **swap the monitor with one that you know works** to determine if the problem is with the monitor or the video card.

4. **Resolve trouble ticket 296005.**

   a. **Determine whether noise is crackling or whining noise.**

   b. If it is a crackling noise, **clean the monitor and try to vacuum or blow dust out of monitor vents. Do not open the monitor!** If necessary, send it out for more in-depth cleaning.

   c. If it is a whining noise, try the following to fix it: **move the monitor or change the refresh rate.** If it won't stop whining, send it out for adjustment and **replace the monitor with a quieter one.**

TOPIC B
Maintain and Troubleshoot Input Devices

In the previous topic, you corrected problems with display devices. You might also need to troubleshoot mice, keyboards, and other input devices. In this topic, you will maintain and troubleshoot input devices.

Input device problems can bring users to a standstill. If they cannot interact with their computer systems, they can get very little work done. They will turn to you as a computer support professional to resolve this issues for them very quickly. Fortunately, most input device troubleshooting is straightforward and relies most on common sense. Plus, you can avoid many input device problems if you can help computer users to care for these devices properly.

Common Input Device Issues

Common input devices such as keyboards and mice are inexpensive to replace if they are damaged beyond repair. Most routine troubleshooting involves cleaning the device or ensuring that it is properly connected. Specialty input devices such as a touch-screen monitor may have device-specific issues; if common troubleshooting techniques are not effective, check the device documentation for the appropriate next steps.

 Keyboards and pointing devices are so inexpensive, that unless the device is a special one designed for a specific need, it is more cost-effective to simply replace the device.

Specific Keyboard Problems
There are some common problems you will encounter that are specific to keyboards.

Symptom	Possible Problems	Solutions
Keys stick.	Foreign matter under the keys causes contact to be made with the wrong key or not at all. Spilled liquid has dried and become sticky.	Physically shake the keyboard upside down or use compressed air to blow out debris. Take care using compressed air on delicate laptop or mini keyboards; the force of the air can blow off the keys and may break the key mechanism. Keep the air can upright to keep the propellant in liquid form, and keep it at a safe distance. For liquid spills, remove the keys and use rubbing alcohol and a lint-free swab to remove the buildup. (You might have to scrape away thick accumulations of liquid.)

Symptom	Possible Problems	Solutions
User with physical limitations is currently unable to use the standard keyboard.	Accessibility features for the keyboard have not been enabled.	In Control Panel, enable the Accessibility options such as StickyKeys, FilterKeys and/or ToggleKeys to enable handicapped users to more easily use the keyboard.
No input is sent when keys are pressed.	Keyboard unplugged. Keyboard plugged into mouse port. Keyboard interface contains bent or broken pins. User attempted to connect the keyboard using a PS/2-to-USB adapter on a keyboard that doesn't support this translation. Keyboard port on the computer is damaged.	Physically check the connections and reseat cables if necessary. Make sure a PS/2 keyboard is not plugged into the PS/2 mouse port. For wireless keyboards, there may be connectivity issues, interference, or frequency conflicts from other nearby devices such as cell phones, baby monitors, and so on. Wireless devices also require batteries, so you might need to replace the batteries. For USB devices on a hub, make sure the hub is plugged in and is supplying power. If other devices are using too much power, the USB hub or port might shut down.
Keyboard-related message or beep codes given during computer boot.	Keyboard might be disconnected or plugged into the mouse port. Keyboard might be damaged.	Physically check the connections. Replace the keyboard.
Wrong characters are displayed on the screen when user inputs information.	The language was changed in the Keyboard Properties within Windows. Short or incorrect contacts being made due to beverage spilled into the keyboard or another foreign matter in the keyboard. Keyboard interface on the computer is damaged.	Check the Keyboard Properties settings, then physically check the keyboard for foreign matter under the keys.
Multimedia buttons not working properly.	Device driver needs updating. File related to the button has been moved, renamed, or modified in some way.	Make sure the proper driver is installed. Check for and download updated drivers from the manufacturer's website. Verify that the file associated with a given button is correctly named, and if any options are needed, that they are correctly formatted.

Symptom	Possible Problems	Solutions
New keyboard won't plug into the same port as the old keyboard.	Very old keyboards used a large 5-pin DIN connector. Today's keyboards use either the smaller 6-pin mini-DIN connector, also called a PS/2 style connector, or a USB connector.	In some cases, because the keyboards are the same except for the connector, you can buy an adapter to allow you to plug the new keyboard into the old port on the system board. The simplest approach is to make sure your system and peripherals have compatible ports and connectors.

Specific Pointing Device Problems

There are some common problems that you will encounter that are common to mice, trackballs, and other pointing devices.

Symptom	Possible Problems	Solutions
Mouse pointer jumps around on the screen.	Mouse ball or rollers are dirty. Mouse has reached the end of its useful life. Mouse is not being rolled over a flat surface. Mouse is being rolled over a dirty mouse pad. Mouse settings are incorrect.	Visually inspect the mouse, the mouse pad, and the area around the mouse. Clean the mouse; replace the mouse pad. An optical mouse might need a different mouse pad because white, light-colored, or patterned pads might interfere with the optical sensor. Use the Device Manager and Help And Support Center utilities to check the status of the pointing device. With an older mouse, regular maintenance might reduce this problem, but not eliminate it. From Control Panel, open Printers And Other Hardware. Click Mouse. Check the pointer speed, click speed, and other settings that might affect performance.

Symptom	Possible Problems	Solutions
Wireless mouse is in use and mouse pointer is jumping around or not moving.	Batteries low. Obstruction between the mouse and the receiver. Connection lost.	Check the batteries and replace if necessary. Verify that there is no obstruction between the transmitter and the receiver. Press the Reset or Connect buttons on each device to try to re-establish the connection. Replace the batteries in the mouse. Press the Reset or Connect buttons on each device again. Verify that the receiver device is connected to the port. Try a corded mouse connected to the port. If this works, replace the cordless mouse with either a corded mouse or another cordless mouse.
Mouse works sometimes, but not others.	IRQ conflict between the mouse and the modem (or another device). (This is a rare occurrence in modern computer systems.)	Use Device Manager to check for hardware conflicts; change the mouse to an open IRQ such as IRQ 12. For wireless mice, there may be connectivity issues, interference, or frequency conflicts from other nearby devices such as cell phones, baby monitors, and so on. Wireless devices also require batteries, so you might need to replace the batteries.
Mouse is not working.	Mouse is not plugged in. Mouse is plugged in to the keyboard port. Mouse was connected after the computer was started. Some pointing devices require special drivers and possibly additional software to function properly. Pointing device is not supported in the operating system. Driver for the pointing device was corrupted or outdated.	Physically check the pointing device connection. Use Device Manager to verify that the correct driver is installed. Check the pointing device's documentation to see if any additional software is required for it to function properly. Check the website of the device manufacturer to see if newer drivers or software should be installed.

Symptom	Possible Problems	Solutions
USB mouse is not working properly.	A problem with the root hub or USB host controller. Mouse is plugged into an unpowered USB hub and is not getting enough power to operate properly.	Check the status of the root hub or USB host controller in Device Manager. Plug the mouse directly into a USB port on the computer; if this works, and the hub is working properly, the mouse is probably not getting enough power. Physically remove some of the devices on the same hub as the mouse to another port or hub or use a powered USB hub.

Input Device Maintenance Techniques

You can avoid many input device problems if you maintain common devices properly.

● Occasionally disconnect keyboards and mice and gently wipe them clean.

● Clean loose debris from inside a trackball or mouse.

● Gently shake an upside-down keyboard to remove debris.

● Provide a clean, flat mouse pad or other mousing surface.

● To avoid spills that can damage input devices, keep food and liquids away from computer systems.

● Replace cordless device batteries regularly.

Cleaning Mice and Trackballs

To clean a standard mouse or trackball, remove the ball, clean the rollers with rubbing alcohol and a lint-free swab, wipe the mouse ball down with the alcohol, and reassemble the mouse once it is dry.

To clean a wireless mouse, use a soft brush or compressed air to clean dust or debris around the optical sensor. Keep the compressed air at a distance to avoid freezing the sensor plastics.

How to Maintain and Troubleshoot Input Devices

Procedure Reference: Troubleshoot Keyboard and Pointing Device Problems

To troubleshoot some of the most common problems with keyboards and pointing devices:

1. If the keyboard is not working at all:
    a. Verify that the keyboard is plugged in to the keyboard port.
    b. Verify that the keyboard cable is securely connected. Some keyboard cables need to be plugged in to the keyboard as well as to the system's keyboard port.
    c. If the keyboard still does not work, switch it with a known good keyboard. Pull the connector straight out of the port so as not to bend any of the pins.
    d. If the keyboard still does not work, verify that CMOS is configured to recognize the keyboard.
    e. If the keyboard still does not work, test the keyboard port with a multimeter. Pin 4 should have a reading of +5 V and pin 3 is ground. If the port is damaged, you will need to replace the system board.

2. If the keyboard is producing the wrong characters when the user types:
    a. Verify that no Function key, Scroll Lock, or other key is enabled or stuck down.
    b. Verify that the correct drivers are in use.
    c. If that is not the problem, replace with a known good keyboard. Unplug the keyboard and plug in the replacement keyboard.

3. If liquids are spilled on the keyboard, it is most likely permanently damaged. Remind users that all drinks must be covered when used near computer equipment. However, you can try:
    a. Unplugging the keyboard and turning it upside down over a wastebasket.
    b. Moving the keyboard around to remove as much liquid as possible.
    c. Rinsing keyboard in running water if the liquid was sticky (soda pop or sweetened drinks).
    d. Setting it on end to dry for several days.
    e. Replacing the keyboard with another keyboard so that the user can get back to work until the keyboard is ready to use again.

4. If the mouse pointer is jumping around on the screen:
    a. Clean the rollers inside the mouse.
    b. Replace the mouse. Unplug the mouse and plug in the new mouse.

5. If a cordless mouse is in use and the mouse pointer is not moving on the screen:
    a. Verify that there is no obstruction between the transmitter and the receiver.
    b. Press the Reset or Connect buttons on each device to try to re-establish the connection. Replace the batteries in the mouse. Press the Reset or Connect buttons on each device again.
    c. Verify that the receiver device is connected to the port.
    d. Try a corded mouse connected to the port. If this works, replace the cordless mouse with either a corded mouse or another cordless mouse.

ACTIVITY 6-2

Maintaining and Troubleshooting Input Devices

Scenario:

Several users have opened trouble tickets with the support center about problems with their keyboards and pointing devices. All of the users need their systems fixed before they can continue with their work. You need to resolve the problems and get the users back to work. The following is a list of the trouble tickets you are responding to.

Ticket No.	Location	User Name	Issue
299001	Elmwood Place, cube 24	Al Mikels	The user's keyboard is not working at all.
299002	Training center, room 1	Andy Potarnia	User's keyboard is producing the wrong characters when he types.
299003	Main building, 42B31	Toma Wright	User's mouse jumping around on the screen.
299004	Main building, 31C93	Jason Zeh	User has a cordless mouse, and the mouse pointer is not moving on the screen.
299005	Main building, 26B15	Daniel Bidlack	Root beer has been spilled on user's keyboard.

 There is a simulated version of this activity available on the CD-ROM that shipped with this course. You can run this simulation on any Windows computer to review the activity after class, or as an alternative to performing the activity as a group in class. The activity simulation can be launched either directly from the CD-ROM by clicking the Interactives link and navigating to the appropriate one, or from the installed data file location by opening the C:\085820Data\Simulations\Lesson#\Activity# folder and double-clicking the executable (.exe) file.

What You Do	How You Do It
1. If you have been assigned trouble ticket 299001, **resolve trouble ticket 299001.**	a. **Verify that the keyboard is plugged in to the keyboard port.** b. **Verify that the keyboard cable is securely connected.** c. If the keyboard still does not work, **switch with a known good keyboard.** d. If the keyboard still does not work, **verify that the keyboard is recognized by the CMOS.** e. If the keyboard still does not work, **replace the system board.**
2. If you have been assigned trouble ticket 299002, **resolve trouble ticket 299002.**	a. **Verify that no Function key, Scroll Lock, or other key is enabled or stuck down.** b. If that is not the problem, **replace keyboard with a known good keyboard.**
3. If you have been assigned trouble ticket 299003, **resolve trouble ticket 299003.**	a. **Make sure the surface the mouse is being rolled on is clean and smooth.** b. **Clean the rollers inside the mouse.** c. **Clean the mouse ball by blowing on it or by using warm water and mild detergent.** d. From the Start menu, **choose Control Panel. Click Printers And Other Hardware. Click Mouse. Check the pointer speed, click speed, and other settings that might affect performance.** e. If the problem is not resolved, **replace the mouse.**

4. If you have been assigned trouble ticket 299004, **resolve trouble ticket 299004.**

    a. **Verify that there is no obstruction between the transmitter and receiver devices.**

    b. **Press the Reset or Connect buttons on each device to try to re-establish the connection.**

    c. **Replace the batteries in the mouse.**

    d. **Press the Reset or Connect buttons on each device.**

    e. **Verify that the receiver device is connected to the port.**

    f. **Try reinstalling the latest software or driver for the cordless mouse.**

    g. If it still has not been resolved, **try a corded mouse connected to the port.**

    h. If the previous step worked, **replace the cordless mouse with either a corded or another cordless mouse.**

5. If you have been assigned trouble ticket 299005, **resolve trouble ticket 299005.**

    a. **Remind users that all drinks must be covered when used near computer equipment.**

    b. **Unplug the keyboard and turn it upside down over the wastebasket.**

    c. **Move the keyboard around to remove as much liquid as possible.**

    d. **Rinse the keyboard in running water.**

    e. **Set on end to dry for several days.**

    f. **Swap in an alternate keyboard so the user can get back to work until the original keyboard is ready.**

TOPIC C
Troubleshoot Adapter Cards

In the last topic, you resolved problems with input devices. Adapter cards can also have problems. In this topic, you will troubleshoot adapter cards.

Your mechanic often knows just what component in your car is acting up based on your description of the way your vehicle is acting. Knowing the common problems associated with adapter cards will enable you to quickly correct the problems your users encounter. Being able to quickly resolve problems for your users will make them more productive.

Common Adapter Card Issues

Other than hardware or system resource conflicts, there are several common problems you will encounter with adapter cards.

Symptom	Possible Causes and Solutions
Adapter works until you replace the system case.	• Possible cause: Adapter card is damaged or grounded against the case, or the cables are pinched, compressed, or pulled out if there is not enough room for all components in a low-profile or compact case. • Solution: Visually inspect card and case for bent or damaged areas. If the card is in contact with the case, it can cause electrical shorts or other faults.
Card works in all slots but one.	• Possible cause: Bus slot damaged. • Solution: Visually inspect the bus slot. Test the bus slot with a multimeter; voltages should be within prescribed ranges for the slot and adapter card. Take care when testing voltages on a PCI slot; if you short pins you can damage the system board or other components. If the damage is confirmed, use another slot or replace the system board. • Possible cause: Grounding or heat-related problems due to proximity to another card. This is very likely with the larger video cards with large heat sink/fan assemblies. Some cards can take up two slots and will generate considerable heat, which can overheat a card fractions of an inch away and with little if any airflow. • Solution: Move the cards to slots that are further apart. • Possible cause: Certain cards can conflict with cards in other slots. This is more common in older systems. • Solution: Check the manufacturer's recommendations for spacing out cards, or using a specific recommended slot (for example, install a particular card in the slot closest to the processor).
Card tests fine and slot tests fine, but services are unavailable.	• Possible cause: Cables not connected, loose, or damaged. • Solution: Visually inspect cards and cables and reconnect if necessary.

Symptom	Possible Causes and Solutions
Services or devices work intermittently.	Possible causes: • Adapter card (or cards) not seated properly. • Hardware resource conflict. • Adapter card physically damaged. • Adapter card electronically damaged. Solutions: • Reseat adapter card (or cards). • Resolve any hardware resource conflicts. • Replace any adapter card that is physically damaged. • Replace any adapter card that is electronically damaged.

How to Troubleshoot Adapter Cards

Procedure Reference: Troubleshoot PC Adapter Card Problems

To troubleshoot some of the most common problems with adapter cards:

1. If you are having adapter card problems:

   a. Locate the adapter card and make sure that it is fully seated into the slot, and then see if this fixed the problem.

   b. If a video card is having troubles, determine if it is in a PCI, ISA, or AGP slot. If it is not in the AGP slot, try moving the card to another slot. Because there is only one AGP slot on the system board, you cannot move an AGP card to a different slot.

   c. Remove the card and press down on all four corners of socketed chips to verify that they are fully seated, and then reinstall the card.

   d. If another hardware device has recently been added to the system, check Device Manager and verify that there is not a resource conflict between the device and the adapter card.

   e. Verify that the drivers are properly installed. You could use the Add/Remove Hardware Control Panel utility to remove all the drivers for the card, then restart the system. It should detect the "new" hardware and install the drivers again. You can also remove the card, then restart to remove the drivers. Then, reinstall the cards. When you restart, the drivers should be installed. If you're servicing a legacy system that doesn't support PnP configuration, consult your adapter card's documentation to determine how to verify, remove, or install the necessary drivers.

   f. If necessary, update the firmware or drivers associated with the device.

2. If you suspect a resource conflict between devices:

   a. Open Device Manager and display the Resources By Connection view.

   b. Determine if there is a conflict between any devices. ISA cards cannot use the same IRQ as another card. IRQs have been set aside for PCI cards to share with each other. However, the PCI cards cannot share that IRQ with ISA cards.

   c. Change the conflicting resource to an unused setting. This might be the IRQ, DMA, or I/O address.

   d. Verify that both devices now work properly.

3. If you suspect a card was damaged due to electrostatic discharge (from improper handling, power surges, or a lightning storm):

   a. Check whether the card in question is listed in Device Manager.

   b. Display Properties for the card and verify whether the Device Status indicates that it is working properly.

   c. If the device is not working properly, click Troubleshoot and follow the Troubleshoot Wizard steps.

   d. If the problem is not resolved, replace the card and verify that the problem has been resolved.

4. If you have a problem with a device, and replacing the device, device cable, and device power cord doesn't fix it, then you should suspect the adapter card. This applies to any adapter card, including ISA, PCI, AGP, and others. To test if this is the problem:

   a. Remove the problem device from the port.

   b. Connect a replacement device to the port.

   c. If necessary, install drivers for the new device. If it works, then the adapter card is okay. If it doesn't work, then try replacing the cable between the device and the port.

ACTIVITY 6-3

Troubleshooting Adapter Cards

Scenario:

The call center has received several trouble calls that are related to internal PC adapter card problems. You need to help resolve the problems and get the users back to work. The following is a list of the current trouble tickets.

Ticket No.	Location	User Name	Issue
399001	Main building, 33J27	Aminah Sinclair	The user is still having problems with his video system. All monitor problems were reviewed and none of these resolved the problem. Therefore, it points toward a problem with the video card.
399002	Elmwood Place, cube 14	Conroy Ives	Last night a lightning storm struck. Most equipment was fine, but this user is having problems with getting on the network. All other users in the area are connecting without problems.

 There is a simulated version of this activity available on the CD-ROM that shipped with this course. You can run this simulation on any Windows computer to review the activity after class, or as an alternative to performing the activity as a group in class. The activity simulation can be launched either directly from the CD-ROM by clicking the Interactives link and navigating to the appropriate one, or from the installed data file location by opening the C:\085820Data\Simulations\Lesson#\Activity# folder and double-clicking the executable (.exe) file.

What You Do	How You Do It
1. If it has been assigned to you, **respond to trouble ticket 399001.**	a. **Locate the video card and make sure it is fully seated into the slot, then see if this fixed the problem.**
	b. **Determine if the video card is in a PCI, PCI-E, or AGP slot.** If it is not in an AGP slot, **try moving the card to another slot.**
	c. If you are still having problems, **remove the card and press down on all four corners of socketed chips to verify they are fully seated, then reinstall the card.**
	d. If a hardware device has been recently added to the system, **check Device Manager and verify that there is not a resource conflict between the device and the video card.**
	e. If you are still having problems, **try a known good working video card.**
2. If it has been assigned to you, **respond to trouble ticket 399002.**	a. **Check whether the network card is listed in Device Manager.**
	b. **Display properties for the network card and verify whether the Device Status indicates it is working properly.**
	c. If the device is not working properly, **click Troubleshoot and follow the Troubleshoot Wizard steps.**
	d. If the problem is not resolved, **replace the network card.**
	e. **Verify that the system can now connect to the network.**

TOPIC D
Troubleshoot Multimedia Devices

In the last topic, you resolved problems with adapter cards. Another group of peripheral devices that you need to be able to troubleshoot is multimedia devices. In this topic, you will troubleshoot multimedia devices.

Although multimedia devices typically aren't critical for a user to complete his or her work, they are usually the devices that give the user the most satisfaction while working. As an A+ technician, you can keep your users happy by making sure they're able to take full advantage of the multimedia components included with their computers.

Common Multimedia Device Issues

There are common symptoms that you can encounter when troubleshooting multimedia devices.

Symptom	Possible Problem and Solution
No sound coming out of the speakers. However, the speakers worked previously.	**Problem:** • Power for the speakers isn't turned on. • Volume for the speakers has been turned down too low. • The speaker cord has come unplugged from the computer or is plugged into the wrong port. • The volume has been muted within Windows. • If you're playing an audio CD, the cable that should connect the sound card to the CD drive might have been disconnected. • Damaged wire or plug. • Missing or corrupt audio driver/mixer device. • Damaged electronics in powered or amplified speakers. • If you are playing an optical disk, the disk might be unbalanced. A user might have placed a label on the disk, or the disk could be cracked or chipped. If it is cracked in the center, it will not remain clipped in the spindle. **Solution:** • Verify that the speakers are plugged into the correct port, turned on, and connected to the computer. • Plug the speakers into another device to verify that you can hear audio. • Check the basic Windows audio functions by playing a WAV file (such as a Windows system sound) or by changing the master volume slider setting; you should hear a sound confirming the setting change. • Replace cables or plugs. • Install or reinstall drivers. • Check the volume settings within Windows using Control Panel or the Volume System Tray icon. • Check the cable that connects the CD drive to the sound card; reseat or replace. • If speakers are damaged, replace. • Make sure the CD/DVD drive is balanced. If necessary, turn the computer case so that the drive is horizontal. If a disk is physically damaged, discard it.

Symptom	*Possible Problem and Solution*
No sound coming out of the speakers. The speakers have never worked.	Problem: • The drivers are not installed or are corrupt. • The speakers, sound card, or both are bad. Solution: • Verify that the speakers are plugged into the correct port, turned on, and connected to the computer. • Check the volume settings within Windows using Control Panel or the Volume System Tray icon. • Verify that you've configured the sound card properly within Windows by using the Sounds And Audio Devices Properties dialog box. • Check Device Manager to make sure it is reporting any problems with the sound card and its drivers. • Install or reinstall the most current drivers for the sound card and computer operating system. • Try plugging the speakers into a sound card that you know works to determine if they're bad. • Try plugging a known good pair of speakers into the suspect sound card to determine if it is bad.
The microphone doesn't work or is too low.	Problem: • The microphone is plugged into the wrong port on the sound card. • The microphone is muted within Volume Control. • The microphone is bad. • The microphone is not selected as the input device. • The microphone is not sensitive enough, or the microphone came from another system and its sensitivity does not match the sound device's specifications. Solution: • Verify that the microphone is connected to the correct port on the sound card. • Check the microphone volume settings by choosing Start→All Programs→Accessories→Entertainment→Volume Control. • Test the microphone on a computer with a properly functioning sound card and microphone. • Connect a known good microphone to the computer. • Switch the audio mixer software to Recording and verify that the microphone is selected as the input device. In Windows, you can use the Sounds And Audio Devices Control Panel application to manage audio settings. • In Windows, you can enable Mic Boost in the Sounds And Audio Devices Control Panel application.

How to Troubleshoot Multimedia Devices

Procedure Reference: Troubleshoot Multimedia Devices

To troubleshoot multimedia devices:

1. If the speakers do not come on and the power light is not lighting up either, verify that the speakers' power cord is plugged in. Some steps to take in resolving this problem might include:

   - Plugging in a lamp or other device to the electrical outlet to verify that the outlet is working. If it is not, contact the electrician to fix the outlet and plug the speakers into another outlet.

   - If the speakers are plugged into a UPS, power strip, or surge protector, verify that the power source is turned on and has power.

   - Verify that the connections of the power cord and speaker cable are secure on the speakers as well as on the PC and electrical outlet.

   - If the speakers still aren't working, replace them with known good speakers.

2. If the speakers' power light is on, but no sound comes out, you might:

   - Verify that the volume on the speakers is turned up high enough to be audible.

   - Verify that the volume within Windows isn't muted or set too low.

   - Make sure the speaker cable is connected to the speakers and to the appropriate port on the computer's sound card.

   - Verify that the cable used to connect the CD drive to the sound card is connected properly.

   - Make sure that the CD drive is functioning properly. Test whether the speakers work by using the Sounds tab of the Sounds And Audio Devices Properties dialog box in Control Panel.

   - Check the configuration of the sound card within the Sounds And Audio Devices Properties dialog box.

   - Install the most current version of the sound card drivers for the computer's operating system.

   - Try the speakers on a known good sound card. If they work, the computer's sound card must be bad.

   - Swap the potentially faulty speakers with known good speakers. If the known good speakers work, the original speakers must be bad.

3. If a user is unable to use his or her microphone with voice recognition software, you should:

   - Check that the microphone is plugged into the correct port on the sound card.

   - Verify the microphone volume settings using Volume Control.

   - Connect a known good microphone to the computer. If it works, the original microphone is bad.

   - Connect the problematic microphone to a known good sound card. If it works, the original sound card is bad.

ACTIVITY 6-4

Troubleshooting Multimedia Devices

Scenario:

Two users have opened trouble tickets with the support center about problems with their speakers. You have been asked to resolve these problems. The following is a list of the trouble tickets.

Ticket No.	Location	User Name	Issue
325145	Main building, 31H21	Reilly Smith	No sound is coming out of the user's speakers. The power light on the speakers is not lit.
325146	Main building, 13B19	Alice Griffin	No sound is coming out of the user's speakers. The power light on the speakers is lit.

What You Do	How You Do It
1. If it has been assigned to you, **respond to trouble ticket 325145.**	a. **Make sure that the speakers are plugged into a power source.**
	b. **Verify that the power source is working properly by plugging a known good device into the power source.**
	c. **Try the speakers on a known good sound card.** If the speakers don't work, **replace the failed speakers on the computer.**

2. If it has been assigned to you, **respond to trouble ticket 325146.**

a. **Verify that the volume on the speakers is turned up high enough to be audible.**

b. **Verify that the volume within Windows isn't muted or set too low.**

c. **Make sure the speaker cable is connected to the speakers and to the appropriate port on the computer's sound card.**

d. **Update the speaker drivers.**

e. **Check the configuration of the sound card.**

f. **Try the speakers on a known good sound card.** If the speakers work, **replace the failed sound card on the computer.** If the speakers don't work, **replace the failed speakers.**

Lesson 6 Follow-up

In this lesson, you maintained and corrected problems with peripheral components. Knowing how to prevent and solve problems with computer peripherals enables you to help your users perform their duties.

1. **What types of maintenance tasks will be part of your daily routine?**

2. **Which peripheral components would you prefer to troubleshoot?**

7 Troubleshooting System Components

Lesson Time: 4 hour(s)

Lesson Objectives:

In this lesson, you will troubleshoot system components.

You will:

- Troubleshoot storage devices.
- Test and troubleshoot power supplies.
- Test and troubleshoot memory.
- Test and troubleshoot CPUs.
- Test and troubleshoot system boards.

Introduction

In the last lesson, you maintained and troubleshot peripheral components. Internal system components also cause problems for users. In this lesson, you will maintain and troubleshoot system components.

It's only a matter of time before a personal computer's internal system components experience problems. As an A+ technician, many of the service calls that you respond to will involve troubleshooting system components, and your ability to quickly and effectively diagnose and solve the problems will be essential in maintaining the satisfaction level of the users you support.

This lesson covers all or part of the following CompTIA A+ (2006) certification objectives:

- Topic A:
    - Exam 220-601 (Essentials): Objective 1.3, Objective 3.3
    - Exam 220-602 (IT Technician): Objective 1.2, Objective 1.3, Objective 3.1
    - Exam 220-603 (Remote Technician): Objective 1.2, Objective 1.3

- Topic B:
    - Exam 220-601 (Essentials): Objective 1.3
    - Exam 220-602 (IT Technician): Objective 1.2
    - Exam 220-603 (Remote Technician): Objective 1.2
    - Exam 220-604 (Depot Technician): Objective 1.2

- Topic C:
    - Exam 220-601 (Essentials): Objective 1.1, Objective 1.3
    - Exam 220-602 (IT Technician): Objective 1.2
    - Exam 220-603 (Remote Technician): Objective 1.2
    - Exam 220-604 (Depot Technician): Objective 1.2

- Topic D:
    - Exam 220-601 (Essentials): Objective 1.3
    - Exam 220-602 (IT Technician): Objective 1.2
    - Exam 220-603 (Remote Technician): Objective 1.2
    - Exam 220-604 (Depot Technician): Objective 1.2

- Topic E:
    - Exam 220-601 (Essentials): Objective 1.3
    - Exam 220-602 (IT Technician): Objective 1.2
    - Exam 220-603 (Remote Technician): Objective 1.2
    - Exam 220-604 (Depot Technician): Objective 1.2

TOPIC A
Troubleshoot Storage Devices

In this lesson, you will troubleshoot system components. The first component inside the computer case that might need troubleshooting are the storage devices. In this topic, you will troubleshoot storage devices.

Storage devices, because they are one of the few system components that contain moving parts, are particularly susceptible to wear and damage. There is a saying that there are two types of storage devices: the ones that have failed and the ones that are failing. Because these devices support so many system functions, it is not always obvious that the device is the culprit, yet storage device problems (particularly those involving hard drives) can have a truly devastating effect on a system and on a user's productivity. Therefore, being able to spot, identify, and correct storage device problems early, before they cause data loss, will be an important skill for you as a support technician.

Common Storage Device Issues

Each type of storage device has issues specific to that device. You will need to recognize the symptoms, problems, and solutions for each issue.

Troubleshooting Hard Drives

There are many problems you might encounter when troubleshooting hard drives.

Hard Drive Symptom	Possible Problem and Solution
Boot error message: Drive Not Ready—System Halted	Drive is damaged. Drive is not configured for Master or Cable Select as appropriate to the system. Data cable is not connected or incorrectly connected to the drive. Solution: Visually inspect the drive and its connections, correct as needed.
POST error codes in the 17xx range	1701: Drive not found. 1702: Hard drive adapter not found. 1703: Hard drive failure. 1704: Hard drive or adapter failure. 1780, 1790: Hard drive 0 failed. 1781, 1791: Hard drive 1 failed. 1782: Hard drive controller failed. Solution: Visually inspect connections and reconnect drive. Replace failed component.

Hard Drive Symptom	Possible Problem and Solution
Can't read from or write to the drive	Bad sectors on the drive. IRQ conflicts. Drive failure. Virus attack. Some problems that appear to be storage device problems are actually virus infections. These can cause physical damage as well, but they usually just damage the files on the storage device and not the device itself. Solution: • Run chkdsk to try to recover information from bad sectors and to mark those sectors as unusable. • Check Device Manager for hardware resource conflicts and for indications of drive failure. • Run virus check software and remove any viruses found.
Computer will not boot	Drive disconnected, damaged, not recognized by the BIOS. Solution: Visually inspect and reconnect drive. Enable drive in CMOS setup utility.
Repeated grinding noises	Physically damaged drive, most likely due to a head crash. Solution: Replace the hard drive. Remind users and technicians not to move a machine while it is in use because that is the most common cause of head crashes.
Data corruption or utilities not running properly	System not being shut down properly, drive is in the process of failing, virus. Solution: Educate users on how to properly shut down the system. Run virus protection software. Back up the data, replace failed or failing drive.
Hard drive is slow	Drive is too full or fragmented. The hard drive controller is too slow. An incorrect (and slower) cable was used to connect the drive. Solution: Delete all unneeded files. Defragment the drive. Verify and replace the hard drive cable if necessary.

Troubleshooting Optical Drives

There are some common problems you will encounter with optical drives.

Optical Drive Symptom	Possible Problem and Solution
Cannot insert optical disc into drive	Misaligned case, which prevents drive door from opening and the tray from moving in and out properly. Solution: Realign the optical drive within the computer case.
Drive mechanism won't pull disc or tray in	The gears may be stripped, especially if the user pushed on the tray directly rather than using the buttons to manipulate the drive. Solution: Replace the drive and educate the user on how to properly insert and remove discs.

Optical Drive Symptom	*Possible Problem and Solution*
Unable to read an optical disc	Inexpensive trays in drives or stickers that don't cover the entire surface of the disc can cause it to wobble because it throws the balance of the drive off. Data can be difficult or impossible to read because of the wobble. Solution: Remove the sticker if it is uneven. If the tray is the problem, replace the drive.
Drive will not release the disc	Sometimes this occurs because the software is still accessing the disc, or the tray can simply be stuck. Solution: Carefully insert a straightened paper clip in the hole in the front of the drive and gently push in to release the catch on the drive so that you can remove the disc.
Can't hear sound or music when playing an audio CD	The wires from the CD drive to the sound card are disconnected. Other possibilities are that the speakers are turned off or down or that the sounds were muted through the Windows settings. Solution: Connect the wires between the CD drive and the sound card. Verify that sound is not muted and that the speakers' volume is set properly.
Intermittent optical drive problems	Corrupted or outdated drivers. Solution: Uninstall and reinstall the drivers. Install updated drivers.
Unable to read CDs you have burned	Possibly data corruption in the burn process, attempting to burn at higher speeds than the media supports, overtaxing the processor by running other programs while burning, problem with the CD burning application. Most programs will warn the user of any such problems, but sometimes users turn off such notifications (or verification of the burn) and will not be informed there is a problem. Solution: Re-create the CD with proper settings.
Unable to view DVD movies	Solution: Make sure that your drive, video card, and its drivers support DVD video, and that you have the necessary software to play a movie.

Troubleshooting Floppy Drives and Tape Drives

There are some common problems you will encounter with other drive types.

Other Drive Type Symptom	*Possible Problem and Solution*
Unable to write to a floppy disk	The disk might be write-protected, not yet formatted, or the floppy disk drive might have failed. Solution: Remove write protection from the disk. Format the disk. Replace the floppy disk drive.
Unable to read a floppy disk	The disk might be corrupt or infected with a virus. Solution: Scan the floppy disk for viruses. Check to see if you can read the disk in another computer's floppy disk drive. Verify that the disk wasn't formatted with another operating system.

Other Drive Type Symptom	Possible Problem and Solution
Unable to remove floppy disk	If you insert a floppy disk with a damaged metal shield, it might not come out all the way when extracted. Do not yank it out and leave the shield and spring inside the drive; you might need to remove and open the drive to remove the disk. Solution: Back up data from damaged floppies and discard them.
Unable to insert a tape cartridge into an internal tape drive	The computer case is not properly aligned with the chassis, making the opening for the internal drive difficult to access. Solution: Check the alignment of the computer case and correct it if necessary.
Unable to read from or write to a tape cartridge	The tape drive might be dirty or the tape cartridge itself might be damaged. There might be foreign material or a broken door flap obstructing the drive. Solution: Clean the tape drive. Remove or repair obstructions. If possible, attempt to read the tape cartridge in another tape drive. If you can't read the tape cartridge, odds are it is corrupted and might not be recoverable. If the tape cartridge is physically damaged, discard it. (Always keep multiple backups of important data.)

ATA Drive Troubleshooting Tips

There are some important points to keep in mind as you troubleshoot PATA drive problems.

PATA Issue	Description
Configuring single drives	If you have one drive on a channel, depending on the manufacturer, it might need to be configured as single—not master or slave. Alternatively, set it to cable select and plug it in to the Parallel ATA cable connector furthest from the motherboard. Check your manufacturer's documentation for the proper procedures and settings for your drive.
Configuring two drives	With two drives on a channel, set both to cable select or configure them both manually, setting one to master and the other to slave. Don't mix these settings by setting one to be cable select and the other as either master or slave. Make sure both aren't set to master or slave.
Removing a drive	If you remove the second Parallel ATA hard disk from a computer with two drives installed, verify that the disk that remains in the computer is set as single. The Master/Slave setting should be used only when there is more than one hard disk in a system; otherwise, a disk-controller error will occur when you restart the computer.

PATA Issue	Description
Moving to another system	If you need to move a Parallel ATA drive from one computer to another, you likely won't run into problems. However, especially if there is a great difference in age between the computers, you might run into problems. The BIOS of another computer might not support LBA or Large (ECHS), or the computer might not be set up for it. In that case, data on the hard drive would be lost if you install it in that system. You can change the mode for a hard drive (from LBA to Large, or vice versa), but this poses a risk of data loss. Typically, you should only set the mode when you first install the disk. If you do need to change it, make sure you have a working backup of all of the data on the disk before doing so.

There are several points to keep in mind when troubleshooting SATA drive problems.

SATA Issue	Description
Controller card	Not all SATA controller cards are supported on all operating systems. Check the vendor specifications for the operating system or software you are using.
Controller driver	SATA drives themselves do not require drivers, but the SATA controller does. Ensure that you are using the latest version.
Drive not detected	If you install a fresh copy of your operating system and the SATA drive is not detected, then restart the setup process and press F6 when prompted to install the driver.
Drive size limitation	If the SATA controller drivers are not loaded during the operating system installation, then the drive will only report the 137 GB capacity supported natively by the operating system.
Speed limitation	1.5 gigabits per second (gbps) SATA cards do not always auto negotiate with newer 3.0 gbps drives. Use jumper settings on the drive to limit the transfer rate to 1.5 gps.

SCSI Drive Troubleshooting Tips

Keep some basic points in mind as you troubleshoot SCSI drive problems.

Issue	Description
IDs and termination	The vast majority (up to 95 percent) of problems with SCSI disks are due to incorrect ID settings and improper termination. Verify that all SCSI devices have unique SCSI ID numbers and are properly terminated.
Resetting system	When a SCSI system is booted or reset, SCSI controllers generally need to renew all SCSI device connections before activating the devices, causing a delay during POST.

Issue	Description
Cables	SCSI cables should be handled carefully to minimize problems. For instance, rolling SCSI cable onto itself can cause crosstalk and impede the signal. Running long lengths of it next to metal or past power supplies can also cause errors due to signal impedance.
SCSI BIOS	If you intend for a SCSI disc to be bootable after you install it, you must enable the SCSI BIOS by using jumper settings or software configuration.
Connectors	If you are installing an additional SCSI hard drive into a computer where only one connector is available on the SCSI cable and the cable itself is terminated, remove and replace the cable with one that has multiple connectors.

How to Troubleshoot Storage Devices

Procedure Reference: Troubleshoot Hard Drive Boot Problems

To troubleshoot some of the most common issues with a hard drive that won't boot:

1. Examine the POST codes and other messages displayed at boot time.

    *   The numbers in the 17xx range indicate that the hard drive or controller were not found. Check that both devices are connected and functional.

    *   The message No Boot Device Available indicates that the BIOS could not find an installed operating system on the hard drive or on a bootable floppy disk, optical disk, or thumb drive. Verify that the operating system was installed. If it was, try to boot from a bootable floppy disk and access the hard drive, then check the boot partition for errors.

    *   The messages No Operating System Found and Ntldr Can't Load are often caused by the presence of non-bootable media in a boot device, such as a non-bootable floppy disk being left in the floppy disk drive.

    *   A configuration or CMOS error indicates that the information reported by CMOS is different than the hard drive found by the POST. Check CMOS settings. If the settings won't stick, check the battery on the system board.

    *   The message Hard Drive Not Found or Fixed Disk Error indicates that the hard drive was not found during the POST. Check all hard drive and hard drive controller connections. The hard drive or controller might be dead.

    *   The message Reboot And Select Proper Boot Device Or Insert Boot Media In Selected Boot Device indicates that the BIOS found no bootable device in the system. It could also indicate that a removable media drive does not contain media if no hard disk was found and it found a removable media drive (such as a floppy disk drive, Zip drive, SuperDrive, or so on).

2. If the drive is newly installed, verify that it has an operating system by booting with a DOS boot floppy disk and entering the drive letter at the command prompt.

    *   If the drive letter is recognized, it might need an operating system installed.

    *   If the drive letter is not recognized, the drive might need to be partitioned and formatted, and then have an operating system installed. If the `fdisk` and `format` utilities are on the DOS boot floppy, you can use them to partition and format the drive.

3. Otherwise, diagnose and correct the boot problem.

- Perform a cold boot.

- Verify that CMOS lists the correct device settings for the hard drive. This includes the correct drive type, whether LBA is enabled, and the CHS (cylinders, heads, and sectors) settings.

- Verify that CMOS is set to boot from the hard drive.

- Listen to the drive or touch the drive to determine if it is spinning during POST. It should be spinning up to full speed during this time. It usually makes noise during this time and you can feel the vibrations of the drive while it is spinning.

- Use your multimeter to verify that the power connection readings are correct. They should be +12 V for Pin 1 and +5 V for Pin 4. Pins 2 and 3 should be grounded.

- Verify that the data cable is correctly oriented. Pin 1 is almost always on the side nearest the power connection. Pin 1 on the cable is on the side with the stripe.

- Check drive settings. For an IDE drive, verify that it is set to master, slave, or cable select as appropriate to the drive and its location in the drive chain within the system. For a SCSI drive, verify that the termination is correct for its location in the chain and that it has a unique device ID. For a SATA drive, jumpers can be moved to enable or disable features. Verify that the jumper settings are correct for the level of features you need.

- Look for data recovery options. There are some built-in recovery capabilities in some operating systems. You can also purchase software to assist you in recovering data. In many cases, though, you will need to resort to sending the drive out to a company that specializes in recovering data from damaged drives.

- If none of these fix the problem, replace the drive.

4. Verify that the drive now works.

- Boot the system.

- Verify that you can read from and write to the drive you repaired.

Procedure Reference: Troubleshoot Why a Newly Installed Second Hard Drive Isn't Recognized

To troubleshoot some of the most common problems with a newly installed second hard drive:

1. Verify that the CMOS settings are correct.

2. Verify that the drive was installed correctly.

3. Access the drive by drive letter in My Computer or at a command prompt to verify that the drive was partitioned and formatted. You can use DOS utilities from a bootable DOS floppy disk or Windows XP's disk management utilities.

Procedure Reference: Troubleshoot Hard Drive Data Access Problems

To troubleshoot some of the most common hard drive data access problems:

1. Document the symptoms.

   - If the system boots and the drive is recognized, but you can't access data and the message Can't Access This Drive is displayed, this could be a problem with the letter assigned to the drive or an indication of drive damage.

   - If the user attempts to access a drive or files on a drive, which causes the system to lock up, and you hear a clicking sound, this indicates drive damage.

   - If the user reports that some folders have disappeared and folder and file names are scrambled with strange characters in their names, this indicates either a computer virus or drive damage.

2. If you suspect a drive letter problem, verify that the drive letter assigned to the drive matches the letter the user is entering, and copy a file to and from the drive to verify that it is working.

3. If you suspect a computer virus, run virus-scanning software.

4. If you suspect drive damage, repair or replace the disk.

   - Run the Windows XP Error-checking option in the Tools pane of the Local Disk Properties dialog box.

   - Use an older version of Scandisk from floppy disk to try to identify and repair the errors it encounters.

   - Open My Computer, right-click the drive letter in question, and then display the Hardware pane. Use the Troubleshooting Wizard to attempt to locate the problem.

   - Back up the data from the drive if possible, and then reformat the drive. Remember, reformatting will destroy any data on the drive.

   - If you cannot repair the errors using these methods, back up the data if possible, and replace the drive.

Procedure Reference: Troubleshoot the Wrong Drive Size Being Reported

To troubleshoot some of the most common reasons why a system reports the wrong hard drive size:

1. If the system contains an older BIOS that does not recognize large drives, it will report that there is only about a 500 MB drive in the system. To resolve this problem, update the BIOS so that the entire drive can be recognized. If the BIOS cannot be upgraded, a Dynamic Disk Overlay driver can be installed to enable the older BIOS and the large drive to work together.

 You can use a manufacturer's install program such as Maxblast or Maxtore to enable an older BIOS to work with a large drive.

2. Users are often misled about the exact size of a drive. When talking in general terms, most people round 1,024 bytes to 1,000 because it is easier to talk in round numbers. By the time you get up to billions of bytes, as you will with the newer drives, those 24 bytes for each 1,000 bytes start to add up to significant amounts.

For more information about binary multiples as used in denoting drive sizes, see **http://physics.nist.gov/cuu/Units/binary.html**.

Procedure Reference: Troubleshoot Floppy Drive Problems

To troubleshoot some of the most common problems with floppy drives:

1. If, when attempting to read data from the floppy disk, the user receives the error message This Disk Is Not Formatted. Do You Want To Format It Now Or Insert Disk Now?, you should:

   ● Check that the disk is readable. You can do this by trying to read it in another floppy disk drive.

   ● Try reinserting the floppy disk in the drive.

   ● If you received the floppy disk from another user with data on it, determine if it was formatted on another operating system such as Macintosh or Linux. If it was, you will not want to format it as this would erase all of the data on the disk.

   ● Verify that the floppy disk functions properly. The shuttle window should open and shut easily. There should be no foreign matter on the Mylar disk surface. The Mylar disk should spin easily within the plastic case.

   ● Check the floppy disk for viruses.

   ● Check the floppy disk for bad sectors.

   ● Check whether or not other floppy disks can be read in the drive.

2. If the user cannot write to a floppy disk in the drive, you should:

   ● Check that the floppy disk is not write-protected. If it is, move the switch to unprotect the floppy disk. Looking at the back side of the floppy disk, the slider on the upper-left corner should be down, blocking the write-protect hole, in order to write to the floppy disk.

   ● Verify that the floppy disk has been properly formatted. A floppy disk formatted using the native format on a Macintosh or Linux system, for example, cannot be read on a Windows system.

   ● Verify that the floppy drive is working properly. Open the system and verify that the floppy drive cable and power connections are properly connected and that the floppy drive mechanisms (you can often see some of them through the holes in the floppy drive case) are functioning properly when you insert a floppy disk in the drive.

   ● Clean the floppy drive read/write heads. You can purchase a special cleaning disk with a cleaning solution to insert in the drive. With the cleaning disk in the drive, you attempt to access the drive, causing the disk to spin and thus cleaning the drive.

3. The error message The System Cannot Find The Drive Specified indicates that the operating system cannot locate the floppy disk drive. You should check the CMOS settings to verify that the system knows there is a floppy drive, and then clean the drive, check the alignment of the drive, and check all connections (power and data cables) for the drive.

4. If you attempt to read a floppy disk and receive a message that the disk is not formatted, it was most likely formatted using a different operating system such as Macintosh or Linux. If so, then the original owner of the disk will need to provide the information to you on a medium that Windows can read. This might be over the network or on a Windows-formatted floppy disk (both Macintosh and Linux can read and write to Windows-formatted floppy disks).

5. If you can read and write to floppy disks on this system, but they cannot be read on another system, you should suspect that the drive is out of alignment. In a drive that is out of alignment, the read/write head is not properly aligned with the tracks on the disk and covers parts of tracks rather than a single track. While there are tools for adjusting the drive alignment, it is often cheaper to simply replace the drive. More information about the types of misalignment, causes, and methods for repairing the damage can be found at **www.accurite.com/FloppyPrimer.html**.

6. If none of the previous solutions fixed the problem, you might need to replace the floppy drive.

Procedure Reference: Troubleshoot Optical Drive Problems

To troubleshoot some of the most common optical drive problems:

1. If the optical drive door won't open:
   - Verify that there is power to the drive.
   - Press the eject button on the drive.
   - Verify that no applications are attempting to read from the drive.
   - Open My Computer and right-click the drive icon, then choose Eject.
   - If all else fails, insert a straightened paper clip in the hole on the drive to manually push the gears that drive the drawer open. You may need to press firmly.

2. If the optical drive reads data and program disks, but the user can't hear audio CDs:
   - Verify that you can read a data CD.
   - Verify that the speakers are connected properly to the sound card.
   - Verify that the speakers are powered and turned on.
   - Verify that the volume is turned up on the physical speakers.
   - Right-click the Volume icon in the System Tray and choose Open Volume Control. Verify that Volume Control is not all the way down and that Mute is not checked. You can also adjust the volume through Control Panel.
   - Play a system sound.
     a. Open Control Panel.
     b. Click the Sounds, Speech And Audio Devices link.
     c. Click the Adjust The System Volume link.
     d. Click the Sounds tab.
     e. Select an event, and then click the Play button next to Sounds to see if the associated sound for the event is played.
   - Verify that the audio cable inside the system case that connects the CD-ROM drive to the sound card is properly installed and that there are no broken wires.
   - Verify that the correct sound drivers are installed.

    a.   In Control Panel, display the Sounds, Speech, And Audio Devices dialog box, and then click the Hardware tab.

    b.   Verify that the Devices list includes the proper driver and that Audio Codecs is listed.

    c.   If not, use the Add Hardware Wizard to add the appropriate drivers.

- Use the Troubleshooting Wizard for the Sounds, Speech, And Audio Devices. (You access this Wizard from the Hardware tab in the Sounds And Audio Devices Properties dialog box. To open this dialog box, open Control Panel, click the Sounds, Speech, And Audio Devices link, and then click the Sounds And Audio Devices link.)

- Attempt to play the default song in the Windows Media Player.

    a.   From the Start menu, choose All Programs→Accessories→Entertainment→ Windows Media Player.

    b.   Choose Tools→Options.

    c.   Click the File Types tab and verify that all File Types are checked.

    d.   Click OK.

    e.   Click the Play button to attempt to play the default song.

- Verify the default audio is set to the system audio drive.

    a.   In Control Panel, open Sounds And Audio Devices.

    b.   Click the Audio tab.

    c.   Under Sound Playback, verify the driver for the sound card is listed below Default Device.

    d.   Click OK.

- Verify that the user can now play the audio CD.

3.   If, after upgrading to Windows XP, a user can no longer access his or her CD/DVD drive:

- Verify that the drive is on the Windows XP hardware compatibility list.

- Verify that the drive is properly installed.

- Verify that Windows Explorer lists a drive letter for the CD/DVD drive.

- Verify that the appropriate driver is installed.

    a.   Open My Computer.

    b.   Right-click the CD/DVD drive icon and choose Properties.

    c.   Click the Hardware tab.

    d.   Verify that the appropriate driver is listed.

- Use the Drives And Network Adapters Troubleshooter within the Help And Support Center.

    a.   Open My Computer.

    b.   Right-click the drive icon and choose Properties.

    c.   Click the Hardware tab.

    d.   Click the Troubleshoot button and follow the prompts to troubleshoot the problem.

4. If there is a drive letter conflict, specify a free drive letter for the drive.

    a. From the Start menu, right-click My Computer, and then choose Manage.

    b. In Computer Management, select Disk Management.

    c. In the list of drives in the right pane, right-click the CD/DVD drive and then choose Change Drive Letter And Paths.

    d. Click Change, and in the Assign The Following Letter drop-down list, select a new drive letter for the Removable Device, choosing one that is not assigned to local or mapped network drives.

    e. Click OK twice.

5. If the user inserts a blank CD/DVD in the CD-RW or DVD-RW drive, and the drive ejects it before the user can write to it:

- Confirm that the user has a CD-R, CD-RW, DVD-R, or DVD-RW drive and not just a CD-ROM or DVD-ROM drive in his or her computer.

- Make sure the media is rated for the speed at which you are trying to write.

- Make sure the user is not trying to write more than the disc can hold.

- Check for software error messages that indicate what the problem might be.

- There might be debris inside the drive. Dust and other foreign matter can cause a drive to constantly eject the disc.

- Check whether the operating system or the hardware is causing the problem by unplugging the data cable from the drive before inserting the disc. If there is a pause before the disc is ejected or if the drive light blinks steadily, it might be because the media is defective or not high enough quality for the drive to use. Try a different brand of discs.

- If the hardware appears to be fine, the operating system might be causing the problem. Try pressing and holding Shift and inserting a disc; pressing Shift temporarily disables the AutoRun feature for the CD/DVD devices. If the CD/DVD plays properly, the operating system is the cause of the problem. You can disable AutoRun permanently by editing the registry. See **http://support.microsoft.com/kb/155217/en-us** for the steps to accomplish this task.

- See if the CD-RW or DVD-RW drive will write after the system has been off for a while. Some systems overheat and have trouble writing when the drive gets too hot.

6. If you can't get video from a DVD disc, you might need to install decoder software to emulate the hardware decoder in standalone DVD players.

Procedure Reference: Troubleshoot Removable Cartridge Drive Problems

To troubleshoot some of the most common problems with removable cartridge drives:

1. If no drive letter is displayed in Windows Explorer for a removable cartridge drive, verify that the drivers for the drive have been installed on the system. If that is not the problem, verify that the drive is connected to the proper port with the proper cable. After fixing either of these problems, you should restart the system.

2.   If the user cannot write to the removable media:

●   Check that it has not been write protected. There might be software-enabled write protection or physical-write protection on the disk, depending on the media you are using.

●   If the disk still cannot be written to, try another disk in the drive.

●   If the disk still cannot be written to, verify that the drive is properly connected to the system and that the power supply is plugged in for external models.

●   If the disk still cannot be accessed, try moving the drive as far from the monitor, speakers, power supplies, or other electronic devices as possible. There might be interference from the devices.

3.   If the media was formatted under an operating system other than Windows, you might have problems reading or writing to it. You can sometimes view the properties of the drive to determine the format of the disk.

4.   If the disk will not come out of the drive, you can try using a straightened paper clip. Most drives have a hole that you can insert the paper clip wire into and then press it to manually release and eject the disk from the drive mechanism.

5.   The original Zip drive used the parallel port. The parallel cable that it came with is not always compatible with the default settings on current parallel ports. You might need to change the settings so that the port is not using unidirectional or ECP settings. It should use bidirectional settings. After making the change, restart the computer and now that ECP has been disabled, you should be able to access the drive.

ACTIVITY 7-1

Troubleshooting Hard Drive Problems

Scenario:

In this activity, you will troubleshoot hard drive problems.

 There is a simulated version of this activity available on the CD-ROM that shipped with this course. You can run this simulation on any Windows computer to review the activity after class, or as an alternative to performing the activity as a group in class. The activity simulation can be launched either directly from the CD-ROM by clicking the Interactives link and navigating to the appropriate one, or from the installed data file location by opening the C:\ 085820Data\Simulations\Lesson#\Activity# folder and double-clicking the executable (.exe) file.

What You Do	How You Do It

A Computer Cannot Boot

1. **Diagnose and correct the problem** when a computer cannot boot and the user sees an error message at POST.

    a. **Perform a cold boot.**

    b. **Verify that CMOS lists the correct drive settings.**

    c. **Listen to the drive or touch the drive to determine if it is spinning during POST.**

    d. **Using your multimeter, verify that power connection readings are +12v for Pin 1 and +5v for Pin 4.** Pins 2 and 3 should be grounded.

    e. **Verify that data cable is correctly oriented.**

    f. **Check drive settings:**
        • PATA: Master, slave, or cable select
        • SCSI: Termination and device ID

    g. If nothing else corrects the problem, **replace the drive.**

2.	Test that the drive now works.	a.	**Boot the system.**
		b.	**Verify that you can read and write to the drive you repaired.**

A Second Hard Drive Isn't Recognized

3. You have installed a second hard drive and it is not recognized. You know that one of the things you need to check when a newly installed drive isn't recognized is the CMOS settings for the drive. What in particular do you need to check in CMOS for this problem?

4. Another thing you should check when a second hard drive isn't recognized is that the drive was installed correctly. What exactly would you be checking?

5. A second hard drive was properly installed but you cannot access it by its drive letter. What should your next step be?

Hard Drive Data Access Problems

6. A user is encountering the following problem: Her computer boots fine and every-thing works until the user tries to access data on the second hard drive, the D drive. The message "Can't Access This Drive" is displayed when she tries to access the D drive. The user would also like an explanation about what the error message means. List some of the steps you might take to resolve this problem.

7. When a user tries to access the hard drive containing his data, the system locks up and makes a clicking sound. From the DOS prompt, he can change to drive D, but when he tries to access a file or list the files on the drive, it locks up and begins clicking again. What steps might you take to attempt to resolve this problem? What is the most likely cause of the problem?

8. A user reports that some of his folders have begun disappearing and some folder and file names are scrambled with strange characters in their names. What steps might you take to attempt to resolve this problem? What is the most likely cause of the problem?

Wrong Drive Size Reported

9. **A 30-GB hard drive was installed, but the system reports that the drive is about 500 MB. What can be done to resolve this problem?**

10. **A user is questioning the difference between the sizes in GB and bytes. Why is there such a big difference? The disk reports in some places as 9.33 GB and in others as 10,025,000,960 bytes. Why isn't it 10 GB?**

DISCOVERY ACTIVITY 7-2

Troubleshooting Floppy Drive Problems

Activity Time: 20 minutes

Scenario:

Users have opened trouble calls with the help center for the following problems that are related to the floppy drives on their systems.

Ticket No.	Location	User Name	Issue
235001	Main building, 23D41	Angharad Phatek	When the user attempts to access the floppy drive, he sees the message This Disk Is Not Formatted. Do You Want To Format It Now Or Insert Disk Now?
235002	Main building, 32G37	Gary Toomey	The user cannot write to a disk in the floppy drive.
235003	Elmwood Place, cube 37	Zoe Isaacs	When trying to access the floppy drive from the command prompt, she sees the message The System Cannot Find The Drive Specified.
235004	Elmwood Place, cube 42	Etta Romero	User received a floppy disk containing important information from another user. When Etta tries to access the disk through Windows Explorer, she receives a message that the disk is not formatted.

 There is a simulated version of this activity available on the CD-ROM that shipped with this course. You can run this simulation on any Windows computer to review the activity after class, or as an alternative to performing the activity as a group in class. The activity simulation can be launched either directly from the CD-ROM by clicking the Interactives link and navigating to the appropriate one, or from the installed data file location by opening the C:\ 085820Data\Simulations\Lesson#\Activity# folder and double-clicking the executable (.exe) file.

1. Identify some issues you should check in resolving trouble ticket 235001.

2. List the issues to check in resolving trouble ticket 235002.

3. What might cause the user to receive the error message shown in trouble ticket 235003?

4. What would you recommend to the user to resolve trouble ticket 235004?

ACTIVITY 7-3

Troubleshooting Optical Drive Problems

Scenario:

The following are the trouble tickets related to CD-ROM, CD-R/RW, DVD, and DVD-R drives that have been assigned to you for resolution.

Ticket No.	Location	User Name	Issue
232001	Main building, 31A57	Nichole Lombard	The door will not open on the CD-ROM drive. The user needs the CD that is in the drive.
232002	Main building, 41A23	Ruth Dalton	User needs to be able to listen to audio CDs. The system reads data and program CDs just fine but there is no audio.
232003	Main building, 11A10	Richard Alston	The user's CD-RW drive was listed as D. A new drive was added to the system and now the D drive does not point to the CD-ROM drive. Some applications cannot find the CD-ROM when he attempts to run the application, even though the CD is in the drive.
232004	Main building, 12D52	Mark Glick	User needs to burn a CD and the drive keeps ejecting the CD media before he can write the disc.
232005	Elmwood Place, cube 7	Jennifer Kulp	The user needs to be able to watch DVDs on her system. She can read CDs, play audio CDs, and read data DVDs in the drive, but does not see any video.

 There is a simulated version of this activity available on the CD-ROM that shipped with this course. You can run this simulation on any Windows computer to review the activity after class, or as an alternative to performing the activity as a group in class. The activity simulation can be launched either directly from the CD-ROM by clicking the Interactives link and navigating to the appropriate one, or from the installed data file location by opening the C:\ 085820Data\Simulations\Lesson#\Activity# folder and double-clicking the executable (.exe) file.

What You Do	How You Do It
1. **Resolve trouble ticket 232001.**	a. **Verify that there is power to the drive.**
	b. **Press the Eject button on the drive.**
	c. **Verify that no applications are attempting to read from the CD-ROM.**
	d. **Open My Computer. Right-click the CD-ROM drive icon and choose Eject.**
	e. **Straighten out a small paper clip, and then insert the end into the hole on the front of the CD-ROM drive.**

2. **Resolve trouble ticket 232002.**

a. **Verify that you can read a data CD.**

b. **Verify that the speakers are connected properly to the sound card.**

c. **Verify that the speakers are properly powered and turned on.**

d. **Verify that the volume is turned up on the physical speakers.**

e. In the System Tray, **right-click the Volume icon and choose Open Volume Controls.**

f. **Verify that Volume Control is not all the way down and that Mute is not checked.**

g. **Play a system sound such as the Asterisk.**

h. **Verify that the proper sound device drivers are installed.**

i. **Verify that the audio drive is the default sound playback device.**

j. In the Sounds And Audio Devices window, **click the Hardware tab and then click Troubleshoot. Follow the prompts in the Troubleshooting Wizard to attempt to resolve the problem.**

k. **Open the Windows Media Player and attempt to play the default song.**

l. **Verify that the audio cable inside the case that connects the CD-ROM to the sound card is properly installed and that there are no broken wires.**

m. **Verify that you can now play the audio CD.**

3. Regarding trouble ticket 232003, explain to the user what the reason for the problem is and what needs to be done to correct it.

4. What would you suggest that the user try in resolving trouble ticket 232004?

5. After checking over the hardware for the DVD drive on the system, you find no problems. What else might the problem be in trouble ticket 232005?

TOPIC B
Troubleshoot Power Supplies

In the last topic, you identified and corrected problems with storage devices. Another personal computer component that is required for the system to operate is the power supply. In this topic, you will troubleshoot power supplies.

Underpowered systems, especially older systems with relatively small power supplies, can experience lockups, random reboots, and other quirky behavior. As an A+ technician, you will be required to test and troubleshoot power supplies.

Common Power Problems

Power problems can result in data loss, erratic behavior, system crashes, and hardware damage, and the more severe the problem, the more severe the consequences.

Power Problem	Possible Causes
Line noise	EMI interference. RFI interference. Lightning. Defective power supply.
Power sag	Many electrical systems starting up at once. Switching loads at the electric company utility. Electric company equipment failure. Inadequate power source.
Power undervoltage or brownout	This symptom can last from several minutes to several days and can be caused by any of the following: • Decreased line voltage. • Demand exceeds power company supply. • Utility company reduced voltage to conserve energy. A variation on this is switching transient or instantaneous undervoltage that lasts only a matter of nanoseconds.
Frequency variation	Usually occurs when using a small power generator. As loads increase or decrease, the power frequency varies. Generators are not recommended for supplying direct power to computers and other sensitive equipment. The variance in frequency (square wave instead of sinusoidal wave) and the instability of the voltage will cause severe instability in computers, leading to crashes, data loss, and possible equipment damage. Using a power conditioner or an inverter with a generator will prevent these issues by stabilizing the voltage and frequency.

Power Problem	Possible Causes
Overvoltage	Suddenly reduced loads.
	Equipment with heavy power consumption is turned off.
	Power company switches loads between equipment.
Power failure	Lightning strikes.
	Electrical power lines down.
	Overload of electrical power needs.

Common Power Supply Issues

Power supply damage from overheating, lightning strikes, or short circuits can produce a number of symptoms.

 POST error codes from 020 and 029 are related to the power supply.

Symptom	Possible Cause and Solution
Fan will not work.	The fan and openings around the power supply bring in air to cool system components, but they also allow dirt and dust to gather around the power supply. This can cause the fan bearings to wear and the fan to turn more slowly. You can use compressed air to remove this debris from the system. If the fan becomes damaged due to dust, replace the power supply or have qualified personnel replace the fan.

Symptom	*Possible Cause and Solution*
Computer won't start or reboots after startup.	• If the computer doesn't start at all, make sure that there is power to the outlet. You can do so by plugging in a lamp or other device that you know works. If that doesn't turn on, you know that you have a bad outlet and not necessarily a bad power supply.
	• Check that the connections from the power supply to the system board are secure, especially on ATX systems. Make sure the master switch to the power supply, at the rear of the system, is on, before pressing the computer's power button. Also on ATX systems, check the voltage of the power being supplied.
	• A loose power supply rail landing on exposed metal can short-circuit the power supply. The power supply can detect this problem and disable itself. If you fix the short (by putting the power cable onto the drive correctly), the power supply should start working again. Unused rails should be either covered (some bring rubber end caps) or tie-wrapped to a safe location (not too tight to avoid damaging the wire). Also check for loose screws or foreign metallic objects that can cause shorts.
	• Check power supply rail voltages with a digital multimeter, to verify that the necessary voltages are being provided to the board. This will not measure voltage under load, but will allow you to determine whether the rails are working properly. Most motherboards also provide a voltage reading within the BIOS. If the system boots, access this BIOS option to obtain readings as detected by the motherboard.
Noise coming from power supply.	Other components, especially drives, can also sometimes make a lot of noise. Make sure this isn't where the noise is coming from. A whine or squeal from the power supply area is usually from the fan. A damaged fan with worn bearings will cause a grinding whine that worsens with time. Sometimes, when the bearings begin to fail, the fan blade assembly will shift, rubbing against the fan grill or the case, and produce a high-pitched noise. Also possible, after cleaning with compressed air, a wire inside the power supply unit was shifted by the forced air and is now touching the fan, causing the very loud grinding noise, possibly stopping the fan altogether. With the power supply off, you can attempt to carefully shift the wire away from the fan by using a plastic tool (metal not recommended so as to avoid damaging any components). If the noise is not from the fan, but from another power supply component, replace the power supply or take it out and send it for service.

How to Troubleshoot Power Supplies

Procedure Reference: Test a Power Supply With a Multimeter

To use a multimeter to test a power supply for proper output voltage:

1. Prepare the computer.

    a. Shut down the computer.

    b. Disconnect all cables externally connected to the chassis.

    c. Remove the computer enclosure (cover).

    d. Locate a spare Molex connector, and remove it from the bundle if necessary so that you can easily access it without having to reach inside the case to work with the connector.

    e. Reconnect the power cable.

    f. Power on your computer.

     Be sure to not touch the case, internal components, or multimeter probe contacts while measuring the power supply voltage. You could be seriously injured or killed.

2. Measure the 5 volt output from the power supply.

    a. Set your multimeter to measure DC voltage with a scale that will permit readings in the +5 volt range.

    b. Insert the multimeter's black probe into the black (GND) lead of the power connector.

    c. Insert the multimeter's red probe into the red (+5) lead of the power connector.

    d. Examine the voltage measured by the multimeter. It should be approximately +5 volts.

3. Measure the 12 volt output from the power supply.

    a. If necessary, set your multimeter to measure DC voltage with a scale that will permit readings in the +12 volt range.

    b. Insert the multimeter's black probe into the black (GND) lead of the power connector.

    c. Insert the multimeter's red probe into the yellow (+12) lead of the power connector.

    d. Examine the voltage measured by the multimeter. It should be approximately +12 volts.

4. Restore the PC to service.

   a. Shut down the computer.

   b. Disconnect the power cable.

   c. Rebundle wires and return the Molex connector to the location from which you got it.

   d. Replace the computer enclosure (cover).

   e. Connect all cables externally connected to the chassis.

   f. Power on your computer.

Power Supply Wire Color Conventions

System components cannot use the 120-volt power coming directly from the electrical outlet. The power supply steps the voltages down to 3.3-, 5-, and 12-volt connections for system components. Wires are color-coded as to their voltages. The following table shows the wire color for each voltage connection.

Color or Component	*Voltage*
Yellow wire	+12
Blue wire	-12
Red wire	+5
White wire	-5
Motor	+/-12
Circuitry	+/-5

Power Supply Testers

Although you can use multimeters to test power supplies, there are also specialized tools called power supply testers that are simpler to use for this purpose, and that perform more comprehensive tests. For instance, you can test the various power connectors (Berg, Molex, AT, and ATX). You can also use them to test the power supply under load.

Procedure Reference: Troubleshoot Power Problems

To troubleshoot power problems:

1. If the fan does not appear to be working and the system doesn't come on or abruptly shuts itself down, address the problem as soon as possible. Leaving the problem alone would allow heat to build up to dangerous levels, causing serious damage to the system, and possibly fire.

   a. Unplug the system and remove the system cover.

   b. Using compressed air, blow out any dust around the fan spindle.

   c. Verify that there is no obvious reason that the fan is not spinning.

   d. If these suggestions do not fix the problem, replace the power supply. Remember, do not open a power supply as there is a high danger of electrocution.

2. If there are power-related startup errors, such as the system, fan, and power light not coming on:

   a. Verify that the power cord is securely connected to the power supply and to the electrical outlet on the UPS or surge protector (or the wall, but you should always protect it through a UPS or surge protector).

   b. Verify that the UPS or surge protector is turned on and plugged in.

   c. Verify that the UPS or surge protector is working by plugging in a lamp with a known good light bulb and turning on the light.

   d. If the lamp did not light, check to see whether any reset buttons need to be reset on the UPS or surge suppressor, or check the electric outlet's circuit breaker.

   e. If none of these fixed the problem, replace the power supply.

3. If an ATX motherboard will not power up, use a multimeter or power supply tester to check the voltage of the power being supplied. Check the connectors to the system board as well.

ACTIVITY 7-4

Troubleshooting Power Supplies

Setup:

Before you begin this activity, shut down your computer.

Scenario:

The following are the trouble tickets related to power problems that have been assigned for you to resolve.

Ticket No.	Location	User Name	Issue
125001	Elmwood Place, cube 20	Sylvania Rawleigh	One of the other hardware technicians has been trying to troubleshoot a power problem. The system will not come on when the user turns on the power switch. He determined that the user has an ATX system board and power supply. You have been assigned to take over this trouble ticket.
125002	Main building, 51B24	Darlene Burley	When the user turns on the PC, it doesn't always come on and sometimes it just shuts itself down abruptly, with no warning. When she turns on the system again, there is no fan noise. She is using a legacy database application and the data is being corrupted during the improper shutdowns.
125003	Main building, 21K37	Earle Washburn	The user turns on the power switch, but the system does not come on. He does not hear the fan, there is no power light on, and he hears no beeps or other sounds coming from the system. His system is plugged into a surge protector.

 There is a simulated version of this activity available on the CD-ROM that shipped with this course. You can run this simulation on any Windows computer to review the activity after class, or as an alternative to performing the activity as a group in class. The activity simulation can be launched either directly from the CD-ROM by clicking the Interactives link and navigating to the appropriate one, or from the installed data file location by opening the C:\085820Data\Simulations\Lesson#\Activity# folder and double-clicking the executable (.exe) file.

What You Do	How You Do It
1. Resolve trouble ticket 125001.	a. Set the multimeter for DC volts over 12V.
	b. Locate an available internal power supply connector. If none are free, power off the system and unplug it, then remove one from a floppy drive or CD drive, then power on the system again.
	c. Insert the black probe from the multimeter into one of the two center holes on the internal power supply connector.
	d. Insert the red probe from the multimeter into the hole for the red wire.
	e. Verify that the multimeter reading is +5V DC.
	f. Move the red probe into the hole for the yellow wire.
	g. Verify that the multimeter reading is +12V DC.
	h. Check the documentation for the ATX motherboard to see if there is a logic circuit switch that signals power to be turned on or off, that it is properly connected, and how it should be set.
	i. Verify that the motherboard, processor, memory and video card are all correctly installed and working.

2. What would you do to resolve trouble ticket 125002?

3. If the computer did not start, what would your next action be?

4. **List the steps you would use to resolve trouble ticket 125003.**

5. **If the computer did not start, what would your next action be?**

TOPIC C
Troubleshoot Memory

In the last topic, you resolved problems with power supplies. Memory issues can also be the cause of generalized computer problems. In this topic, you will troubleshoot memory.

Memory plays a huge role in every operation done by a personal computer. An issue with memory can result in a wide range of problems and symptoms. As an A+ technician, your ability to identify and solve memory problems will be crucial in providing your users with the optimal computing environment.

Error Checking

Many memory modules include error-checking mechanisms to protect data. The most common are *parity* and *Error Correcting Code (ECC)*.

Error-Checking Mechanism	Description
Parity	Parity is an error correction method that is used for electronic communications. For memory modules, the use of a parity bit can detect some of the errors that can be introduced during a data transmission. Eight bits are for data, and the ninth bit is the parity bit. Parity can be odd or even, meaning that the total number of 1s is an odd or an even number. If an error is detected, nothing is done to fix it. The system simply tries again after discarding the data. Parity is rarely used; other system components are relied on to verify that the data contained in memory is accurate when non-parity memory is used. Some chips use fake parity. In this case, the values are always 1s and it is assumed that there are never any memory problems. Other pieces of hardware and/or software take over in verifying that the information contained in the memory is correct.
Error Correction Code (ECC)	Error Correction Code (ECC) is an error correction method that uses several bits for error-checking. A special algorithm is used to detect and then correct any errors it finds. ECC is used only in upper-end systems such as high-end workstations and servers; other desktop systems use non-ECC memory.

Common Memory Issues

Memory problems typically show themselves as memory-specific errors, erratic behavior of the system, or frequent crashes.

Symptom	Possible Causes
Computer crashes or reboots; data is corrupted.	ESD, overheating, or other power-related problems that can affect memory. Registry writing to bad memory, General Protection Faults (GPFs), and exception errors caused by software and operating system.

Symptom	Possible Causes
Memory errors appear on screen.	Memory address errors at boot time. Memory mismatch errors in which you are prompted to specify how much RAM is installed to clear the message. Applications that require large amounts of memory or that don't properly release memory.
Computer appears to boot; screen remains blank.	Memory is not correct for the system. For instance, the computer is expecting memory that uses error checking and you installed non-parity memory. Memory module is not fully inserted into the slot.
Computer does not boot. POST beep codes sound.	CPU cannot communicate with memory due to the memory being improperly installed or the BIOS not recognizing the memory. Beep codes are specific to the BIOS manufacturer and the ones for memory can be found in the manufacturers' beep codes list.
Some or all newly installed memory is not recognized.	You exceeded the maximum amount of RAM that can be addressed by the system. Even though the slots can accept SIMMs containing more memory, the system can only recognize a certain amount of memory on most systems. The wrong memory type was installed. The memory was not installed in the proper sequence. You might need to leave empty slots between multiple modules, or you might need to install modules containing more memory in lower-numbered slots than smaller modules.

How to Troubleshoot Memory

Procedure Reference: Troubleshoot Memory Problems

To troubleshoot memory problems:

1. Perform a virus scan. Viruses can cause symptoms that mimic those of a memory problem.

2. Verify that the correct memory modules were installed in the system. You can check the part numbers against the memory or PC manufacturer's website. For example, be sure that you aren't trying to use DDR2 RAM in a DDR RAM system.

3. Verify that the memory was installed and configured properly. Older systems required that memory be installed in pairs. In all cases, verify that the memory modules are fully seated. Always start with memory in the first bank. Check your documentation for other requirements specific to your system.

4. Try swapping the memory between slots. For example, if you only experience problems when many applications are open, the chance is that one of the memory modules in the higher banks is the problem. If the system won't boot, try one of the other modules in the first bank to see if it then boots. Try putting a known good module in the first slot and removing all of the other memory modules.

5. Check for BIOS upgrades. If there are known problems, then a fix has probably been issued. This usually applies to older systems.

DISCOVERY ACTIVITY 7-5

Troubleshooting Memory

Scenario:

The following are the trouble tickets to which you have been assigned. All of the users are experiencing some type of problem related to the memory installed in their systems.

Ticket No.	Location	User Name	Issue
401001	Main building, 12B52	Roger Wheaton	The user is experiencing corrupted data in his database application. The hard drive has been checked and no problems were found with it. The application was reinstalled and the database was reindexed and all data problems have been corrected. No other users are experiencing this problem when they enter data. He has been successfully entering data until just recently.
401002	Elmwood Place, cube 6	Rory Waldon	The user is complaining of application crashes. He is fine if he is only running his email and word processing programs. If he also opens his graphics program at the same time, then the applications are crashing.
401003	Main building, 22G42	Hazel Beech	Additional memory was installed in her system and now it won't boot.

There is a simulated version of this activity available on the CD-ROM that shipped with this course. You can run this simulation on any Windows computer to review the activity after class, or as an alternative to performing the activity as a group in class. The activity simulation can be launched either directly from the CD-ROM by clicking the Interactives link and navigating to the appropriate one, or from the installed data file location by opening the C:\085820Data\Simulations\Lesson#\Activity# folder and double-clicking the executable (.exe) file.

1. **After troubleshooting trouble ticket 401001, you have discovered symptoms of a memory problem. What could cause sudden memory problems?**

   a) New virus

   b) Power loss

   c) New memory not compatible

   d) Power surge

2. **You are attempting to resolve trouble ticket 401002. Why is the user only experiencing the problem when additional applications are opened?**

   a) There is not enough memory in the system.

   b) Memory errors are occurring in higher memory than is normally used.

   c) The memory modules are incompatible with one another.

3. **Resolve trouble ticket 401003 by placing the steps in the proper order.**

   Verify that the correct memory was installed in the system.

   Check to see if the BIOS manufacturer has released any upgrades that would resolve the problem.

   Try swapping memory around in the memory banks.

   Verify that memory was installed and configured correctly.

TOPIC D
Troubleshoot CPUs

In the last topic, you resolved memory problems. In addition to memory, the processor is involved in every computer operation and can cause problems throughout the system if it is compromised. In this topic, you will troubleshoot CPUs.

Because the processor provides the computational power that drives everything that a personal computer does, the ability to recognize and resolve processor issues is a critical skill for computer technicians.

Common CPU Issues

Most problems with CPUs can be attributed to overheating or outright failure. The main solution to CPU problems is to replace the CPU or the entire system board. When you replace a processor, you must select a processor that is compatible with the type supported by the system board.

 Older prcessors in unsecured sockets could experience *chip creep,* which is the phenomenon of vibrations and movements causing the chip to become loose. In today's ZIF sockets, this is no longer an issue.

 All processors today use some type of socket installation. For older slot-based systems, it was possible to purchase adapters to use a socketed processor in the slot-based system board.

CPU Replacement Tips

Today's ZIF sockets enable the chip to drop in, which ensures that Pin 1 on the processor is properly aligned with Pin 1 on the socket and that you do not bend the pins when removing or inserting the processor. The chip will fit easily and does not need to be forced; once the chip is in place, you can lower and secure the retaining clip.

CPUs and Cooling Systems

Because CPUs are prone to damage from overheating, you should always consider the cooling system components when you are troubleshooting CPU issues. For instance, if a user is experiencing intermittent problems during operation, there could be inadequate airflow within the computer chassis that can be corrected by providing space in front of the vents and fans. Also, dust can often accumulate on the CPU's heatsink, and can reduce the efficiency of the heatsink, possibly causing the CPU to overheat.

When thermal problems cause a system to shut down or fail to boot, it could be that the overall system cooling is inadequate, a cooling device has failed, or the processor is overclocked, whether intentional or not.

- If you suspect the cooling system is a problem, you can add more cooling devices, upgrade to more efficient devices, or replace failed devices.

- If you suspect the CPU is overclocked, use BIOS or jumper settings to reduce the CPU speed.

How to Troubleshoot CPUs

Procedure Reference: Troubleshoot CPUs

To troubleshoot CPUs:

1. If you suspect that overheating is causing CPU problems, verify that the CPU fan is installed and functional. If the fan doesn't work, replace it.

2. On older systems, chip creep can occur over time. Reseat the CPU if you think that chip creep might be the source of your CPU problems.

3. Processors have no serviceable parts. When a processor is defective, you need to install a new one. Thus, CPU failure usually requires you to replace the processor.

Procedure Reference: Troubleshoot Cooling Systems

Problems with cooling systems can often manifest themselves as CPU problems. To troubleshoot cooling systems:

1. Verify that the air vents in the computer chassis are not blocked.

2. Move the system further from the wall if airflow is not sufficient.

3. Use compressed air to remove dust and dirt from fan components and the CPU heatsink.

4. Verify that the fan blades are turning freely; remove debris or obstructions.

5. Make sure the heat sink is securely clipped to the CPU.

6. If a cooling component has failed, replace it.

7. Configure the processor to eliminate overclocking.

8. Inadequate system cooling can create ongoing thermal problems that cause the system to shut down or not to boot at all. If cooling is an ongoing issue, the ultimate solution is to upgrade the cooling system by replacing or adding cooling devices.

DISCOVERY ACTIVITY 7-6

Discussing CPU Troubleshooting

Scenario:

You are attempting to resolve problems for a user who has been reporting intermittent but severe system errors such as frequent unexpected shutdowns. The problems have been getting more frequent, and you have been unable to pinpoint a cause within the system software, power supply, memory, or any adapter cards. You are starting to suspect that there is a bad CPU, and you need to proceed accordingly to get the user back to work with as little downtime and cost as possible.

---

1. **What initial steps should you take to identify and resolve a potential CPU problem?**

   a) Replace the CPU with a known good processor.

   b) Verify that the CPU fan and other cooling systems are installed and functional.

   c) Replace the system board.

   d) Reseat the CPU.

   e) If the CPU is overclocked, throttle it down to the manufacturer-rated clock speed.

---

2. **All other diagnostic and corrective steps have failed. You need to verify that it is the CPU itself that is defective. What should you do?**

   a) Replace the system board.

   b) Reinstall the operating system.

   c) Remove all the adapter cards.

   d) Replace the CPU with a known good chip.

TOPIC E
Troubleshoot System Boards

In previous topics, you resolved problems with the majority of the components of a personal computer. Because this is the main circuitry in the personal computer, problems with the system board will affect other components. In this topic, you will troubleshoot system boards.

As an A+ technician, it's likely that you will be asked to troubleshoot many different hardware components, including system boards. Identifying and solving system board problems can be difficult, but doing so efficiently can alleviate the need to replace an entire personal computer, saving both money and user downtime.

Common System Board Issues

System board problems can be among the most difficult to recognize and diagnose. Typically, the computer will not boot, or the computer will display erratic behavior that cannot be resolved otherwise. If you have eliminated all other hardware components, applications, and the operating system as the source of the problem, then you should check to see if the system board is the cause.

Causes of System Board Problems

Common sources of system board-related problems include:

● Computer viruses infecting the system, including the BIOS.

● Loose connections between system components and the system board.

● Out-of-date BIOS.

● CMOS battery is not holding the BIOS information.

● Damage to the CPU due to overheating or electrical damage. Use a temperature sensor along with cooling systems to combat overheating, and utilize standard ESD prevention methods.

● Electrical shorts on the system board due to improperly seated components, power surges, or ESD. This is the most common cause of system board problems.

● Physical damage to the system board.

Preventing System Board Problems

When you have to touch the system board, you can prevent damage by handling it with care. When you install components into the system board, be sure not to bend or break any of the pins. This includes the pins on the cards as well as the system board. Also, the system board could be cracked if you pushed down too hard. When you secure the system board to the case, be sure not to overtighten the screws as this could also crack or damage the system board. ESD damage, from handling or from electrical surges such as lightening strikes, can ruin the system board electronics. Be sure to use proper surge protection as well as ESD-prevention techniques to help prevent such problems.

Repair vs. Replace

Today's system boards are highly integrated and generally not repairable. When you examine a system board, you will find that there are very few components on the board that are actually repairable. For example, if a built-in port fails, you will have to install an expansion card that provides that port's functionality. If an integrated circuit fails, you will have to replace the system board. Even if you are highly skilled in the use of a soldering iron, in most cases, when a system board fails, you will replace it. Other than the battery, there is virtually nothing you can repair.

How to Troubleshoot System Boards

Procedure Reference: Troubleshoot System Board Problems

To troubleshoot system board problems:

1. If the computer displays error messages, research the messages to determine a possible cause.

2. Eliminate problems with all other system components.

3. Perform a virus scan.

4. Reseat all components on the system board, including both cables and connector pins.

5. Update the system BIOS.

6. Update device drivers.

7. Replace the CMOS battery.

8. If you suspect overheating, implement further CPU cooling measures.

9. If you suspect electrical damage to the CPU, replace the CPU.

10. If you suspect electrical or physical damage to the system board, replace the system board or the entire system unit.

DISCOVERY ACTIVITY 7-7

Troubleshooting System Boards

Scenario:

The following list of trouble tickets are system board problems that you have been assigned to resolve.

Ticket No.	Location	User Name	Issue
135095	Main building, 51B24	Jennifer Bules	When the user turns on the PC, it doesn't always come on and sometimes it just shuts itself down abruptly, with no warning. When she turns on the system again, there is no fan noise. Her data is becoming corrupted from the frequent reboots.
135096	Main building, 21K37	Edward Wever	When the user turns on the computer, he sees a message stating that the computer's date and time are incorrect. He must reset this information in the computer's BIOS each time he starts the computer.
135097	Elmwood Place, cube 20	Sarah Wesson	One of the other hardware technicians has been trying to troubleshoot a power problem. The computer periodically and randomly reboots. The other technician has determined that the user has an ATX system board and power supply. You have been assigned to take over this trouble ticket.

1. **What should you do to resolve trouble ticket 135095?**

2. **What should you do to resolve trouble ticket 135096?**

3. **What should you do to resolve trouble ticket 135097?**

Lesson 7 Follow-up

In this lesson, you resolved problems with system components. Solving problems with storage devices, power issues, memory, CPUs, and system boards is a critical skill for any hardware technician.

1. **With what types of system components do you have troubleshooting experience?**

2. **What system components do you expect to have to troubleshoot most often at your workplace?**

8 Installing and Configuring Operating Systems

Lesson Time: 3 hour(s)

Lesson Objectives:

In this lesson, you will install and configure operating systems.

You will:

- Install Microsoft Windows.

- Upgrade Windows from a given version to a later version.

- Add devices to an installation of Microsoft Windows.

- Optimize an installation of Microsoft Windows.

Introduction

So far in this course, you have installed and configured the physical components of a system, and you have worked with the operating system only in a high-level general way. Now it is time to put the system hardware and software together. In this lesson, you will install and configure operating systems.

Because so many computers today come with operating system software installed by the vendor, an ordinary user might never need to install an operating system. As a trained computer support professional, however, your needs are different. You might be called upon to install and configure operating systems if the original installation does not meet your needs; if you are upgrading a system; if you have constructed a computer from scratch; or if you are redeploying a system from one use to another. In all these cases, you will need the skills to install, configure, and optimize the computer so it meets your business needs.

This lesson covers all or part of the following CompTIA A+ (2006) certification objectives:

- Topic A:

  - Exam 220–601 (Essentials): Objective 1.2, Objective 3.1, Objective 3.2, Objective 3.3, Objective 3.4

  - Exam 220–602 (IT Technician): Objective 3.1, Objective 3.2, Objective 3.3, Objective 3.4, Objective 4.2

  - Exam 220–603 (Remote Technician): Objective 2.1, Objective 2.4, Objective 3.2

  - Exam 220–604 (Depot Technician): Objective 1.1

- Topic B:

  - Exam 220–601 (Essentials): Objective 3.2

  - Exam 220–602 (IT Technician): Objective 3.2

  - Exam 220–603 (Remote Technician): Objective 2.2, Objective 2.4

- Topic C:

  - Exam 220–601 (Essentials): Objective 3.2, Objective 3.3

  - Exam 220–602 (IT Technician): Objective 3.3

- Topic D:

  - Exam 220–601 (Essentials): Objective 3.1, Objective 3.2, Objective 3.3, Objective 3.4

  - Exam 220–602 (IT Technician): Objective 3.1, Objective 3.2, Objective 3.4

  - Exam 220–603 (Remote Technician): Objective 2.1, Objective 2.2, Objective 2.4

TOPIC A

Install Microsoft Windows

In this lesson, you will install and configure operating systems. The fundamental installation method is to install the operating system from scratch. In this topic, you will perform a fresh installation of Microsoft Windows.

Being able to perform a fresh installation of Windows can be important if you have built a custom computer system from scratch, if the system you purchased from a vendor did not have the correct system installed, or if you are completely redeploying existing hardware from one purpose to another. The skills and information in this topic will help you plan and perform a fresh installation properly whatever your technical and business requirements might be.

Windows System Requirements

Before installation, you must make sure that your hardware meets or exceeds the minimum requirements for the version of Windows you will install.

Operating System	Requirements
Windows 2000 Professional 	• Processor: Pentium 133 MHz or greater • RAM: 32 MB required (64 MB recommended) • Hard disk: 2 GB with 1 GB free space • Video adapter: VGA • Local installation source: 12X CD-ROM • Input devices: Keyboard; mouse or other pointing device
Windows XP Professional 	• Processor: 233-MHz minimum required; 300 megahertz (MHz) or higher recommended. Intel Pentium/Celeron family, AMD K6/Athlon/Duron family, or compatible processor recommended • RAM: 64 MB required (128 MB recommended) • Hard disk: 1.5 GB available space • Video adapter: Super VGA 800x600 resolution • Local installation source: CD-ROM or DVD-ROM • Input devices: Keyboard; mouse or other pointing device

Operating System	Requirements
Windows XP Home Edition 	• Processor: 233-MHz minimum required; 300 megahertz (MHz) or higher recommended. Intel Pentium/Celeron family, AMD K6/Athlon/ Duron family, or compatible processor recommended • RAM: 64 MB required (128 MB recommended) • Hard disk: 1.5 GB available space • Video adapter: Super VGA 800x600 resolution • Installation source: CD-ROM or DVD drive • Input devices: Keyboard; mouse or other pointing device
Windows XP Media Center Edition 	Media Center Edition is intended for installation on a specially-configured media-ready Media Center PC that will connect to and interact with other home media devices such as a TV, music center, or game system. Media Center PCs are available from many major retailers and computer manufacturers. For information about the different Media Center PC models and options as well as purchasing information, see the Media Center web page at **www.microsoft.com/windowsxp/mediacenter/ default.mspx**.

Mac OS System Requirements

The system requirements for Mac OS X Tiger are:

• A Macintosh computer with a PowerPC G3, G4, or G5 processor.

• Built-in FireWire support.

• A built-in display or a display connected to an Apple-supplied video card supported by your computer.

• A DVD drive for installation.

• 256 MB of RAM.

• 3 GB of available hard disk space minimum; 4 GB to install all developer tools.

Linux System Requirements

The hardware requirements for installing Linux will depend upon the distribution of Linux you choose. Linux is a portable operating system, and there are versions available for many different processor types, including Intel x86 and Pentium; Itanium; DEC Alpha; Sun Sparc; Motorola; and others. In general, a basic installation of Linux on a workstation might require as little as 16 or 32 MB of memory and 250 MB of disk space, but you might need several gigabytes of disk space for complete installations including all utilities.

Hardware Compatibility

You should check all your hardware to ensure that it is compatible with the version of Windows you plan to install. Microsoft tests and verifies hardware devices for different versions of Windows and maintains the results in the Windows Marketplace Tested Products List. For Windows XP Professional, you can also run the Microsoft Windows Upgrade Advisor from the product compact disc to generate compatibility reports.

 The Tested Products List is available on the Microsoft website at **http:// testedproducts.windowsmarketplace.com/**.

 Previously, Microsoft issued a list of all supported hardware in a file called the Hardware Compatibility List (HCL). For current versions of Windows, the HCL has been replaced by the Tested Products List. You still can access the HCLs for legacy versions of Windows from the HCL Home Page at **http://www.microsoft.com/whdc/hcl/default.mspx**.

Macintosh Hardware Compatibility

If your Macintosh computer meets the minimum requirements for Mac OS installation, the hardware should all be compatible with the operating system. You can verify that your hardware is supported by checking the list at **http://www.apple.com/macosx/upgrade/ requirements.html.**

Linux Hardware Compatibility

Because Linux is a portable operating system, it is compatible with a wide range of hardware. You will need to check with the vendor or provider of your Linux distribution to verify if your particular system hardware is supported by that distribution.

One web resource you can use to research general Linux hardware support is the Linux Hardware Compatibility HOWTO site at **www.tldp.org/HOWTO/Hardware-HOWTO.** You can find additional Linux hardware compatibility lists at **www.linux-drivers.org.**

Installation Methods

You can choose any of several methods to install Windows operating systems.

Installation Method	Description
Local installation source	You can launch the Setup program by booting the computer from a local installation CD-ROM.
Network installation source	You can launch the Setup program by connecting to a shared network folder that contains the installation source files and running the installation program file manually. In this case, you will need another operating system with networking capability already installed on the computer, or you will need bootable media such as a floppy disk, USB drive, or CD-ROM drive, with network connection software included.

Installation Method	Description
Unattended installation	You can automate an installation of Windows so that it requires limited or no user intervention. An *unattended installation* requires you to create an *answer file,* which is a text file that provides configuration information to the Windows Setup program. Microsoft provides a utility called the Setup Manager Wizard that can assist you in creating answer files as well as a batch file that includes the correct Setup command syntax. There are some advanced customization settings you can only implement by using unattended installation. For general information about unattended installations, see the article "Overview of Unattended Installation" at **technet.microsoft.com.**
System imaging	A *computer image* is a file containing a sector-by-sector replica of a computer's hard disk that can be replicated onto the hard disks of one or more other computers. The image contains the operating system software, such as Windows XP Professional, and also the applications, files, desktop settings, and user preferences from a single computer. Imaging provides a rapid way to deploy standardized computer installations. To use system imaging to install Windows, you will need:

- A *reference computer* to provide a baseline configuration for other computers. The contents of the reference computer are stored in the computer image.

- A third-party *disk imaging application*, such as PowerQuest Drive Image Pro or Symantec Ghost, to create the image itself.

- A *software distribution point* to store the image. This can be a network share point, or removable media, such as a CD-ROM.

- *Target computers,* the new or existing computers on which you deploy an image. Target computers must have the same disk controller type and mass-storage device driver as the reference computer. For example, if the reference computer has a small computer system interface (SCSI) controller with a non-generic driver, then the target computer must have a SCSI controller and use the same driver.

To use imaging to install Windows systems, follow the instructions in your drive imaging software's documentation.

Problems can arise from differences in the hardware between the reference computer and the install computer. Not everyone has the same exact computer throughout a company, so it's not uncommon for slight variances in network and video cards to exist. For these systems, the best thing to do is to create the image without these drivers installed, then install them after the machine is imaged. Bigger concerns that are difficult to overcome deal with motherboard differences at the system board level which can cause the installation to fail. This would necessitate different images for each system type.

If your network environment supports Microsoft Active Directory, you can use Microsoft's Remote Installation Services (RIS) to deploy Windows automatically on multiple computers throughout your organization. The RIS process is somewhat similar to deploying ghost images, but requires a number of Microsoft services and system tools rather than third-party software.

Installation Options

There are various options you can choose during Windows operating system installation.

Option	Description
Disk and file system preparation	You can set up and format one or more disk partitions during installation. If you make an entire disk one partition, you cannot repartition the disk later without either reinstalling the operating system or using a third-party tool. NTFS is the recommended Windows file system because it is well-suited to today's large partition sizes and provides security and enables file compression and encryption.
Regional and date and time settings	You can set the date and time for your locale and select the appropriate regional settings, such as the appropriate local display format for currency.
Computer name	You can give the computer a descriptive name of up to 15 characters. The Setup program might suggest a default name for you.
Network configuration	You can decide how you want to configure networking settings for the computer. You can accept a Typical configuration or you can configure Custom settings that are appropriate to your environment.
Workgroup or domain membership	Domains and workgroups are two different organizational and security models for Windows networking. Domains require a specially-configured Windows Server computer called a domain controller and are most often used in corporate environments with centralized administration. Workgroups are unstructured named collections of individual computers and are usually deployed in homes and small offices.
Internet connection method	You can indicate whether the computer will connect to the Internet using the local network connection or if it will connect to an account from an Internet Service Provider (ISP).
Local user accounts	For Windows XP, if you are installing into a workgroup, you can create local user accounts during installation. You can create additional local users and groups after installation. For Windows 2000, if you are installing into a workgroup, you can set logon options for local users. You can configure the system to require each user to log on individually, or you can configure it to log on automatically as a specific user whenever the computer boots.

Default Administrator Account

In addition to the local user accounts you create during or after installation, there is a default user account named Administrator on all Windows XP and Windows 2000 systems. If you are installing Windows XP Professional or Windows 2000 Professional, you can assign this default account a password during the installation process. On all Windows systems, you can use this account to log on and administer the system if there is not another suitable administrative account available.

Windows Update

After you have installed Windows, you should obtain the latest updates for that version from Microsoft Windows Update website. The appearance and functionality of the website will be customized for the particular version of Windows you are using, but the updates will fall generally into one of three categories: critical updates, including Service Packs and security-related system patches; optional software updates that provide new tools and functionality; and optional hardware updates such as new device drivers.

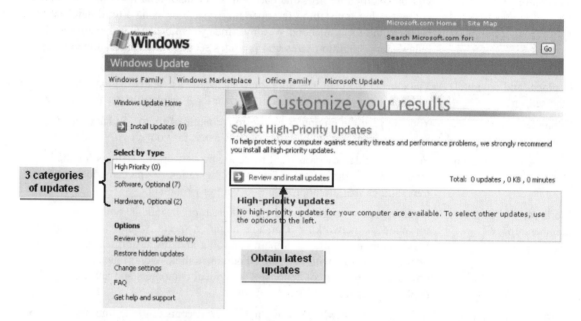

Figure 8-1: Windows Update.

 The Windows Update website is located at **windowsupdate.microsoft.com**. You can also connect to the Windows Update website by choosing Windows Update from the Start menu. You can run either an Express or Custom update; if you run a Custom update, you will be able to choose from updates in each of the three main categories.

 Microsoft Update is an alternative Microsoft website you can use as a comprehensive source of updates for not only Windows operating systems but also for other Microsoft software products as well. You can access Microsoft Update at **update.microsoft.com/microsoftupdate.**

Service Packs and Patches

Patches are targeted operating system updates that Microsoft releases on an as-needed basis to provide enhancements to the operating system or to address security or performance issues. *Service Packs* are comprehensive updates that generally include all prior patches and updates, but which can also include important new features and functions.

Windows Genuine Advantage (WGA)

Every time you access the Microsoft site, it goes through a process of validating your installation. If Microsoft deems the install to be invalid, you will not be able to proceed with updates and will be instructed to contact Microsoft.

Service Pack 2

Windows XP Professional Service Pack 2 (SP2) was a major update that Microsoft released to address security threats against Windows computers. Most of the enhancements in Service Pack 2 are aimed at increasing the default level of security of the operating system, including the Windows Firewall and the Security Center Control Panel application. SP2 also includes some improvements to Internet Explorer such as a pop-up advertisment blocker and other system functionality enhancements.

You can add Service Pack 2 to existing Windows XP installations. However, for new installations, the Service Pack is typically slipstreamed into the media, which means that it is included with the Windows XP installation files and installed concurrently with the base operating system.

Microsoft Product Activation

Microsoft Product Activation is an anti-piracy technology that verifies that software products are legitimately purchased. Product activation reduces a form of piracy known as casual copying. For example, you must activate Windows XP within a given number of days after installation. After the grace period, users cannot access the system until you activate Windows XP.

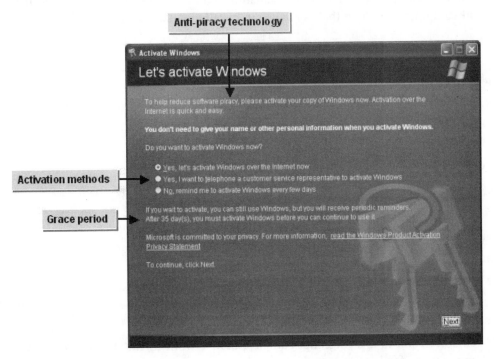

Figure 8-2: Product activation.

 You must have an activated installation of Windows to download updates and add-ons from Windows Update.

Activation Methods

For individual installations of Windows, you can activate the installation over the Internet. If you do not have an Internet connection, you can activate over the phone although this takes a little longer. If you wish, you can postpone product activation and activate later in the activation grace period.

In large organizations, you can use a Volume License Product Key that eliminates the need to individually activate each installation of Windows. You can also activate Windows as part of an automated installation.

How to Install Microsoft Windows

Procedure Reference: Install Windows Manually

To install Windows XP or Windows 2000 Professional:

1. Verify that your hardware meets the requirements for your version of Windows.

2. Access the Windows installation source files.
   - If you are installing from CD-ROM, insert the disc.
   - If you are installing from a network installation source, connect the computer to the network and open the share that contains the installation source files.

3. Run the Setup program.
   - If you are installing from compact disc, the Setup program should launch automatically.
   - If you need to launch the program manually, open the CD-ROM or the installation source files share. Run Setup.exe from the root folder, or run Winnt32.exe from the \I386 subfolder.

4. Complete the Setup Wizard.
   a. Prepare the disks for installation by partitioning and formatting the drive.
   b. Use the Setup Wizard to select the appropriate installation options for your system.

5. Complete the post-installation steps for your operating system.
   - Configure the Internet connection method.
   - For Windows XP, select the desired choice for product activation.
   - For Windows XP in a workgroup, enter names for any local user accounts you want to create.
   - For Windows 2000 in a workgroup, complete the Network Identification Wizard to set logon options for local users.

6. Log on to Windows, connect to Windows Update, and install any current Service Packs or critical security updates.

7. Test the Windows installation to verify that the Setup program properly detected your hardware and that all system devices are working properly. If devices are not working, download and install any new or updated drivers from the hardware vendor or from the Microsoft website.

Procedure Reference: Create a User Account with User Accounts

To create a user account with the User Accounts Control Panel utility:

1. From the Start menu, choose Control Panel. Open User Accounts.

2. Click Create A New Account.

3. Enter the account name and click Next.

4. Select the account type. Selecting Computer Administrator will make the account a member of the default Administrators group. Selecting Limited will make the user a member of the default Users group.

5. Click Create Account.

Procedure Reference: Create a User Account with Local Users and Groups

To create a user account with Local Users and Groups:

1. Open Computer Management.

2. Under System Tools, expand Local Users And Groups and select the Users folder.

3. Choose Action→New User, or right-click the Users folder and choose New User.

4. In the New User dialog box, enter the user name. This name uniquely identifies the account. It can contain up to 20 characters.

5. If desired, enter a full name for the user. This is a descriptive name that can be longer than the user's logon name. The full name will display on the Welcome screen. If you do not enter a full name, the full name will be set to match the user name.

6. If desired, enter a description to be displayed next to the user account in Local Users and Groups.

7. If desired, enter and confirm a password for the user. Otherwise, the default password will be blank.

8. Select the desired account options.
   - User Must Change Password At Next Logon
   - User Cannot Change Password
   - Password Never Expires
   - Account Is Disabled

9. Click Create, and then click Close.

Procedure Reference: Change a User's Password in Windows 2000/XP

To change a user's password in Windows XP:

1. Log on as a local computer administrator.

2. Open Computer Management.

 In Windows XP, resetting a user's password will prevent them from accessing any encrypted files. You should reset a user's password only as a last resort.

3. Expand Local Users And Groups and select the Users folder.

4. Right-click the user for whom you want to change the password and choose Set Password.

5. If you're using Windows XP, click Proceed.

6. In the New Password text box, type the new password for the user.

7. In the Confirm Password text box, type the password again.

8. Click OK.

9. Close Computer Management.

Procedure Reference: Create a Local Group

To create a local group:

1. Open Computer Management.

2. Expand Local Users And Groups and select the Groups folder.

3. Choose Action→New Group.

4. Enter the group name and an optional description of the group.

5. Enter and verify the user names and click OK.

6. Click Create, and then click Close.

Procedure Reference: Modify a User's Group Memberships

To modify a user's group memberships in Windows XP:

1. Log on as a local computer administrator.

2. Open Computer Management.

3. Expand Local Users And Groups.

4. Select the Users folder.

5. Double-click the user for whom you want to change group memberships.

6. Click the Member Of tab.

7. Click Add.

8. If you know the name of the group to which you want to add the user, enter it under Enter The Object Names To Select and click OK.

   If you want to search for the group to which you want to add the user:
   a. Click Advanced.
   b. Click Find Now to display a list of groups.
   c. Select the desired group or groups and click OK.

9. Click OK to close the Select Groups dialog box.

10. Click OK to close the user's Properties dialog box.

11. Close Computer Management.

Workgroup Logon Methods

There are two different methods that you can use for user logons in a workgroup environment:

- *The Welcome Screen*, which is the default logon method. The Welcome Screen lists the local logon account names; a user simply has to click the account name to initiate the logon process. If the Welcome Screen is active, then you can also choose to use *Fast User Switching*, which enables users to switch from one account to another without closing programs or logging off. This feature is useful in a home environment, in which several trusted users share a computer.

- *The Log On To Windows dialog box*, in which users enter their own user credentials. Only the name of the last user who logged on is visible by default. This method, which is also known as the *classic logon prompt*, does not support Fast User Switching.

To configure the logon method:

1. Choose Control Panel→User Accounts.

2. Click Change The Way Users Log On Or Off.

3. Check or uncheck Use The Welcome Screen.

4. If you check Use The Welcome Screen, then you also can choose to check or uncheck Fast User Switching.

5. Click Apply Options.

Logging on as the Default Administrator Account

If you are using the Welcome screen, the default Administrator account name will not be listed unless it is the only account on the system. If you need to log on as the default Administrator, press the Ctrl+Alt+Del key combination twice to bring up the Log On To Windows dialog box, and enter the user name and password.

OPTIONAL ACTIVITY 8-1

Installing Windows XP Home

Setup:

You will install Windows XP Home on your existing system as if there were no operating system present. Your instructor will provide you with the installation CD-ROM. Your computer system is configured so that the CD-ROM drive is the primary boot device. You have a unique two-digit classroom number.

Scenario:

You have built a custom computer system for a client's home using individual hardware components. You now need to install an operating system. Because this client only needs the system for private home use, you think that Windows XP Home is the operating system choice that will best meet his requirements.

 There is a simulated version of this activity available on the CD-ROM that shipped with this course. You can run this simulation on any Windows computer to review the activity after class, or as an alternative to performing the activity as a group in class. The activity simulation can be launched either directly from the CD-ROM by clicking the Interactives link and navigating to the appropriate one, or from the installed data file location by opening the C:\085820Data\Simulations\Lesson#\Activity# folder and double-clicking the executable (.exe) file.

What You Do	How You Do It
1. **Run the Windows XP Home setup program.**	a. **Insert the Windows XP Home installation CD-ROM in your CD-ROM drive.**
	b. **Choose Start→Turn Off Computer.**
	c. **Click Restart.**
	d. When prompted, **press any key on the keyboard to boot from the CD-ROM drive.**
	e. The first part of Setup proceeds in text mode. **Observe as the system detects the basic hardware and loads files for Setup.**

2. Partition and format the disk.

a. On the Welcome to Setup screen, **press Enter.**

b. To accept the license agreement, **press F8.**

c. You will delete the existing partition. With the C partition selected, **press D.**

d. To confirm the deletion, **press Enter and then press L.**

e. To create a partition, **press C.**

f. **Press the Backspace key to delete the existing value for the partition size.**

g. **Type *6000* and then press Enter.**

h. To set up Windows in the new partition, **press Enter.**

i. **Select Format The Partition Using The NTFS File System (Quick) and press Enter.**

j. **Observe as the format proceeds, the system copies files, and the system restarts.**

 Do not boot from the CD-ROM once the setup files have been copied to the hard disk. If you do, you will start the text mode of Setup over again.

3. **Use the Setup Wizard to select installation options.**

a. The system restarts in graphic mode and the first stages of the installation proceed without user intervention. When the Windows XP Home Edition Setup Wizard launches, on the Regional and Language page, to accept the default settings, **click Next.**

b. On the Personalize Your Software page, in the Name box, **type** *Software Manager* and in the Organization box, **type** *Information Technology*

c. **Click Next.**

d. On the Your Product Key page, **enter your product key and click Next.**

e. On the What's Your Computer's Name page, **type** *Client##* **and click Next.**

f. On the Date And Time Settings page, **verify the date and time, select your time zone, and click Next.**

g. The Wizard will pause, installation will proceed, and the Wizard will reappear. On the Networking Settings page, **verify that Typical Settings is selected and click Next.**

4. Complete the post-installation steps.

a. The system will restart in Windows. If prompted to adjust your screen resolution, **click OK twice.**

b. On the Welcome To Microsoft Windows screen, **click Next.**

c. On the Checking Your Internet Connectivity Screen, **click Skip.**

d. If Service Pack 2 is slipstreamed into your Windows XP installation files, on the Help Protect Your PC screen, **select Not Right Now and click Next.**

e. On the Ready To Activate Windows screen, **select No, Remind Me Every Few Days and click Next.**

f. On the Who Will Use This Computer screen, in the Your Name box, **type** *Admin##* **and click Next.**

g. **Click Finish.**

h. **Remove the installation CD-ROM from the drive.**

---

5. What additional steps should you perform at this point to complete the installation?

a) Create additional user accounts.

b) Install applications.

c) Install Service Packs and other critical updates.

d) Install a printer.

---

6. **Verify the installation.**

    a. The system will automatically log you on as the Admin## user. The Start menu will open. From the Start menu, **right-click My Computer, and choose Manage.**

    b. In Computer Management, under System Tools, **select Device Manager.**

    c. **Expand each of the hardware categories and verify that there are no devices displayed with Error or Warning icons.**

    d. **Close Computer Management.**

7. **Create a password for your user account.**

    a. **Choose Start→Control Panel.**

    b. **Click User Accounts.**

    c. **Click the Admin## account.**

    d. **Click Create A Password.**

    e. **Type and confirm *!Pass1234* and click Create Password.**

    f. **Click Yes, Make Private.**

    g. **Close User Accounts and Control Panel.**

OPTIONAL ACTIVITY 8-2

Exploring the Windows XP Home Interface

Scenario:

You have just installed Windows XP Home. Previously you worked mostly with Windows XP Professional, and you want to identify some of the areas where the two operating systems are different.

 There is a simulated version of this activity available on the CD-ROM that shipped with this course. You can run this simulation on any Windows computer to review the activity after class, or as an alternative to performing the activity as a group in class. The activity simulation can be launched either directly from the CD-ROM by clicking the Interactives link and navigating to the appropriate one, or from the installed data file location by opening the C:\ 085820Data\Simulations\Lesson#\Activity# folder and double-clicking the executable (.exe) file.

What You Do	How You Do It
1. **Identify user interface differences between Windows XP Home and Windows XP Professional.**	a. **Choose Start.**
	b. By default, The Start menu arrangement is slightly different. There is no My Recent Documents link and no Printers and Faxes link. **Click My Computer.**
	c. By default, the Address bar is not displayed. **Choose Tools→Folder Options.**
	d. **Click the View tab.**
	e. **Scroll to the bottom of the Advanced Settings list.**
	f. There is no option to turn off Simple File Sharing. **Click Cancel.**
	g. **Right-click the C drive and choose Properties.**
	h. There is no Security tab. You cannot see or modify the NTFS permissions on the drive. **Click Cancel.**
	i. **Close My Computer.**

TOPIC B
Upgrade Windows

In the previous topic, you installed Microsoft Windows from scratch. The other primary type of installation is an upgrade installation. In this topic, you will upgrade Windows.

As a system professional, you'll probably be called upon to upgrade systems even more often than performing from-scratch installations. Software vendors such as Microsoft are constantly coming out with new operating system versions, and it is much more economical to upgrade existing systems when possible rather than to purchase new computer hardware with the new version pre-installed. Whether you are upgrading for an individual user or as part of a company-wide migration plan, the skills in this topic should help you upgrade older versions of Windows to the current version successfully.

Supported Upgrade Paths

Existing Windows installations can be directly upgraded to specific other versions of Windows.

Current Operating System	Can be Upgraded To
Windows 95	Windows 98, Windows 2000 Professional
Windows 98/98 SE/Me	Windows 2000 Professional, Windows XP Professional
Windows NT Workstation 4.0	Windows 2000 Professional, Windows XP Professional
Windows 2000 Professional	Windows XP Professional; will be upgradeable to Windows Vista
Windows XP Home Edition	Windows XP Professional
Windows XP Professional	Windows Vista

Unsupported Upgrades

Upgrading Windows 95 directly to Windows XP Professional is not supported. It was possible to upgrade a Windows 95 computer to Windows 2000 Professional and subsequently to Windows XP Professional. However, Windows 2000 Professional is no longer commercially available. If you still have installation media for Windows 2000 you can follow this indirect upgrade path. Generally, it is best to perform a clean installation of Windows XP Professional on any systems that are still running Windows 95.

Hardware Upgrade Compatibility

If you are upgrading an existing computer to a different version of Windows, you will need to check your existing hardware against the Tested Products List to ensure that the existing computer hardware is compatible with the target operating system. For Windows XP Professional, you can also run the Microsoft Windows Upgrade Advisor from the product compact disc to generate compatibility reports. The Setup program will also run a compatibility check during the upgrade process.

Network Compatibility Considerations

As part of the hardware compatibility check, you should verify that the new version of Windows will support the existing network adapter card. In most cases, the network configuration settings will upgrade smoothly to the new version of Windows if the card is supported.

However, when you are upgrading an older version of Windows, there may be cases in which you find that the old system is still running legacy protocols, such as NetBEUI and NWLink, that are not supported by current Windows network implementations. Because the current *de facto* standard network protocol is TCP/IP, you will need to plan to upgrade and configure these systems for TCP/IP during the upgrade process.

Software Upgrade Compatibility

Before upgrading, you should check the Tested Products List or run the Microsoft Windows Upgrade Advisor to verify that your existing applications will run properly on the new version of Windows. The Setup program will also run a compatibility check during the upgrade process. Applications written for Windows 2000 should work well on Windows XP; legacy applications might require one or more of the compatibility fixes built in to Windows XP. You can select an appropriate application compatibility mode for the application after you have upgraded the operating system.

Application Compatibility Modes

The Windows XP application compatibility modes are Windows 95, Windows 98/Windows Me, Windows NT 4.0, Windows 2000, 256 colors, and 640 x 480 screen resolution. You can set the appropriate mode for a particular application by running the Program Compatibility Wizard from Windows XP Help and Support Center. See the article "Windows XP Application Compatibility Technologies" at **www.microsoft.com/technet/prodtechnol/winxppro/plan/appcmpxp.mspx** for more information.

Macintosh Software Compatibility

Applications that ran in previous releases of Mac OS X should be supported when you upgrade to any current release.

If you need to use Mac OS 9 applications on a Mac OS X system, you can do so in the Classic environment in Mac OS X. To use the Classic environment, you must have a Mac OS 9 System Folder installed on your computer, either on the same hard disk as Mac OS X, or on another disk or disk partition. For more information on the Classic environment in Mac OS X, see **www.apple.com/support/panther/moretopics/**.

Apple also provides tools to enable IBM PC users to transfer files and software when migrating from an IBM Windows PC to a Macintosh. For more information on moving from Windows to Macintosh, see **www.apple.com/macosx/switch**.

Linux Software Compatibility

Check your Linux vendor's website and read the technical documentation for the distribution of Linux you plan to upgrade to in order to determine if your existing applications will be supported under the new version. You can also check the resources at **www.linux.org/apps** for lists of Linux-compatible applications in various categories from a number of vendors. You can also register as a user at **www.linux.org/user** and post questions about particular applications in the online user forums.

How to Upgrade Windows

Procedure Reference: Upgrade to Windows XP Professional

To upgrade to Windows XP Professional:

1. Verify that the computer meets the hardware requirements for Windows XP. You can run compatibility checks by clicking Check System Compatibility on the opening screen of the Windows XP installation CD-ROM.

2. Back up any existing user data files.

3. Insert the Windows XP Professional CD-ROM. The setup program should launch automatically. (You can also launch the winnt32.exe installation program manually from the installation source files.)

4. Click Install Windows XP and select Upgrade as the installation type.

5. Accept the license agreement and enter the Product Key.

6. On the Get Updated Setup Files page, make the appropriate choice depending on whether or not you want to check for updated files on the Internet.

   - Yes, Download The Updated Setup Files (Recommended).

   - No, Skip This Step And Continue Installing Windows.

7. Follow the remaining steps in the Setup Wizard to complete the installation.

8. Log on to Windows XP.

9. Connect to Windows Update and install any current Service Packs or critical security updates.

10. Test the Windows installation to verify that the Setup program properly detected your hardware and that all system devices are working properly.

11. If not all devices are functioning, use the Add Hardware tool in Control Panel to add any additional devices, or install new or updated device drivers from the Microsoft or manufacturer's website.

12. Use the Add Or Remove Programs tool in Control Panel to add any desired additional Windows XP components to your system.

OPTIONAL ACTIVITY 8-3

Upgrading Windows XP Home to Windows XP Professional

Setup:

Your instructor will provide you with the Windows XP Professional installation CD-ROM. If Service Pack 2 is not slipstreamed into your Windows XP Professional installation source, your instructor will provide you with the Service Pack 2 CD-ROM as well.

Scenario:

A customer purchased a computer that came preinstalled with Windows XP Home, but after using it for a while, the customer has decided that she prefers to use the more advanced functionality of Windows XP Professional. The computer system vendor has provided an installation CD for Windows XP Professional, and the customer would like you to upgrade her system.

 There is a simulated version of this activity available on the CD-ROM that shipped with this course. You can run this simulation on any Windows computer to review the activity after class, or as an alternative to performing the activity as a group in class. The activity simulation can be launched either directly from the CD-ROM by clicking the Interactives link and navigating to the appropriate one, or from the installed data file location by opening the C:\ 085820Data\Simulations\Lesson#\Activity# folder and double-clicking the executable (.exe) file.

What You Do	How You Do It
1. **Run the Microsoft Windows Setup Advisor.**	a. **Insert the Windows XP Professional Installation CD-ROM.**
	b. The Setup program should launch automatically. **Click Check System Compatibility.**
	c. **Click Check My System Automatically.**
	d. **Select, No, Skip This Step And Continue Installing Windows and click Next.**

e. There should be no incompatibilities. **Click
    Finish.**

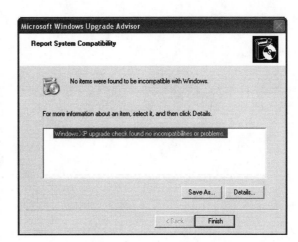

f. In the Windows XP Setup program, **click
    Back.**

2. **Run the Windows XP Professional upgrade program.**

    a. **Click Install Windows XP.**

    b. **Verify that the Installation Type is Upgrade (Recommended) and click Next.**

    c. **Select I Accept This Agreement and click Next.**

    d. On the Your Product Key page, **type your product key and click Next.**

    e. To save time at this point in the installation, **select No, Skip This Step And Continue Installing Windows and click Next.**

3. **Complete the post-installation steps.**

    a. The system will restart, load the Windows XP Professional Setup program, and Setup will continue. The installation program might reload more than once. When the upgrade is complete, the system will restart in Windows. On the Welcome To Microsoft Windows screen, **click Next.**

 Do not boot from the CD-ROM when the system restarts. If you do, you will start Setup over again.

b. If Service Pack 2 is slipstreamed into your Windows XP installation files, on the Help Protect Your PC screen, **select Not Right Now and click Next.**

c. On the Ready To Activate Windows screen, **select No, Remind Me Every Few Days and click Next.**

d. **Click Finish.**

e. **Remove the installation CD-ROM.**

4. If Service Pack 2 is not slipstreamed into your Windows installation, **install Service Pack 2.**

    a. To log on as your Admin## account, in the Password field, **type *!Pass1234* and press Enter.**

    b. **Insert the Windows XP Service Pack 2 CD-ROM.**

    c. The Service Pack 2 installation should run automatically. **Click Continue.**

    d. **Click Install Now.**

    e. In the Windows XP Service Pack 2 Setup Wizard, **click Next.**

    f. **Select I Agree and click Next.**

    g. To accept the uninstall folder location, **click Next.**

    h. When the installation is complete, **click Finish.**

    i. The system will restart. On the Help Protect Your PC screen, **select Not Right Now and click Next.**

    j. To log on as your Admin## account, **type *!Pass1234* and press Enter.**

    k. The Windows Security Center window will open. **Close the Windows Security Center.**

5. If your Windows system has been activated, **update the system from Windows Update.**

a. **Choose Start→All Programs→Windows Update.**

b. If prompted to install Windows Update software, **click Install, and then click Install Now.**

c. To see the list of available and recommended updates, **click Custom.**

d. If an Internet Explorer dialog box appears, **verify that the In The Future, Do Not Show This Message check box is checked and click Yes.**

e. If prompted to install the latest version of Windows Update, **click Download And Install Now.**

f. When the installation is complete, **click Restart Now.**

g. **Log in as your Admin## account.**

h. **Choose Start→All Programs→Windows Update.**

i. To see the list of available and recommended updates broken down by category, **click Custom.**

j. To review optional software updates, under Select By Type, **click the Software, Optional link.**

k. To review optional hardware updates, under Select By Type, **click the Hardware, Optional link.**

l. **Click the High Priority link.**

m. All high-priority updates should be selected by default. **Click Review And Install Updates. Click Install Updates.**

n. **Follow any prompts or dialog boxes and restart the system as necessary.**

6. **Verify the installation.**

    a. **Choose Start, right-click My Computer, and choose Manage.**

    b. In Computer Management, under System Tools, **select Device Manager.**

    c. **Expand each of the hardware categories and verify that there are no devices displayed with Error or Warning icons.**

    d. **Close Computer Management.**

ACTIVITY 8-4

Creating and Managing Local User Accounts

Setup:

There are two administrative user accounts on the computer: the default Administrator account and an account named Admin## that you created when you installed Windows.

Scenario:

You have been called in to configure a client's new Windows XP computer. After interviewing the client, you've determined that she needs accounts on the computer for the following users:

- Susan Williams (the client)
- Jeff Bernard (Susan's employee in her home-based business)

For consistency, you recommend that your client use the following naming convention for user accounts: the user's first name plus the first initial of his or her last name. In addition, you recommend that each user have a reasonably complex password. Susan does not want her employee to be able to change his password. Because Susan is the owner of the computer, you plan to add her account to the Administrators group.

 There is a simulated version of this activity available on the CD-ROM that shipped with this course. You can run this simulation on any Windows computer to review the activity after class, or as an alternative to performing the activity as a group in class. The activity simulation can be launched either directly from the CD-ROM by clicking the Interactives link and navigating to the appropriate one, or from the installed data file location by opening the C:\085820Data\Simulations\Lesson#\Activity# folder and double-clicking the executable (.exe) file.

What You Do	How You Do It
1. Create the local accounts.	a. **Open Computer Management.**
	b. **Expand Local Users And Groups.**
	c. **Select the Users folder.**
	d. **Choose Action→New User.**
	e. In the User Name text box, **type *SusanW***

f. In the Full Name text box, **type** *Susan Williams*

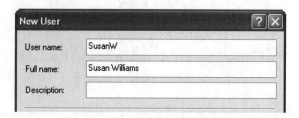

g. In the Password text box, **type** *!Pass1234*

h. In the Confirm Password text box, **type** *!Pass1234*

i. **Uncheck the User Must Change Password At Next Logon check box.**

j. **Click Create.**

k. **Enter the account information for the user Jeff Bernard.**

l. **Click Create.**

		m.	**Click Close.**
2.	**Add SusanW to the built-in Administrators group.**	a.	**Select the Groups folder.**
		b.	**Double-click the Administrators group.**
		c.	**Click Add.**
		d.	**Type *SusanW* and then click OK.**
		e.	To close the Administrators Properties dialog box, **click OK.**
		f.	**Close Computer Management.**
3.	**Verify that you can log on as SusanW.**	a.	**Choose Start→Log Off.**
		b.	**Click Log Off.**
		c.	**Click Susan Williams.**
		d.	In the Password text box, **type *!Pass1234***
		e.	**Press Enter.**
		f.	**Log off and log back on as Admin##.**

TOPIC C
Add Devices to Windows

In the first part of this lesson, you installed and upgraded Windows. After installation, you might need to make various modifications to the system, such as adding devices. In this topic, you will add devices to Windows.

Although the installation process should detect and install any devices present on the system at the time of installation, what if it does not do so? And what if you need to add devices to the system later? You know how to accomplish the physical installation of most devices, but the other half of the equation is to make sure that Windows properly detects the device and adds the correct drivers. The information and skills in this topic should ensure that you can add devices to Windows regardless of the device type or the source of the device drivers.

Driver Signing

Definition:

A *signed device driver* is a driver that has been tested and verified for a particular operating system, and has a piece of encrypted data, called a *digital signature*, attached to it by a signing authority. The digital signature ensures that the driver files have not been altered or overwritten by another program's installation process, and that the drivers will not overwrite system files with older and sometimes incompatible versions, which can cause system instability. For the best performance and stability, Microsoft recommends that you use only hardware devices with signed drivers.

 Some hardware manufacturers do not provide signed drivers so there will be no option for using signed drivers in some installs. Proceed with the understanding that the drivers could cause problems.

Example:

Has not been altered
Will not overwrite files

Figure 8-3: Signed device drivers.

Unsigned Driver Installation Options

Because unsigned drivers can cause system instability, Windows XP enables you to configure settings that limit unsigned driver installation. There are three driver-signing options:

- *Ignore* permits installation of both signed and unsigned drivers.

- *Warn* displays a warning message when a user attempts to install an unsigned driver. This is the default setting.

- *Block* prevents installation of unsigned drivers.

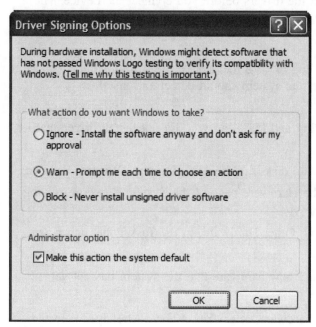

Figure 8-4: *Unsigned driver installation options.*

Installation Permissions

You need Administrator level permissions to be able to install new permanent devices in Windows. However, ordinary users can generally add and remove common Plug and Play devices, such as USB-based removable storage drives, that have support built in to Windows. If you find that you have difficulty installing a device, log on with an account that is a member of the Administrators group.

How to Add Devices to Windows

Procedure Reference: Install a Device

To install a device:

1. Check with your device vendor's documentation to see if the vendor recommends installing the latest device drivers before connecting the device, so that the Plug and Play auto-detect function works with the latest device definitions. If they so recommend, run the manufacturer's setup program to install the drivers before you connect the device. The specific steps in the program will vary according to the manufacturer's programming.

2. Attach the device to the computer.

3. If necessary, turn on the computer and log on as a member of the Administrators group. If the device is Plug and Play compatible, the system should detect and install it automatically.

4. If the device is not detected through Plug and Play, and you did not install drivers earlier, run the manufacturer's setup program.

5. If you do not have a manufacturer's setup disk, run the Add Hardware Wizard. You can:
   - Click Add Hardware Wizard on the Hardware page of the System Properties dialog box.
   - In Control Panel, click Printers And Other Hardware. In the Task Pane, under See Also, click Add Hardware.

6. Click Next. The wizard will scan for any new hardware that the system has not yet detected.

7. If the wizard does not locate any new hardware, select Yes, I Have Already Connected The Hardware and click Next. (Select Yes even if you are installing a driver without a physical device attached. If you select No, the wizard will end so that you can connect the hardware.)

8. From the bottom of the Installed Hardware list, click Add A New Hardware Device. Click Next.

9. Do one of the following:
   - If the device is physically attached, select Search For And Install The Hardware Automatically and click Next to force another detection cycle. If the device is not found, click Next to select the device from a list.
   - If the device is not physically attached, select Install The Hardware That I Manually Select From A List, and click Next.

10. Select the type of hardware and click Next.

11. Select the device driver to install:
    - For Microsoft-supplied device drivers, select the manufacturer and model to install. Click Next.
    - For manufacturer-supplied drivers, click Have Disk and browse to select the location of the driver (this location should contain the driver's *information (INF) file*, the file that contains the information that the system needs to install the device). Click Next.

12. Click Finish.

13. In Device Manager, verify that the device is working properly.

Procedure Reference: Use Device Manager to Verify Hardware Device Status

To use Device Manager to verify that a hardware device is working properly:

1. Log on as a local administrator.

2. Open Device Manager.

    a. On the Start menu, right-click My Computer.

    b. Choose Properties.

    c. Click the Hardware tab.

    d. Click Device Manager.

3. Expand the category of a hardware device (for example, Network Adapters).

4. Right-click the hardware device and choose Properties.

5. Review the Device Status portion of the Properties dialog box. You use this information to determine if the device is working properly.

Procedure Reference: Use Device Manager to Install a Different Device Driver

To use Device Manager to install an updated device driver:

1. Log on as a local administrator.

2. Open Device Manager.

3. Right-click a device and choose Update Driver.

4. Choose Install From A List Or Specific Location. Click Next.

5. Select Search Removable Media or specify a location to search, or both. Click Next.

6. If the wizard finds another driver, you will be prompted to use that driver or keep the current driver. Make your selection and click Next and complete the wizard to install the driver.

7. If the wizard can't find a driver, the wizard will end. Click Finish.

Procedure Reference: Uninstall Devices

To uninstall a device:

1. Right-click the device in Device Manager and choose Uninstall to remove the driver.

2. Turn off the computer and physically remove the device.

Procedure Reference: Identify Unsigned Drivers

You can use File Signature Verification (sigverif.exe) to identify unsigned drivers on a system. To identify unsigned drivers:

1. To run File Signature Verification, from the Start menu, choose Run and enter Sigverif. exe, or run Sigverif.exe at a command prompt.

2. Click Advanced if you want to set search and logging options. Otherwise, skip to step 6.

If you want to start the scan immediately without configuring options, you can also run the command sigverif.exe /defscan.

3. On the Search page, select one of the following:

- Select Notify Me If Any System Files Are Not Signed to scan all system files and drivers.

- Select Look For Other Files That Are Not Digitally Signed to specify a file type and search location to scan. Enter the file type information and search location in the Search Options area.

4. On the Logging page, specify the name of the log file, and whether to append data to the log or overwrite the log each time you scan.

5. Click OK to close the Advanced File Signature Verification Settings dialog box.

6. Choose Start to start the scan. When the scan is complete, any unsigned drivers will be listed in the Signature Verification Results dialog box.

7. Click Close to close the Signature Verification Results dialog box.

8. Click Close to close File Signature Verification.

Procedure Reference: Configure Driver Signing Verification

To configure driver signing verification:

1. On the Hardware page of the System Properties dialog box, click Driver Signing.

2. Choose the appropriate option:

- *Ignore* to permit installation of all drivers.

- *Warn* to display a warning message when a user attempts to install an unsigned driver. This is the default setting.

- *Block* to prevent installation of unsigned drivers.

3. Click OK twice.

ACTIVITY 8-5

Installing Hardware Manually

Scenario:

You have a desktop computer with a single network adapter, but you need to do some testing on the system as if it had two network adapters. You decide to install The Microsoft Loopback Adapter, which is a software interface that can simulate the presence of a network adapter.

 There is a simulated version of this activity available on the CD-ROM that shipped with this course. You can run this simulation on any Windows computer to review the activity after class, or as an alternative to performing the activity as a group in class. The activity simulation can be launched either directly from the CD-ROM by clicking the Interactives link and navigating to the appropriate one, or from the installed data file location by opening the C:\085820Data\Simulations\Lesson#\Activity# folder and double-clicking the executable (.exe) file.

What You Do	How You Do It
1. **Install the Microsoft Loopback Adapter.**	a. **Choose Start→Control Panel.**
	b. **Click Printers And Other Hardware.**
	c. To run the Add Hardware Wizard, in the Task Pane, **click Add Hardware.**
	d. **Click Next.**
	e. The wizard searches for new hardware. **Select Yes, I Have Already Connected The Hardware and click Next.**

f.   **Drag the scroll box to the bottom of the Installed Hardware list and select Add A New Hardware Device. Click Next.**

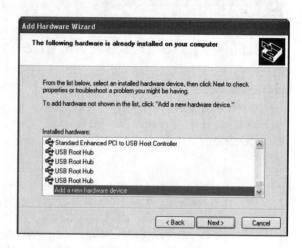

g.   **Select Install The Hardware That I Manually Select From A List. Click Next.**

h.   **Scroll down to select Network Adapters. Click Next.**

i.   In the Network Adapter list, **select Microsoft Loopback Adapter. Click Next.**

j.   This is an adapter driver that you can install without manufacturer's driver files. To install the hardware, **click Next.**

k.   **Click Finish.**

2.   **Verify the device installation.**

a.   In the Task Pane, **click System.**

b.   **Click the Hardware tab and click Device Manager.**

c.   In Device Manager, **expand the Network Adapters category.**

d. Both the adapters are listed. **Close Device Manager.**

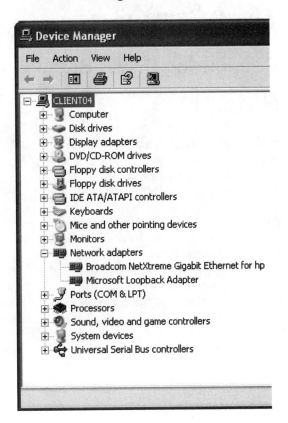

e. In the System Properties dialog box, **click Cancel.**

f. **Close the Printers And Other Hardware window.**

ACTIVITY 8-6

Configuring Driver Signing Verification

Scenario:

You work in a lightly managed Windows XP Professional environment. Users have a lot of autonomy and occasionally make changes to the hardware configurations of their own systems. To protect your environment, you first want to make sure that all the current drivers on each user's computer are safe. Then, you want to make sure that users cannot install any hardware with unsigned device drivers.

 There is a simulated version of this activity available on the CD-ROM that shipped with this course. You can run this simulation on any Windows computer to review the activity after class, or as an alternative to performing the activity as a group in class. The activity simulation can be launched either directly from the CD-ROM by clicking the Interactives link and navigating to the appropriate one, or from the installed data file location by opening the C:\085820Data\Simulations\Lesson#\Activity# folder and double-clicking the executable (.exe) file.

What You Do	How You Do It
1. **Determine the signing status of current system and driver files.**	a. **Choose Start→Run.**
	b. **Type *sigverif* and click OK.**
	c. **Click Advanced.**
	d. Use this dialog box to verify the files that will be included in the scan. You could also set logging options in this dialog box. **Click OK.**

e. **Click Start.**

f. The system builds a list of files and then scans the selected files. This takes a few moments. If you had any unsigned files, a results window would appear listing the files. This information is also logged to the Sigverif.txt log file. To close the message box and return to the File Signature Verification dialog box, **click OK.**

g. If any unsigned drivers are reported, make a note of the driver file names and close the results list. In the File Signature Verification dialog box, **click Close.**

2. **If you discovered any unsigned files during the scan, how would you use this information?**

3. **Configure the system to block the installation of unsigned drivers.**

   a. **Choose Start, right-click My Computer, and choose Properties.**

   b. **Click the Hardware tab.**

   c. On the Hardware page of the System Properties dialog box, **click Driver Signing.**

   d. **Select Block – Never Install Unsigned Driver Software.**

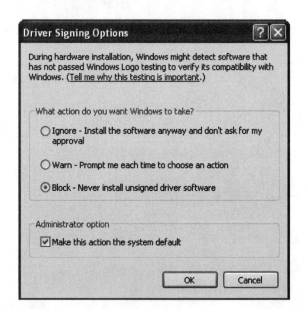

   e. **Click OK twice.**

TOPIC D
Optimize Windows

In the previous topics, you installed and configured Windows and the devices running on Windows. Once the system software and hardware has been completely installed, you might find that you need to make adjustments so that the system performs at an optimal level. In this topic, you will optimize Windows.

Installing and configuring Windows goes beyond making sure all the hardware and software is installed and working. As a support professional, others will be looking to you to ensure that their systems are functioning at their highest possible level. The skills and information in this topic should help you meet users' needs by optimizing the performance of many aspects of the Windows environment.

Virtual Memory

Definition:
Virtual memory is the ability of the computer system to use a portion of the hard disk as if it were physical RAM. Windows can manage enough memory addresses to fill 4 GB of memory, but few systems have this much physical RAM installed. The Windows *Virtual Memory Manager (VMM)* component is responsible for translating this virtual range of addresses into a physical memory location. When all physical memory locations are assigned, the VMM can transfer some of the memory data to a designated location on the hard disk called the *pagefile*.

Example:

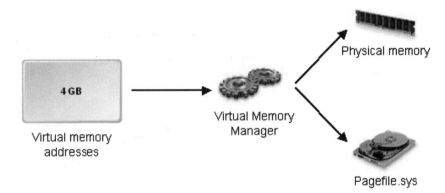

Figure 8-5: Virtual memory.

The Virtual Memory Process

When data is stored in virtual memory:

1. An application loads and requests memory from the system.

2. The VMM assigns it a *page* of memory addresses from within the virtual memory space.

3. The application stores information in one or more of the virtual memory locations.

4. The VMM maps the virtual address the application uses to a physical location in RAM.

5. As physical RAM becomes full, the VMM moves inactive data from memory to the pagefile in a process called *paging* or *swapping*.

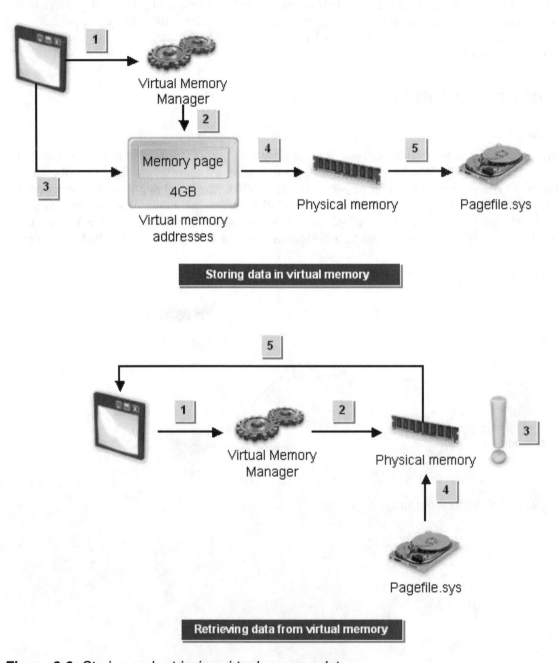

Figure 8-6: Storing and retrieving virtual memory data.

When data is retrieved from virtual memory:

1. An application requests data from its virtual memory location.

2. The VMM determines which physical RAM location was mapped to this virtual memory address.

3. If the VMM finds that the data is not present in the RAM location, it generates an interrupt called a *page fault*.

4. The VMM locates the data in the pagefile, retrieves the data from the hard disk, loads it back into RAM, and updates the virtual-to-physical address mapping for the application. If necessary, the VMM swaps other data out of RAM to release space.

5. The application retrieves the data from RAM.

Optimizing the Pagefile

When you install Windows, the system automatically creates a pagefile named Pagefile.sys at the root of the drive. The size of the pagefile varies within a range determined by the pagefile's Initial Size value and Maximum Size value. The system sets the size values of the pagefile using an algorithm that takes into account the amount of physical memory and the space available on the disk. When the system starts, the pagefile is set to the initial size; if more virtual memory space is needed, the system adds it to the pagefile until it reaches the maximum size. An administrator can alter the initial and maximum size values to optimize the pagefile and virtual memory performance. In modern systems, there is rarely a severe shortage of either physical RAM or disk space, so optimizing the pagefile might not be an issue, but you can consider the following tips:

● Although Microsoft recommends an initial pagefile size of 1.5 times the amount of RAM, the more RAM you have, the smaller a pagefile you need.

● If the initial size of the pagefile is too low, the system will waste resources as it adds more space to the pagefile. Adding space to the pagefile after startup also increases disk fragmentation. If the initial size is too high, however, the pagefile will be mostly empty, which wastes disk space.

● If you get a lot of "low virtual memory" errors, increase the maximum size of the pagefile.

● If you have multiple drives, you can move the pagefile off the drive that contains the Windows system files, so that the computer can access system files and pagefile information simultaneously. Put the pagefile on the fastest drive that doesn't contain Windows.

● If there is not a noticeable speed difference between drives, create additional pagefiles on multiple drives. This speeds access time because the system can read and write from multiple drives simultaneously. However, there is no performance advantage to putting the pagefile on different partitions on the same disk.

Windows Services

Definition:

A Windows *service* is a background process that performs a specific operation. Services can run whether or not a user is logged on. Unlike applications, services do not run in visible windows. Services enable the system to perform functions that are not included in the operating system kernel. This keeps the kernel small and streamlined, and it enables an administrator to optimize the performance of the system by running only necessary services.

Services and Daemons

Windows services are equivalent to daemons on UNIX or Linux systems. Some UNIX daemons are supported on Windows or other operating systems; for example, Windows can run the Line Printer Daemon (LPD) that provides print services on a UNIX server.

Example:

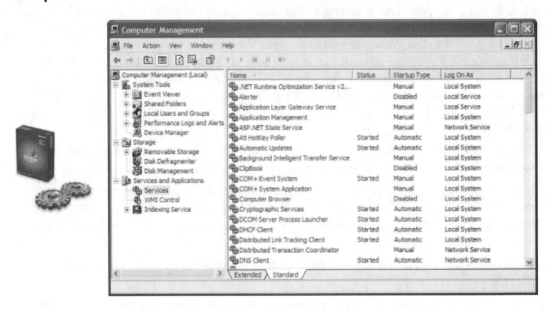

Figure 8-7: Windows services.

Windows Service Startup Values

Based on the configuration you select when you install Windows XP, Setup automatically configures a core set of its services to automatically start whenever the computer boots. In addition, if you install other Windows features and some third-party software, you will find that these applications add their own services to the operating system. You can manage the services in Windows XP by setting their Startup values.

Service Startup Type	Configures the Service To
Automatic	Start automatically when Windows boots.
Manual	Start manually. In some instances, Windows starts these services for you when you perform an action that requires the service. In other instances, you must open the Services console and manually start the service.

Service Startup Type	Configures the Service To
Disabled	Not start under any circumstances. In order to start this service, you must change its startup type to either Automatic or Manual and then start it.

Windows XP also enables you to configure the operating system to attempt to automatically restart a service when it fails. You can do so by using the Recovery tab in the Properties dialog box for each service.

The Windows XP Boot Process

There are five major sequences that occur during the Windows XP Professional boot process.

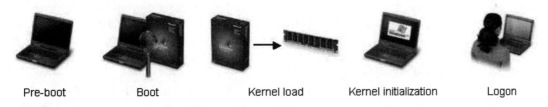

Pre-boot   Boot   Kernel load   Kernel initialization   Logon

Figure 8-8: *The Windows XP boot process.*

Sequence	Description
Pre-boot sequence	The *pre-boot sequence* begins when the power is turned on. The computer runs Power-On Self Test (POST) routines to determine the amount of physical memory and the other hardware components present. If the computer has a Plug and Play BIOS, the hardware is recognized and configured. The computer's BIOS locates the boot device, and then loads and runs the Master Boot Record (MBR).

Sequence	Description
Boot sequence	The *boot sequence* is when the operating system is selected, and the hardware configuration is detected and loaded. It has four sub-phases: Initial Boot Loader, Operating System Selection, Hardware Detection, and Configuration Selection. The boot sequence uses six files during its four sub-phases: Ntldr, Boot.ini, Ntdetect.com, Ntoskrnl.exe, Ntbootdd.sys, and the optional Bootsect.dos file.
	• During the *Initial Boot Loader* phase, the operating system loader file, Ntldr, switches the microprocessor from real mode, in which 640 K of RAM is reserved for MS-DOS and the rest is designated as extended memory, to 32-bit flat memory mode, in which Windows XP Professional uses all of the available memory. Ntldr starts the built-in mini-file system drivers, so that it can find partitions formatted to FAT or to NTFS and begin the startup process on them.
	• During the *Operating System Selection* phase, if there are multiple operating systems installed on the computer, and the Boot.ini file is configured to present a list of operating systems, the Please Select The Operating System To Start menu appears so that the user can select a system. If Windows XP is chosen, Ntldr runs Ntdetect.com. If a non-Windows operating system is chosen, Ntldr runs Bootsect.dos and relinquishes control of the system. If the user makes no selection, the default operating system loads.
	• During the *Hardware Detection* phase, Ntdetect.com collects a list of currently installed hardware components and returns the list to Ntldr. This list will later be used to create the Hardware key in the registry. The components detected include bus and adapter types, video adapters, communications ports, parallel ports, floating-point coprocessors, removable media, keyboards, and pointing devices.
	• During the *Configuration Selection* phase, if the computer has multiple hardware profiles configured, Ntldr displays the Hardware Profile/Configuration Recovery menu. Otherwise, Windows XP loads using the default hardware profile.
Kernel load sequence	During the *kernel load sequence,* the operating system components are loaded into memory. Ntldr loads Ntoskrnl.exe, containing the Windows XP kernel, but does not initialize it. Ntldr then loads the HAL.dll file. Next, the HKEY_LOCAL_MACHINE\SYSTEM registry key loads, and Ntldr reads the SELECT key to determine which control set to load. Control sets are areas of the registry that contain the low-level configuration information for the system, such as the list of device drivers and services to start. If the system includes any BIOS-disabled SCSI drives, Windows XP will load the Ntbootdd.sys device driver.
Kernel initiation sequence	In the *kernel initiation sequence,* the Windows XP Professional kernel takes control of the system. Ntldr passes control to the Windows XP kernel. At this point, the Microsoft Windows XP logo appears, along with a status bar. During this sequence:
	• The HKEY_LOCAL_MACHINE\HARDWARE registry key is created from the information gathered in the hardware detection phase.
	• A copy of the current control set, called Clone, is created.
	• Device drivers are loaded and initialized based on entries in the HKEY_LOCAL_MACHINE\System\CurrentControlSet\Services key. First, drivers with a registry Start value of 0 load, then drivers with a Start value of 1.
	• Next, the Session Manager starts higher-order subsystems and services. This includes the Win32 subsystem, which controls all input/output devices, provides access to the video display, and enables the Graphical User Interface (GUI). The Session Manager also starts the Winlogon process.

Sequence	Description
Logon sequence	During the *logon sequence,* Winlogon.exe starts the Local Security Authority (LSA), and the Logon screen or Logon dialog box appears. Users can now log on, while Windows XP continues to load low-level drivers and services in the background. The boot process is considered complete when a user successfully logs on. The Clone control set built earlier is copied to a new control set called LastKnownGood, thus preserving a copy of the settings in the successful boot sequence.

 The Please Select The Operating System To Start menu is also known as the Boot Loader menu and the OS Choices menu.

Startup Settings and The Boot.ini File

Boot.ini is a hidden, read-only text file stored in the root of the Windows system partition. The Boot.ini file has two functions: to store the load paths to the operating system or systems installed on the computer, and, if there are multiple operating systems installed, to build and display the Please Select The Operating System To Start menu during the boot process. (Note that it is no longer common to boot multiple operating systems on a single computer, and therefore it is seldom necessary to edit the startup settings in Boot.ini to optimize boot performance on multi-boot systems. Currently, the common way to host multiple operating systems on a single physical system is to employ virtualization technologies such as VMware® or Microsoft Virtual PC.)

There are two sections in the Boot.ini file.

- The [boot loader] section contains the timeout parameter, which determines how long the Please Select The Operating System To Start menu is displayed. The default value is 30 seconds. It also contains the default parameter, which stores the path to the default operating system, which loads if no other operating system is selected.

- The [operating systems] section lists the path to each operating system installed on the computer. Each entry includes descriptive text, which is displayed as the choice for that operating system on the Please Select The Operating System To Start menu. The path also includes any special boot switches to use for that operating system. The path to a Windows installation appears in Advanced RISC Computer (ARC) syntax, and tells the system which disk controller, disk, and disk partition contains the operating system.

You can edit the Boot.ini file to change the list of operating systems that appears on the Please Select The Operating System To Start menu, adjust the amount of time the menu is displayed, change a boot switch for an operating system, or change the boot partition for an operating system.

- You can edit the file directly by opening it in Notepad.

- You can modify boot settings from the Advanced page of the System Properties dialog box. Under Startup And Recovery, click Settings.

ACTIVITY 8-7

Examining Startup Settings

Scenario:

In this activity, you will examine the startup settings that are controlled by the Boot.ini file.

 There is a simulated version of this activity available on the CD-ROM that shipped with this course. You can run this simulation on any Windows computer to review the activity after class, or as an alternative to performing the activity as a group in class. The activity simulation can be launched either directly from the CD-ROM by clicking the Interactives link and navigating to the appropriate one, or from the installed data file location by opening the C:\085820Data\Simulations\Lesson#\Activity# folder and double-clicking the executable (.exe) file.

What You Do	How You Do It
1. **Examine the current startup settings.**	a. **Choose Start, right-click My Computer, and choose Properties.** b. **Click the Advanced tab.** c. Under Startup And Recovery, **click Settings.** d. If there is more than one operating system installed, you can choose which one will load by default when the system starts up. **Verify that the Default Operating System is Microsoft Windows XP Professional.**

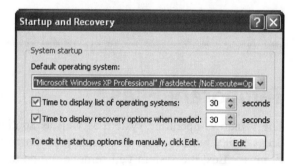

	e. If there were more than one operating system installed, the user would see a list of operating systems and could choose one to load. The list would be displayed for a fixed amount of time before the default operating system loads. **Verify that the Time To Display List Of Operating Systems value is 30 seconds.**

2. Examine the Boot.ini file.

a. Click Edit.

b. The settings in the Startup And Recovery dialog box are stored in the Boot.ini file. You could edit the file manually if you chose. **Close Notepad** without saving any changes.

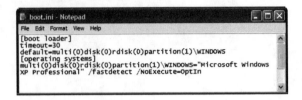

c. To close the Startup And Recovery dialog box and leave the System Properties dialog box open, **click Cancel.**

Temporary Files

The Windows operating system as well as applications and services that run on the system occasionally need to store information in temporary files in various locations on the hard disk. In most cases, the system will remove temporary files after use, but if too many temporary files remain on the disk it, can take up hard disk space and slow performance. You should occasionally remove old temporary files if they exist.

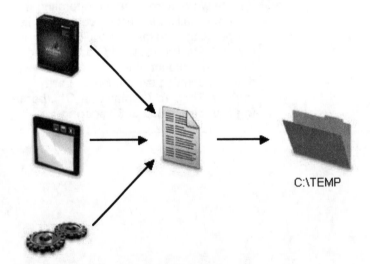

Figure 8-9: *Temporary file storage.*

Temporary File Storage Locations

Temporary files often have an extension of *.tmp or *.temp. Windows may store temporary files in a folder called \Windows\Temp or \Tmp. The location is determined by the value of the Path variable in the system's environment variables. You can access the environment variables from the Advanced tab of the System Properties dialog box.

Applications can have their own temporary file storage locations. For example, the Internet Explorer web browser application stores temporary copies of downloaded web files in a Temporary Internet Files folder. This helps web pages load faster. Files in the Temporary Internet Files folder usually have a functional extension such as .htm or .gif.

ACTIVITY 8-8

Viewing Windows Temporary Files

Scenario:

You are unsure where your Windows system stores its temporary files. You would like to find the temporary file storage location and open it to determine if an inordinate number of temporary files has accumulated on the system.

 There is a simulated version of this activity available on the CD-ROM that shipped with this course. You can run this simulation on any Windows computer to review the activity after class, or as an alternative to performing the activity as a group in class. The activity simulation can be launched either directly from the CD-ROM by clicking the Interactives link and navigating to the appropriate one, or from the installed data file location by opening the C:\ 085820Data\Simulations\Lesson#\Activity# folder and double-clicking the executable (.exe) file.

What You Do	How You Do It
1. Determine the value of the Path variable.	a. On the Advanced page of the System Properties dialog box, **click Environment Variables.**
	b. **Verify that the TEMP variable points to the local administrator's user profile.**

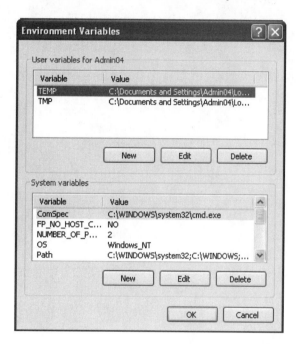

c. To view the complete path TEMP variable, **click Edit.**

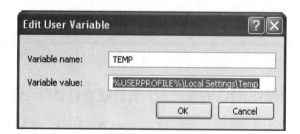

d. **Click Cancel three times.**

2. **View the files in the temporary file storage location.**

    a. **Choose Start→My Computer.**

    b. **Open the C drive.**

    c. If necessary, **click Show the Contents Of This Folder.**

    d. **Open the Documents And Settings folder.**

    e. **Open the Admin## folder.**

    f. The temporary files folder is hidden. **Choose Tools→Folder Options.**

    g. **Click the View tab.**

    h. In the Advanced Settings list, **select Show Hidden Files And Folders and click OK.**

       Hidden files and folders
         ○ Do not show hidden files and folders
         ◉ Show hidden files and folders

    i. **Open the Local Settings folder.**

    j. To view temporary files, **open the Temp folder.**

    k. **Close the Temp window.**

Windows Optimization Software Tools

You can use a number of system tools to optimize different areas of Windows system performance.

Optimization Category	Tools
Virtual memory optimization	Use the Virtual Memory dialog box to adjust settings for virtual memory, including pagefile locations and initial and maximum size for each pagefile.

Optimization Category	*Tools*
Hard drive optimization	Disk Management is the primary tool you will use to optimize hard disks on your system by creating, deleting, or formatting partitions to create the most functional disk configuration. For example, you might want to break a large hard disk into one operating system partition and a data partition; when users search for files or documents they can limit the search to the data partition only and save time. You might also use the Disk Defragmenter utility or its command-line version, defrag.exe, to reduce fragmentation on the disk.
Temporary file optimization	You can use the Advanced tab of the System Properties dialog box to set or change the Path variable that determines where Windows stores temporary files. To optimize storage of temporary Internet files in Internet Explorer, open the Internet Options dialog box and click Settings. You can view or delete the existing temporary files, and you can set the percentage of disk space allotted to temporary Internet files. You can manually delete temporary files from the \Temp folder. Windows XP also provides the Disk Cleanup tool to assist you in locating and removing unnecessary files. This also helps improve drive performance overall.
Windows services optimization	Running only the necessary services saves system resources such as memory and processor time and improves efficiency. Use the Services node in Computer Management to view the list of running services, start or stop services, and set the startup type (Manual, Automatic, or Disabled) for services.
Startup optimization	• Using the Services node in Computer Management to set only necessary services to start automatically will also improve startup time. • You can use the System Configuration Utility, available from the Tools group in the Help And Support Center, to selectively disable legacy configuration files such as System.ini and Win.ini. These text-based configuration files are present primarily to support backward-compatibility with older Windows programs. However, because the processing time required to load these small files is negligible, this also could affect system stability without effectively reducing boot time. For further information, see Windows XP Help on the System Configuration Utility. • On multi-boot systems, you can you can edit the Boot.ini file reduce the timeout value for the boot loader menu. You can also suppress the display of the Boot Loader menu completely by reducing the timeout value to zero or by removing all but one operating system entry from Boot.ini. Use the Startup And Recovery dialog box to configure startup settings in Boot.ini.
Application optimization	The best approach you can take to ensure optimum performance for all applications is to: • Make sure the system is configured with sufficient processor, memory, and hard disk resources. • Perform routine system-wide optimization and tuning. • Keep the computer clear of viruses and other malicious software. • Follow any application-specific optimization procedures documented by your software vendor.

How to Optimize Windows

Procedure Reference: Change the Pagefile Size

To change the size of the pagefile:

1. In the System Properties dialog box, click the Advanced tab.

2. In the Performance area, click Settings.

3. Click the Advanced tab.

4. In the Virtual Memory area, click Change to open the Virtual Memory dialog box. You can see the current size of the pagefile in the Currently Allocated area at the bottom of the dialog box.

5. Verify that Custom Size is selected.

6. Enter the new values in the Initial Size and Maximum Size text boxes.

7. Click Set.

8. Click OK three times.

Procedure Reference: Add a Pagefile

To add a pagefile:

1. In the Virtual Memory dialog box, select a volume from the Drive list.

2. Under Paging File Size For Selected Drive, select Custom Size.

3. Enter the initial and maximum sizes for the pagefile on this drive.

4. Click Set.

5. Click OK three times.

Procedure Reference: Move the Pagefile

To move the pagefile:

1. In the Virtual Memory dialog box, create a new pagefile on another disk.

2. In the Virtual Memory dialog box, select the original pagefile.

3. Under Paging File Size For Selected Drive, select No Paging File.

4. Click Set.

5. You will see a message informing you that you need to restart your computer. Click OK.

6. Click OK twice more.

7. Restart the computer when prompted.

Procedure Reference: Clean Up Temporary Files

To use Disk Cleanup to clean up a hard disk:

1. Run Disk Cleanup.

   - From the Start menu, choose Control Panel, click Performance And Maintenance, and then click Free Up Space On Your Hard Disk.

   - Choose Accessories→System Tools→Disk Cleanup.

2. If you have multiple drives, select the drive you want to clean up and click OK.

3. On the Disk Cleanup page, check the check boxes for any categories of files that you want to clean up. Disk Cleanup displays the number of KB in the category; if you want to see the actual files you will be deleting, click View Files.

4. To compress old files, check Compress Old Files and click Options to set the length of the expiration window.

5. As an Administrator, you can use Disk Cleanup as a central access point to removing unused software components. Click the More Options tab and click Clean Up in the following areas:

   - Windows Components to launch the Windows Components Wizard.

   - Installed Programs to launch Add Or Remove Programs.

   - System Restore to delete all but the last restore point.

6. Click OK to perform the disk cleanup steps.

7. Click Yes to confirm.

Procedure Reference: Optimize System Services

To optimize settings for system services:

1. Open Computer Management and select the Services node.

2. Locate and double-click the service you need to manage.

3. Select the desired Startup Type and click Apply.

   - Select Automatic startup for services that need to load at boot time.

   - Select Manual startup for services that do not need to load at boot time. This will reduce startup time and the service can be started later during system operation.

   - Select Disabled for a service that should never start. If you need to start a Disabled service, you will need to change its startup type first.

4. To start, stop, pause, or resume a service, click the appropriate button.

   - When you stop a service, no user or process can access the service. Also, services that depend upon the service will also stop.

   - When you pause a service, members of the Administrators and Server Operators groups can still connect to the service, and dependency services can still run.

5. Click OK.

Procedure Reference: Configure Startup Settings in Boot.ini

To optimize the boot time on multi-boot systems:

1. Open the System Properties dialog box.

2. On the Advanced page, under Startup And Recovery, click Settings.

3. In the Startup And Recovery dialog box, in the System Startup section, perform the desired optimization task.

   ● To reduce the display time, enter the new timeout value in the Time To Display List Of Operating Systems text box. Be sure to configure enough time for the user to select an alternate operating system.

   ● To turn off the Boot Loader menu, uncheck the Time To Display List Of Operating Systems check box. (This is the same as setting the display time to 0.) Verify that the correct operating system is selected from the Default Operating System drop-down list.

   ● To remove an operating system entry, in the Startup And Recovery dialog box, in the System Startup section, click Edit. Notepad will run and open the Boot.ini file. Select and delete all but one line in the [operating systems] section. Make sure that the path in the default= line matches the path to the remaining operating system. Save the file and close Notepad.

4. Click OK to save your changes to the Boot.ini file and close the Startup And Recovery dialog box.

5. Click OK to close the System Properties dialog box.

ACTIVITY 8-9

Configuring Virtual Memory

Scenario:

You manage Windows XP Professional desktop systems for a group of desktop-publishing specialists who use highly memory-intensive applications for developing, editing, and printing graphics. They have been receiving some low-memory errors. Until you can purchase and install more RAM, you want to ensure that you have adequate pagefile space allocated on your system to meet their virtual memory needs. There is quite a bit of empty space on their hard disks.

 There is a simulated version of this activity available on the CD-ROM that shipped with this course. You can run this simulation on any Windows computer to review the activity after class, or as an alternative to performing the activity as a group in class. The activity simulation can be launched either directly from the CD-ROM by clicking the Interactives link and navigating to the appropriate one, or from the installed data file location by opening the C:\085820Data\Simulations\Lesson#\Activity# folder and double-clicking the executable (.exe) file.

What You Do	How You Do It
1. **Open the Virtual Memory dialog box.**	a. **Choose Start, right-click My Computer, and choose Properties.**
	b. **Click the Advanced tab.**
	c. On the Advanced tab of the System Properties dialog box, under Performance, **click Settings.**
	d. In the Performance Options dialog box, **click the Advanced tab.**

e. Under Virtual Memory, **click Change.**

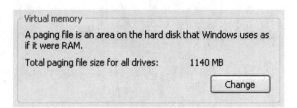

2. **Adjust the virtual memory settings.**

a. To select the text, **double-click in the Initial Size text box.**

b. **Type a value that is 100 MB greater than the existing initial size.**

c. To select the text, **double-click in the Maximum Size text box.**

d. **Type a value that is 100 MB greater than the existing initial size.**

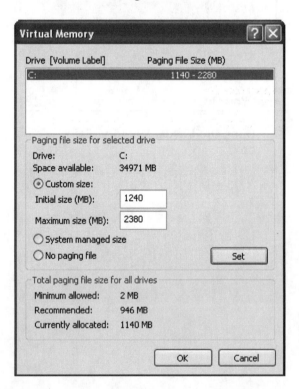

e. **Click Set.**

f. **Click OK three times.**

ACTIVITY 8-10

Disabling the Remote Registry Service

Scenario:

You have users who complain that their systems are running slowly and take a long time to start up. You want to improve system performance and the boot time by preventing unnecessary services from loading. After examining the list of running services, you determine that there is no need for administrators to edit the registry on these machines from elsewhere on the network, so you decide that it would be advisable to disable the Remote Registry service.

There is a simulated version of this activity available on the CD-ROM that shipped with this course. You can run this simulation on any Windows computer to review the activity after class, or as an alternative to performing the activity as a group in class. The activity simulation can be launched either directly from the CD-ROM by clicking the Interactives link and navigating to the appropriate one, or from the installed data file location by opening the C:\085820Data\Simulations\Lesson#\Activity# folder and double-clicking the executable (.exe) file.

What You Do	How You Do It
1. Open Computer Management.	a. Choose Start, right-click My Computer, and choose Manage.
	b. Expand Services And Applications and select Services.
2. Disable the service.	a. Scroll the services list to locate the Remote Registry service.
	b. Double-click the Remote Registry service.

c. **Click the Startup Type drop-down arrow and choose Disabled.**

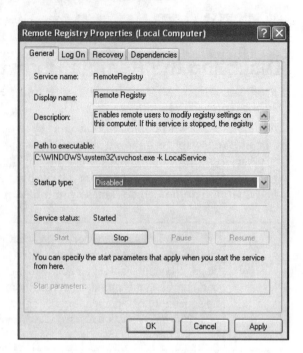

d. **Click Stop.**

e. **Click OK.**

f. **Close Computer Management.**

Lesson 8 Follow-up

In this lesson, you installed and configured operating systems. Whether you are upgrading, installing from scratch, or redeploying a system, you will need the skills that enable you to install, configure, and optimize computer operating systems to meet your business needs.

1. **Have you done operating system installations prior to this training? Do you feel you will be able to perform installations more efficiently as a result of the information in this lesson?**

2. **Which of the configuration and optimization procedures in this lesson do you think will be of the most use to you in your professional environment?**

9 | Maintaining and Troubleshooting Microsoft Windows

Lesson Time: 3 hour(s)

Lesson Objectives:

In this lesson, you will maintain and troubleshoot installations of Microsoft Windows.

You will:

- Identify Windows operating system utilities to use in maintenance and troubleshooting.
- Perform backups.
- Troubleshoot Windows.
- Recover a damaged installation of Windows.

Introduction

In the previous lesson, you installed and configured Microsoft Windows. Once the system has been installed, you will need to maintain it on an ongoing basis and correct any problems that may occur. In this lesson, you will maintain and troubleshoot Microsoft Windows.

It would be nice if you could install a system, configure it, verify it, and walk away and never touch it again. But in the real world, systems need attention both for ongoing maintenance tasks as well as to resolve the problems that can, unfortunately, arise. As a professional computer support technician, you will be the main point of contact for customers and clients who have systems that need fine-tuning or have problems they need an expert to solve. You will need to be ready with the tools, knowledge, and skills to resolve the users' issues quickly.

This lesson covers all or part of the following CompTIA A+ (2006) certification objectives:

- Topic A:
    - Exam 220–601 (Essentials): Objective 3.1, Objective 3.3, Objective 3.4
    - Exam 220–602 (IT Technician): Objective 1.3, Objective 3.1, Objective 3.3, Objective 3.4, Objective 6.2
    - Exam 220–603 (Remote Technician): Objective 1.3, Objective 2.1, Objective 2.3, Objective 2.4

- Topic B:
    - Exam 220–601 (Essentials): Objective 3.3, Objective 3.4, Objective 6.2
    - Exam 220–602 (IT Technician): Objective 3.1, Objective 3.3, Objective 3.4
    - Exam 220–603 (Remote Technician): Objective 2.1, Objective 2.3

- Topic C:
    - Exam 220–601 (Essentials): Objective 1.3, Objective 3.3
    - Exam 220–602 (IT Technician): Objective 3.1, Objective 3.3, Objective 6.1
    - Exam 220–603 (Remote Technician): Objective 2.1, Objective 2.3, Objective 5.2

- Topic D:
    - Exam 220–601 (Essentials): Objective 3.3
    - Exam 220–602 (IT Technician): Objective 3.1, Objective 3.3
    - Exam 220–603 (Remote Technician): Objective 2.1, Objective 2.3

TOPIC A
Operating System Utilities

In this lesson, you will maintain and troubleshoot Microsoft Windows. To prepare yourself for these tasks, you should start by reviewing the maintenance and troubleshooting utilities that are available on the system. In this topic, you will identify operating system utilities to use in maintenance and troubleshooting.

As a competent computer support professional, you don't want to have just a few tools in your toolkit; you want to have a wide range of options available so that you can choose the most appropriate one to use in a particular situation. Some tools are physical items that you can touch, but a lot of them are software utilities that are built in to the operating system. This topic will prepare you to make the best use of the wide range of tools and utilities that you can use to perform file, disk, and system management on Microsoft Windows.

File Management Tools

You can use command-line tools or the graphical Windows Explorer interface to manage files and folders on Windows systems.

File Management Tool	Description
Windows Explorer	Windows Explorer is the primary graphical utility that you can use to perform all basic file and folder management tasks. With Windows Explorer, you can:
	● Create files and folders.
	● Delete files and folders.
	● Rename files and folders.
	● Move files and folders.
	● Copy files and folders.
	● View file and folder properties such as file size or the date and time the file was modified.
	● View or change file or folder attributes.
Command-line tools	There are command-line utilities that enable you to perform most file-management tasks at a command prompt or in a script file. These include:
	● `del`, `deltr` to delete files and folders.
	● `ren` (`rename`) to rename files and folders.
	● `copy`, `xcopy` to copy files .
	● `dir` to display file size and date and time modified.
	● `attrib` to view or change file attributes.
	● `cd` to change to a different location in the folder hierarchy.
	● `md` to create folders
	● `rd` to delete folders.
	● `edit` *filename* to edit a text file.
	For the syntax of these commands, see the Windows Help system.

Disk Management Tools

There are several command-line and graphical utilities you can use to perform disk management tasks in Windows.

Disk Management Tool	Description
Disk Management	A comprehensive graphical tool that you can use to manage disk drives themselves as well as the partitions the drives contain. With Disk Management, you can: • Display the drives attached to the system. • Display, create, and remove partitions on the drives. • Assign drive letters to partitions. • Determine the amount of free space on a partition. • Reformat partitions. • Convert partitions from the FAT or FAT32 file system to NTFS.
chkdsk.exe	Verifies the logical integrity of a file system. With the /f switch, chkdsk can repair the file system data. Enter chkdsk /f *drive letter* in the Run dialog box or at the command line.
format.exe	Use to format disks to a selected file system. You can run the format command at the command line, or right-click a drive in Windows Explorer and choose Format.
diskpart.exe	A command-line tool that enables you to manage disks and partitions by issuing direct commands, or by creating script files to automate disk operations.
Disk Defragmenter (defrag.exe)	Arranges stored data on a disk in contiguous blocks. Because individual files are stored on disks in multiple separate blocks, the used and empty storage areas on a disk can become fragmented and scattered. This can affect disk performance. Windows provides the Disk Defragmenter tool to realign the stored files. You can run Disk Defragmenter from Computer Management, from the All Programs→Accessories→System Tools menu, or by issuing the command defrag.exe in the Run dialog box or at the command line.

ACTIVITY 9-1

Exploring Disk Management Tools

Setup:

There are at least two NTFS partitions on the primary hard disk. If you did not do the lab for the *Installing and Configuring Operating Systems* lesson, you will need to create a second NTFS partition.

Scenario:

As a computer support professional, you will be responsible for managing and maintaining hard disk configuration and performance for your customer. To prepare yourself for professional disk-management tasks, you plan to review the status of the disks on your own local system.

 There is a simulated version of this activity available on the CD-ROM that shipped with this course. You can run this simulation on any Windows computer to review the activity after class, or as an alternative to performing the activity as a group in class. The activity simulation can be launched either directly from the CD-ROM by clicking the Interactives link and navigating to the appropriate one, or from the installed data file location by opening the C:\085820Data\Simulations\Lesson#\Activity# folder and double-clicking the executable (.exe) file.

What You Do	How You Do It
1. Check the status of your disk.	**a. Choose Start→All Programs→ Accessories→Command Prompt.**
	b. Enter *chkdsk*

	c. Examine the chkdsk results and enter *cls* to clear the screen.
2. Did chkdsk find any bad sectors?	
3. Use diskpart.exe to examine the partitions on your disk.	**a. Enter *diskpart***
	b. At the DISKPART prompt, to see a list of DISKPART commands, enter *help*
	c. Enter *list disk*
	d. To move the focus to disk 0, enter *select disk 0*
	e. To see details about the disk configuration, enter *detail disk*
	f. To exit DISKPART, enter *exit*
	g. Close the Command Prompt window.

4. **Check the fragmentation status of your disk.**

   a. **Choose Start→Control Panel.**

   b. **Click Performance And Maintenance.**

   c. In the Performance And Maintenance window, under Pick A Task, **click Rearrange Items On Your Hard Disk To Make Programs Run Faster.**

   d. The Disk Defragmenter window opens. With the C drive selected, **click Analyze.**

   e. When the analysis is complete, a Disk Defragmenter message box appears. In the Disk Defragmenter message box, **click View Report.**

   f. To determine the overall fragmentation percentage, in the Volume Information area, **scroll to the Volume Fragmentation statistics.**

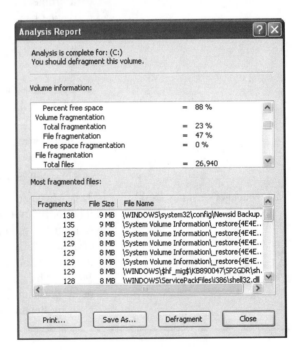

   g. To sort the list to determine which files are most fragmented, in the Most Fragmented Files list, **click twice on the Fragments column heading.**

   h. To determine whether or not you should defragment, **view the top section of the report. Click Close.**

i.   **Close Disk Defragmenter.**

5.   **Based on the analysis, should you defragment?**

System Management Tools

There are several important utilities you will use to manage Windows computers, as shown in the following table.

System Management Tool	Description
Device Manager	Device Manager is the primary tool you will use to manage and configure system devices in a hardware profile. The default Device Manager view displays a categorized list of all devices attached to the system. You can use Device Manager to:
	• See the status of a device. An exclamation point means there is a problem with a device; a yellow question mark means the device has been detected but a driver is not installed, or there is a resource conflict.
	• Enable or disable a device. A disabled device appears with a red X.
	• Determine the device driver a device is using; upgrade a device driver; roll a device driver back to a previous version.
	• Determine any system resources that the device is using, such as interrupt request lines (IRQs) or Direct Memory Access (DMA) ports.
	• Uninstall or re-install devices.
Task Manager (taskmgr.exe)	Task Manager is a basic system-diagnostic and performance-monitoring tool included with Windows XP. You can use Task Manager to monitor or terminate applications and processes; view current CPU and memory usage statistics; monitor network connection utilization; and manage logged-on local users. Run Task Manager by right-clicking the taskbar and choosing Task Manager, or by pressing Ctrl+Alt+Del and clicking Task Manager. Task Manager, by default, will always remain on top of other applications.

System Management Tool	Description
System Configuration Utility (msconfig.exe)	The System Configuration Utility, available from the Tools group in the Help And Support Center, is a graphical tool intended to help automate some routine troubleshooting steps. You can use it to: • Select files and system services to process at startup. • Selectively disable legacy configuration files such as System.ini and Win.ini. • View and enable or disable services or applications that load automatically at startup. For further information, see Windows XP Professional Help on the System Configuration Utility.
System Information Utility (msinfo32.exe)	The System Information utility, available from the Tools group in the Help And Support Center and also from System Tools on the Start menu, displays detailed information about the current system configuration, including a general summary of the system components, hardware resource assignments by category, installed hardware devices, the software environment, and Internet Explorer settings.
Event Viewer	Use Event Viewer to view the contents of event logs, which are system files that contain information about significant events that occur on your computer. There are three default event logs on Windows 2000 Professional and Windows XP computers: • The *Application log* records Information, Warning, or Error messages generated by specific applications, and by some Windows services. The application developer determines whether or not a particular application will post entries to the log. • The *Security log* records Success Audit or Failure Audit events if an administrator has configured security auditing on the system. If you have not configured an audit policy, this log will be empty. • The *System log* records Information, Warning, or Error messages generated by system components. For example, this log will show you if a driver or service has failed to load. To access the Event Viewer from the command line enter eventvwr.exe.
Registry Editor (regedit.exe)	Use Registry Editor to view, search, or modify the contents of the registry. Use extreme caution if you decide to modify the registry directly. It is generally best to modify the registry indirectly by using other applications and system tools.
Computer Management	The pre-configured MMC console that serves as a central location for accessing major system administration and information tools.

ACTIVITY 9-2

Exploring System Management Utilities

Scenario:

As a computer support professional, you will be responsible for managing and maintaining system configuration and performance for your customers. To prepare yourself for professional system-management tasks, you plan to review the status of the system components on your own local computer.

 There is a simulated version of this activity available on the CD-ROM that shipped with this course. You can run this simulation on any Windows computer to review the activity after class, or as an alternative to performing the activity as a group in class. The activity simulation can be launched either directly from the CD-ROM by clicking the Interactives link and navigating to the appropriate one, or from the installed data file location by opening the C:\ 085820Data\Simulations\Lesson#\Activity# folder and double-clicking the executable (.exe) file.

What You Do	How You Do It
1. View device status in Device Manager.	a. In the Control Panel Performance And Maintenance window, **click System.**
	b. **Click the Hardware tab.**
	c. **Click Device Manager.**
	d. **Expand the Keyboards node.**
	e. **Verify that the keyboard device icon appears normal and double-click the icon to open the keyboard's property sheet.**

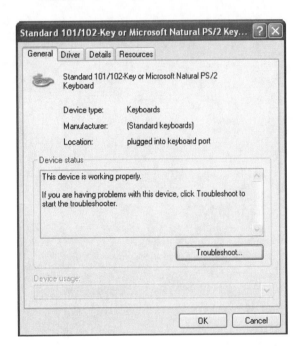

f. **Click the Driver tab.**

g. You can view details about the driver, update or roll back the driver, or uninstall the device on the Driver page. **Click the Resources tab.**

h. The Resources page shows the resource settings for the device. It is rare that you would have to adjust resource allocation manually. **Click Cancel.**

i. **Expand other categories and view the status and properties of other devices.**

j. **Close Device Manager.**

k. **Close System Properties.**

l. **Close Performance And Maintenance.**

2. **Did any devices have any problems?**

3. Examine the system status with Task Manager.

a. **Right-click the taskbar and choose Task Manager.**

b. The Applications page is blank because there are no application windows open. To start an application, **click New Task.**

c. To run Notepad, **type _notepad_ and click OK.**

d. Notepad opens in the background and the Notepad task appears on the Applications page. **Verify that a running process count, CPU usage percentage, and committed memory value appear in the Task Manager status bar.**

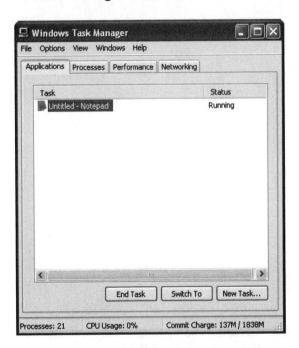

e. **Verify that the CPU usage gauge appears in the notification area of the taskbar.**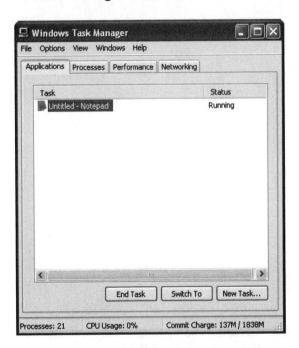

f. In Task Manager, **right-click the Notepad application and choose Go To Process.**

g. There are many processes running on the system. Most are running in the background, not in their own windows, and so they do not appear on the Applications page. To close Notepad, with the Notepad process selected, **click End Process.**

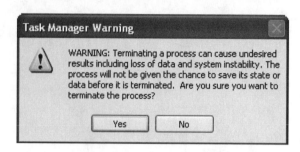

h. **Click Yes.**

i. **Click the Performance tab.**

j. The Performance page provides a graphical report on system performance statistics. **Click the Networking tab.**

k. The Networking tab provides a graphical report on network activity. **Click the Users tab.**

l. When Fast User Switching is enabled, the Users tab is available and shows any users who are currently logged on. **Close Task Manager.**

4. **Examine the system configuration settings with msconfig.**

a. **Choose Start→Help And Support.**

b. Under Pick A Task, **click Use Tools To View Your Computer Information And Diagnose Problems.**

c. In the Tools list, **click System Configuration Utility.**

d. **Click Open System Configuration Utility.**

e. System Configuration is a diagnostic and troubleshooting utility that can help automate routine troubleshooting steps. The General page controls overall startup behavior. **Click the System.ini tab.**

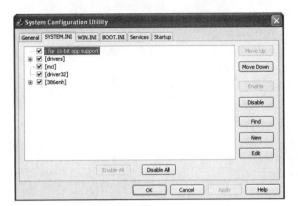

f. System.ini and Win.ini are legacy configuration files from earlier DOS shell versions of Windows. Windows will process these files if they are present. You can use System Configuration to enable or disable portions of these files. **Click the Boot.ini tab.**

g. System Configuration provides another way to modify the startup settings in Boot. ini. **Click the Services tab.**

h. You can use System Configuration to enable or disable services. **Click the Startup tab.**

i. You can view and manage items that are configured to load at system startup. To close System Configuration, **click Cancel.**

5. **Examine the system information with msinfo32.**

   a. In the Help And Support Center, in the Tools list, **click Advanced System Information.**

   b. **Click View Detailed System Information (Msinfo32.exe).**

   c. **Maximize System Information.**

   d. In the System Summary, **verify that the system is running Windows XP Professional with Service Pack 2. Expand Hardware Resources.**

   e. You can see the assignments for each category of hardware resources. To view the assigned interrupts, **select IRQs.**

   f. **Collapse Hardware Resources.**

   g. You can see detailed information about all aspects of the computer system. **Expand Components and select CD-ROM.**

   h. **Collapse Components.**

   i. **Expand Software Environment and select System Drivers.**

   j. **Collapse Software Environment.**

   k. **Expand Internet Settings, Internet Explorer.**

   l. **Select Summary.**

   m. **Close System Information.**

   n. **Close the Help And Support Center.**

6. **Review the system logs.**

    a. **Choose Start, right-click My Computer, and choose Manage.**

    b. Under System Tools, **select Event Viewer.**

    c. **Double-click the System log.**

    d. **Double-click the first Information entry in the log.**

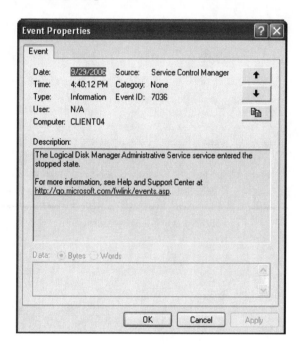

    e. This shows you the basic structure of an event log entry. In the Event Properties window, **click the Down arrow and then the Up arrow to scroll through the event log entries.**

    f. To close the Event Properties window, **click Cancel.**

    g. **Choose View→Filter.**

h. **Uncheck all event types except Warning and Error.**

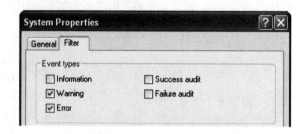

i. **Click OK.**

j. Now the Warning and Error messages, if any, appear in sequence. It's perfectly normal to see a few Error and Warning messages in a log. Most of these problems are either minor or due to some external condition, such as a server being unavailable. **Close Computer Management.**

TOPIC B
Maintain Microsoft Windows

In the previous topic, you identified the general operating system management utilities that you will employ in a range of activities as a computer support technician. One of those common support tasks is to perform basic system maintenance. In this topic, you will maintain Windows systems by performing data and system backups.

Maintaining an operating system is an ongoing task that might not seem as exciting or interesting as performing a new installation or replacing a hard disk, but it is actually one of the most crucial tasks for a support technician. System maintenance is important for two reasons; first, proper maintenance can prevent system problems from arising. Second, proper maintenance of the system, including the creation of appropriate backups, can make recovery or troubleshooting operations much easier in the event that problems do arise. As an A+ technician, you can use the skills and information in this topic to perform backups as part of your ongoing operating system maintenance tasks.

Backup and Restore

Definition:

Data backup is a system maintenance task that enables you to store copies of critical data on another medium for safekeeping. *Data restoration* is a system recovery task that enables you to access the backed-up data. Backups protect against loss of data due to disasters such as file corruption or hardware failure. Restored data does not include any changes made to the data after the backup operation. Data backups can be accomplished simply by copying individual files and folders to a local or network location or by using dedicated software and hardware to back up large amounts of data. Large backups are usually stored on specialized backup media such as magnetic tape drives.

Example:

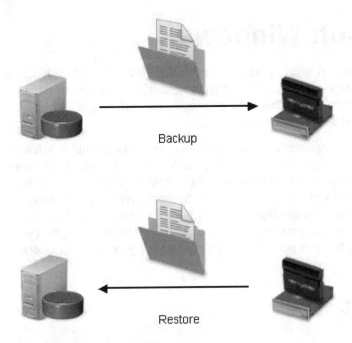

Figure 9-1: *Backup and restore.*

Backup Schemes

Backups should be performed systematically and on a regular basis for the best protection against data loss. Most large organizations will implement a structured backup scheme that includes a backup schedule and specifications for how much data is backed up, where it is stored, and how it can be retrieved. The backup scheme will specify the backup *rotation method,* which determines how many backup tapes or other media sets are needed, and the sequence in which they are used and reused. Designated administrators will have the responsibility for designing and managing the backup scheme and for restoring data when needed.

The Windows Backup Utility

The built-in Windows Backup utility enables you to back up and restore files on local and remote Windows systems. Windows Backup stores data in *backup sets* on a wide variety of backup media types, including hard and floppy disks, writable CD-ROMs, tape drives, and other compact storage media. Backup sets can be stored in single files or can be spread across one or more backup media.

 You can access the Windows Backup Ulitility from the command line using the ntbackup.exe command.

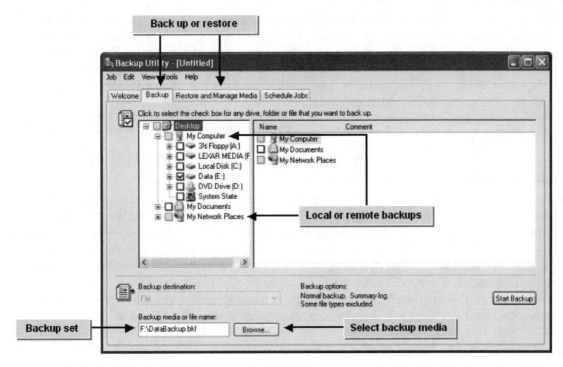

Figure 9-2: *Windows Backup.*

 There are also many third-party backup utilities available for backing up and restoring data on Windows computers.

Backup Types

Windows Backup supports a variety of backup types.

Backup Type	Backs Up
Copy	Selected files, without marking them as backed up by clearing the Archive file attribute.
Daily	Files modified the day the backup is performed, without marking them as backed up.
Differential	Files changed since the last normal or incremental backup, without marking them as backed up. *since last full backup*
Incremental	Files changed since the last normal or incremental backup, marking them as backed up. *since last backup*
Normal	Selected files, marking them as backed up.

Backup Requirements

You must be a member of the Backup Operators group, be a file owner, or have at least Read NTFS permissions to back up file data.

Windows File Protection (WFP)

Windows File Protection is a Windows XP Professional system service that automatically maintains backup copies of key system files. Files protected by WFP include all SYS, DLL, TTF, FON, OCX, and EXE files installed by Windows Setup. If a key boot file or a Boot or System level driver or service is altered or deleted, WFP simply replaces the file from a backup copy, either from the hidden %systemroot%\System32\ Dllcache folder or from the Windows XP Professional installation media.

You might see a Windows Protection error if a driver or service under Windows File Protection fails to load. This generally occurs at startup.

System File Checker

The System File Checker utility (sfc.exe) enables you to scan all protected operating system files and replace any incorrect files with the correct Microsoft versions. To use this command-line utility, open a Command Prompt window and enter `sfc /scannnow`. When the System File Checker detects a file that was overwritten by a method other than a Service Pack installation, a hotfix installation, or an operating system upgrade, it replaces the file. When it replaces the file, it attempts to restore it from a locally cached copy. If that copy isn't available, it installs the file from the installation media. This means that you might find it necessary to reinstall the latest Service Pack and hotfixes after using System File Checker.

Windows Backup Limitations

There are a couple limitations you should be aware of when using the Microsoft Windows Backup utility. First, it only supports floppy drive, tape drive, hard drive, or external drives (Zip, USB, IEEE 1394 (FireWire)). There is no direct support for writable CDs or DVDs. The only way to make use of these is to back up to the hard rive first, then manually transfer to a DVD or CD. Another limitation of this utility is when you are installing Windows XP Home, it is not installed by default for you. You will need to manually install this utility.

System State Data

You can use the Windows Backup utility to back up System State data on Windows computers. The *System State* is a subset of crucial system components that is backed up as a unit. On Windows XP Professional systems, the System State data consists of:

- Boot files.
- System files protected by Windows File Protection.
- The Registry.
- And, COM+ object registrations, a database of program components that are shared between applications.

 Backing up the System State data requires approximately 400 MB of space. You must back it up to a tape, a folder on the local computer, or a shared folder on a server.

System State Backup Set

In Windows XP, backing up the System State is the only way to back up and restore the registry. You cannot remove any items from the System State backup set. You must have administrative privileges to back up and restore the System State, and you cannot back up or restore the System State remotely.

How to Perform Backups

Procedure Reference: Back Up Files on Windows XP

To back up data files on Windows XP Professional:

1. Run Windows Backup.

    *   From the Start menu, choose All Programs→Accessories→System Tools→Backup.
    *   In Control Panel, click Performance And Maintenance, and then click Back Up Your Data.

2. Click Next.

3. Select Back Up Files And Settings. Click Next.

4. Select one of the following to back up user data:

    *   My Documents And Settings to back up the current user's My Documents folder, Favorites list, desktop settings, and Internet cookie files.
    *   Everyone's Documents And Settings to back up this information for all users.
    *   Let Me Choose What To Back Up to select the files to back up.
    *   All Information On This Computer to back up all user data and create an Automated System Recovery (ASR) backup set.

5. Click Next.

6. If you selected Let Me Choose What To Back Up, expand the source location of the files in the Items To Back Up list, and check the check box for each item that you want to back up. Click Next.

7. Enter a path and file name for the backup storage location, or select the storage location by clicking Browse. The default backup file name is Backup.bkf. The descriptive name for the backup will match the file name.

8. If you do not want to use the default backup name, enter a different descriptive name in the Type A Name For This Backup text box. The descriptive name can help you uniquely identify backup sets when you need to restore files from a backup.

9. Click Next.

10. To create the backup using the default settings, click Finish. Otherwise, click Advanced.

11. If you clicked Advanced, select the type of backup and click Next.

12. Check the check boxes for each backup option you want to use:

    *   Verify Data After Backup reads the data after it is backed up.
    *   Use Hardware Compression, If Available can save space if hardware compression if supported on the media.
    *   Disable Volume Shadow Copy disables Windows Backup's ability to back up files while they are open or being written to. In rare circumstances, you might choose to disable Volume Shadow Copy to reduce the size of a backup set, or to increase the speed of the backup. However, in general, you should not disable it.

13. Click Next.

14. Select whether to append the data to an existing backup or to overwrite the backup. Click Next.

15. Select Now to run the job immediately. Click Next.

16. Click Finish.

Procedure Reference: Schedule Backups

You can use Windows Backup to schedule backups to occur at a selected time. To schedule a backup:

1. Use Windows Backup to create a backup job.

2. On the last page of the wizard, click Advanced.

3. Select any advanced options on the Type Of Backup, How To Back Up, and Backup Options pages.

4. On the When To Back Up Page, select Later.

5. Click Set Schedule.

6. Select your scheduling options. You can schedule a task to run Once, Daily, Weekly, Monthly, At System Startup, At Logon, or When Idle. For Daily, Weekly, or Monthly schedules, you can configure specific times and days.

7. To configure advanced properties for Daily, Weekly, or Monthly tasks, click Advanced, configure the properties, and then click OK. You can configure start and end dates for the task, and configure the task to run more than once at the scheduled time.

8. If you want this task to run on more than one schedule (for example, weekly and also at system startup), check Show Multiple Schedules and click New to create additional schedules.

9. To configure how this task will respond to system conditions such as a low battery, click the Settings tab and configure the settings. See the Windows Backup Help system for specific information.

10. When you have finished creating and configuring all the schedules, click OK.

11. In the Backup Or Restore Wizard, enter a name for the scheduled job and click Next.

12. Enter the credentials for a user with the permissions and rights necessary to back up the files, and click OK. The job will run in this user's context at the scheduled time.

13. Click Finish.

Procedure Reference: Back Up System State Data

To back up System State data in Windows XP:

1. Log on as a user who's either a member of the Backup Operators or Administrators groups, owner of a file, or a user who has at least the Read NTFS permissions to back up file data.

2. If you plan to back up to tape, insert a tape into the tape drive.

3. If you plan to back up to a folder, verify that you have enough available disk space. Create the folder.

4. From the Start menu, choose All Programs→Accessories→System Tools→Backup.

5. Click Next.

6. Verify that Back Up Files And Settings is selected and click Next.

7. On the What To Back Up page, select Let Me Choose What To Back Up.

8. Click Next.

9. Below Items To Back Up, expand My Computer and check System State.

10. Click Next.

11. On the Backup Type, Destination, And Name page, complete the following tasks:

    a. From the Select The Backup Type drop-down list, select the type of backup you want to create (if you do not have a local tape backup device, your only choice will be File).

    b. Next to Choose A Place To Save Your Backup, click Browse to browse for the folder in which you will store the backup. If you're backing up to file, you must store the System State data backup on a hard disk because you will need approximately 400 MB of storage space.

    c. In the Type A Name For This Backup text box, type a name for the backup file.

    d. Click Next.

12. To create the backup using the default settings, click Finish (click Advanced if you want to schedule the backup to run on a regular basis).

13. Review the Backup Progress dialog box to verify that the backup completed successfully.

14. Click Close to close the Backup Progress dialog box.

Advanced Mode

You can also run Windows Backup in Advanced Mode. Advanced Mode enables you to enter your backup configuration options on separate pages of a dialog box instead of through the wizard. However, all the same options are available through either method. To run in Advanced Mode, click the Advanced Mode link on the first page of the Backup Or Restore Wizard. A Backup Utility window will open. To switch back to Wizard Mode, click the Wizard Mode link on the Welcome page in the Backup Utility window.

Managing Backup Media

Windows Backup provides commands for formatting, re-tensioning, and erasing backup tape media, and for creating and managing catalogs of the contents of backup sets. See Windows Backup Help for more information on maintaining backup media.

Ntbackup

You can also use the `ntbackup` command to back up folders from the command line. This is useful if you want to create a batch file to back up data. See Windows Backup Help for the syntax and usage of the `ntbackup` command.

ACTIVITY 9-3

Backing Up System State Data

Setup:

You will need approximately 400 MB of free space on your C drive to complete the backup.

Scenario:

One of your clients uses his computer 100 percent of the time to do his job. His computer uses the Windows XP operating system. He is very concerned about a computer crash. He wants to make sure that you will be able to reconstruct his computer as quickly as possible in the event of an operating system failure.

There is a simulated version of this activity available on the CD-ROM that shipped with this course. You can run this simulation on any Windows computer to review the activity after class, or as an alternative to performing the activity as a group in class. The activity simulation can be launched either directly from the CD-ROM by clicking the Interactives link and navigating to the appropriate one, or from the installed data file location by opening the C:\085820Data\Simulations\Lesson#\Activity# folder and double-clicking the executable (.exe) file.

What You Do	How You Do It
1. Create a folder for storing the System State data backup.	a. **Open Windows Explorer.**
	b. **Select the C drive.**
	c. **Choose File→Properties.**
	d. **Verify that you have enough free disk space to store the System State data backup.**

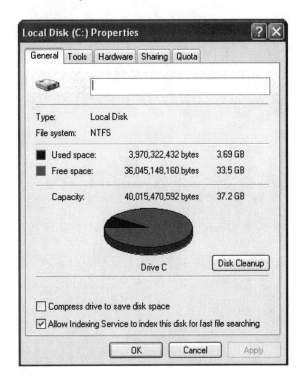

	e. To close the Properties dialog box, **click Cancel.**
	f. **Choose File→New→Folder.**
	g. **Type** *Backup* **and press Enter.**
	h. **Close Windows Explorer.**

2. **Back up the System State data.**

   a. From the Start menu, **choose All Programs→Accessories→System Tools→Backup.**

   b. **Verify that the Always Start In Wizard Mode check box is checked.**

   c. **Click Next.**

   d. **Verify that Back Up Files And Settings is selected. Click Next.**

   e. **Select Let Me Choose What To Back Up and click Next.**

   f. Below Items To Back Up, **expand My Computer.**

   g. **Check the System State check box.**

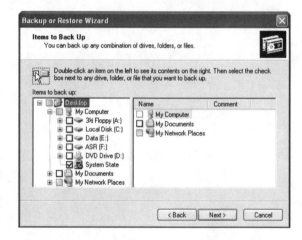

   h. **Click Next.**

   i. **Click Cancel.** In the Save As dialog box, from the Save In drop-down list, **select Local Disk (C:). Open the Backup folder and click Save.**

   j. **Click Next.**

k. **Click Finish.**

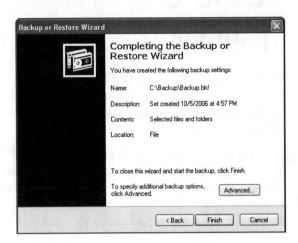

l. When the backup is complete, **click Close.**

TOPIC C
Troubleshoot Microsoft Windows

In the previous topic, you performed basic Windows system maintenance tasks. By maintaining the system properly, you can avoid many problem conditions and you will be in a good position to correct errors efficiently when they arise. In this topic, you will diagnose and correct various Windows system errors.

As a computer support professional, you will be the first line of response to help users when problems arise with their systems. You will need the knowledge to recognize and diagnose problem conditions, and you will be need to respond to those problems with the appropriate corrective action. The information, utilities, and skills in this topic should provide you with the diagnostic and troubleshooting toolkit you will need to identify and correct a range of possible system problems.

System Stop Errors

Definition:

System *stop errors* are errors severe enough to stop all processes and shut the system down without warning. File system errors, viruses, hard disk corruption, or controller driver problems can cause stop errors. Stop errors are rare in Windows XP, but when they occur, they are normally preceded by a blue error screen containing a summary statement about the error condition and also hexadecimal memory data. Because of the blue background, a stop error is often referred to as a blue-screen error.

Example:

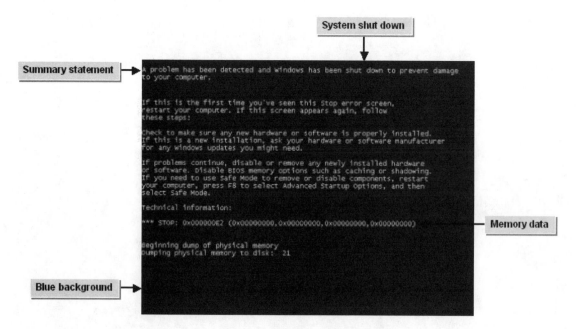

Figure 9-3: Stop errors.

Responding to Stop Errors

If you experience a blue-screen error, you should try to capture as much information as possible from the error summary information at the top of the screen. You can sometimes use this information to diagnose the problem. You can record the error codes and then search for the meaning of the error codes in the Microsoft Knowledge Base.

You can also configure Startup And Recovery settings to perform a *memory dump,* which means that the system writes the contents of memory at the time of the stop error to a *dump file* on the hard disk for diagnostic purposes. You would need special tools and support from Microsoft technical engineers to interpret a dump file. To configure Startup And Recovery settings, go to the Advanced page of the System Properties dialog box and, under Startup And Recovery, click Settings.

If you want to prevent the system from restarting automatically after the stop error, reboot and press F8 during the boot sequence to bring up the Windows Advanced Options Menu. Select Disable Automatic Restart On System Failure and allow the system to restart. Another way of preventing the system from restarting automatically is to change the settings for the computer. To do this right click My Computer, then click Properties, Advanced Tab, in Startup and Recovery, click Settings. Uncheck Automatically Restart and click OK.

For more information on interpreting stop errors, see the Windows XP Professional Resource Kit, and Microsoft Knowledge Base articles Q314084 and Q314103.

System Lockup Errors

Definition:

A *lockup error* is an error condition that causes the system or an application to stop responding to user input. The system display "hangs" or "freezes" in a particular state, or sometimes the contents of a window go blank. The system might return to normal after a short wait for other processes to execute, or it might be necessary to terminate an unresponsive process. Application lockup errors are more common than complete system lockups.

Example:

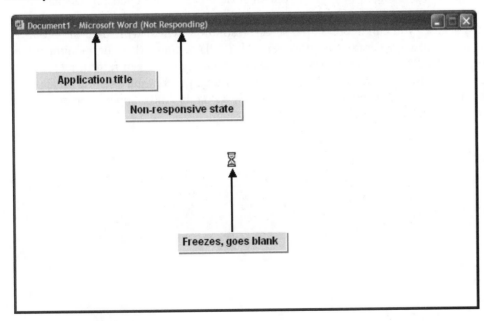

Figure 9-4: Lockup errors.

Responding to Lockup Errors

If your system or an application locks up, sometimes waiting a few minutes is sufficient for the system to recover resources and begin responding. If not, you can sometimes identify the particular offending process by running Task Manager. On the Applications tab, look for applications with a Not Responding status. You can then use the End Task button to shut them down. On the Processes tab, look for processes that are monopolizing the CPU, and use the End Process button to shut them down. Sometimes it's necessary to restart the system.

Although applications might occasionally hang without indicating any serious problem, repeated system lockups or stop errors are a sign of trouble, and you should investigate them to see if there is an underlying hardware problem or if they could be caused by malicious software, such as a computer virus. In addition to hardware or malicious software, it could also be caused by unstable/incompatible drivers, applications conflicting with each other, resource allocation issues (multiple video-intensive applications trying to access the same resource), memory limitations (not enough memory or too many applications running at the same time), etc.

Input/Output Device Issues

Some of the input/output device issues that can affect Windows operation include:

- A missing or loose mouse or keyboard connection.
- Blocked signals for wireless devices.
- A missing or incorrect driver for a specialty input or output device.
- And, misconfigured monitor settings resulting in display anomalies.

Display Configuration Issues

You can usually configure some settings for the monitor using controls on the device itself. For example, you can set the contrast and brightness, screen size, and screen rotation. If any of these are set to incorrect or extreme values, the display might not appear as desired.

You can also configure output settings from within Windows. Open the Display Properties dialog box from within Control Panel, or by right-clicking the desktop and choosing Display. For example, the screen resolution might make items too small for some users to view comfortably. In this case, you can decrease the screen resolution, which will solve the problem, but a better solution is to increase the font dots per inch (DPI) setting. Also, the monitor might not display properly if advanced settings such as the color quality or screen refresh rate are set to a value that is not appropriate for the display device. You can reconfigure settings manually or use the Video Display Troubleshooter in the Windows XP Help And Support Center to walk through common problem scenarios.

Application Errors

There are some common error messages that indicate problems with applications.

Symptom	Suspected Problem
Application won't install	You are trying to install an application that needs to overwrite a file that is currently in use on the computer.
Application won't start or load	The application was installed incorrectly, a version conflict between the application and other applications on the computer exists, or your computer is experiencing memory access errors.
Application not found	One or more of the application files has been deleted, moved, or become corrupt.
General Protection Fault (GPF)	An application is accessing RAM that another application is using, or the application is attempting to access a memory address that doesn't exist.
Illegal operation	An application is attempting to perform an action that Windows does not permit. Windows forces the application to close.
Invalid working directory	The application can't find the directory for storing its temporary files (typically \Temp). This can happen if you delete the folder that an application needs for storing its temporary files.

Boot Errors

There are several errors that can occur during the boot process or Windows startup.

Error	Description
POST errors	If there are errors during the POST, the system might display a numeric error message. Typically, you can press F1 to acknowledge the error and continue booting. For other POST errors, a series of audible beeps will tell you if a problem has been detected. The sequence of beeps is a code that indicates the type of problem.
Invalid boot disk	The most common cause of this is a non-bootable disk in a drive. If your system has floppy-disk drives, check to see if you need to remove a disk from the drive. However, there could be a hardware problem with the hard disk. Also verify that CMOS is set to boot from the hard drive. Most BIOS allow for the configuration of 4 or more boot devices as 1st, 2nd, 3rd, etc. If one fails, it will automatically try the next in line. The only way this process will fail is if the boot devices are set to None or all the same (which many don't allow). Also, it can't be assumed that the user will want the CMOS to be set to "boot from the hard drive" since many times there is a need to boot from CD, or even boot through the network.
Inaccessible boot device	There might be a hardware problem with the hard disk or hard disk controller. Check hard drive and hard drive controller connections.
Missing NTLDR	The NTLDR file might be missing or corrupt, in which case you might need to copy it from the Windows CD-ROM. However, the most common problem is that there is a non-bootable disk in the drive.

Error	Description
Other missing Windows startup files	If Ntoskrnl is missing, you can copy it from the Windows installation CD-ROM. This error can also indicate a problem in the ARC path specifications in the Boot.ini file. If Bootsect.dos is missing on a dual-boot system, you will have to restore it from a backup file, as its contents are specific to a particular system. System files should not be deleted or become corrupt during normal system operation, so these errors are rare. They might indicate an underlying hardware problem, a disk error, or the presence of a computer virus.
Device or service failed during startup	There might be a problem with a missing or corrupted device driver, or there could be hardware resource conflicts (although this is rare on a Plug and Play system).
Device or program in registry not found	A device driver or related file might be missing or damaged. You might need to reinstall the device.

POST Beep Error Codes

POST beep codes vary from one BIOS manufacturer to another. The following table lists some typical POST beep error codes and their meanings.

Beep Error Code	Video Output	Problem	Solution
One or more short beeps	Command prompt	None (normal startup beep)	None.
None	None	Power	Check power cords, wall voltage, PC's power supply.
None	Cursor	Power	Check the PC's power supply; check for sufficient wall voltage.
None	Command prompt	None	May be a defective speaker.
One short, one long beep	None	Display	Check for monitor power; check video cable; check display adapter.
Two short beeps	None or incorrect display (garbage)	Display	Check for monitor power; check video cable; check display adapter.
Two short beeps	None	Memory	Check to see that all RAM chips are seated firmly, swap out RAM chips to determine which is defective, and replace the defective chip.
Repeating short beeps	Probably none	Power	Check the PC's power supply; check for sufficient wall voltage.
Continuous tone	Probably none	Power	Check the PC's power supply; check for sufficient wall voltage.

Beep Error Code	Video Output	Problem	Solution
One long, one short beep	Probably none	System board	Check to see that all adapters, memory, and chips are seated firmly; check for proper power connections to the system board; use diagnostics software or hardware to further troubleshoot the system board.
One long, two short beeps	Probably none	Display	Check for monitor power; check video cable; check display adapter.
One long, three short beeps	Probably none	Display	Check for monitor power; check video cable; check display adapter.
Two short beeps	Numeric error code		Varies depending upon the source of the problem as indicated by the numeric error code.

POST Numeric Error Codes

The following table lists common POST numeric error codes and their meanings.

POST Error Code	Problem
02#	Power
01##	System board
0104	Interrupt controller
0106	System board
0151	Real-time clock or CMOS RAM
0162	CMOS checksum error
0163	Time and date (clock not updating)
164 or 0164	System memory configuration incorrect
199 or 0199	User-indicated device list incorrect
02##	Memory
201 or 0201	Memory error (may give memory address)
0202	Memory address error
03##	Keyboard
0301	Stuck key (scan code of the key may be indicated)
0302	Keyboard locked
06##	Floppy disk driver or controller
0601	Floppy disk adapter failure
0602	Disk failure
17##	Hard disk or adapter
1701	Drive not ready or fails tests

POST Error Code	Problem
1704	Hard drive controller failure
1707	Track 0 failure
1714	Drive not ready
1730-1732	Drive adapter failure

CMOS Error Codes

In addition to the POST error codes, you might also see a CMOS error code. The following are examples of CMOS error codes that you might see displayed after the POST.

- The error `Display Type Mismatch` is displayed if the video settings don't match the monitor attached to the system.

- The error `Memory Size Mismatch` is displayed if the amount of RAM detected and the amount specified in CMOS don't match. This error is usually self-correcting, although you might need to reboot to fix it. Other devices such as hard drives can also generate mismatch errors. This generally happens when the physical device is different than what is specified in CMOS.

- The error `CMOS Checksum Failure` is generated if the CMOS memory is corrupted. This can happen from a bad or dead battery, or a loose connection to the battery. Try replacing the battery to see if it clears up the problem. If it doesn't, the system board might be bad (or going bad).

Error and Warning Messages in Event Viewer

Warning and error messages in the System or Application event logs do not necessarily indicate a major problem on your system. Some common sources of error messages, such as the Windows time service or the ACPI service, are usually benign. If you review the contents of your own system's logs regularly, you will be familiar with the events logged by normal system operations and be able to distinguish these from true problem conditions that require action.

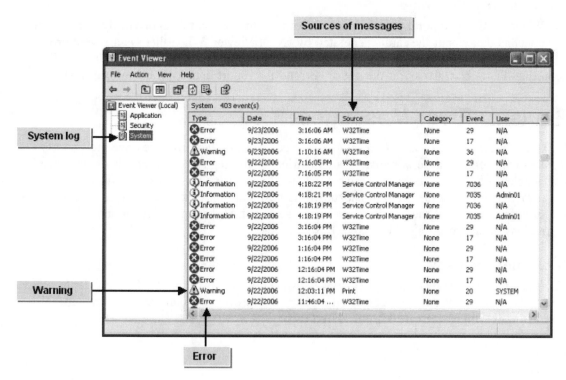

Figure 9-5: *Error and warning messages in Event Viewer.*

The Structure of Event Log Entries

All Information, Warning, Error, Success Audit, and Failure Audit entries in the event logs contain similar information.

Item	Description
Type	The type of log entry: Information, Warning, Error, Success Audit, or Failure Audit.
Source	The software that logged the event; this could be an application, service, or driver.
Category	Classifications for security events, such as Logon and Logoff, Policy Change, Object Access, and so on.
Event	An identifying number for the type of event. Events with the same number are of the same nature.
User	The name of the user that generated the event, if applicable. (Many events are generated by the system itself.)
Computer	The name of the computer where the event occurred.
Description	A text description of the event. These descriptions tend to be quite short; in many cases, there is a link to more specific information on the Microsoft Help and Support website.
Data	Binary event data. Not all events generate binary data.

Windows Error Reporting

The Windows Error Reporting node in the Software Environment category in System Information contains data about the faults generated by Event Viewer. When there is a severe error, Windows will also display an Error Reporting dialog box and generate report data. The Error Reporting dialog box gives you the option to send the report data to Microsoft for analysis.

Registry Error Messages

In extremely rare cases, you may receive a stop error or another error message that reports a problem with registry access, registry value entries, or the registry files. For example, a hard disk problem or power failure may have corrupted the registry hive files. To protect the registry, always maintain proper system backups. The best solution to a specific registry problem is to search for the text of the specific error message at **support.microsoft.com** and follow the instructions in any resulting Knowledge Base article.

Recovering the Registry

There is a process for recovering a corrupt registry. For information, see the Knowledge Base article "How to recover from a corrupted registry that prevents Windows XP from starting" at **http://support.microsoft.com/kb/307545/en-us**.

DISCOVERY ACTIVITY 9-4

Identifying System Errors

Scenario:

In this activity, you will interpret system errors and discuss possible appropriate responses to error conditions.

---

1. **A user calls saying that her screen occasionally goes blue and the system shuts down. What should you advise her to do?**

   a) Call the Help Desk the next time the shutdown is in progress.

   b) Reboot manually after the automatic restart.

   c) Record as much information on the top of the blue screen as she can so that you can research the particular error.

   d) Run the system in Safe Mode.

---

2. **A user reports that his Microsoft Word window has gone blank and he cannot type text. What are possible approaches to resolving his problem?**

   a) Reboot the computer.

   b) Run another copy of Microsoft Word.

   c) Wait a few minutes to see if the application returns to normal.

   d) Use Task Manager to shut down the application if it has a status of Not Responding.

---

3. **A user reports her monitor display is "fuzzy" and hard to look at. What is a possible cause of this problem?**

   a) Display settings for the monitor are incorrectly configured.

   b) The power cord is unplugged.

   c) The monitor cable is not properly seated.

   d) The monitor device is disabled in Windows.

---

4. **A user reports that while she is editing a document, she receives an "invalid working directory" message from her application. What is a good diagnostic question to ask in response to this error?**

   a) Did the application work yesterday?

   b) Is anyone else having this problem?

   c) Who installed the application?

   d) Have you deleted any files or folders lately?

---

5. **Match the error message with its most likely cause.**

___	Invalid boot disk	a.	Corrupted device driver
___	Inaccessible boot device	b.	POST failure (related to the hard disk)
___	Device failed during startup	c.	Non-bootable disk left in the drive
___	Registry file failure	d.	Hard disk controller failure
___	Numeric error code 1701	e.	Disk problem leading to corrupted hive files

Remote Diagnostic and Troubleshooting Tools

Windows XP includes utilities that enable you to remotely administer and troubleshoot users' computers.

Remote Tool	Use To
Remote Desktop	Remote Desktop is a remote management tool that allows you to operate the computer as if you were in front of it. Depending on the permissions you define, you will have full access to all resources, including printers, storage drives, and the network that machine is attached to. You are even capable of accessing multiple machines at once or hopping to multiple machines in a chain, by running remote desktop on each machine on the daisy chain. The problem with Remote desktop for troubleshooting an end user's computer is that it must be enabled and a user must be granted privileges to log in. If a user does not have a password set up to log in to their computer, remote desktop will not allow that username to be used to log in. If no other username exists, there is no opportunity for remote desktop to work. The biggest limitation of remote desktop is that only one person can be logged on to the machine at once, so once you log in using remote desktop, the monitor at the local computer will go to the log in screen. If a local user logs in, the remote user will be disconnected. Remote desktop is not really a remote diagnostic and troubleshooting tool as much as a management tool.
Remote Assistance	Enable a user to request remote assistance. This enables a user to get help from an expert over the Internet. The expert is able to access the user's desktop remotely, and troubleshoot specific problems a user is having. Unlike remote desktop, the remote person shares a view of the desktop with the local user and retains control of the machine. The user must then allow the remote person access (control) of the mouse and keyboard to allow the assistance to begin. Otherwise, the user can simply allow the remote person to observe the problem and chat using the built-in chat services or some other form of communication. The end user can request assistance either via e-mail or via MSN Messenger.

How to Troubleshoot Windows

Procedure Reference: Use Task Manager for Troubleshooting

To use Task Manager to diagnose and troubleshoot Windows:

1. Right-click the taskbar and choose Task Manager.

2. Examine the Applications tab. If any application displays a status of Not Responding, select the application and click End Task. When prompted, click End Now to close the problematic application.

3. Click the Processes tab. You can click any of the column headings to sort the list of processes by that parameter. For example, to sort the list of processes in descending order by processor utilization, click the CPU column heading twice. (By default, the first click of the column heading sorts the list in ascending order.) If necessary, select a process and click End Process to force it to close. Click Yes to confirm.

4. On the Performance tab, use the information displayed to evaluate the computer's performance. Key statistics on this page include:

    *   CPU Usage. The current CPU utilization on the computer.

    *   CPU Usage History. The history of CPU utilization on the computer for roughly the last 30 seconds.

    *   PF Usage. The amount of space in use (in MB) in the paging file. If this is particularly high, consider increasing the minimum paging file size. You should also consider adding more RAM to the computer.

    *   Page File Usage History. The history of paging file use for the last 30 seconds.

    *   Commit Charge (K). The amount of memory allocated to programs and the operating system (in KB).

    *   Physical Memory (K). The amount of physical RAM installed in the computer. Available indicates the amount of RAM that is available for use by applications and data.

    *   Kernel Memory (K). The amount of memory in use by the operating system and its device drivers. Paged indicates the amount of RAM currently occupied by Windows that it can swap to the paging file if necessary. Non-paged indicates the amount of RAM containing the Windows operating system that can't be swapped out to disk.

5. On the Networking tab, use the statistics displayed here to determine the workload generated by network traffic. If the traffic is excessive, consider upgrading to a faster network card.

6. On the Users tab, if it appears, review the list of connected users and whether their status is active or idle. If necessary, you can use this page to disconnect or force a logoff of users.

Procedure Reference: Use Event Viewer for Troubleshooting

To use Event Viewer to diagnose and troubleshoot Windows:

1. Open Computer Management.

2. Select each log and examine it for errors.

3. If necessary, you can filter the events in the log to help you identify the cause of the problem. To do so, select the appropriate log and then choose View→Filter. Make the appropriate selections to filter the log. Criteria on which you can filter include:

- The type of message (information, warning, error, success audit, or failure audit).
- The source of the message (an application, service, or driver).
- Category of the message.
- The event ID, an identifying number for the type of event.
- The user who generated the event (if applicable).
- The name of the computer where the event occurred.
- A text description of the event.

4. If you're unsure as to the cause of an error message, try researching the message in the Microsoft KnowledgeBase at **http://support.microsoft.com/search/?adv=1**.

Procedure Reference: Enable Remote Desktop Support

To configure a computer to permit you to remotely administer it:

1. Open the System Properties dialog box.

2. Check the Allow Users To Connect Remotely To This Computer check box.

3. Click OK to close the message box warning you to be careful of user accounts without passwords.

4. By default, all members of the local Administrators group can connect to a computer on which you've enabled Remote Desktop. If you want to permit other users to remotely administer the computer, click Select Remote Users.

5. Click Add, and enter the names of the user(s) you want to remotely administer the computer. Click OK twice to save your changes.

6. Click OK to close the System Properties dialog box.

Procedure Reference: Troubleshoot a User's Computer with Remote Desktop

To use Remote Desktop to troubleshoot a user's computer:

1. On your computer, choose Start→All Programs→Accessories→Communication→Remote Desktop Connection.

2. In the Computer text box, type the name of the remote computer you want to troubleshoot and then click Connect.

3. When prompted, enter a valid user name and password for the remote computer.

When you establish the connection to the remote computer, Windows XP automatically switches to the user logon screen at that system to prevent the remote user from interfering with the troubleshooting steps you perform.

4. Perform any necessary diagnostics and troubleshooting using the desktop displayed. You can work as if you were seated at the remote computer.

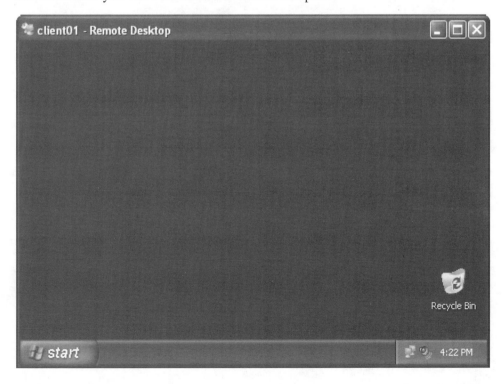

5. When you are done, make sure you log off from the remote computer. Then, disconnect or shut down the remote desktop application.

Procedure Reference: Request Remote Assistance

To configure a computer so that a user can request Remote Assistance:

1. Open the System Properties dialog box.

2. If necessary, check the Allow Remote Assistance Invitations To Be Sent From This Computer check box.

3. Click OK.

4. To request assistance, open the Help And Support Center and click Invite A Friend To Connect To Your Computer With Remote Assistance, then complete the following steps:

   a. Click Invite Someone To Help You.

   b. On the Remote Assistance page, select the method for sending the invitation. You can send the request using either an instant message in Windows Messenger or an email in Outlook Express, or you can transfer it as a file.

   c. Use the appropriate steps to send the invitation. When prompted, be sure to define a password for the Remote Assistance session.

   d. When the person to whom you sent the invitation receives the request, he or she can open the invitation and enter the password you defined when you sent the invitation.

   e. On the computer that issued the invitation, click OK to enable the remote user to connect to the computer.

ACTIVITY 9-5

Troubleshooting a Remote Computer with Remote Desktop

Setup:
You are going to work with a partner to complete this activity. You will take turns playing the role of the helper and the user needing assistance. First, the user needing assistance will enable Remote Desktop. Then, the helper will connect to that computer using Remote Desktop Connection and the Administrator user account.

Scenario:
You have been assigned to support a user whose office is several floors away from yours. You would like to be able to troubleshoot this computer without having to go to the user's office.

There is a simulated version of this activity available on the CD-ROM that shipped with this course. You can run this simulation on any Windows computer to review the activity after class, or as an alternative to performing the activity as a group in class. The activity simulation can be launched either directly from the CD-ROM by clicking the Interactives link and navigating to the appropriate one, or from the installed data file location by opening the C:\ 085820Data\Simulations\Lesson#\Activity# folder and double-clicking the executable (.exe) file.

What You Do	**How You Do It**
Computer Needing Help:	
1. At the computer needing help, **configure the computer to support Remote Desktop connections.**	a. **Open the System Properties dialog box.**
	b. **Click the Remote tab.**
	c. **Check the Allow Users To Connect Remotely To This Computer check box.**

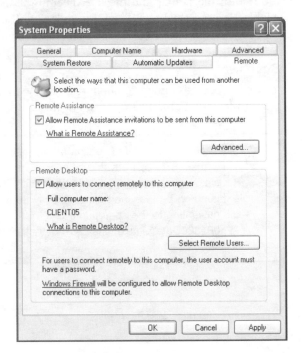

 You're going to connect to your partner's computer as Administrator, so you don't have to grant permissions to a user account to use Remote Desktop by clicking Select Remote Users.

d. **Click OK.**

Helper Computer:

2. At the helper computer, **connect to the other computer using Remote Desktop Connection.**

   a. On your computer, **choose Start→All Programs→Accessories→ Communications→Remote Desktop Connection.**

   b. In the Computer text box, **type** *the name of your partner's computer*

   c. **Click Connect.**

   d. **Log on as** *Administrator* **with a password of** *!Pass1234* **and press Enter.**

   e. **Verify that you can see the other computer's desktop.**

    When you make the connection, your partner will see the logon screen.

   f. **Log off from your remote session with your partner's computer.**

   g. If time permits, **reverse roles and repeat the activity.**

TOPIC D
Recover Microsoft Windows

In the previous topic, you performed troubleshooting tasks to correct various Windows error conditions. If you cannot correct the error condition using normal troubleshooting means, you might need to recover all or part of the system data or configuration. In this topic, you will recover Microsoft Windows from various system problems.

As a computer support professional, it will be your responsibility to recover systems from severe problems when they arise. Windows provides a wide range of techniques for recovering from all types of error conditions. You will need to know which recovery technique is the most appropriate to use in a given situation, as well as to be able to employ it properly. The information and skills in this topic should prepare you to respond in a professional and competent manner to correct system issues, recover the system, and get users working again.

System Restore

A *system restore point* is a snapshot of the system configuration at a given moment in time. The System Restore utility monitors the system for changes to core system files, drivers, and the registry. It automatically creates restore points that contain information about any changes to these components and stores the restore points on the computer's hard disk. You can also create manual restore points. Restore points include information about changes to system files, but not data files or the contents of the My Documents folder. You can use a restore point to restore system settings to an earlier state without affecting changes in user data since that time.

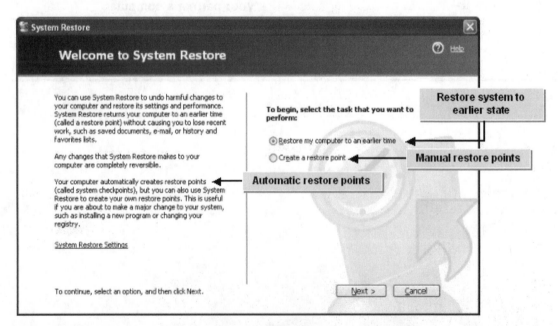

Monitors for changes to core system components

Figure 9-6: System Restore.

For a complete list of file types that are excluded from System Restore monitoring, see "Appendix D – Tools for Troubleshooting" in the Windows XP Professional Resource Kit.

 Restore points also do not completely remove installed software. Use Add Or Remove Programs to remove all files, settings, and Registry entries for an installed application.

Types of Restore Points

The following table lists all the possible types of restore points.

Type of Restore Point	Created When
Initial System Checkpoints	Windows XP is installed. Can be used to roll the system back to its state just after installation.
System Checkpoints	Every 24 hours. If the computer is off for more than 24 hours, one is created at the next reboot.
Program Name Installation	Programs are installed with installer tools such as InstallShield and Windows XP Installer.
Auto Update	Before installing any update from the Microsoft website that is automatically downloaded with the Auto Update feature.
Manually Created	Users manually create restore points.
Restore Operation	You restore the system to a restore point.
Unsigned Device Driver	An unsigned driver is installed.
Backup Utility Recovery	The Windows Backup utility is used to recover files.

Safe Mode

Safe Mode is a Windows system startup method that loads only a minimal set of drivers and services. If a non-critical driver or service on your system is causing a severe error, you can use Safe Mode to omit all non-critical drivers and services from the boot sequence; start the system; load additional drivers, services, and applications as needed; and correct the problem.

Figure 9-7: Safe Mode.

An example of a Safe Mode error is when the display fails to initialize during startup. This can produce stop errors or the screen will appear blank or distorted. You can start the computer in Safe Mode, and then roll back or uninstall the display adapter driver. When you restart the computer, the display should initialize.

Safe Mode Boot Options

To display Safe Mode boot options, press F8 during the boot sequence just after the POST. There are three different Safe Mode boot options.

Option	Description	Use When
Safe Mode	Starts the computer with a minimal set of drivers and services, including the mouse, keyboard, VGA display, and hard disk.	The system problem might be with the networking components.
Safe Mode with Networking	Starts the computer with Safe Mode drivers and services, plus networking drivers and services.	You need to use files on a network server to repair the system.
Safe Mode with Command Prompt	Starts the computer with Safe Mode drivers and services, but with a command-prompt interface.	A system problem prevents the system from creating the Windows GUI desktop.

Step By Step Mode

Windows 9*x* supported an additional startup option, step by step confirmation. If you pressed Shift+F8 during the boot sequence, you could choose which commands to execute during the boot sequence. On Windows XP systems, you should use the Selective Startup option on the General page of the System Configuration Utility to selectively control which items the system processes during the boot sequence.

Last Known Good

Last Known Good is an advanced boot option that you can use to revert the system to the state it was in on the last successful startup and user logon. Each time you restart a computer and log on successfully, the system stores a copy of the *control set* containing the successful startup parameters in the Last Known Good area of the registry. If the system fails on a subsequent boot and you do not log on, you can use the Last Known Good boot option to load the control set from the previous successful boot.

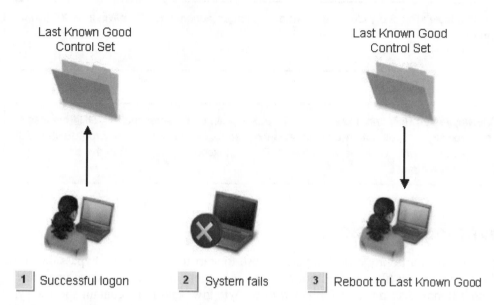

Figure 9-8: *The Last Known Good process.*

 Remember that Windows startup is not considered successful until a user logs on. Therefore, the Last Known Good control set is not created until user logon. This also means that once you have restarted and logged on to a damaged system, you can no longer use Last Known Good to revert to a previous configuration.

Recovery Console

The *Recovery Console* is a minimal, non-graphical administrative version of Windows. You can boot to Recovery Console and use a command-line interface to manage the system even if Windows will not start normally.

```
Microsoft Windows XP(TM) Recovery Console.

The Recovery Console provides system repair and recovery functionality.

Type EXIT to quit the Recovery Console and restart the computer.


1: C:\WINDOWS

Which Windows installation would you like to log onto
<To cancel, press ENTER>? 1
Type the Administrator password:
C:\WINDOWS>_
```

Figure 9-9: *Recovery Console.*

In Recovery Console, you can:

● Enable and disable services.

● Manage files and disks.

● And, correct boot problems.

You can install Recovery Console as a boot option or launch it from the Windows XP installation CD-ROM.

 One way to use Recovery Console is to fix a disk problem that prevents NTLDR from loading. The Recovery Console has two commands that can fix the master boot record (MBR) and the boot sector: Fixmbr, which rewrites the MBR, and Fixboot, which rewrites the boot sector of the system volume.

Windows Boot Disk

A Windows *boot disk* is a floppy disk that you can use to start the system and bypass damaged or missing Windows startup files. It does not contain a complete and self-contained operating system. The boot floppy disk must be formatted using Windows and must contain specific system files:

● Boot.ini.

● Ntldr.

● Ntdetect.com.

● Bootsect.dos, if present.

● And, Ntbootdd.sys, if present.

Automated System Recovery (ASR)

 Automated System Recovery (ASR) is a process that uses backup data and the Windows installation source files to rebuild a failed computer system. To perform ASR, you will need:

● The Windows installation CD-ROM.

● An *ASR floppy disk*, which provides the information Windows Setup needs to run ASR recovery.

● And, an *ASR backup set* that contains a complete copy of the Windows system files and all configuration information.

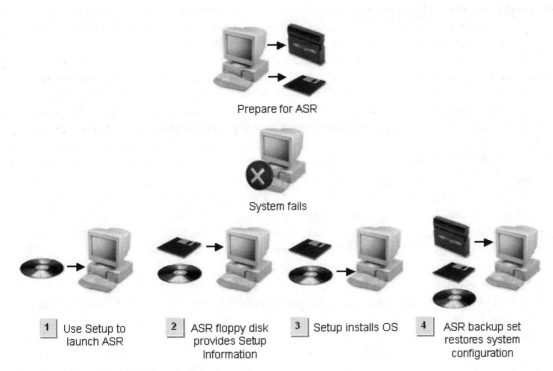

Prepare for ASR

System fails

| 1 | Use Setup to launch ASR | 2 | ASR floppy disk provides Setup Information | 3 | Setup installs OS | 4 | ASR backup set restores system configuration |

Figure 9-10: *The ASR process.*

If a system fails completely, an administrator can use the ASR option in Windows Setup to reinstall Windows and provide the ASR floppy disk and ASR backup set to reconfigure the system.

Phases in the ASR Process

The ASR process consists of the following phases:

1. To prepare for ASR, an administrator uses Windows Backup to create an ASR backup set and ASR floppy disk.

   - The ASR backup set must be stored on local backup media, not on a network drive.

   - The ASR backup set cannot be stored on the same hard disk as the Windows installation, as this disk can be re-initialized during the ASR process.

2. If the system suffers a complete and catastrophic failure, the administrator selects a computer to use to restore the system.

3. The administrator runs Windows Setup from the Windows installation CD-ROM and initiates ASR.

4. The administrator provides the ASR floppy disk.

5. The system passes the information in the Setup Information Files (SIF) on the ASR floppy disk to Windows Setup.

6. Windows Setup installs the operating system as specified on the ASR floppy disk.

7. The administrator provides the ASR backup set.

8. ASR configures the system according to the information in the backup set.

Repair Installations

Although ASR is not supported in Windows 2000, both Windows 2000 and Windows XP support an alternate recovery method called Emergency Repair. When you install Windows, the system stores information about the configuration of the operating system in a hidden folder called \Windows\Repair. If your installation is damaged, you may be able to repair it by using this information and the Windows Setup program. You might want to try a repair installation as an intermediate step before attempting ASR or a complete reinstall.

Emergency Repair Disk

In Windows 2000, you can create a copy of the Repair information on a floppy disk called an *emergency repair disk (ERD).* When you create an ERD, the system also updates the contents of the \Repair folder. To create an emergency repair disk in Windows 2000, insert a blank floppy disk, choose Programs→Accessories→System Tools→Backup, and click Emergency Repair Disk. Be sure to back up the Registry along with the other repair information.

Recovery Partitions

Sometimes a computer manufacturer will supply a recovery partition or CD-ROM that you can use to restore a computer to the configuration it was in when it shipped from the manufacturer. Note that the Recovery Partition/CD-ROM not only restores the operating system, but also all applications that came pre-installed on the computer. Some manufacturers store the necessary information in a hidden partition on the computer's hard disk. Others store this information on a CD-ROM. The steps you use to perform this type of recovery are manufacturer-specific. Review the documentation that came with the computer to determine how to perform the recovery.

Windows System Issues

When you troubleshoot performance problems, you will need to identify the cause of the problem, categorize it, and take appropriate actions.

Category of Problem	Possible Causes and Actions to Take
General issues	• For boot process issues, use standard Safe Mode and boot-process trouble-shooting techniques. • Viruses can cause a variety of general system problems. Install or update the user's virus software and perform a complete virus scan. • If the problem occurs when a specific application runs, use Task Manager to terminate the application and then troubleshoot its installation and configuration.
Memory issues	An application or service might be leaking memory, which means that it is not releasing previously allocated memory back to the system after use. • Use Task Manager to see which applications are using memory. Have the user reboot and run for a period of time, then check again to confirm. • Use the System Configuration Utility to disable problem applications at startup. • Use system monitoring techniques to check the overall memory performance.

Category of Problem	Possible Causes and Actions to Take
Disk issues	Low disk space can slow system performance. If there is less than 100 MB of free disk space: • Delete temporary Internet files in the Internet Explorer cache. • Empty the C:\Temp and C:\Tmp directories. • Search for and delete .chk files. • Run the Disk Defragmenter, Disk Cleanup, and Check Disk utilities.
CPU issues	Use Task Manager to identify processes that dominate the available CPU usage. Use System Configuration to disable any unnecessary processes at startup.

 The ultimate solution to some performance problems might be upgrading the system hardware by adding more memory or a larger hard disk. As a support technician, you might or might not be able to request this type of upgrade.

How to Recover Microsoft Windows

Procedure Reference: Troubleshoot System Problems

When you diagnose and resolve any system problem in Windows, always follow a structured troubleshooting process:

1. Gather information from the user and other resources to identify the problem. Resources include vendor manuals, web-based research materials, and operating system tools such as the Event Log and Device Manager.

2. Analyze the problem and try to isolate a potential cause.

3. Test the related components to confirm the possible cause.

4. Implement a solution and evaluate the results.

5. Verify with the user that the problem has been solved.

6. Document your activities.

Procedure Reference: Restore Data from Windows Backup

To restore data in Windows Backup:

1. Log on as a user who is either a member of the Backup Operators or Administrators groups, owner of a file, or a user who has at least the Write NTFS permissions to restore file data.

2. Load your backup media.

3. Run Windows Backup.

4. Click Next.

5. Select Restore Files And Settings and click Next.

6. Below Items To Restore, expand the backup media (File or Tape).

7. Expand the backup set you want to restore.

8. Check the check boxes for the files and folders you want to restore from the backup set.

9. Click Next.

10. If you want to configure advanced options such as the destination for the restored files, what you want Backup to do if the files already exist on the computer's hard disk, and whether you want to restore security permissions, click Advanced.

11. Click Finish to restore the backup.

12. Click Close to close the Restore Progress dialog box.

13. Close Backup.

14. Verify that the files, folders, or both were restored successfully.

Procedure Reference: Restore System State Data

To restore System State data:

1. Log on as a local administrator.

2. If you can't start Windows XP in normal mode, boot to Safe Mode.

3. Load your backup media.

4. Run Backup.

5. Click Next.

6. Select Restore Files And Settings and click Next.

7. If you don't see the backup set containing the System State data backup, click Import File. In the Catalog Backup File text box, type the path and file name for the backup file and click OK.

8. Below What To Restore, complete the following steps:
   a. Expand the backup media (File or Tape).
   b. Expand the backup set you want to restore.
   c. Check the System State check box.

9. Click Next.

10. Click Finish to restore the backup.

11. Click Close to close the Restore Progress dialog box.

12. Click Yes to restart the computer. (You might need to close some processes manually.)

13. When the computer reboots, log on and verify that the problem has been corrected.

Procedure Reference: Use Safe Mode or Last Known Good

To boot the system using Last Known Good or one of the Safe Mode options:

1. Restart the computer (by turning the power off and on if necessary).

2. Just after the POST phase of the boot sequence, and during the display of the Boot Loader menu if you have one, press F8.

3. Select Last Known Good or the desired Safe Mode option from the Windows Advanced Options menu.

4. Start Windows and log on.

5. If you are in Safe Mode, click OK in the message box.

6. If you are in Safe Mode, perform the appropriate configuration or troubleshooting tasks and restart the system in normal mode.

Procedure Reference: Configure a Manual Restore Point

To configure a manual restore point:

1. Run System Restore.
   - From the Start menu, choose All Programs→Accessories→System Tools→System Restore.
   - Or, in the Help and Support Center, click Undo Changes To Your Computer With System Restore.

2. Select Create A Restore Point and click Next.

3. Enter a descriptive name for the restore point and click Create.

4. To verify that the restore point was created, click Home.

5. Select Restore My Computer To An Earlier Time and click Next.

6. Verify that your restore point appears on the calendar for the current day.

7. Click Cancel to close System Restore.

Procedure Reference: Restore the System to a Restore Point

To restore a system to a restore point:

1. If you cannot boot the computer to a normal mode, boot to Safe Mode.

2. Run System Restore.

3. Select Restore My Computer To An Earlier Time and click Next.

4. Select the date on the calendar that contains the restore point you want to use.

5. Select the restore point you want to use. Click Next.

6. Click Next to confirm the system restoration.

7. After the system has restarted, log on and click OK to close System Restore.

Procedure Reference: Install Recovery Console as a Boot Option

To install the Recovery Console as a startup choice:

1. From the Windows XP installation source files directory (this is the \I386 directory if you are using the Windows XP installation CD-ROM), run the command `winnt32.exe /cmdcons`.

2. Click Yes to confirm the Recovery Console installation.

3. Follow the prompts to complete the Recovery Console installation, and click Finish.

Procedure Reference: Use Recovery Console

To use Recovery Console to correct system problems:

1. Boot to Recovery Console:
   - If the Recovery Console is installed as a boot option, restart the computer and select Recovery Console from the Boot Loader menu.
   - Otherwise, boot the computer from the Windows XP CD-ROM. On the Welcome To Setup screen, press R to boot to Recovery Console.

2. When prompted, enter the number of the Windows XP installation you want to log on to. (On a single-boot system this will be installation number 1.)

3. Enter the Administrator password to log on to Windows XP.

4. Use the appropriate Recovery Console commands to correct the system problem.

5. To end the Recovery Console session and restart the computer, type exit and press Enter.

Procedure Reference: Create and Test a Boot Floppy Disk

To create a Windows boot floppy disk:

1. Put a floppy disk in the disk drive.

2. In Windows Explorer or My Computer, right-click the floppy-disk drive and choose Format.

 Even if the disk is already blank and formatted, you must format it again under Windows. The Windows formatting routine writes required boot information to the boot sector of the floppy disk.

3. Choose Start to format the disk. (Checking Quick Format is optional.)

4. Click OK to confirm the format.

5. When the format is complete, click Close.

6. If you have not already done so, configure Windows Explorer's View options to show file extensions, hidden files, and hidden system files:
   a. In My Computer or Windows Explorer, choose Tools→Folder Options.
   b. Click the View tab.
   c. Select Show Hidden Files And Folders.
   d. Uncheck Hide File Extensions For Known File Types.
   e. Uncheck Hide Protected Operating System Files (Recommended).
   f. Click Yes to confirm the change.
   g. Click OK.

7. Copy the following required boot files from the C:\ folder to the floppy disk:
   - Boot.ini
   - Ntldr
   - Ntdetect.com
   - Bootsect.dos (if present)
   - Ntbootdd.sys (if present) (This is the device driver for BIOS-disabled SCSI disk drives.)

8. Restart the computer with the floppy disk in the drive to verify that you can boot successfully.

9. Remove the boot floppy disk, label it, and store it in a secure location.

Procedure Reference: Use a Boot Floppy Disk

To use a boot floppy disk to correct a boot problem:

1. Insert the boot floppy disk in the floppy drive.

2. Restart the computer.

3. Boot and log on to Windows.

4. Correct the problem by replacing the corrupted file with a good copy from the boot floppy disk, from the Windows installation CD-ROM, or by altering incorrect entries in Boot.ini.

5. Remove the boot floppy disk and restart the computer normally.

Procedure Reference: Recover a Computer Using the Recovery Partition/CD-ROM

To reset a computer to its default installation configuration:

1. Follow the computer manufacturer's instructions to boot from either the recovery partition or CD-ROM.

2. When prompted, follow the instructions on the screen to recover the computer.

Procedure Reference: Prepare for ASR

You cannot perform ASR unless you have prepared the ASR data in advance. To prepare for ASR:

1. Format a floppy disk, and verify that you have sufficient space on your backup media to hold the complete Windows XP system (between 1 and 2 GB of data).

2. Run Windows Backup in Advanced Mode.

3. On the Welcome page of the Backup Utility, click Automated System Recovery Wizard.

4. In the Automated System Recovery Preparation Wizard, click Next.

5. Select a backup location and enter a name for the backup file. Click Next.

6. Click Finish. The backup set is created.

7. When you are prompted, insert the formatted floppy disk and click OK.

8. Click OK to close the message box when the floppy disk is complete.

9. Click Close to close the Backup Progress dialog box.

10. Remove the floppy disk, label it, and store it in a secure location.

 To create an ASR backup set while also backing up all user data, run Windows Backup in Wizard mode, select Back Up Files And Settings, and select All Information On This Computer. You will need enough storage space to back up the complete contents of your computer.

Procedure Reference: Perform ASR

To perform ASR:

1. Run the Windows Setup program by booting from the Windows XP installation CD-ROM, or by running the Winnt32.exe command manually.

2. When the Press F2 To Run Automated System Recovery (ASR) message appears in the status bar, press F2 (this message appears very briefly).

3. When prompted, insert the ASR boot floppy disk and press any key. (You can also initiate ASR with the ASR floppy disk already in the drive.)

4. If prompted, press C to confirm that your disk partitions will be deleted and re-created.

5. When prompted, after the disk is scanned and configured, Windows Setup runs, and the Automated System Recovery Wizard runs, insert the ASR backup media, and complete the Automated System Recovery Wizard. The restoration will proceed automatically.

 To support unattended system recovery, the screens in the Automated System Recovery Wizard are configured to advance automatically after a time-out.

6. If you are prompted for an installation directory (for example, if you are installing to a clean hard disk) provide the path (typically you will install to C:\Windows). When the installation and restoration are complete, the computer will restart.

7. Log on and verify the system configuration.

Procedure Reference: Perform an Emergency Repair

To perform an Emergency Repair:

1. Boot the computer from the Windows CD-ROM and press R when prompted to repair the computer.

2. Press R from the Repair Options menu.

3. In Windows 2000, the Windows Setup program will offer repair options; in Windows XP, Recovery Console will launch. You can then attempt to repair the computer with the emergency repair information on the ERD or from the Repair folder on the hard disk.

ACTIVITY 9-6

Restoring System State Data

Setup:

You have backed up the System State data for Windows XP to C:\Backup\Backup.bkf.

Scenario:

A programmer just installed a custom application he developed on one of your client's computers. The client has contacted you because he's now experiencing problems with his computer. You aren't sure what the custom application changed on the computer. Fortunately, you scheduled a System State data backup to take place on a regular basis; the last backup occurred last night.

There is a simulated version of this activity available on the CD-ROM that shipped with this course. You can run this simulation on any Windows computer to review the activity after class, or as an alternative to performing the activity as a group in class. The activity simulation can be launched either directly from the CD-ROM by clicking the Interactives link and navigating to the appropriate one, or from the installed data file location by opening the C:\ 085820Data\Simulations\Lesson#\Activity# folder and double-clicking the executable (.exe) file.

What You Do	How You Do It
1. **Restore the System State data.**	a. **Open Backup.**
	b. **Click Next.**
	c. **Select Restore Files And Settings and then click Next.**
	d. **Expand the media set and check the System State check box.**
	e. **Click Next.**
	f. **Click Advanced.**
	g. On the Where To Restore page, to accept the default of Original Location, **click Next and then click OK.**
	h. On the How To Restore page, **select Replace Existing Files and click Next.**
	i. On the Advanced Restore Options page, **click Next.**
	j. To start the restoration process, **click Finish.**
	k. When the restore is complete, **click Close.**
	l. When prompted, to restart the computer, **click Yes.**
	m. The restart might take longer than normal. When it completes, **log back on to the computer.**

ACTIVITY 9-7

Restoring the System to a Restore Point

Setup:

In this activity, you will create a restore point and restore the system to that restore point.

Scenario:

One of your hardware suppliers has just posted some updated device drivers to their website, and they recommend that all their clients install these drivers. However, none of the drivers are signed. You know that you could roll back a single driver if you have problems with it, but in this case, you have several different files to update. You're not sure exactly what the ramifications to the system will be. Before you start installing the new drivers, you would like to be sure that you have a way to bring the system back to its current state if you encounter problems. You decide to use a restore point; because you have not created a manual restore point before, you want to test the restore point after you create it.

 There is a simulated version of this activity available on the CD-ROM that shipped with this course. You can run this simulation on any Windows computer to review the activity after class, or as an alternative to performing the activity as a group in class. The activity simulation can be launched either directly from the CD-ROM by clicking the Interactives link and navigating to the appropriate one, or from the installed data file location by opening the C:\085820Data\Simulations\Lesson#\Activity# folder and double-clicking the executable (.exe) file.

What You Do	How You Do It
1. **Configure a manual restore point.**	a. **Choose Start→All Programs→ Accessories→System Tools→System Restore.**
	b. **Select Create A Restore Point. Click Next.**
	To begin, select the task that you want to perform:
	○ Restore my computer to an earlier time
	◉ Create a restore point
	c. In the Restore Point Description text box, **type New Drivers**
	d. **Click Create.**

2. **Verify the restore point by restoring the system.**

    a. **Click Home.**

    b. **Select Restore My Computer To An Earlier Time. Click Next.**

    c. Dates listed in bold contain restore points. **Verify that the New Drivers restore point is selected in the list for the current day. Click Next.**

2. On this list, click a restore point.

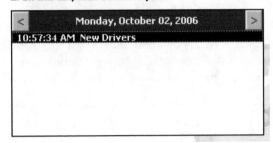

    d. **Read the Confirm Restore Point Selection information and click Next.**

    e. The system shuts down and restarts, and files are restored from the restore point. When the system has restarted, to log on, enter *!Pass1234*

    f. To close System Restore, **click OK.**

ACTIVITY 9-8

Recovering the System With Last Known Good

Objective:

In this activity, you will create a boot problem with the keyboard, and then correct the problem by using Last Known Good.

Scenario:

A change to the configuration of the keyboard driver is completely preventing user logons. Because the keyboard is not responding, even the Administrator can't log on to fix the problem. You need to restore system functionality so that users can log on again.

 There is a simulated version of this activity available on the CD-ROM that shipped with this course. You can run this simulation on any Windows computer to review the activity after class, or as an alternative to performing the activity as a group in class. The activity simulation can be launched either directly from the CD-ROM by clicking the Interactives link and navigating to the appropriate one, or from the installed data file location by opening the C:\ 085820Data\Simulations\Lesson#\Activity# folder and double-clicking the executable (.exe) file.

What You Do	How You Do It
1. Modify the Registry to prevent the Kbdclass device from loading.	a. To run Registry Editor, **Choose Start→ Run, type** *regedit* **and click OK.**
	b. In Registry Editor, **expand HKEY_ LOCAL_MACHINE\System\ CurrentControlSet\Services.**
	c. **Scroll down and select the Kbdclass subkey.**
	d. **Double-click the Start value entry.**

e. A Start value of 4 will prevent the driver from loading, which simulates a corrupt keyboard driver. In the Value Data text box, **type *4* and click OK.**

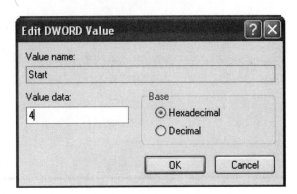

f. **Close Registry Editor.**

2. **Test the keyboard problem.**

a. **Choose Start→Turn Off Computer. Click Restart.**

b. The computer boots and the Welcome Screen appears. **Attempt to type your password. You will be unable to do so.**

3. **Why are you unable to log on?**

4. **Why won't Safe Mode work in this situation?**

a) Because the keyboard is one of the Safe Mode devices. If you disable the driver, the keyboard won't work even in Safe Mode.

b) Because you have already logged on.

c) Because Safe Mode is not a troubleshooting tool.

d) Because you have not configured a Restore Point.

5. **Use the Last Known Good configuration to start the computer.**

    a. **Use the power button to turn the computer off and on again.**

    b. **After the POST sequence and before the progress bar, press F8.**

    c. **Select Last Known Good Configuration, and then press Enter.**

    d. **Verify that Microsoft Windows XP Professional is selected and press Enter.**

    e. **Enter your password to log on.**

ACTIVITY 9-9

Testing the Recovery Console

Setup:
You have the Windows XP Professional installation CD-ROM available.

Scenario:
You are spending your day visiting the desktops of a number of users who have reported severe system problems. Not all the systems have Recovery Console installed as a boot option, so you have a copy of the Windows XP Professional CD-ROM available. Once you boot to Recovery Console, however, you need to select the appropriate tools and techniques to correct the specific problem for each system.

There is a simulated version of this activity available on the CD-ROM that shipped with this course. You can run this simulation on any Windows computer to review the activity after class, or as an alternative to performing the activity as a group in class. The activity simulation can be launched either directly from the CD-ROM by clicking the Interactives link and navigating to the appropriate one, or from the installed data file location by opening the C:\085820Data\Simulations\Lesson#\Activity# folder and double-clicking the executable (.exe) file.

What You Do	How You Do It
1. **Use Recovery Console to start the computer.**	a. **Insert the Windows XP Professional CD-ROM.**
	b. **Choose Start→Turn Off Computer and click Restart.**
	c. When prompted, **press any key to boot from the CD-ROM.**
	d. On the Welcome To Setup screen, to boot to Recovery Console, **press R.**
	e. At the Which Windows Installation Would You Like To Log On To prompt, **enter *1***
	f. If you reinstalled Windows XP Professional earlier in this course, the Administrator password is blank. To log on, **press Enter.**
	If you did not reinstall Windows XP Professional, the Administrator password is !Pass1234. To log on, **type *!Pass1234* and press Enter.**
2. **View Help system entries on various Recovery Console commands.**	a. At the C:\Windows prompt, to display a list of supported Recovery Console commands, **enter *help***
	b. **Press the Spacebar key to scroll to the end of the list.**
	c. To view the Help information on the bootcfg command, **enter *help bootcfg***
	d. **View Help information on other Recovery Console commands of your choice.**
	e. To exit Recovery Console and restart the computer, **enter *exit***
	f. **Enter your password to log on.**
	g. **Remove the installation CD-ROM.**

3. **Use the Help information to match the system problem with the most likely method for correcting it in Recovery Console.**

___ After performing some disk management tasks, a user has been unable to restart his computer. The user sees an Unreadable Boot Disk message.

a. Use the enable command to enable the service.

___ A user has manually disabled a key startup service.

b. Use the delete command to delete pagefile.sys. The file will be re-created at the next startup.

___ A user installed a new, unsigned driver and the system will not start.

c. Use Fixmbr, which rewrites the MBR, or Fixboot, which rewrites the boot sector of the system volume.

___ A user deleted the Ntdetect.com file.

d. Use the expand and copy commands to copy a new version of the file from the Windows XP Professional installation media.

___ The Windows pagefile has become corrupt.

e. Use the disable command to disable the driver. When you reboot, you can remove the driver.

___ NTLDR will not load.

f. Use the bootcfg command.

ACTIVITY 9-10

Creating and Testing a Windows XP Boot Floppy Disk

Setup:

You will need a blank floppy disk for this activity. Your computer system BIOS is configured to boot from the floppy drive.

Scenario:

You're updating your troubleshooting toolkit, and you realize that you don't have a boot floppy disk for the new Windows XP Professional installations in your company. You decide to use your desktop computer to create a Windows XP Professional boot floppy disk.

There is a simulated version of this activity available on the CD-ROM that shipped with this course. You can run this simulation on any Windows computer to review the activity after class, or as an alternative to performing the activity as a group in class. The activity simulation can be launched either directly from the CD-ROM by clicking the Interactives link and navigating to the appropriate one, or from the installed data file location by opening the C:\085820Data\Simulations\Lesson#\Activity# folder and double-clicking the executable (.exe) file.

What You Do	How You Do It
1. **Format a floppy disk.**	a. **Place a blank floppy disk in your computer's floppy-disk drive.**
	b. **Open My Computer.**
	c. **Right-click the floppy drive icon and choose Format.**
	d. **Check Quick Format and click Start.**

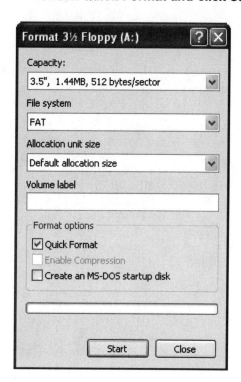

e. To confirm the format, **click OK.**

f. When the format is complete, **click OK.**

g. **Click Close.**

2. **Configure Windows Explorer options to show protected operating system files.**

a. In My Computer, **open the C drive.**

b. **If necessary, click Show The Contents Of This Folder.**

c. **Choose Tools→Folder Options.**

d. **Click the View tab.**

e. **If necessary, select Show Hidden Files And Folders.**

f. **If necessary, uncheck Hide Extensions For Known File Types.**

g. **Uncheck Hide Protected Operating System Files (Recommended).**

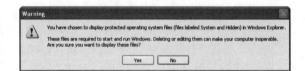

h. To confirm the change, **click Yes.**

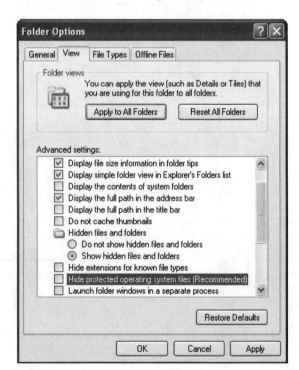

i. **Click OK.**

		j.	**Verify that you can now see the system files.**

3.	**Copy the required files to the boot floppy disk.**	a.	In the C:\ folder, **select the Boot.ini, Ntldr, and Ntdetect.com files.**
		b.	**If you have a Bootsect.dos file or an Ntbootdd.sys file, select those files as well.**
		c.	**Right-click any selected file and choose Send To→3 1/2 Floppy (A).**
		d.	**Close the window.**

4.	**Test the boot floppy disk.**	a.	**Choose Start→Turn Off Computer and click Restart.**
		b.	The system will locate the disk in the floppy drive and boot from that drive instead of the C drive. **Enter your password to log on.**
		c.	**Remove the floppy disk from the drive and label it.**

Lesson 9 Follow-up

In this lesson, you performed maintenance and troubleshooting on Microsoft Windows systems. You will be the main point of contact for customers and clients who have maintenance issues or system problems, and the skills and tools you used in this lesson should help you resolve those problems for your clients quickly.

1. **Were any of the management or recovery tools and utilities presented in this lesson familiar? Which ones?**

2. **Have you ever had to recover a damaged computer system? What was the situation, and what approach did you use? Do you think your approach will be different from now on?**